THE
CONFESSIONS
OF
st. AUGUSTINE

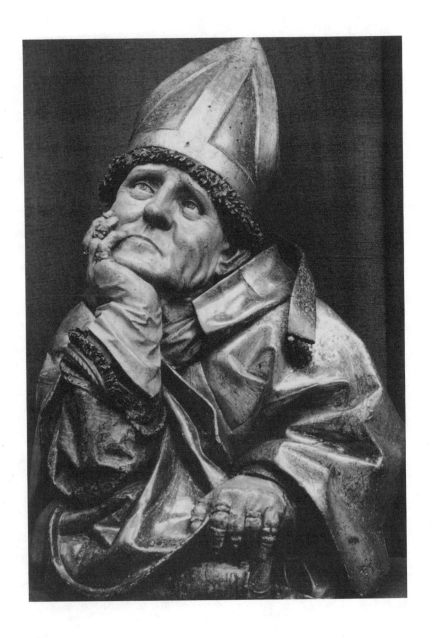

THE
CONFESSIONS
OF
St. AUGUSTINE
BOOKS I-IX (SELECTIONS)

WITH INTRODUCTION, NOTES AND VOCABULARY
BY
JAMES MARSHALL CAMPBELL
AND
MARTIN R.P. MCGUIRE

ADDITIONS BY RAYMOND V. SCHODER, S.J.
AND
THOMAS P. HALTON

FOURTEENTH PRINTING

BOLCHAZY-CARDUCCI PUBLISHERS, INC.
WAUCONDA, IL 1994

COVER AND PAGE 4:

St. Augustine Pondering: German Wood
Carving, circa 1510.
Liebighaus Museum, Frankfurt.

Cover Design by Leon Danilovics.
Photography by Raymond V. Schoder, S.J.

Reprint of the Edition:
Prentice-Hall, Inc. 1931

Fourteenth Printing 1994
© Copyright 1984

Bolchazy-Carducci Publishers, Inc.
1000 Brown St.
Wauconda, IL 60084

Printed in the United States of America

International Standard Book Number
Hard Bound   0-86516-057-0
Soft Bound   0-86516-058-9

FOREWORD

I am glad to see back in print this excellent edition of Latin selections from St. Augustine's *Confessions*, with its helpful introduction, notes, and vocabulary. This is another good service by this publisher to the cause of Classical and Christian education, by way of making available again textbooks for the study of our great cultural tradition.

The *Confessions* rightfully rank among the most splendid and influential works of Western Man. Here is one of the most illuminating and moving autobiographies, a profound treatise on the way of God with men, a pioneer essay in psychological analysis of human motives and ideals, and a noble example of the grandeur, power, and rhetorical beauty of the Latin language. To read Augustine in his own words is to come to know a magnificent human being, a brilliant master of literary style, and the rich mellowness and sublimity of mind and spirit which results from giving divine grace its full scope in its potential impact on human life. Anyone who knows enough Latin to read this timeless masterpiece will be inspired and humanized by the experience. Making that experience possible is a contribution to civilization. The world today has much to learn from Augustine's story, his humility, his spiritual perspective and insights, and his authentic love. His is a voice and a message little heard in our time — and therefore all the more imperative to hear.

Reasons for enthusiasm for Augustine the man and his thought are many. Reading his own meditations in the selections here provided will justify my claims. I am happy also to have been able to provide illustrations of places connected with Augustine's life, and the delightful portrait of him wrapped in thought that deserves to be better known.

LOYOLA UNIVERSITY OF CHICAGO   RAYMOND V. SCHODER, S.J.
1984

Hippo Regius. Punic tombstones.

PREFACE

THE beginnings of this edition of the *Confessions* reach back to the year 1924, when Sister M. Constance Mooney, M.A., of the Sisters of St. Mary of Namur of Fort Worth, presented to Professor Deferrari's Latin Seminar a paper entitled "A Suggested College Course in St. Augustine's Confessions." In the summer of that year Sister Inviolata Barry, Ph.D., Professor of Latin in Our Lady of the Lake College, San Antonio, and the editor whose name appears first upon the title-page began gathering materials for an edition of the *Confessions* suitable for the college and the preparatory seminary. Sister Inviolata had scarcely determined upon the selections to be used, however, when her promotion to a strenuous deanship compelled her to abandon the enterprise. The work was begun anew by the present editors in 1926.

The only other annotated edition of the *Confessions* in whole or in part readily available in English differs apparently in purpose and certainly in execution from the present work. Whatever class of readers Gibb and Montgomery had primarily in mind, their commentary emphasizes the literary, philosophical, and historical interests of the *Confessions* rather than the syntactical and linguistic. For college students, if for no others, adequate notes upon the latter are as indispensable as adequate notes upon the former, and it is for college students that the present edition is intended, although advanced high-school students can use the text without difficulty. The selections, therefore, constitute the equivalent of a normal semester's reading in college Latin, and aim to include the most interesting passages of the narrative portions of the *Confessions*. Besides the usual notes upon historical, religious, philosophical, and Biblical matters, every syntactical difficulty is considered, classical and non-classical, and a

baldly literal translation is ventured wherever interpretation
seems to demand it. Frequent reference is made to stylistic
devices of St. Augustine, and definitions of such devices are
given. An especially prepared vocabulary is appended. We
have failed of our resolution to write no "learned" notes in
the single instance of the question of St. Augustine's knowledge
of Greek, because of a wide misconception upon the subject
prevalent among the educated. The "Selected Bibliography"
may be of use to novices in Augustinian studies, while its
remarks may suggest how largely pioneer even a school edition
of the *Confessions* may be, despite all the Augustinian labors
of recent years.

De Labriolle's text is used throughout. His paragraph
divisions, we believe, will facilitate immensely the understanding of the text. We have taken the liberty of inter-
spersing the text with headings designed to recall the student
always to the prayerful character of the *Confessions*.

We are indebted to the following editors and translators of
the *Confessions* and in the order given: Professor De Labriolle,
of the Sorbonne; the late Graf von Hertling; Drs. Wolfschläger and Koch, of Münster in Westphalia and of Dortmund
respectively; the Rev. John Gibb and the Rev. William
Montgomery, the Cambridge editors of the *Confessions*.
Materials furnished by the foregoing entered into the composition of about a score of our notes. Acknowledgment is
made by appropriate symbol in each case.

We must finally thank Professor Deferrari for suggesting the
enterprise, for constant encouragement and advice during its
execution, and for the wealth of materials put at our disposal
by his Seminar in Patristic Latin; our colleague, Brother
Giles, C.F.X., Ph.D.; the Rev. Felix M. Kirsch, O.M.Cap.,
Ph.D., of the Capuchin College, The Catholic University of
America, who read the work in manuscript; and Mrs. Flor-
ence B. McGuire, M.A., for assistance in preparation of the
Vocabulary.

JAMES MARSHALL CAMPBELL
MARTIN R. P. McGUIRE

TABLE OF CONTENTS

ILLUSTRATIONS

INTRODUCTION

Church of St. Augustine. Thagaste (Souk Ahras), where Augustine was born.

INTRODUCTION

I. AUGUSTINE'S LIFE IN OUTLINE BEFORE HIS CONVERSION

1. Aurelius Augustinus was born on November 13, 354, at Thagaste, in the province of Numidia, in North Africa. His father, Patricius, a magistrate of the town, was still a pagan at the time of Augustine's birth; his mother, Monica, or more correctly Monnica (after the manner of the Inscriptions), was a Christian. Though he was thus exposed from his earliest years to contrary religious impressions, he was completely subject to his mother in formal spiritual training, becoming while still quite young a catechumen in the local church. He was not baptized, however, until near his thirty-third year, after he had lived that part of his life which forms the narrative portion of his *Confessions*.

2. The talents of the son aroused the hopes of the father, and after the usual primary instruction, taken at Thagaste, Augustine was sent to the larger city of Madaura, some twenty miles away and locally eminent in commerce and in the arts and sciences. After a period of study there of unknown duration, he returned to Thagaste for a year's sojourn while Patricius raised money for his further schooling. Augustine was between fifteen and sixteen at the time, and in the enforced idleness of this interval at home evil habits grew up, which were finally renounced only at his conversion seventeen years later. With the aid of a rich fellow townsman, Romanianus, Patricius at the end of this year had funds sufficient for his purpose and Augustine went to Carthage, the greatest town in all North Africa and one of the glories of the fourth-century Empire in luxury and learning. Augustine embraced both, if we may take his own story literally. To his after-self these years at Carthage were a time of depravity never sufficiently bewailed To at least one contemporary, however, he ap-

3

peared modest and studious at the time.[1]   It is only the degree
of his waywardness, however, that can well be called into
doubt.   Patricius meanwhile died, a Christian on his deathbed,
and Augustine continued at Carthage, supported by Monnica
and Romanianus.

3. In his nineteenth year Augustine was recalled for a time
from his dissolute beginnings by a perusal of a lost dialogue of
Cicero's, called the *Hortensius*, a work intended by its author
as an exhortation to the pleasures of philosophy, though
studied at Carthage chiefly as a model of style.   So far did
the youthful Augustine seize its deeper import that it produced
a revolution in his thinking.   From now on he was ceaselessly
in quest, amid philosophical and moral aberrations, of that
higher, enduring happiness which, in his ignorance of self, he
thought could be found in the possession of knowledge alone.
The influence of his mother's earliest instructions was indelible
in him, however blurred over by recent indulgences, and, upon
reading the *Hortensius*, he resorted to the Scriptures as a
possible source of the wisdom and contentment which he was
seeking.   But their bald, unadorned style seemed so inferior
to the cadences of Cicero that the pupil of the rhetorical art
turned elsewhere.   That love of the Sacred Scriptures, so
aboundingly evident in the *Confessions*, was to awaken only
in Milan during the last stages of his spiritual wanderings.

4. His search for intellectual peace now led him, as it was
leading so many of his contemporaries, into the strange syn-
cretism of the Manichees.[2]   The accommodative theology of
Manichaeism was calculated to have some appeal for everyone.
The sect made a great point of scientific independence, among
other things, and singled out the Old Testament for deprecia-

[1] The schismatic bishop, Vincentius, writing thirty years afterwards,
thus recalls him.   Cf. Augustine, *Epistola* XCIII, 51, in *Corpus Scriptorum
Ecclesiasticorum Latinorum* XXXIV, Pars II, 494–495.

[2] For a detailed description of Manichaeism cf. F. C. Burkitt, *The
Religion of the Manichees*, Cambridge, 1925; Gibb and Montgomery, *The
Confessions of Augustine*, Cambridge, 1927, XXI–XXXIII.   The following
references in the present work may also prove useful, p. 109, note 1;
p. 115, note 97; p. 125, note 40.

tive criticism. On both scores Augustine was attracted. And
the fact that Our Saviour was numbered among its prophets
appealed to one of the latent affections of his childhood. For
nine years he was a Manichaean disciple.

5. Soon after joining the sect he returned to his native
Thagaste as a teacher of rhetoric. After a short period there
he was back in Carthage again, with opportunities more
suited to his gifts. He quickly made a name for himself in
this larger field and sustained this name by his studies in the
tireless quest of wisdom. Gradually he began to doubt the
sufficiency of the Manichaean system, particularly when he
compared its cosmology with the results of Greek astronomical
science. His associates strove to allay his growing misgivings
by the prospects of a visit from Faustus, a man famed among
them for resourcefulness in defending the Manichaean faith.
Finally Faustus came and shattered completely, by his superficial answers to Augustine's questions, all his hopes of finding
peace among the Manichees. He remained in outward com-
munion with them, however, while in search of a better system.

6. Augustine was now approaching his thirtieth year in
great spiritual unrest. At the same time the unruly conduct
permitted Carthaginian students was becoming too much for
him. Attracted by the reports of a more rigorous discipline
in the traditional capital of the Empire, he sailed away in the
night, without the knowledge of his mother. His sojourn at
Rome was not a pleasant one. His African reputation was of
no avail against the fame of teachers already in residence; he
suffered a severe illness; he was living with Manichees, in
whose religion he no longer believed. Tossed to and fro
intellectually, despising the Catholic Church and the doctrine
of the Incarnation especially, tortured by the problem of evil
and by man's responsibility thereto, Augustine began to specu-
late in earnest on the possibility of certain knowledge and to
veer towards the New Academy,[3] which taught that truth
was unattainable for man.

[3] For a sketch of the New Academy, cf. Windelband, *History of Ancient
Philosophy*, English translation by H. E. Cushman, 2nd ed., New York,
1901, 332–349.

7. In this state he eagerly and successfully tried for a professorship of rhetoric vacant at Milan in 384. Soon after his arrival there he fell under the spell of Milan's great and eloquent Bishop Ambrose, easily the first man in the city where the imperial authority was centered. The magnetism of Ambrose, and not his doctrine, at first attracted Augustine, but after a time the doctrine too began to break in upon his soul, as he returned again and again to Ambrose's sermons. He came to perceive that the Catholic doctrine could be defended credibly. Finally he saw that it could be true. But was it true? That was the question. In his doubts he made some decisions. He broke off his remaining connections with the Manichees. He found the skeptical philosophers of the Academy unsatisfactory because, as he said, "the wholesome name of Christ was lacking to them." He resolved, therefore, to return to the catechumenate of his childhood, there to await clearer guidance.

8. About this time Monnica came to Milan, to add her fervent prayers in the city's churches to the action of grace within her son. Meanwhile he was studying ardently Neoplatonic works.[4] Through these he slowly arose above his materialistic conception of God. He began to perceive that there is a spiritual method of knowledge, distinct from and superior to the senses. He was led on by degrees from the perceptible to the imperceptible world. He finally came to the idea of the creator, single, spaceless, unchangeable. The problem of evil vanished for him under this concept, and the idea of an authority, to be accepted for its own sake, began to grow in his soul. He saw the possibility of contentment without completeness of knowledge. In fact the higher his ideal of knowledge became, the more insufficient appeared to him the indulgence of earthly passion—and in this he was unconsciously approaching the deepest root of his troubles.

[4] On Neoplatonism, cf. *Catholic Encyclopedia*, X, 742–745, s. v. *Neoplatonism;* Windelband, op. cit., 365–383; and Gibb and Montgomery, XXXIX–XLIX.

9. Unconscious it remained to him for a long time, however. Meanwhile he entertained the idea of marriage as a remedy for his soul, encouraged to it by Monnica, who saw in it a possible step towards his conversion. A young lady was chosen; the marriage was scheduled to take place two years thereafter, when she would be of age; Augustine, in anticipation of the event, gave up living with a woman who had been his companion from early years at Carthage, and who was the mother of his son, Adeodatus. This renouncement proved too much for him, however, and he was soon living with another woman outside the bonds of wedlock.

10. Augustine had a genius for friendship, and there gathered around him at Milan a group, partly from his native Africa, all bent like himself upon the earnest seeking for truth. There were many discussions in this circle and several hesitations in the tendency of Augustine's thinking, but his Neoplatonic readings served always to recall him to lofty planes of thought. He had developed a liking for the language of the Scriptures after Ambrose had given him respect for their doctrines. Now he discovered many agreements between the Scriptures and the Neoplatonists. Presently he found in them what the Neoplatonists could not give, a motive for his will in grace and redemption and the following after Christ. It was no longer a question of the truth of Christian doctrine nor of the consolations it certainly held in store. It was now a question of accepting the moral restrictions which Christianity imposed. Augustine therefore hesitated.

11. At length from out the Egyptian East and in a most roundabout manner came the impulse for a crisis. Pontici-anus, an officer from Africa in attendance at court and a pious, sincere Christian, was visiting Augustine's circle one day, when he fell to speaking of St. Anthony, the famous Egyptian hermit, who had died about thirty years before and whose fame was already spreading through the West. He related how one day, while at Trèves, he was strolling with three companions outside the city and how two of them, taking a route by themselves, came by chance upon the hut

of a hermit, where they found a little book which told the
story of St. Anthony. This was probably St. Athanasius'
life of the hermit, which had been recently translated into
Latin. One of the two fell to reading it and both were so
gripped by the narrative that they renounced their imperial
offices and devoted themselves to God. This story, as told
by Ponticianus, was decisive for Augustine. When the nar-
rator had departed, he rushed out into the garden, followed
only by his friend, Alypius. He sat down and pondered over
the futilities of his past life. The final scene is one of the
classics of literature—how he moved by himself to a fig tree,
threw himself under it, burst into a flood of tears, heard the
voice of a child near by cry, "Take and read, take and read";
how he returned to Alypius, seized a copy of the Epistles of
St. Paul, unrolled it and began to read what first his eyes lit
upon, "not in rioting and drunkenness, not in chambering
and impurities, not in contention and envy: But put ye on
the Lord Jesus Christ and make not provision for the flesh
with its concupiscences." With these words he ceased. His
decision was made. He resigned his professorship, he retired
with his mother, his son, and some other members of his
circle to the villa of Cassiciacum in the hills near Milan,
which his friend Verecundus owned, and there passed the
winter of 386–387 in prayer, study, and writing. In Easter
week of 387, in the thirty-third year of his age, he was baptized
by Ambrose at Milan, and the long catechumenate of Augustine was over.

12. St. Monnica died in the same year at Ostia on their way
home to Africa. Augustine returned to Rome. He was
ordained a priest in 391 and became bishop of the African see
of Hippo about 396. Sometime thereafter,[5] but not later
than the turn of the century, he wrote his *Confessions*, the
best known of his works today, but only one of a vast output
of sovereign importance for his own time and still a masterly,
though hidden, influence, after the march of fifteen centuries.

[5] On the date of the *Confessions*, cf. De Labriolle, P., *Saint Augustin
Confessions*, vol. I, Paris, 1925, pp. v-vi.

II. ST. AUGUSTINE IN THE WORLD OF THOUGHT

13. The latter half of the fourth century and the first decades of the fifth combine to form one of those times of transition so frequent in the history of the West. Within this three-quarter century the Latin half of the world empire plunges formally to predestined ruin, and the uncertain beginnings of the Middle Ages commence to emerge from the chaos. The civilization of many centuries, long suffering a slow decay, is precipitated towards far-flung destruction by devastating barbarian invasions. The ancient pagan religion, disprivileged now but still powerful, makes its last great stand against the Church, and the Church, at grips with the deadliest heresies, defines doctrine vital to her mission. Italy, Gaul, Spain, Rome, all fall before the hordes from the North, and finally even Augustine's own Africa, as Augustine is breathing his last. In abiding significance for the after-world this period is scarce second to any, and that the years of Augustine (354–430) spanned its limits is one of its major claims on the future.

14. The importance of Augustine to the story of civilization is not to be easily exaggerated. His name is the last in point of time of the great names of antiquity; in influence on the thought of after-ages his name is one of the first. He was not the most learned of the Latin Fathers; St. Jerome was in this his superior. In the subtle play of dialectical argument Tertullian was at least his equal. There are several Latin Fathers whom as a stylist he does not surpass, and yet Augustine in sheer greatness of stature towers above them all, and not only above them, but above all the Fathers of the Church Universal. Until his time the Greek domination of the intellectual West was a fact not seriously challenged, a tradition already ancient before Christianity came. The first three centuries of the Church had but added to the Greek hegemony. It was as accepted a feature of the standing order as the political solidarity of the Empire. No Latin Father, no Latin writer, had arisen to whom the Greeks were not sovereign in thought. Not even the protesting Tertullian had avoided his tribute of homage. And then Augustine came and the Greek Fathers lost forever their primacy in Western theology. This achievement is as startling in retrospect as the fall of the West which it survived. But it is not the full measure of Augustine in the history of ideas.

15. To assess the parts of Greece and Rome in the formation of our present-day culture is a fruitful preoccupation of contemporary classical scholarship. While the originality of Rome in certain respects emerges in correction of venerable errors, the originality and predominance of Greece in most things of the spirit is stated with always clearer precision. In almost every department, the leading, the creative names are Greek. But it is the unique fact that in that department in which Greece most obviously outreached Rome—the field of speculative philosophy—the name of one Latin is coupled with the greatest of the Greeks in any survey of Graeco-Roman civilization. Some critics, according to their prejudice, will call the greatest Greek thinker Plato, others will call him Aristotle. In either case his Latin companion is always St. Augustine. Cicero and Vergil among the Latins can rival, and in our day surpass, him in after-world popularity; but not even Cicero and Vergil attain to his influence in the world of thought.

16. Long before the birth of Christ an intellectual decline had come over the ancient world, and the ancient mind tended to move in heavy dependence on the past. Into this relatively inferior intellectual life came that new principle of living which is Christianity. And some philosophers were converted to Christianity and applied the method of philosophy to the new message and thus became numbered among the Fathers of the Church. In varying degree these Fathers, from the second century on, were masters of the older heritage and in varying degrees they were masters of the new. But the greatest of them were typical of the intellectual traditionalism that was a mark of later antiquity. And then Augustine came and the ancient mind found in him once more an Athenian elasticity and freedom, and it seized at the same time the meaning of Christianity with an insight which has never been surpassed. This is the unique distinction of Augustine as a thinker. He had not the pioneering, creative originality of Plato nor the systematizing power of Aristotle, but he was creative and he was systematic as was no one of their ancient successors, and he came in time to possess what their unaided reason had never achieved—the supernatural message of Christianity. Because he surpassed all ancient thinkers, save Plato and Aristotle, in philosophic power, he surpassed all other Fathers in philosophic appreciation of Christianity; because his talents were enriched by this appreciation, by this philosophic experience unknown to Plato and Aristotle, he came to have a place by their side as a determining force in thought. His superlative gifts, forever focussed upon God as the center of the universe, constitute the peculiar mark of Augustine's originality. Because of it he was able to discuss God, God's relation to the world, the Trinity, Providence, Freedom, Grace, with a mastery unapproached hitherto and surpassed in part only when St. Thomas Aquinas in the thirteenth century brought Aristotle to the service of the Gospel. And because St. Thomas' task was chiefly a harmonization of Platonic-Augustinian theology with contemporary Aristotelian science, St. Augustine's thought lives in that Thomistic philosophy in which the Roman Catholic Church still sees her intellectual self. And because Protestantism developed from the medieval tradition dominant in its formative years, traditional Protestantism has borne at least traces of Augustine from Luther's day to our own. Outside formally religious circles Augustine is the hope of many present-day philosophers who can find neither in St. Thomas nor in Kant a basis for the natural knowledge of God. And into the realm of psychology the originality of Augustine ventured. That tireless theocentric impulse which led him to trace out man's relations to God drove him inevitably to the depths of man's heart and made of him the first great writer in the field of descriptive psychology—the most "modern," perhaps, of his many claims to a place beside Plato and Aristotle.

17. Of all the Fathers of the Western Church, Augustine was the most voluminous. Three years before his death in 430 he wrote his *Retractations,* a work that aimed to give an account in chronological order of all his writings and to correct, especially in questions of dogma, such errors as he believed them to contain. Ninety-three works were thus reviewed and they did not include his large output of sermons and letters nor about ten other works, written after the completion of his *Retractations.* Impressive as this total is, it cannot suggest the huge dimensions of some of the writings it embraces. There is scarcely a branch of theology which has not received at least some enrichment from his works and, though few of them are read today, even by specialists, their content has become a part of the living traditions of the West. Among them the *De Trinitate* is one of the most ambitious and influential, being the authoritative prelude to all that the Middle Ages did in exposition of the doctrine of the Trinity. The *De Doctrina Christiana,* explaining the method proper for an effective exposition of the Bible, was the model for Christian hermeneutics during all the Middle Ages. The *De Civitate Dei,* unfolding on a colossal scale his concept of Christianity in the environment of the world, is a philosophy of history, remarkable for its profundity of thought and for the synthetic power it reveals and, again, a dominant book in the Medieval period, particularly on questions of the relation between church and state; a book that is read and admired for its own sake today.

18. Augustine is, therefore, our contemporary, as he has been of every age since his own. In some of his works he seems the contemporary of his own age scarcely at all. And of no work of his is this more true than of his *Confessions,* a work whose title would promise us much on the context of his times and whose development ignores, wherever possible, the world through which he moved. In this, however, is another token of the creative originality of St. Augustine, and out of it came a type of literature unknown to the world before.

III. THE CONFESSIONS

19. Towards the end of 397 or the beginning of 398, when St. Augustine was about eleven years in the Faith, he wrote a work treating, for the most part, the story of his progress thereto [6] and called his book *Confessions*. Much has since been made of the lapse of time and of the change of viewpoint which an eleven-year interval could produce in the mid-life of a strenuously busy man, and it is admitted generally that St. Augustine was at least severe in this picture of his earlier self. In any case he wrote a book unique among the achievements of antiquity.

20. If Augustine had intended mere autobiography, models were at hand for the taking. Xenophon, Caesar, and Marcus Aurelius among the pagans; Aquilius Severus, Ephraem the Syrian, St. Gregory of Nazianzus among the Christians, had all recorded epochs and phases of their lives. How many of these writings Augustine knew is a highly dubious matter. What seems certain is that he did not use them, nor, in fact, any autobiography, as a model. Christian Greek and Latin literature borrowed mostly from its pagan counterpart the other literary forms which it used as vehicles for its thought, and Christian Latin was immediately dependent in many instances upon Christian Greek. But with the *Confessions* there came a type which in its purpose, its outline, its content, its general manner of exposition was something new—a prayer in the form of a spiritual autobiography, a work written primarily to God, to praise Him, to thank Him, and to petition Him in memory of that event for which Augustine was before all else grateful, his conversion. It traces his spiritual experiences from his birth in 354 to his baptism and the death of St. Monnica in 387.[7] It is the grateful record of the action

---

[6] Books I–X treat of himself (**de me scripti sunt**) according to his *Retractations*, II, 6; Books XI–XIII are a treatise on the History of Creation. Books I–IX treat of his spiritual wanderings; Book X, of his state of soul at the time he wrote the *Confessions;* Books XI–XIII, while not autobiographical, are pertinent to the subject of his conversion as a scientific proof of the knowledge of God that had come to him.

[7] Cf. note 6 above.

of Grace in him during these years and it is so exclusively
this that the stirring environment in which Grace unfolded is
ignored, beyond the irreducible minimum necessary for a
proper account of the author's spiritual Aeneid.

21. The *Confessions* are the most widely read of his works.
The timelessness and universality of their appeal lies in their
power to paint the moods of the soul with such penetration and
accuracy, with such freedom from the prepossessions peculiar
to a given age that in them every age can see its most secret
self depicted.   And all is told with such profundity and truth
of feeling that St. Augustine has been one of the most widely
read authors of Latin antiquity.   And of all the vast deposit
of Patristic writings, in whatever tongue composed, only the
City of God of the same Augustine has a place alongside the
Confessions in the literature which all the civilized world
appropriates as its own.

IV. THE STYLE OF ST. AUGUSTINE

22. It seems almost trite to insist that Augustine in style, as
in all things else, was conditioned by the age in which he lived.
How he could have dominated his own time if his style had
been strange to his contemporaries passes the limits of the
imagination.   This point is usually made, however, in discussion of Augustine's style, and sometimes in his defense—
as if to differ from the "Golden" Latin of some four hundred
years before was necessarily to be decadent, as if there were
an absolute norm evaluating style for all time.   It is a fact
that Augustine is markedly different from the classic prose of
Cicero; that he indulges devices which Cicero would not have
tolerated and which we do not allow.   But his own age did
allow them—demanded them, in fact—and every age accepts
his *Confessions*, regardless of what "decadence" it perceives,
and even holds up certain chapters as examples of surpassing
beauty.   Are we to assume, as is sometimes done,[8] that the
Confessions enjoy their world position unsupported in any

[8] Cf. A. Gudeman, *Geschichte der altchristlichen lateinischen Literatur
vom 2.-6. Jahrhundert*, Berlin and Leipzig, 1925, 84–85.

respect by the allurements of what we call style? This is not the place to attempt to answer so mighty a question. It involves the central problem of just what style is. It suggests that much loose thinking enters into evaluations of style, that an unconsciously subjective element is a factor in our conclusions, that there is something confusing and unsatisfactory in trying to be absolute about it. It is sufficient to remark here that the expressed canons of taste change, but that the appeal of the *Confessions* endures amid all the changes and that if style has nothing to do with the universal prestige of the *Confessions*, they are the only work, besides the Bible, of which such a statement can be made.

23. Regardless of what is to be thought of them, certain features of Augustine's style are determined, of course, by his times and by the circumstances of his life. Born an African and educated thoroughly in the rhetorical manner of his day and place, eventually becoming a teacher of rhetoric himself, he exhibits even in his matured prose traits that impress us as bombastic and puerile; a love of metaphor that seems to us unmeasured, a fondness for word-play that is soon wearisome to us and that at times is downright repulsive; deliberate repetitions of single words and phrases that sometimes are not musical to us. The educated world of his day and of the three centuries preceding had retained a love of the older rhetoric, though the occasions that had made that rhetoric serious and dignified had faded with the rise of Roman absolutism. Form had been exalted, therefore, to make up for poverty of content, and Augustine was the heir of a long tradition of rhetorical frivolity, when he entered the rhetorical schools. Later in life he tried to shake off some of these mannerisms on the grounds that they were devices of display and concessions to pride. They persisted with him, however, to the end.

24. But the mighty subjects which engaged the maturity of Augustine assured form a secondary place in his stylistic economy. While we of today, with our different tastes, are offended by some of the devices he employs, we must admit

them subordinate to the march of his thought, even when they pall upon us most, and frequently they present that thought in a texture which strikes us as hauntingly beautiful. The language of the Latin Bible, particularly of the Latin Psalter, enters here—that acquisition of Augustine so tardy in his intellectual development, yet so powerful an instrument in his delicate hands for profound emotional suggestion.

25. The most striking fact about the style of Augustine is the richness of viewpoint it reflects. Even in its most emotional flights a passion for truth controls it, a philosophical anxiety to express every element in its proper relation to the universal; an everlasting effort to phrase all things in their exact place in God's scheme. Augustine would have been far more attractive to us, had he not been so careful; if the subjective had only found occasional play amid his universal caution. But this theocentric consciousness conditions his style throughout, and gives even his *Confessions*, despite all their passion, an impersonal, objective tone. It is also the secret, however, of the exalted heights which he reaches, the source of some of the sublimest passages resident in the traditions of the West.

26. A final feature of Augustine's style, which no summary of it can ignore, is its adaptability to the person or persons whom he addresses. His *Sermons*, though extemporized, never lose sight of the lay audience for which they are chiefly intended and of the love of flowery devices so strong in uncultured minds. His *Letters* too are remarkable for their consistent effort to reach the cultural level of the recipient. The *City of God* is cast in a brilliance of form calculated to appeal to those best capable of grasping its profound argument.

27. The appropriateness of the style of the *Confessions* is not obvious at first glance; there is so much in them reflecting the rhetoric of the schools and so much that clearly ignores that rhetoric. Parallelisms abound and more than abound, at least to our standards of taste. Word-play and repetition are everywhere. Other devices of sound are frequent throughout. But the sentence structure and the word order, as a

whole, exhibit an informality, an arbitrariness almost, which is strange to the practices of rhetoric in his day, while the constant infiltration of Biblical quotations is an added violation of unity of style as the rhetors conceived it. But the *Confessions* are first and foremost a prayer. God is the auditor whom Augustine has first and chiefly in mind, and, after God, only those friends of his who could follow the informalities of his prayer. The features of the contemporary culture abound in his work, therefore, but the freedom of prayer is its outstanding and appropriate characteristic.

V. SOME STYLISTIC DEVICES IN THE CONFESSIONS

28. The following is a list of some of the favorite devices used by Augustine in the *Confessions*. It does not pretend to be exhaustive,[9] but the definitions [10] and illustrations it includes, together with references made to this list in the notes, may serve to give some accurate impressions of the style of the *Confessions*.

29. Adjective substantive abstract. An idea properly adjectival is raised to substantive rank as an abstract noun. *Conf.* III, 4, 7, **immortalitatem sapientiae.**

30. Alliteration. The recurrence of the same initial letter or letters in succeeding words. *Conf.* I, 4, 4, **Reddis debita nulli debens, donas debita nihil perdens.**

31. Anadiplosis. Cf. **Geminatio** below.

32. Antimetathesis. The repetition of the same word in a sentence with a change of meaning. *Conf.* I, 13, 20, **tenere cogebar Aeneae nescio cuius errores** (travels), **oblitus errorum** (religious aberrations) **meorum.**

[9] A definitive treatment of the style of the *Confessions* is scheduled to be published in *The Catholic University of America Patristic Studies*, in June of 1931, by the Rev. Clement L. Hrdlicka, O.S.B., of St. Procopius College, Lisle, Illinois.

[10] The definitions are based upon J. M. Campbell's *The Influence of the Second Sophistic on the Style of the Sermons of St. Basil the Great*, Washington, 1922, and upon Sister M. Inviolata Barry's *St. Augustine the Orator*, Washington, 1924. For the theory of style in Late Latin, cf. Norden, *Die Antike Kunstprosa*, Leipzig and Berlin, 1922, 573–624.

33. Antonomasia. The designation of a person by one of his qualities or accomplishments. *Conf.* IV, 2, 2, **diligentibus vanitatem et quaerentibus mendacium.**

34. Asyndeton. The ellipsis of grammatical connectives to obtain energy of style and staccato emphasis. *Conf.* I, 4, 4, **Summe, optime, potentissime, omnipotentissime, misericordissime,** etc.

35. Chiasmus. Two or more successive clauses wherein the succession of words in the first clause is reversed in the second and the succession of words in the second is reversed in the third, etc. *Conf.* I, 4, 4, (with repetitive paronomasia) **opera mutas nec mutas consilium.**

36. Epanaphora. The repetition of the same word or words at the beginning of two or more successive clauses. *Conf.* I, 1, 1, **Magnus es, domine,** . . . **magna virtus tua** . . . .

37. Geminatio. The repetition, either immediately or after an interval, of the same word or phrase. *Conf.* I, 1, 1, **Et laudare te vult homo, aliqua portio creaturae tuae** . . . **Et tamen laudare te vult homo, aliqua portio creaturae tuae.**

38. Hendiadys. The placing on an equal grammatical plane of two expressions, one of which is logically subordinate to the other. *Conf.* III, 11, 19, **ex fide et spiritu = ex spiritu fidei.**

39. Hyperbaton. A transposition of a word (or words) from its natural position either for emphasis or for elegant affectation. *Conf.* II, 2, 4, **cum accepit in me sceptrum et totas manus ei dedi vesania libidinis.**

40. Oxymoron (paradox). An expression self-contradictory when separated from its context. *Conf.* II, 2, 2, **superba deiectione et inquieta lassitudine.**

41. Parison. Successive clauses having the same general structure. *Conf.* I, 4, 4, (with epanaphora and paradox) **numquam novus, numquam vetus.**

42. Parechesis. A similarity in the sound of words of different roots plus a dissimilarity of sense. *Conf.* III, 1, 1, **Veni Carthaginem, et circumstrepebat me undique sartago flagitiosorum amorum.**

43. Paronomasia. A similarity in the sound of words of the same root, plus a dissimilarity of sense. *Conf.* II, 3, 7, **Quid dignum est vituperatione nisi vitium? Ego ne vituperarer, vitiosior fiebam.**

44. Pleonasm. The joining of several words or phrases which have about the same meaning. *Conf.* III, 4, 8, **ut diligerem et quaererem et adsequerer et tenerem atque amplexarer.**

45. Polyptoton. A repetition of the same word in different cases, either directly or after an interval. *Conf.* IX, 11, 28, (with paronomasia) **ut coniuncta terra amborum coniugum terra tegeretur.**

46. Polysyndeton. The artistic multiplication of connectives. *Conf.* VIII, 6, 15, **Quam legere coepit unus eorum et mirari et accendi et inter legendum meditari.**

47. Repetitive paronomasia. The rhetorical repetition of the same word in the same sense. *Conf.* I, 4, 4, **aut quid dicit aliquis, cum de te dicit?**

48. Rhetorical question. A question asked for effect rather than information. *Conf.* I, 4, 4, **et quis habet quicquam non tuum?**

49. Zeugma. An adjective made to modify, or a verb to govern or be governed by, two nouns with one of which it is logically connected and with the other of which it is connected only by an extension of meaning. *Conf.* I, 6, 8, **Itaque iactabam et membra et voces.**

VI. NOTES ON THE VOCABULARY OF THE CONFESSIONS

50. In the period of four hundred and fifty years that separates the *Confessions* from the masterpieces of Cicero, Latin, like any living tongue, experienced an evolution in its vocabulary. This evolution is particularly marked in the Christian writers, whose language is permeated with words introduced into or developed within Latin itself to give adequate expression to the doctrines and ideas of Christianity. If we except this special Christian vocabulary, however, it is really surprising how relatively few striking innovations in vocabulary are to be found in the carefully written works of highly cultured Christian authors of the Late Empire like St. Ambrose, St. Jerome, and St. Augustine. These men in their language and style reflect very clearly the Ciceronian tradition of their age.

51. All words occurring in the present Selections are listed and defined in the Vocabulary at the end of the book. An indication here, however, of the more important elements that have entered directly or indirectly into the composition of St. Augustine's vocabulary may serve to give the student a more concrete and discerning appreciation of the divergences of the word-content in the *Confessions* and in other Christian Classics from the norms of Ciceronian and Caesarian prose. The elements mentioned may be grouped conveniently under two heads: general innovations in the Latin vocabulary, and special innovations introduced by or under the influence of Christianity.

General Innovations

52. The employment in prose of poetical words and phrases. This practice, already initiated by Livy, who borrowed from Vergil, was continued without restraint by subsequent prose writers of Silver and Late Latin. Horace and Vergil were the schoolbooks of succeeding generations and left an indelible stamp on Silver and Late Latin prose and verse. This merging of the vocabulary of prose and poetry was promoted actively also by the stylistic tendencies dominant in the schools of rhetoric under the Empire.

53. The employment of archaic words. Sallust and Varro already reveal a marked fondness for archaic words and expressions, and we meet this again in Tacitus, an imitator of Sallust, but especially in Fronto, Gellius, and Apuleius, who were avowed archaists. Even in Augustine's own age, we find men like Symmachus drawing materials from the old comic poets and Sallust. Through the efforts of the archaists a number of old words were put back into circulation.

54. The introduction into both prose and verse of many words borrowed from the language spoken by cultured circles and from the language spoken by the rank and file of the people—the racy *Sermo Plebeius*, with its varied shades and elements. A number of popular words were already passing into the literary language in the Golden Age, as we know from Cicero's *Letters* and Horace's *Satires*, and even from Propertius and Ovid. The tendency to borrow words from the popular speech continued during the Silver Age, and with the decline of Latin culture in the Late period, the popular element became steadily more prominent in the literary language.

55. The introduction of provincialisms. The great writers who arose in Spain, North Africa, and Gaul under the Empire unquestionably introduced some local elements into the Latin literary language, particularly in vocabulary. It is extremely difficult, however, for us to single out such provincialisms. It was once thought that the works of the African writers from Fronto to St. Augustine exhibited such peculiarities in common that one could speak of a well-defined African Latin. But a searching examination of every shred of possible evidence has convinced our best contemporary scholars that there is nothing peculiarly African in the language of these writers. At most they reveal certain peculiarities of style, due to the cultivation of Asiatic tendencies in rhetoric in the African schools.

56. Greek loan words. Words continued to be borrowed from the Greek in the Silver Age, when the Greek language was well known and Greek literature was cultivated intensely in the West. The more numerous literary borrowings, however, were made subsequently by the Christian writers.

57. The coining of new words, especially nouns of agency and abstracts. Classical Latin is remarkably poor in the latter. The deficiency in substantives of these two types was made up as necessity demanded in the Silver and Late Latin by an ever-increasing number of new formations. Numerous verbs both simple and compound continued to be created throughout the Silver and Late periods, and the same holds true in the case of adjectives and adverbs. In all these instances, it is of interest to note that St. Augustine himself made contributions.

58. Changes in meaning. Many Classical and Silver Latin words changed their meanings in the long interval before St. Augustine. Hence the student should be very careful when he meets Classical words. In numerous cases, they have taken on quite different meanings from those which they have in Caesar, Cicero, Vergil, and the Silver authors.

Innovations Produced by Christianity

59. Christianity exercised a far-reaching influence on the vocabulary of the Latin language by the introduction of a large number of Hebrew and Greek loan words, first given a Latin form by the early Latin translators of the Scriptures, who aimed above all else at a literal rendering of their original. It is thus that words like **apostolus, baptismus, ecclesia, episcopus, evangelium, paracletus, propheta, psalmus, zizania,** became a part of the Latin vocabulary. These early translators, moreover, because of their own lack of cultural training or because of their desire to make their translations intelligible even to the most lowly of their hearers, employed quite freely the language of the people in their versions, and as a result a number of popular words and expressions came to form an essential element of Ecclesiastical Latin. The influence of these early Latin translations on the Ecclesiastical Latin Literature of the third and fourth centuries was enormous. They were only gradually superseded in the fifth century by the great translation made by St. Jerome—our *Vulgate Version.*

60. Old Latin words themselves were made to do service for Christianity through changes or restrictions in their meanings. Thus **dominus** came to signify *the Lord;* **gentes,** *the gentiles, the pagans;* **gratia,** *grace;* **fides,** *the Christian Faith;* **fidelis,** *a faithful Christian;* **oratio,** *prayer;* **praesul,** *bishop;* **praedico,** *preach;* **salus,** *salvation;* **Spiritus,** *the Holy Ghost,* etc.

61. Ecclesiastical Latin received a constant enrichment also, apart from the translators of Scripture, from the Christian Latin writers who, beginning with Tertullian, continued to borrow from the Greek and at the same time coined a very large number of words themselves. Tertullian in particular created so many new words that he may be justly considered as practically the founder of a Christian vocabulary in Latin, adequate for the needs of the most subtle speculation and controversy.

62. From this brief sketch of the elements that have contributed in varying degrees to form the vocabulary of a Christian Latin writer of the Late Empire, the student should be enabled to evaluate with some understanding the words which he will meet in his reading of the *Confessions*. To sum up: the vocabulary of the *Confessions* is composed basically of words drawn from Classical Latin as it was handed down and thoroughly inculcated in the schools of the Empire— Augustine himself, as a professor of rhetoric before his conversion, was one of the most brilliant representatives of the Classical tradition in his age —; of a large number of non-Classical words and expressions which, borrowed from the Greek or from the popular language or coined from time to time, had become a part of the current literary vocabulary in Augustine's age; of a large number of words and phrases which had been borrowed, coined, or adapted in meaning by the early translators of the Scriptures and by the Ecclesiastical writers to express Christian concepts in Latin, and which by Augustine's time had already come to constitute a special Ecclesiastical vocabulary; and lastly, of a number of words coined by Augustine himself.

VII. SYNTACTICAL SUMMARY [11]

63. The following pages contain a brief summary of the syntactical divergences from the common norms of the Classi-

[11] In the treatment of syntactical divergences an attempt has been made to indicate at least briefly the historical development of certain constructions, particularly those that belong entirely or almost entirely to

cal prose of Caesar and Cicero. In the long interval between these writers and St. Augustine, it was only natural that the syntax of Latin, like that of any living tongue, should undergo numerous modifications. On the whole, however, Latin syntax was rather conservative, and the student will be surprised to find so few striking changes. Moreover, the majority of the deviations which he will observe in the *Confessions* are not peculiar to Late Latin but already occur in the poetry of Vergil and Horace and in the prose writers of the Silver Age, who, following the example of Livy, introduced the syntactical constructions of poetry quite freely into prose. The remaining innovations, relatively restricted in number, belong to Late Latin in general and especially to the Latin of the Christian writers, which was influenced by the syntax of the Latin Versions of the Bible. The early translators, in their striving for a literal rendering, introduced a number of Greek and Hebrew idioms—the latter indirectly through the Greek— into Latin, and these became current in all Ecclesiastical Latin. The number of genuine Hebraisms in Ecclesiastical Latinity, however, is often exaggerated.

The Substantive

64. As an adjective. The adjectival use of the substantive is restricted in Class. Latin, but becomes freer in the later

Late Latin writers. For the syntax of Late Latin the student will receive almost no help from the standard school grammars, as they seldom go beyond Suetonius. The teacher, however, may be referred to the great *Lateinische Grammatik* of Stolz-Schmalz revised by M. Leumann and J. B. Hofmann, 5th ed. Munich, 1928. The second half of this work contains a scientific and comprehensive exposition of Latin syntax to the sixth century A.D. It is the only adequate historical treatment of Latin syntax that has appeared to date in any language. In the syntactical summary below, *Early* = all Latin before Cicero; *Class.* = the Latin prose of the Golden Age; *Silver* = Latin from the death of Augustus (14 A.D.) to the death of Suetonius; *Late* = Latin from Apuleius on; *Ecclesiastical* = Latin peculiar to the Latin translations of the Scriptures and to the Christian writers As Livy is a writer who marks the transition from the Golden to the Silver Age, he is mentioned specifically when he is the first to employ a certain construction in prose.

writers. Cf. *Conf.* I, 17, 27, sacrificatur transgressoribus angelis; *Conf.* IX, 7, 15, Iustina, Valentiniani regis pueri mater.

65. Abstracts. As indicated above (§ 57), the greatly extended use of abstract nouns is one of the striking features of the Late Latin vocabulary and style.

66. Adjectives and participles used substantively. In Class. Latin this usage may be summarized as follows: (*a*) *Persons.* The singular is rare and is confined almost entirely to the genitive and accusative cases. The plural is more common, especially in the nominative or accusative. (*b*) *Things.* The neuter singular of the second declension may be used in the nominative or accusative to express an abstract idea. The plural is more common but is confined mostly to the nominative and accusative. The historian Sallust shows a strong tendency to employ adjectives and participles substantively, and from Livy on, this usage becomes extended to all genders and cases. The student will note numerous instances of this usage in the *Confessions.* Particularly to be noted is the substantival use of the neuter, both singular and plural, of the perfect passive participle. All examples of this usage are clearly indicated in the Vocabulary.

The Pronoun

67. Reflexive and reciprocal pronouns. In Class. Latin reciprocal relations are ordinarily expressed by **inter nos, inter vos, inter se.** Beginning with Livy, however, we note innovations. Thus Livy employs **invicem inter se**; Pliny and Tacitus, **invicem** alone or **invicem se**; Silius Italicus, **vicissim**; and Late Latin writers even use prepositions with **invicem** as if it were a true pronoun. The following examples from the *Confessions* reflect the Silver and Late usage: *Conf.* VI, 10, 17, **sibimet invicem,** "to one another"; *Conf.* IV, 4, 8, **ex invicem,** "upon each other"; *Conf.* IV, 8, 13, **docere aliquid invicem aut discere ab invicem,** "to teach one another something or to learn (something) from one another in turn";

Conf. IV, 6, 11, **pro invicem,** "for each other"; *Conf.* IV, 8, 13, **vicissim benivole obsequi . . .** "to one another in turn."

68. The demonstratives. (*a*) **Is.** This weak demonstrative steadily lost ground in the later Latin writers and was largely replaced in some of its case forms by **hic, iste, ille,** and **ipse.**

(*b*) **Hic.** It continued to be employed, but with greatly weakened demonstrative force. In many of its Class. uses it was replaced by the stronger demonstrative **iste.**

(*c*) **Iste.** From the beginning of the first century A.D. this pronoun began to lose its original force and by the time of Tacitus it was no longer thought of specifically as a pronoun of the second person. It increased in usage at the expense of **is, hic,** and even of **ille,** to become one of the favorite demonstratives of Late Latin. It is particularly common in the Ecclesiastical writers, who were influenced by its frequent employment in the Early Latin Versions of the Bible. St. Augustine used **iste** quite freely for **hic** and **ille.** (1) **iste** = **hic:** *Conf.* I, 6, 7, **in istam, dico vitam mortalem;** *Conf.* I, 6, 8, **nam ista mea non memini;** *Conf.* II, 3, 5, **incidere potest in istas meas litteras.** iste—ille = hic—ille: *Conf.* I, 13, 22, **vel potius ista oderam, illa amabam.** ille— iste = ille—hic: *Conf.* I, 13, 22, **cum illa inania istis utilioribus amore praeponebam;** *Conf.* V, 13, 23, **iste . . . docebat salutem;** *Conf.* VIII, 6, 15, **Isti . . . fleverunt se tamen.** (Forms of **ille** precede in the full context of the last two examples.) The substitution of **iste** for **hic** in these combinations is common in the *Confessions* and in Late Latin in general. (2) iste = ille: *Conf.* V, 6, 10, **venturum expectabam istum Faustum;** *Conf.* V, 7, 12, **Noverat enim se ista non nosse;** *Conf.* V, 7, 12, **Iste vero cor habebat;** *Conf.* VIII, 11, 27, **Tu non poteris, quod isti, quod istae . . . .**

(*d*) **Ipse.** In Late Latin **ipse** was a favorite pronoun. In addition to its Class. use as an intensive, it was employed as an equivalent for **is, hic, ille, iste,** and **idem.** The *Confessions* contain numerous examples of some of its late uses. (1) **ipse** = **is** or **ille:** *Conf.* III, 11, 20, **cum mihi narrasset ipsum** visum; *Conf.* III, 4, 7, sed liber ille ipsius exhortationem continet ad philosophiam; *Conf.* V, 14, 24, ipsa defendi posse mihi iam coeperunt videri; *Conf.* V, 7, 12, ille nec ausus est subire ipsam sarcinam. (2) ipse = idem: *Conf.* V, 6, 10, Et per annos ferme ipsos novem. Cf. *Conf.* IV, 1, 1, Per idem tempus annorum novem. It should be observed furthermore that ille and ipse occasionally have little more force than a definite article.

69. **Interrogative and indefinite pronouns and adjectives.** (*a*) quis = uter. *Conf.* I, 13, 22, quid horum . . . quisque obliviscatur? This use of quis, though already occurring in Cicero, becomes relatively common only in Late Latin.

(*b*) quilibet = quicumque: *Conf.* VI, 3, 3, quolibet tamen animo id ageret. This usage is confined to Late Latin.

The Adjective

70. **Comparison.** Positive for superlative: *Conf.* VIII, 6, 13, animi, quem volebat habere liberum et quam multis posset horis feriatum. This use of quam potuit with the positive in place of the superlative is confined to the Silver and Late Latinity.

The Adverb

71. **The adverb as adjective.** *Conf.* III, 4, 7, ego inbecilla tunc aetate discebam; *Conf.* V, 13, 23, ut . . . me probatum praefectus tunc Symmachus mitteret. This adjectival use of the adverb becomes common in Latin Prose only from Livy on.

72. **Adverbs of time.** adhuc = " even," " still," " further." *Conf.* I, 11, 17, quasi necesse esset, ut adhuc sordidarer, si viverem; *Conf.* III, 4, 8, in ipso adhuc lacte matris tenerum cor meum pie biberat; *Conf.* IX, 10, 26, Quid hic faciam adhuc et cur hic sim, nescio. This use of adhuc is confined in prose to Silver and Late Latin.

73. **Adverbs of place.** St. Augustine is very fond of using inde, ubi, unde, and other adverbs of place as the equivalent of a pronoun (with or without a preposition) in its proper case. This usage is not uncommon in Class. Latin, but be-

comes especially frequent in the Silver and Late writers. *Conf.* V, 7, 12, ut . . . libris continebantur, an certe vel par etiam inde (= eis or ex eis) ratio redderetur; *Conf.* I, 13, 20, Nam illas primas, ubi (= quibus or in quibus) legere et scribere . . . discitur; *Conf.* I, 17, 27, Itane aliud non erat, ubi (= quo) exerceretur ingenium . . . ?; *Conf.* IX, 4, 7, dies quo etiam actu solverer a professione rhetorica, unde (= a qua) iam cogitatu solutus eram.

74. **Adverbs of interrogation.** ut quid = quid or cur. *Conf.* I, 17, 27, ut quid mihi illud (sc. erat or some similar verb form) . . . , deus meus?; *Conf.* II, 3, 5, et ut quid hoc (sc. facio or some similar verb form)? ut quid already occurs twice in Cicero but becomes common only in Late Latin, especially in the Ecclesiastical writers, who were influenced by its use in the Latin Versions of the Bible, where it rendered a corresponding Greek expression.

75. **Adverbs of negation.** (*a*) nec = ne . . . quidem. *Conf.* II, 4, 9, nec copiosus adactum inopia. This use of nec is cited in prose first for Livy.

(*b*) nec = neve. *Conf.* I, 15, 24, ne deficiat . . . neque deficiam. The use of neque as a connective in joining a second negative final clause to a preceding negative final clause is cited first for Nepos and Livy, and then becomes increasingly common in later writers.

(*c*) necdum = nondum: *Conf.* III, 4, 8, quoniam necdum mihi . . . nota erant. This usage is cited in prose first for Tacitus and is rare before Late Latin.

(*d*) nec saltem = ne . . . quidem: *Conf.* VIII, 8, 19, et non pudet nec saltem sequi? This usage occurs first in Silver Latin and is rare before the Late writers.

(*e*) non = ne in prohibitions: *Conf.* I, 13, 22, non clament adversus me; *Conf.* IX, 12, 33, non inrideat; *Conf.* IX, 13, 36, non se interponat. This usage, though occurring once in Cicero, is only common in the poets and later prose writers.

(*f*) ut non = ne in a negative final clause: *Conf.* IV, 16, 31, revertamur iam, domine, ut non evertamur. In Class. Latin non is sometimes used when the negative is applied to some

particular word in the clause.   However, in the later Latinity
this nicety of expression is lost, and ut non is often used simply
for ne as here.

76. Other adverbs.   (a) acsi = quasi: *Conf.* IV, 8, 13,
diligendo moriturum acsi non moriturum.   The use of acsi
with a participle as the equivalent of quasi is Late Latin.

(b) quamquam with a participle or adjective: *Conf.* III, 3, 6,
quamquam longe sedatior.   This use of quamquam is Classical
but rare before Silver and Late writers.

The Verb

77. Voice.   In common with other Late writers, St. Augustine uses the passive extensively, and he shows a special
fondness for impersonal passive forms.   Cf., e.g.: *Conf.* I, 9,
15, supplicatur; *Conf.* I, 12, 19, metuebatur; *Conf.* I, 13, 20,
discitur; *Conf.* I, 14, 23, instabatur; *Conf.* I, 17, 27, adclamabatur; *ibid.*, sacrificatur; *Conf.* V, 7, 13, sacrificabatur; *Conf.*
V, 13, 23, missum est; *Conf.* IX, 7, 15, institutum est, etc.

St. Augustine, moreover, is fond of employing the passive
in a middle sense, a usage chiefly poetic in Class. Latin.   Cf.,
e.g., *Conf.* VIII, 6, 15, si adiungi recusarent, " if they refused
to join (to join themselves to the others) "; *Conf.* VIII, 11, 25,
punctumque ipsum temporis . . . admovebatur " and the
moment itself of time was moving nearer "; *Conf.* IX, 4, 12,
insinuati sunt mihi . . . nutus tui, " Thy wishes pushed their
way into me."   All instances of the use of the verb in a middle
sense are indicated in the Vocabulary.

78. Tenses.   (a) *The indicative.*   The pluperfect is occasionally employed for the imperfect or perfect.   Cf., e.g.,
Conf. I, 13, 20, adamaveram enim latinas, non quas primi
magistri, sed quas docent . . . ; *Conf.* IV, 7, 12, et ego
mihi remanseram infelix locus; *Conf.* VIII, 7, 18, remanserat
muta trepidatio et quasi mortem reformidabat restringi.
This use of the pluperfect is confined almost entirely to the
poets before Silver and Late Latin.

(b) *The subjunctive.*   St. Augustine shows a tendency to
employ the imperfect subjunctive in past contrary-to-fact

conditions.   While this is due in some measure to a confusion
of the tenses in Late Latin, it can also be explained in most
instances in the *Confessions* by St. Augustine's desire to secure
greater vividness.   Cf., e.g., *Conf.* I, 12, 19, **non enim discerem, nisi cogerer;** *Conf.* V, 9, 16, **quo enim irem, si hinc
tunc abirem;** *ibid.*, **quo vulnere si feriretur cor matris, numquam sanaretur;** *Conf.* V, 14, 25, **quod si possem . . . cogitare, statim machinamenta illa omnia solverentur.**

(c) *Sequence of tenses.*   Occasionally, as in Class. Latin,
St. Augustine employs primary tenses of the subjunctive after
secondary tenses of the indicative for the sake of vividness.
Cf. *Conf.* I, 17, 27, **proponebatur enim mihi . . . ut dicerem
verba Iunonis irascentis . . . quod non possit . . . avertere;**
Conf. V, 8, 14, **quod audiebam . . . sedari, ne in eius scholam . . . inruant, nec eos admitti omnino, nisi ille permiserit.**
Cf. also, however, *Conf.* VIII, 12, 29, **audieram . . . quod . . .
admonitus fuerit.**   Here **esset** or **fuisset** would be required
by Class. norms.

(d) *Compound tenses.*   The use of **fueram, fuero,** etc., for
eram, ero, etc., in forming the compound tenses of the passive
is rather restricted in Class. Latin, being confined chiefly to
the poets.   Beginning with Livy, however, the usage becomes
common and it is very frequent in Late Latin.   Cf., e.g.,
Conf. III, 12, 21, **narravit se . . . datum fuisse Manichaeis;**
Conf. IX, 4, 12, **nihil enim tale ab ineunte aetate expertus
fueram.**

79. Moods.   The most striking divergences in the use of
the moods from the Class. norms are the following:

(a) The employment of the subjunctive in iterative sentences.

(b) The use of the indicative in the indirect question.

(c) The use of a clause introduced by **quod, quia,** or **quoniam**
with the indicative or subjunctive in place of the accusative
and infinitive in indirect discourse.

(d) The greatly extended use of the complementary infinitive.

All these divergences are treated later in detail under their
several headings.

The Employment of the Cases (Without Prepositions)

80. The vocative. Under Scriptural influence, St. Augustine always employs the nominative **deus meus** as a vocative. Cf., e.g., *Conf.* I, 4, 4. Class. Latin would require **mi deus.**

81. The accusative. There is a great extension in the transitive use of verbs in the Silver and Late Latinity. Hence the student will note a number of verbs in the *Confessions* taking a direct complement in the accusative that are always or mostly intransitive in Class. Latin. Cf., e.g., the following:

excedere: *Conf.* II, 2, 4, **excessi omnia legitima tua.**

ingredi: *Conf.* I, 8, 13, **procellosam societatem altius ingressus.**

invadere: *Conf.* VIII, 8, 19, **invado Alypium.**

praevenire: *Conf.* IX, 6, 14, **ingenio praeveniebat multos . . . viros.**

82. The dative. (*a*) With simple verbs.

misereri: *Conf.* IX, 13, 35, **cui misertus eris.** Late Latin.

(*b*) With compounds.

inspirare: *Conf.* I, 1, 1, **fides . . . quam inspirasti mihi.** Cf. also *Conf.* IX, 6, 14; *Conf.* IX, 13, 37.

suspirare: *Conf.* III, 6, 10, **suspirabant tibi.** Cf. also *Conf.* VIII, 6, 13; *Conf.* IX, 7, 16; *Conf.* IX, 13, 37.

influere: *Conf.* IX, 6, 14, **influebant auribus meis.**

infundere: *Conf.* VIII, 12, 29, **luce securitatis infusa cordi meo.**

inserere: *Conf.* IX, 4, 7, **inseri litteris nostris.**

insinuare: *Conf.* IX, 4, 12, **insinuati sunt mihi . . . nutus tui.**

refundere: *Conf.* VI, 3, 4, **eum . . . cui refunderentur.**

When motion to or into a person or thing is expressed after such verbs in Class. Latin prose, the regular construction is *in* with the accusative, the dative being confined to the poets and later prose writers.

cohaerere: *Conf.* I, 9, 15, **praegrandi affectu tibi cohaerens.** The Class. usage is **cum** with the ablative after this verb, the dative being confined to the poets and later prose writers.

(*c*) *Final dative* (*dative of purpose*). *Conf.* IX, 10, 23, **instaurabamus nos navigationi.** This example marks an extension of the Class. usage, which would require **ad** with the accusative here.

(*d*) *Dative of interest*. This use of the dative, with its various shadings, undergoes a considerable extension in Late Latin. The following examples will indicate the freedom with which St. Augustine employs the construction both in its Class. and later use. *Conf.* I, 6, 7, **nutrices meae sibi ubera implebant**; *Conf.* II, 3, 7, **tacebas mihi**; *Conf.* II, 4, 9, **mihi abundabat**; *Conf.* III, 4, 7, **viluit mihi**; *Conf.* VIII, 11, 25, **haesitans mori morti et vitae vivere**; *Conf.* IX, 12, 33, **matrem oculis meis interim mortuam**; *Conf.* IX, 12, 33, **ut oculis tuis viverem**; *Conf.* I, 4, 4, **vae tacentibus de te**; *Conf.* IX, 13, 34, **vae etiam laudabili vitae hominum** (the dative with **vae** is cited in prose first for Livy); *Conf.* IV, 4, 8, **ille abreptus dementiae meae** (the dative with **abripere** is confined to the Silver and Late Latin); *Conf.* V, 8, 15, **ventus . . . litus subtraxit aspectibus nostris** (the dative of the thing with **subtrahere** is cited first for Vergil, and then from Livy on).

(*e*) *Dative of the agent*. This use of the dative when the agent is a substantive or when it is used with the simple tenses of the verb is chiefly confined to Silver and Late writers. Cf., e.g., *Conf.* III, 3, 6, **perversi deridentibus eos . . . spiritibus**; *Conf.* IX, 4, 12, **ut eis legeretur**.

83. The genitive. There is a great increase in the use of the genitive with substantives in Late Latin, a fact due to a variety of causes, the chief of which may be considered the great increase in the number of substantives employed, especially abstracts, and an ever-growing fondness for abstract expressions. While it is no longer necessary to seek for the explanation of many genitive constructions in Ecclesiastical Latin in the dominating influence of Greek, and particularly of the Hebrew through the Greek versions, since it is now clear that almost all the so-called Graecisms and Hebraisms have their prototypes either in the Early, Class., or Silver Latinity, it should be noted, however, that the influence of similar genitive constructions in the Greek and Hebrew undoubtedly contributed to their relatively greater frequency in the Christian Latin writers.

(a) *Partitive genitive.* The substantive use of the neuter plural of the adjective with a genitive is cited first in Latin prose for Sallust, but becomes frequent only in Livy and later writers. *Conf.* IX, 7, 15, **per cetera orbis;** *Conf.* I, 17, 27, **per inania nugarum.**

The employment of a substantive followed by the genitive plural of that same substantive to express superlative quality passed into Ecclesiastical Latin through the influence of the Latin Versions of the Bible, where it rendered literally a common Hebrew idiom that had been reproduced in the Greek. The construction, however, had an independent growth in Latin itself and is to be met with in Early and Silver writers. Cf. *Conf.* III, 6, 10, **pulchritudo pulchrorum omnium;** *Conf.* VIII, 11, 26, **nugae nugarum et vanitates vanitantium.**

(b) *Appositional genitive.* The appositional genitive of the type **arbor fici** is cited first for Livy. Cf. *Conf.* VIII, 12, 28, **sub quadam fici arbore.**

To the extended development of the appositional genitive belongs the type **crudelitatis saevitia,** i.e., the use of a substantive followed by a synonym in the genitive. This construction, of which isolated examples already occur in the Class. poets, becomes frequent in Late Latin. It was cultivated on stylistic grounds in the schools of rhetoric. Cf., e.g., *Conf.* V, 8, 14, **terrarum locum;** *Conf.* VIII, 6, 13, **officio benivolentiae;** *Conf.* IX, 6, 14, **affectus pietatis;** *Conf.* IX, 12, 30, **grandi dilectionis affectu.** For a somewhat similar tautological use of the genitive, cf. *Conf.* VI, 11, 18, **omnes vanarum cupiditatum spes inanes.**

Another type of the appositional genitive, **odor suavitatis,** i.e., the use of a substantive followed by an abstract substantive in the genitive in place of the corresponding adjective, although having close parallels in Silver Latin, is chiefly confined to the Ecclesiastical writers, who were influenced by this common Hebrew idiom that passed through the Greek into the Latin Versions of the Bible. Cf. *Conf.* I, 13, 22, **spectaculum vanitatis** (= **spectaculum vanum**); *Conf.* II, 4, 9, **de pestilentiae more** (= **de pestilente more**); *Conf.* IV, 4, 8, viribus valetudinis (= viribus validis); *Conf.* IX, 4, 8, sonos pietatis (= sonos pios).

(*c*) From these appositional uses of the genitive mentioned above should be distinguished the employment of a substantive in the genitive after an abstract noun derived (mostly) from an adjective. Through the fondness for abstract expression this usage becomes very common in Late Latin, the abstract in such cases practically having no greater force than a corresponding adjective. Cf. *Conf.* I, 11, 17, a pietate matris (= a pia matre); *Conf.* III, 4, 7, inmortalitatem sapientiae (= immortalem sapientiam); *Conf.* III, 11, 20, interpretationis falsitate (= interpretatione falsa); *Conf.* IV, 1, 1, spectaculorum nugas (= spectacula nugatoria); *Conf.* IV, 1, 1, intemperantiam libidinum (= intemperantes libidines); *Conf.* V, 7, 12, veritatem . . . pietatis (= veram pietatem); *Conf.* V, 3, 3, veritate rerum (= veris rebus); *Conf.* IX, 4, 12, flagelli tui asperitatem (= asperum flagellum tuum).

(*d*) *Genitive of quality.* The employment of the genitive of quality without an accompanying adjective belongs to Late Latin. Cf. *Conf.* IV, 4, 7, deus ultionum; *Conf.* V, 9, 17, deus misericordiarum.

(*e*) *Genitive with adjectives. Conf.* V, 13, 23, rerum autem incuriosus. The genitive with incuriosus is Silver and Late Latin. *Conf.* VI, 4, 6, eorum . . . certum. The genitive with certus is cited first for Vergil and Ovid, from whom it passed into Silver and Late Latin.

84. The ablative. (*a*) *Place relations.* In the poets and later prose writers the simple ablative is used freely to express place relations where Class. Latin Prose would require a preposition. Cf., e.g., *Conf.* I, 13, 22, vela pendent liminibus (= ab, ex or in liminibus); *Conf.* II, 2, 2, mersabat gurgite (= in gurgite or in gurgitem); *Conf.* VI, 1, 1, feretro cogitationis (= in feretro . . .); *Conf.* IX, 12, 31, quid corde premerem (= in corde; cf. Vergil, *Aeneid* I, 209, premit altum corde dolorem).

(*b*) *Ablative of time.* The ablative of duration is relatively restricted in Class. Latin, but it steadily increases in the

Silver Period, and in Late Latin it becomes in many writers the normal usage. Cf. *Conf.* V, 6, 11, **tanto tempore;** *Conf.* VIII, 6, 13, **et quam multis posset horis feriatum;** *Conf.* VIII, 7, 18, **nec decennio et amplius ista meditati;** *Conf.* IX, 12, 33, **flevisse me matrem exigua parte horae;** *Conf.* IX, 12, 32, **toto die . . . maestus eram.** Note also *Conf.* V, 9, 17, **bis die.** The Class. usage is **bis in die.**

(c) *The ablative absolute.* The use of the future participle in this construction is cited only from Livy on. Cf. *Conf.* IV, 4, 8, **tamquam et illo inrisuro mecum baptismum.**

The use of the perfect passive participle of a deponent as an active in the ablative absolute is rare in Class. Latin but becomes common in later writers. Cf. *Conf.* IX, 7, 16, **confessis eisdem daemonibus.**

In the *Confessions* the ablative absolute is occasionally connected with some other element in the sentence by **-que.** This usage is confined to the later Latinity. Cf. *Conf.* V, 6, 10, **cuius adventu conlatoque conloquio;** *Conf.* V, 7, 13, **refracto . . . studio . . . magisque desperans.**

In the following example a clause depends directly on an element in the ablative absolute construction; *Conf.* VIII, 6, 15, **narrato placito et proposito suo, quoque modo in eis talis voluntas orta est.** Cf. also *Conf.* I, 19, 30, **vel gula imperitante vel ut haberem quod darem pueris.** Here the ablative absolute is used as an exact equivalent of a causal clause and is made an integral part of the sentence structure by the correlative **vel.**

The Prepositions

85. The great frequency in the employment of the preposition is a general characteristic of Late Latin. Many relations come more and more to be expressed by prepositions which in Class. Latin are expressed by the cases alone. Beyond frequency in usage, however, the employment of the prepositions in these Selections from the *Confessions* presents few serious innovations that might cause difficulty to the student.

86. Prepositions with the accusative. (a) **ad.** (1) **ad = apud.** Cf., e.g., *Conf.* V, 7, 12, **rectum ad te;** *Conf.* V, 9,

17, **Nusquam nisi ad te.** This usage, already found in Class. Latin, is common in the Late writers. (2) Final use of **ad.** Cf. *Conf.* I, 1, 1, **fecisti nos ad te**; the use of **ad** with a person or with a personal pronoun to express purpose or end is common in the later Latinity. Cf. also *Conf.* I, 9, 14, **non erat ad insipientiam mihi.** Here **ad** with an accusative is employed in place of the dative in a double dative construction. The passage is Scriptural. (3) With certain verbs. Cf. *Conf.* VI, 10, 17, **trium . . . ad te expectantium, ut dares.** If the meaning here is "waiting for thee," the use of **ad** in place of a simple accusative object, is Late. The meaning may be, however, "(turned) toward thee, awaiting that. . . ." Cf. *Conf.* I, 9, 14, **artibus ad honorem hominum . . . famulantibus.** The use of **ad** with the accusative for the dative with **famulari** is Late. Cf. *Conf.* III, 11, 19, **fleret ad te**; *Conf.* IX, 12, 33, **fleat ipse ad te**; *Conf.* III, 11, 20, **de me plangere ad te.** The use of **ad** = "before" or "to" with **flere** and **plangere** is Late. It may have arisen under the influence of a Scriptural phrase like **clamare ad.**

(b) **apud.** The use of **apud** to express "place where" instead of the simple ablative or locative is very rare in Class. Latin. The usage is confined chiefly to Early Latin, to Tacitus, and especially to Late Latin in general. Cf. *Conf.* II, 3, 5, **apud Carthaginem**; *Conf.* VIII, 6, 15, **apud Treveros**; *Conf.* IX, 8, 17, **apud Ostia Tiberina.** Cf. also *Conf.* V, 8, 14; *Conf.* IX, 10, 23.

(c) **per.** (1) Expressing means or instrument. This use of **per** occurs in Class. Latin but becomes common only in Silver and especially in Late Latin. It is frequent in the *Confessions.* Cf., e.g., *Conf.* I, 1, 1, **per humanitatem . . . per ministerium**; *Conf.* I, 6, 7, **per haec ipsa**; *Conf.* I, 8, 13, **per haec**; *Conf.* III, 4, 8, **per philosophiam**; *Conf.* IV, 1, 1, **per doctrinas**; *Conf.* IX, 4, 12, **per baptismum.** (2) Expressing cause (= **propter**). Causal **per** becomes common only in Silver and Late Latin. Cf., e.g., *Conf.* II, 2, 4, **licentiosae per dedecus humanum, inlicitae autem per leges tuas**; *Conf.* III, 4, 7, **per gaudia vanitatis humanae.**

(*d*) **post.** The use of **post** with **currere** and similar verbs to express the idea of "being a follower of," "adhering to," passed into Ecclesiastical Latin from the early Latin Versions of the Bible, where it rendered a Greek idiom. Cf. *Conf.* VIII, 7, 18, **post te ire;** *Conf.* IX, 7, 16, **currebamus post te.**

87. Prepositions with the ablative. (*a*) **a** or **ab.** (1) Place "from which" with names of towns is expressed in Class. Latin by the ablative without a preposition. The later writers frequently use **ab** or **ex.** Cf., e.g., *Conf.* II, 3, 5, **mihi reducto a Madauris.** (2) In the meaning "as regards," "in respect to." This usage is Class., but becomes more frequent in later writers. Cf. *Conf.* II, 3, 5, **essem disertus vel desertus potius a cultura tua, deus meus.** But **a** can also be taken here as indicating agency. (3) The use of **a** with the adjective **sanus** is Late Latin. Cf. *Conf.* III, 2, 2, **a talibus affectibus sanus.** (4) **a longe.** This combination of preposition and adverb passed into Ecclesiastical Latin through the Latin Versions of the Bible, where it renders a Greek usage.

(*b*) **coram.** This preposition, relatively uncommon in Class. Latin, is very frequent in Ecclesiastical writers, who were influenced by its use in the Latin Versions of the Bible. Cf. *Conf.* II, 1, 1, **coram oculis tuis;** *Conf.* V, 6, 11, **Coram te;** *Conf.* VI, 4, 6, **coram sensibus meis;** *Conf.* IX, 4, 7, **coram te,** etc.

(*c*) **cum.** In Cicero **cum** regularly follows the relative pronoun, but beginning with Livy it normally precedes. Cf. *Conf.* II, 8, 16, **cum quibus;** *Conf.* IV, 4, 8, **cum quo;** *Conf.* IV, 8, 13, **cum quibus,** etc.

(*d*) **de.** The great extension in the use of **de** at the expense of **ab** and **ex** and in the expression of many relations expressed in Class. Latin by the simple ablative alone is a general characteristic of Late Latin. (1) To indicate source or separation after certain verbs that are regularly followed by **ab** or **ex** in Class. Latin. Cf., e.g., *Conf.* III, 11, 19, **de hac profunda caligine eruisti animam meam;** *Conf.* IV, 4, 7, **abstulisti hominem de hac vita;** *Conf.* IV, 7, 12, **Et tamen fugi de patria;** *Conf.* IX, 6, 14, **de terra abstulisti vitam eius;** *Conf.* IX, 12,

32, **Neque enim exudavit de corde meo maeroris amaritudo.**
(2) With ablative of material. The regular Class. usage is **ex.**
Cf. *Conf.* IV, 1, 1, **escas, de quibus . . . fabricarent angelos.**
(3) In place of the partitive genitive. The use of **ex** and
especially of **de** in place of the partitive genitive is very common in the later Latinity. Cf. *Conf.* VIII, 6, 14, **putaverat
enim aliquid de libris;** *Conf.* IX, 5, 13, **quid . . . de libris
tuis legendum esset.** (4) In the phrase **se vindicare de.**
This usage is Silver and Late. Cf. *Conf.* I, 6, 8, **et me de illis
flendo vindicabam.**

(e) **ex.** (1) Instrumental. This usage is cited occasionally
in Silver Latin but becomes common only in the Late writers.
Cf. *Conf.* I, 8, 13, **Hoc autem eos velle ex motu corporis
aperiebatur;** *Conf.* III, 11, 19, **Videbat enim illa mortem meam
ex fide et spiritu, quem habebat;** *Conf.* VIII, 12, 29, **ex evan-
gelica lectione . . . admonitus fuerit.** (2) Temporal. **ex
quo** (sc. **tempore**) "since." This phrase is used first by Livy.
Cf. *Conf.* VIII, 7, 17. Cf. a similar use of **ex illo,** "from that
time," "from then," in *Conf.* IX, 7, 15, **et ex illo in hodiernum
retentum.** The latter phrase occurs first in Ovid and is rare
before Late Latin.

(f) **foris a.** The use of this combination as a preposition
"outside," "outside of," is Late Latin. Cf. *Conf.* VI, 1, 1,
quaerebam te foris a me.

(g) **prae.** (1) Local. The use of **prae** with a verb of rest
begins with Livy. Cf. *Conf.* VIII, 6, 14, **miratus est, quod
eas et solas prae oculis meis litteras repente conperisset.** (2)
Causal. The use of **prae** to express cause in positive sentences
is confined to Early, Silver, and Late Latin. Cf. *Conf.* III,
6, 10, **philosophos transgredi debui prae amore tuo;** *Conf.* V,
12, 22, **quibus prae pecuniae caritate iustitia vilis est.** (3) To
express comparison. The use of **prae** in the sense of "more
than," "beyond" (= **praeter**), is Silver and Late Latin. Cf.
Conf. I, 17, 27, **quid mihi recitanti adclamabatur prae multis
coaetaneis?;** *Conf.* V, 6, 11, **prae multis** (sc. **illum hominem**)
laudabam ac ferebam. The use of **prae = quam** or the simple
ablative after a comparative does not occur in Class. Latin

and is rare before the Late writers. Cf. *Conf.* IX, 5, 13, quod prae ceteris evangelii vocationisque gentium sit praenuntiator apertior.

(*h*) **pro.** The use of **pro** to express a purely final relation is Late Latin. Cf. *Conf.* I, 9, 15, **varia tormenta, pro quibus effugiendis tibi per universas terras . . . supplicatur.**

88. Prepositions with the accusative or the ablative. (*a*) in with the accusative. (1) Final. The use of **in** to express purpose is relatively rare in Class. Latin but becomes common in Silver and especially in Late Latin. Cf. *Conf.* I, 9, 14, **et in tuam invocationem rumpebam nodos linguae** (= **ad te invocandum**); *Conf.* I, 11, 17, **confitens in remissionem peccatorum.** The second example is Scriptural. (2) Consecutive. The use of **in** to express an actual effect or result is confined chiefly to the poets before Silver and Late Latin. Cf. *Conf.* V, 9, 16, **in dedecus meum creveram**; *Conf.* IX, 12, 29, **puer Adeodatus exclamavit in planctum.** (3) With certain verbs. **credere in** and **sperare in.** In the Latin Versions of the Bible the preposition **in** followed by the accusative or the ablative was employed with the verbs **credere** and **sperare** to express the idea "believe in," "hope in," in imitation of a Greek idiom, and this usage passed into Ecclesiastical Latin in general. Cf. *Conf.* I, 1, 1, **in quem non crediderunt** (a Scriptural quotation); *ibid.*, **credens in te**; cf. the use of the ablative, *Conf.* VI, 1, 1, **respondit mihi credere se in Christo.** Cf. *Conf.* IV, 4, 9, **Spera in deum**; *ibid.*, **phantasma, in quod sperare iubebatur**; cf. the use of the ablative, *Conf.* I, 11, 17, **speravit in te**; *Conf.* IV, 16, 31, **in velamento alarum tuarum speremus** (a Scriptural passage). **suspendi in.** With verbs signifying "hang," Class. Latin employs **ab, de, ex, in** (with ablative), or the ablative alone. St. Augustine uses **in** with the accusative in *Conf.* VI, 1, 1, **et in Ambrosi ora suspendi.** (4) With adjectives. The use of **in** with the accusative after **benignus** is Late Latin. Cf. *Conf.* V, 13, 23, **hominem benignum in me.** (5) In various phrases. The following phrases are confined mostly to the Silver and Late Latin: *Conf.* VIII, 11, 26, **in aeternum**; *Conf.* IX, 7, 15, **in hodiernum**; *Conf.* VIII, 12, 30,

in melius; *Conf.* VIII, 11, 26, **in obviam** (Late Latin); *Conf.*
VIII, 6, 14, **in quantum.**

(*b*) **in** with the ablative. (1) Local. There are no striking
divergences from the Class. norm. However, the phrase **in
auribus** belongs to Silver and Late Latin. It is especially
common in Ecclesiastical writers through its use in the Latin
Versions. Cf. *Conf.* I, 11, 18, **sonat undique in auribus
nostris;** cf. also *Conf.* I, 14, 23; *Conf.* IX, 12, 31. The phrase
in conspectu (= "in the presence of," "before"), although
occurring in the earlier Latinity, is only common in Ecclesiastical Latin, which was influenced by its use in the Latin
Versions, where it rendered a similar Greek expression. Cf.
Conf. V, 3, 3, **Proloquar in conspectu dei mei.** (2) Temporal.
The use of **in** with the ablative to express time "when" in
place of the simple ablative is characteristic of the late
Latinity. Cf. *Conf.* IV, 2, 2, **Docebam in illis annis;** *ibid.*,
in illis annis . . . habebam; *Conf.* IX, 4, 7, **erga nos benificia
tua in illo tempore.** The normal usage in the *Confessions*,
however, is the simple ablative. (3) To designate the person
or thing with which an action is concerned ("in reference to,"
"in respect of," "in the case of," etc.). This usage, which in
the last analysis is local, is very common in the *Confessions*,
but beyond frequency it presents no striking deviations from
the Class. norms. Cf. *Conf.* V, 8, 15, **illis cruciatibus arguebatur in ea reliquiarium Evae;** *Conf.* V, 9, 16, **tormenta digna
factis meis in veritate ordinis tui;** *Conf.* VIII, 11, 27, **an vero
isti et istae in se ipsis possunt** (here **in** is practically equivalent
to **per**); *Conf.* I, 8, 13, **edomito in eis signis ore;** *Conf.* IX, 4,
12, **gaudens in fide.** (4) Instrumental. The use of **in** to
express means is confined almost entirely to Late Latin, being
especially common in the Ecclesiastical writers, who were
influenced by this use of **in** in the Latin Versions. In the
latter it rendered literally a similar usage that had passed
from the Hebrew into the Greek, where it also existed inde-
pendently. While the present Selections from the *Confessions*
contain no clear-cut instances of instrumental **in,** the following
examples of **in** expressing circumstance border clearly upon it.

Cf. *Conf.* I, 17, 27, dicere aliquid et de ingenio meo, munere tuo, in quibus a me deliramentis atterebatur; *Conf.* III, 3, 6, seducentibus . . . spiritibus in eo ipso, quo alios inridere amant et fallere; *Conf.* V, 9, 16, nec solverat ille in cruce sua inimicitias; *Conf.* VIII, 12, 28, nescio quid enim puto, dixeram, in quo apparebat sonus vocis. (5) Modal. The use of in to express manner is chiefly Silver and Late Latin. Cf. *Conf.* VIII, 12, 28, in hac sententia multa dixi tibi (Class., in hanc sententiam).

(c) sub with the ablative. The use of sub to express a condition or circumstance in phrases such as sub condicione, sub lege, etc., begins in prose with Livy. Cf. *Conf.* I, 15, 24, ne deficiat anima mea sub disciplina tua.

(d) super with the accusative. (1) Local. The use of super to indicate "place where" instead of in with the ablative passed into Ecclesiastical Latin through its employment in the Latin Versions of the Bible, where it rendered literally a corresponding Greek usage. Cf. *Conf.* VIII, 11, 27, Obsurdesce adversus inmunda illa membra tua super terram (= in terra). Cf. also the use of super in the sense of "upon," "over," with the verb invalescere—a usage imitated from the Greek by the Latin translators of the Bible—in *Conf.* II, 2, 2, Invaluerat super me ira tua. (2) super = praeter. This usage is Silver and Late Latin; cf. *Conf.* V, 9, 16, mala, quae conmiseram . . . in te . . . multa et gravia super originalis peccati vinculum. (3) super = "more than." This use is confined to Late Latin, although it has close parallels in Silver writers. It is especially common in Ecclesiastical authors, who were influenced by its employment in the Latin Versions of the Bible, where it rendered literally a corresponding Greek usage. Cf. *Conf.* IV, 4, 7, in amicitia mea, suavi mihi super omnes suavitates illius vitae meae; *Conf.* I, 15, 24, ut dulcescas mihi super omnes seductiones. (4) super = de ("concerning," "about"). This use of super with the accusative is Late Latin. Cf. *Conf.* IX, 6, 14, considerare altitudinem consilii super salutem generis humani.

The Nominal Forms of the Verb (Infinitive, Gerundive, Gerund, Participle, and Supine)

89. The infinitive. While the infinitive in indirect dis-course lost some ground in Late writers, the great extension of its other uses may be considered a general characteristic of Late Latin. The impetus given to the free use of the infinitive by the Augustan poets especially, who often imitated their Greek models in this regard, exerted a great influence on the prose of the Silver Age, and this tendency toward an extension in the employment of the infinitive continued in later writers.

(a) *As an appositive.* The use of the infinitive as an ex-planatory supplement or as the appositive of a substantive or neuter pronoun is relatively rare in Class. prose, being confined chiefly to Cicero (in his philosophical works) and Sallust, who were influenced in their usage by the frequency of this construction in Greek. Cf. *Conf.* IV, 8, 13, **Alia erant, quae . . . capiebant animum, conloqui et conridere et vicissim benivole obsequi, simul legere . . . nugari,** etc.; *Conf.* IX, 6, 14, **dulcitudine mirabili, considerare altitudinem consilii tui.**

(b) *The infinitive as a complement of verbs.* The infinitive is never, or rarely, employed with the following verbs in Class. Latin prose:

accendere. *Conf.* IX, 4, 8. Late Latin.

amare. *Conf.* I, 10, 16; *Conf.* III, 1, 1; *Conf.* III, 3, 6. From Horace on. In prose, mostly Late Latin.

ambire. *Conf.* VIII, 6, 15. The poet Statius, Tacitus, and Late Latin.

ardere. *Conf.* III, 4, 8. First in Sallust, and not in prose again before Late Latin. In poetry, from Vergil on.

cavere. *Conf.* I, 19, 30; *Conf.* VIII, 6, 13. In Class. prose, only in Sallust. Otherwise, Early, Poetic, and Late Latin.

cedere. (= "concede," "agree"). *Conf.* III, 11, 19. Poetic (Propertius and Silius Italicus) and Late Latin.

dare. *Conf.* I, 1, 1; *Conf.* I, 6, 7. With the active forms of **dare** as in these instances, almost entirely poetic before Late Latin.

dedignari. *Conf.* III, 5, 9. Poetic, Silver, and Late Latin.
deligere. *Conf.* IX, 5, 13. Late Latin.
differre. *Conf.* VI, 11, 20; *Conf.* VIII, 7, 17; *Conf.* VIII, 7, 18.
First in Horace. In prose, from Livy on.
dignari. *Conf.* III, 12, 21; *Conf.* V, 9, 17. First in Vergil,
and then in Silver and Late Latin.
disponere. *Conf.* VI, 11, 18. Late Latin.
erubescere. *Conf.* II, 3, 7. First in Vergil. In prose, from
Livy on.
exardescere. *Conf.* II, 1, 1. Late Latin.
formidare. *Conf.* IX, 11, 28. Plautus (once), Cicero (once),
Horace (once), and Late Latin.
haesitare. *Conf.* VIII, 11, 25. Late Latin.
novisse (= "know how"). *Conf.* I, 6, 7; *Conf.* IV, 4, 9; *Conf.*
VI, 3, 3. Early, Poetic, and Late Latin.
petere. *Conf.* VIII, 12, 30. Poetic and Late Latin.
praeterire. *Conf.* V, 8, 14. Plautus (once), and Late Latin.
quaerere. *Conf.* II, 2, 4. Cicero (once). Otherwise Poetic,
Silver, and Late Latin.
recusare. *Conf.* V, 8, 15; *Conf.* VI, 4, 6. Rare in Class.
Latin, and confined to negative sentences.
tardare. *Conf.* VI, 11, 20. Late Latin.
temptare. *Conf.* IV, 4, 8. In prose, only in Hirtius and
Nepos before Livy.
valere (= posse). *Conf.* I, 6, 8; *Conf.* I, 8, 13; *Conf.* I, 14, 23;
Conf. IX, 4, 12. Poetic, Livy (once), then Silver and
Late Latin.
(c) *The infinitive as the complement of certain phrases.*
ascendit in cor meum. *Conf.* IX, 4, 12. Late Latin.
cura est. *Conf.* II, 2, 4. Poetic, Silver, and Late Latin.
mihi venit in mentem. *Conf.* II, 8, 16. Plautus (once),
Cicero (once). The usage is uncommon in later writers.
(d) *With* **piget.** *Conf.* VIII, 6, 15. Early, Sallust (once),
then Livy and later writers.
(e) *As a complement of adjectives.*
avidus. *Conf.* III, 1, 1. Augustan Poets, Silver, and Late.
indignus. *Conf.* I, 12, 19. Poetic before Late Latin.

inpatiens. *Conf.* IV, 7, 12.   Silver Poetry, and Late Latin.

paratus. *Conf.* IX, 7, 15.   Without some form of **sum,** as in this instance, cited only for Caesar in Class. Latin.

peritus. *Conf.* I, 14, 23.   First in Vergil, and in prose, only from Tacitus on.

potens. *Conf.* IX, 6, 14.   Cited in poetry (rarely and not for the Augustan poets) before Late Latin.

(*f*) *The use of the accusative and infinitive after certain verbs.*

dedignari. *Conf.* IX, 4, 7.   Late Latin.

dimittere (= "permit," "allow"). *Conf.* III, 11, 20.   Late Latin.

expetere. *Conf.* IV, 1, 1.   Early Poetry, Cicero (once), Livy (once), and Late Latin.

facere. *Conf.* IX, 8, 17 (in a Scriptural quotation).   The employment of the accusative and infinitive after **facere** in the sense of "make to," "cause to," is found occasionally in Early, Class., and Silver Latin, but becomes common only in Late writers.   It is particularly frequent in the Ecclesiastical authors, who were influenced by this use of **facere** in the Latin Versions of the Bible to translate Greek causatives and also certain Hebrew forms with a causative sense.

inpetrare. *Conf.* IX, 7, 16 (sc. **se** as subject).   First in Tacitus, and then Late Latin.

odisse. *Conf.* I, 12, 19.   Silver and Late Latin.

urgere. *Conf.* III, 12, 21.   Cicero (once), then Tacitus, and Late Latin.

90. The gerundive. (*a*) Attributive use (type: **vir amandus**).   It is very restricted in Class. Latin, but is extended in later writers.   Cf., e.g., *Conf.* VI, 1, 1, **me tamquam mortuum, sed resuscitandum tibi flebat.**

(*b*) Predicate use (type: **trado hominem custodiendum**). The employment of the gerundive in agreement with an accusative object after certain verbs to express purpose is relatively limited in Class. Latin, but it receives a considerable extension in later writers.   Thus the use of this construction with the following verbs is not found in Class. authors: *Conf.* V, 3, 3, adponere; *Conf.* II, 4, 9, auferre; *Conf.* IX, 15, 13, differre; *Conf.* V, 7, 12, proferre; *Conf.* IX, 6, 14, sociare; *Conf.* VI, 4, 6, proponere. In the last example, where the passive of the verb is employed, the gerundive construction, naturally, becomes nominative. This is quite in accord with Class. usage.

(c) *The dative of the gerundive.* The purely final use of the dative of the gerundive is cited first in prose for Livy and is relatively rare. Cf. *Conf.* VI, 3, 3, quod reparandae menti suae nanciscebatur (= ad reparandam mentem suam). The use of the dative of the gerundive after adjectives is cited in prose also first for Livy. Cf. *Conf.* IX, 5, 13, percipiendae tantae gratiae paratior aptiorque (= ad percipiendam tantam gratiam).

(d) *The ablative of the gerundive.* On the final use of the gerundive with pro, see § 87 (*h*) above.

91. The gerund. (a) *The accusative of the gerund.* The accusative of the gerund with inter is poetic and rare before Livy; cf. *Conf.* VIII, 6, 15, inter legendum.

(b) *The ablative of the gerund.* (1) In Class. Latin the use of the ablative of the gerund to express manner or circumstance is rather rare, the present participle performing this function. This use of the ablative of the gerund, however, was given considerable impetus by Ovid and Livy, and thereafter increased steadily, so that in Late authors it is very common. Examples of the ablative of the gerund as the equivalent of the present participle are not uncommon in the *Confessions;* cf., e.g., *Conf.* IV, 8, 13, fuderam . . . animam meam diligendo mortiturum; *Conf.* IV, 8, 13, veniendo et praeteriendo inserebant mihi alias spes; *Conf.* V, 8, 15, mansit orando et flendo; *Conf.* VI, 3, 3, Nec iam ingemescebam orando. The last two citations especially contain clear-cut examples of the usage. (2) The use of an accusative object with the ablative of the gerund is relatively rare in Class. Latin except in Sallust. In the Augustan poets, however, and in Livy it becomes more common, and in Late Latin it is quite frequent. This is certainly due in part to the extension in the use of the ablative of the gerund in place of the present participle. Cf., e.g., *Conf.* I, 15, 24, in confitendo tibi miserationes tuas; *Conf.* I, 19, 30, fallendo . . . paedagogum et magistros; *Conf.* IV, 8, 13, diligendo mortiturum.

92. The participle. Beyond the relatively much greater frequency in the employment of the participle and the extension of its substantive use, which are general characteristics of the later Latinity, the present Selections from the *Confessions* contain no striking deviations from Class. norms. On the substantive use of the participle, cf. § 66; for the use of the future participle in the ablative absolute, cf. § 84 (*c*).

93. The supine. The supine is rare in the later Latinity, except where it is used deliberately on stylistic grounds. In these Selections the supine in -u does not occur, and there are only two instances of the supine in -um. Cf. *Conf.* VIII, 6, 15, **exisse deambulatum;** *Conf.* IX, 12, 32, **irem lavatum.**

Particles

94. Copulative particles. (*a*) **et.** (1) The use of **et** = "also" is restricted to a relatively small number of cases in Class. Latin, while the use of **et** = **etiam** begins only with Livy. St. Augustine employs **et** in both these meanings very freely. Cf., e.g., *Conf.* I, 6, 8, **Post et ridere coepi** (et = "also"); *Conf.* I, 13, 20, **Unde tamen et hoc nisi de peccato** (et = etiam); *Conf.* I, 20, 31, **quia et ut sim tu dedisti mihi** (et = etiam); *Conf.* II, 8, 16, **quia et illud nihil est** (et = etiam); *Conf.* III, 11, 19, **ubi esset illa, ibi esse et me** (et = "also"); *Conf.* IX, 6, 14, **Placuit et Alypio renasci in te mecum** (et = "also"), etc. (2) The adversative use of **et** (= **autem,** or even **sed**) is not common in Latin before Livy. It is rather frequent in the *Confessions.* Cf., e.g., *Conf.* II, 2, 2, **Invaluerat super me ira tua, et nesciebam;** *ibid.,* **et iactabar et effundebar . . . et tacebas;** *Conf.* III, 1, 1, **Nondum amabam et amare amabam.**

(*b*) **nec.** (1) **neque . . . aut = neque . . . neque.** This combination belongs to the poets and later prose writers. Cf. *Conf.* IX, 8, 17, **Neque enim se ipsa fecerat aut educaverat se ipsam.** (2) **neque . . . vel = neque . . . neque.** This usage is rare before Silver Latin. Cf. *Conf.* I, 6, 7, **nec mater mea vel nutrices meae . . . implebant.** For nec = ne . . . **quidem, necdum** = **nondum,** etc., see Adverbs of negation, § 75.

95. Conclusive particles. (*a*) **et ideo.** As a conclusive particle connecting coördinate sentences, **et ideo** is cited once for Varro, and then only for Silver and Late Latin. Cf. *Conf.* III, 1, 1, **Et ideo non bene valebat.**

Apart from frequency or infrequency, or position in the sentence, as, e.g., in the case of **ecce,** the particles occurring in the present Selections do not otherwise show any serious divergences from the Class. norm.

Subordination

96. The indirect question. The employment of the indicative in the indirect question is very rare in Class. Latin, but it becomes common in Late writers. There are several instances of this usage in the present Selections, although St. Augustine ordinarily adheres to the Class. rule and employs the subjunctive. Cf. *Conf.* 1, 8, 13; *Conf.* I, 11, 17; *Conf.* I, 11, 18 (twice); *Conf.* I, 13, 20; *Conf.* I, 17, 27; *Conf.*V, 9, 16 (twice); *Conf.* V, 14, 24; *Conf.* VIII, 6, 15; *Conf.* IX, 11, 27; *Conf.* IX, 11, 28. The use of **utrumnam** to introduce an indirect question is Late Latin. Cf. *Conf.* VIII, 12, 29, **cogitare coepi, utrumnam** solerent.

97. The use of a clause introduced by **quod, quia,** or **quoniam** in place of the accusative and infinitive in indirect discourse. Isolated instances of this usage occur in Early, Classical, and Silver Latin, but it only becomes frequent in Late writers, particularly the Ecclesiastical, who were influenced by its unrestricted employment in the Latin Versions of the Bible. This construction, a regular one in Greek, was rendered literally into Latin. Regarding the use of the moods in such clauses, it may be said in general that the indicative is employed if the speaker himself wishes to state something as actual and certain, while the subjunctive is used either if the content of the dependent clause is considered false or improbable, or if the speaker does not wish to commit himself as to the truth of what is said. Cf. *Conf.* I, 1, 1, testimonium, quia superbis resistis; *Conf.* II, 8, 16, considerare, quia . . . possem; *Conf.* V, 3, 3, Fama . . . praelocuta mihi erat, quod esset; *Conf.* VI, 1, 1, respondit mihi credere se . . . quod . . . me visura esset; *Conf.* VI, 4, 6, ut certus essem, quod septem et tria decem sint; *Conf.* VIII, 12, 29, audieram, . . . quod . . . admonitus fuerit; *Conf.* IX, 10, 26, tu scis, quod . . . tunc ait illa; *Conf.* IX, 11, 28, audivi, quod . . . conloquebatur; *Conf.* IX, 12, 32, hoc confiteor . . . quoniam lavi. In the *Confessions* the Class. accusative and infinitive construction is the predominating one.

98. Causal sentences. (*a*) Introduced by **quod**, and **quia**. As in the later Latinity in general, **quia** is used more frequently than **quod** as a causal particle in the *Confessions*. The Classical principle regarding the use of the indicative and subjunctive in causal clauses is observed.

(*b*) Introduced by **eo quod**. In the later Latinity this combination has little or no more force than the simple **quod**. Cf. *Conf.* III, 12, 21, me adhuc esse indocilem, eo quod inflatus essem novitate haeresis illius.

(*c*) Introduced by **eo . . . quo**. The use of this combination as an equivalent for **eo . . . quod** is Late Latin. Cf. *Conf.* II, 4, 9, dum . . . fieret a nobis quod eo liberet, quo non liceret.

(*d*) Introduced by **propter quod**. The use of **propter quod** as an equivalent for **propterea quod** is Late Latin. Cf. *Conf.* III, 12, 21, multa praetereo, propter quod propero.

(*e*) Introduced by **nisi quia**. This construction occurs once in Class. Latin, being confined otherwise to Early and Late writers. The Class. usage is **nisi quod**. Cf. *Conf.* I, 6, 7; *Conf.* III, 11, 19; *Conf.* IV, 8, 13.

(*f*) Introduced by **dum**. The use of **dum** as a causal particle followed by the subjunctive is Late Latin. In its occasional causal use in Class. Latin it is always followed by the indicative. Cf. *Conf.* VIII, 7, 16, ubi me posueram, dum nollem me adtendere. See also § 101(*b*), below.

99. Final sentences. (*a*) With **visum est**. A final **ut** clause with **visum est** is rare in Class. Latin, becoming frequent only from Livy on.   Cf. *Conf.* IX, 12, 32, **visum etiam mihi est, ut irem lavatum.**

(*b*) Introduced by **quo.**   The use of **quo** as a final particle without a comparative is rare in Class. Latin but becomes common, especially in Tacitus and later writers. Cf. *Conf.* III, 11, 19, **iussisse illum, quo secura esset;** *Conf.* IX, 12, 32, **rogabam te, . . . quo sonares dolorem meum.** It should be noted, furthermore, regarding the first example, that the use of a final clause with **iubere** in place of the accusative and infinitive is rare before Livy and becomes common only in Late Latin.

(*c*) Introduced by **dum.**   The use of **dum** in final clauses belongs to Late Latin, although there are close parallels to this usage in Livy and Tacitus; cf. *Conf.* II, 4, 9, **abstulimus . . . dum tamen fieret a nobis.**

100. Consecutive sentences.   (*a*) **absit, ut.**   The employment of a consecutive **ut** clause after **absit** is cited for Silver Poetry, but is rare before Late writers.   It is especially common in the Ecclesiastical Latinity.   Cf. *Conf.* V, 9, 17, **Absit, ut tu falleres eam.**   The imperfect subjunctive is regular here, as it represents the original past potential.

(*b*) **nisi ut.**   The use of **nisi ut** in which **nisi** combines with the negative expressed or implied in the main clause to produce an affirmative is peculiar to Silver and Late Latin.   Cf. *Conf.* V, 8, 15, **Et quid a te petebat . . . nisi ut navigare me non sineres?**   *Conf.* VI, 10, 17, **nullam ob aliam causam . . . venerat, nisi ut mecum viveret;** *Conf.* VIII, 12, 29, **nihil aliud . . . mihi iuberi, nisi ut aperirem codicem.**   Note also the use of the dative with **iuberi** in the last example.   This is rare before Tacitus and later writers.

101. Temporal sentences.   (*a*) Introduced by **mox ut.**   The use of **mox ut** as an equivalent for **ut primum** is Late Latin.   Cf. *Conf.* IV, 4, 8, **potui autem mox, ut ille potuit;** *Conf.* IX, 4, 12, **Mox ut genua . . . fiximus, fugit dolor ille.**   Note also the use of **ut primo** practically as an equivalent of **ut primum** in *Conf.* IV, 4, 8, **statimque, ut primo cum eo loqui potui.**

(*b*) Introduced by **dum.**   The employment of **dum** with the imperfect subjunctive as an exact equivalent of **cum-circum-**

stantial is not uncommon in Livy, but otherwise it is rare
before Late Latin, where it becomes frequent. The usage
developed by analogy from the **cum** construction. Cf. *Conf.*
V, 14, 24, **Et dum cor aperirem . . . pariter intrabat.**

102. The subjunctive in iterative sentences. Occasionally
in Class. Latin, **cum** (rarely **si**, or **qui**) with the imperfect or
pluperfect subjunctive is employed in sentences containing
an idea of repeated action in the past in place of the indicative
—the normal usage. Beginning with Nepos and Livy, however, the subjunctive becomes frequent, and is extended quite
generally to temporal, relative, and conditional sentences in
past time containing an idea of repeated action. In the primary tenses, the iterative subjunctive is confined in Class.
Latin to the ideal second person. But from the beginning of
the Silver Age, there is to be noted a growing tendency to
employ the subjunctive with the third person also. In Late
Latin the subjunctive in iterative sentences is a normal usage;
cf., e.g., the following instances occurring in the Selections:

(*a*) *In temporal sentences. Conf.* I, 8, 13, **hoc ab eis vocari rem
illam, quod sonabant, cum eam vellent ostendere; *Conf.* III, 6,
10, medullae . . . suspirabant tibi, cum te illi sonarent mihi
frequenter; *Conf.* V, 14, 24, ubi, cum ad litteram acciperem,
occidebar; *Conf.* IX, 8, 17, et erat in eis cohercendis, cum
opus esset, sancta severitate.**

(*b*) *In relative sentences. Conf.* III, 4, 8, **quidquid sine hoc
nomine fuisset . . . non me totum rapiebat; *Conf.* III, 12, 21,
faciebat enim hoc, quos forte idoneos invenisset; *Conf.* V, 6,
10, Ceteri enim eorum, in quos forte incurrissem . . . illum
mihi promittebant; *Conf.* VI, 3, 3, Quolibet tamen animo id
ageret, bono utique ille vir agebat.** In this last instance,
however, the subjunctive could also be taken as potential.

(*c*) *In conditional sentences. Conf.* I, 19, 30, **si deprehenderem, arguebam;** *ibid.*, **si . . . arguerer saevire . . . libebat; *Conf.* III, 2, 2, Et si calamitates . . . agantur, . . .
abscedit;** *ibid.*, **si autem doleat, manet intentus; *Conf.* IV, 8,
13, illa mihi fabula non moriebatur, si quis amicorum meorum
moreretur.**

103. Conditional sentences. The divergences from Class. usage have already been noted in §§ 78(*b*) and 102(*c*), above.

104. Concessive sentences. The employment of **quamquam** with the subjunctive is rare in prose before the Silver Age, but from Tacitus on it is in many writers a normal usage. Cf. *Conf.* IX, 13, 34, **Quamquam illa . . . vixerit.**

VIII. BIBLICAL CITATIONS

105. St. Augustine did not begin to employ St. Jerome's translation, our Vulgate Version, until after 400. Hence, for his *Confessions*, the composition of which most probably should be assigned to the year 398,[12] he had to draw on earlier versions of the Scriptures. Of the earlier Latin versions, he followed particularly the so-called *Itala*, if we are to accept the present reading of the famous passage in his *De Doctrina Christiana*, II, 15: **Plurimum hic quoque iuvat interpretum numerositas collatis codicibus inspecta atque discussa ; tantum absit falsitas ; nam codicibus emendandis primitus debet invigilare solertia eorum qui Scripturas divinas nosse desiderant, ut emendatis non emendati cedant, ex uno duntaxat interpretationis genere venientes.** *In ipsis autem interpretationibus itala ceteris praeferatur, nam est verborum tenacior cum perspicuitate sententiae.* On the basis of this reading, the *Itala* was a revised Latin version of the Bible distinguished for its faithfulness and clearness. This Version was in circulation in Italy, particularly in Northern Italy, in the latter part of the fourth century, and was employed by St. Ambrose and his circle. During his sojourn in Milan, St. Augustine undoubtedly became acquainted with the favored *Itala*, and on returning to Africa took a copy of it with him. This, in brief, is the commonly accepted view of the *Itala* Version and of its employment by St. Augustine.

The vain attempts, however, to find traces of a superior Latin Version in our extant remains of the Latin translations before St. Jerome that could in any way correspond to the

[12] Cf § 19

description of the *Itala* contained in *De Doctrina Christiana*,
have led several prominent contemporary scholars to question
the traditional reading of the crucial passage and to deny the
existence of such a Version.   Thus Dom Leclercq would favor
an emendation of *Itala* to **illa** and Dom Quentin claims that
we should recognize a lacuna in the text just before *Itala* which
is itself, in part, a distortion of the true reading.   We cannot
enter into their arguments here.   Let it suffice to observe that
until more substantial and less subjective arguments are
brought forward it is better simply to accept the reading *Itala*
as it stands.

We know, furthermore, that St. Augustine also consulted
Greek codices of the Bible and often emended the Latin trans-
lation that he used after a careful comparison with the Greek.
Thus he states in *Letter* 261, 5: **Psalterium a sancto Hieronymo
translatum ex Hebraeo non habeo; nos autem non interpretati
sumus, sed codicum Latinorum nonnullas mendositates ex
Graecis exemplaribus emendavimus.**   It should be noted that
before St. Jerome's Vulgate came into wide use, the Greek
Septuagint enjoyed far more prestige than any of the early
Latin Versions.

106. One cannot fail to be impressed by the extremely large
number of Scriptural quotations and allusions in the *Confessions*.   They enter into the very fabric of the whole work
and are in perfect harmony with its plan.   St. Augustine, like
all the Fathers, was familiar with the Bible from end to end,
and he undoubtedly knew whole portions of it, such as the
Psalms and Gospels, by heart.   In citing Scripture he followed
the general practice of the Fathers.   That is, for his longer
quotations he ordinarily consulted a text of the Bible, but for
the shorter and more familiar quotations he usually depended
on his memory.   This citing from memory resulted in some
slips here and there from the exact wording of the passage
quoted.   The sense, however, is invariably preserved.

In the notes to our Selections we have given for the con-
venient comparison of the student the Douai rendering of all
Scriptural passages, although in many cases St. Augustine's

Scriptural text does not exactly correspond to the Latin Vulgate, from which the Douai is made. In a few instances where the context demanded, we have indicated the differences between the Vulgate Version and the earlier Latin Version employed by St. Augustine. The indication of such differences—which are chiefly verbal—in all cases would greatly increase the bulk of the notes and would be of little interest or value to the student.

For further information on the Versions of the Bible used by St. Augustine, the student should consult: F. Vigouroux, *Dictionnaire de la Bible*, art. *Latines (Versions) de la Bible*, columns 96–123, particularly, 120–122, vol. IV, (Paris 1906), and especially Cabrol-Leclercq, *Dictionnaire d'archéologie chrétienne*, columns 1606–1611, vol. 7, Paris, 1927. Lastly, the student will find an excellent sketch of the history of the Old Latin and Vulgate Versions of the Bible in Canon William Barry, *Roma Sacra*, 54–82, New York, 1927.

IX. THE PROBLEM OF ST. AUGUSTINE'S CONVERSION

According to the account of Augustine himself in the eighth and ninth books of the *Confessions*, he submitted his will to the authority of the Church on his Baptism at Milan in 387. Augustine had been taken at his word as thus expressed, with one eccentric exception, down to near the end of the last century.[13]

It will be recalled by those familiar with the outlines of Augustine's life as told in the *Confessions* that after the famous scene in the garden at Milan, during which he had finally determined to live the Christian life, he retired with relatives and other companions to Cassiciacum, the pleasant country house of his friend, Verecundus, there to make a remote, as distinguished from an immediate, preparation for Baptism. Philosophical questions alive in the schools of the time were

[13] Cf Charles Boyer, *Christianisme et Néo-Platonisme dans la formation de Saint Augustin*, Paris, 1920, 2, note 1; 1–18; 189–195, for a summary of the problem; and *ibid.*, 227–229, for a bibliography of it.

one of the concerns of Augustine and his companions there, and we have a memorial of the debates they held in his *Contra Academicos, De Beata Vita,* and *De Ordine,* a faithful memorial beyond a doubt, since a stenographer was in attendance on these debates and since the transcripts he made were the substance of these works as they proceeded shortly afterwards from Augustine's pen. To these must be added a fourth work, his *Soliloquia* or dialogue between Augustine and his own reason. These four dialogues, all written during his fall and winter sojourn at Cassiciacum, together with four letters also composed at the time, are our only strictly contemporary witnesses to the mind and soul of Augustine during his pre-baptismal retirement. The *Confessions,* it will be remembered, came about eleven years afterwards.

It was only in 1888 that this discrepancy in time became significant for scholarship. Two studies [14] appearing in that year called attention to the striking difference between the Augustine described in the *Confessions* as resident at Cassiciacum—peaceful, penitent, bearing all the earmarks of one thoroughly converted to Christianity—and the Augustine reflected in the *Dialogues* and the four letters of his period of retirement—a pronounced and enthusiastic Neoplatonist, it seemed; redeemed from his old manner of life, but with nothing distinctively and exclusively Christian in his compound.

A school has rapidly developed favoring the *Dialogues* and the *Letters* in question as the sole and authentic witnesses to the true Augustine at Cassiciacum because of their chronological advantage. This school implies that Neoplatonism and not Christianity was the master force in his moral reformation and the chief factor in his intellectual development during this crisis of his life; that only much later did he become the Christian whose viewpoint gives us the account of Cassiciacum which we find in the *Confessions.*

[14] Gaston Boissier, *La conversion de Saint Augustin,* in the *Revue des Deux-Mondes,* vol. 85 (1888), 43, reprinted in the author's *La fin du paganisme,* 6th ed., Paris, 1909, Book 3, ch. 3; Adolph Harnack, *Augustins Confessionen,* Giessen, 1888, 3rd ed., 1903.

A large controversial literature has been devoted to the subject, with scholarship tending latterly to accept the historicity of the *Confessions* as well as that of the *Dialogues*. The initial fact of Augustine's scrupulosity as a writer could not lightly be cast aside, and it has gradually become evident to many that the two Augustines are psychologically possible in the same personality, that the one is in fact a supplement of the other, that the apparent contradictions between these writings arise because of the very special purpose which called each forth, that the *Dialogues* contain statements and references that clearly show Augustine a Christian in thought and in practice at the time of their composition, despite the Neoplatonic language, which, as a comparative stranger to the Scriptures and as a deep lover of Neoplatonism, he used as the vehicle of his thought.

X. A SELECTED BIBLIOGRAPHY

1. Bibliographical Surveys

Fichier augustinien (Augustine Bibliography). Institut des études augustiniennes. Paris. *Fichier Auteurs*, I-II; *Fichier Matières*, I-II, Boston, Mass., Hall, 1972. Prémier Supplément (1971-78), Boston, 1981. This is a photographic reproduction of the thematically organized card-index of the Institut des Études Augustiniennes, covering more than four centuries of scholarship.

Bavel, T.J. van. *Répertoire bibliographique de saint Augustin 1950-1960*, Den Haag, Martin Nijhoff, 1963 (*Instrumenta Patristica* 3).

Andresen, Carl. *Bibliographia Augustiniana*, Darmstadt, Wissenschaftliche Buchgesselschaft, 1973. See especially 44-52.

Miethe, Terry L. *Augustinian Bibliography, 1970-1980*. London and Westport, Conn., Greenwood Press, 1982. See especially 21-27.

For regular additions see *s.v.* the issues of *L'Année philologique*, *Bibliographia Patristica*, *Bulletin signalétique*, and especially the annual *Bulletin augustinienne* in *Revue des Études Augustiniennes*, e.g. *REAug* XXVIII, 1982, 303-382, XXIX, 1983, 332-407.

2. On Augustine and the Confessions

Alfaric, Prosper, *L'évolution intellectuelle de saint Augustin, I: Du manichéisme au néoplatonisme*, Paris, E. Nourry, 1918.

Altaner, B. and Stuiber, A. *Patrologie: Leben, Schriften und Lehre der Kirchenväter.* 9 ed., Freiburg, Herder, 1978, 412-449, 636-646.

Balmus, C. *Etude sur le style de saint Augustin dans les Confessions et la Cité de Dieu*, Paris, Société d'édition "Les Belles Lettres," 1930.

Batiffol, P. *Le catholicisme de saint Augustin*, 2nd ed., Paris, Lecoffre, 1920.

Berardino, Angelo di. *Patrologia*. v. 3: *I padri latini*, Torino, Marietti, 1978. This is the continuation of J. Quasten, *Patrology*, written by members of the Institutum Patristicum Augustinanum, Rome. The chapter on Augustine is by A. Trapè.

Bevan, Edwyn. *Hellenism and Christianity*, London, Allen and Unwin, 1921, 109-144.

Boyer, Charles. *Christianisme et néoplatonisme dans la formation de saint Augustin*, Paris, Beauchesne, 1920, rev. ed., Rome, 1953.

— Brown, Peter. *Augustine of Hippo: a Biography*, Berkeley, University of California Press, 1967, 1975. See Bibliography, 435-452.

— Brown, Peter. *Religion and Society in the Age of Saint Augustine*, London, Faber and Faber, 1972.

Brown, Peter. *The World of Late Antiquity, A.D. 150 to 750*, New York, Hartcourt Brace Jovanovich, 1971.

Capánaga, V. *Augustín de Hipona; maestro de la Conversión Cristiana, (BAC 8)*, Madrid, 1974.

Clarke, M.L. *Higher Education in the Ancient World*, London, Routledge and Kegan Paul, 1971.

Courcelle, P. *Recherches sur les Confessions de saint Augustin*, Paris, de Boccard, 1950, 1968.

Courcelle, P. *Les «Confessions» de s. Augustin dans la tradition littéraire: antécédents et postérité*, Paris, Etudes Augustiniennes, 1963.

Du Roy, O. J-B. "Augustine of Hippo, St.," in *New Catholic Encyclopedia*, I. 1041-1058.

Finaert, J. *L'évolution littéraire de saint Augustin*, Paris, "Les Belles Lettres", 1939.

Gilson, E. *Introduction à l'étude de Saint Augustin*, Paris, Vrin, 1929.

Hertling, George. F. von, *Augustin*, Mainz, Kirchheim, 1911.

Markus, R.A., ed. *Augustine. A Collection of Critical Essays*, Garden City, N.Y., Doubleday, 1972.

Markus, R.A. *Saeculum: History and Society in the Theology of St. Augustine*, London, Cambridge University Press, 1970.

Marrou, H.I. *Saint Augustin et la fin de la culture antique*, Paris, 1938. *Retractatio*, Paris, de Boccard, 1949.

Matthews, A.W. *The Development of St. Augustine. From Neoplatonism to Christianity, 386-391 A.D.*, Washington, Catholic University Press, 1980.

Meagher, Robert E. *An Introduction to Augustine*, New York, N.Y.U. Press, 1978.

O'Connell, Robert J. *St. Augustine's Confessions: the Odyssey of Soul*, Cambridge, Mass., Harvard University Press, 1969.

O'Meara, John J. *The Young Augustine*, London, Longmans Green, 1954, New ed., 1980, *The Young Augustine. An Introduction to the Confessions of St. Augustine*.

Ottley, R.L. *Studies in the Confessions of St. Augustine*, London, R. Scott, 1919.

Paronetto, V. *Agostino. La vita, il pensiero, la missione*, Milan, Ed. Accademia, 1977.

Perrini, M. *Agostino Confessioni*, Brescia, La Scuola, 1977. A translation, with a perceptive introduction.

Pincherle, Alberto. "The Confessions of St. Augustine. A Reappraisal." *Augustinian Studies* 7 (1976), 119-133.

Pincherle, A. *Vita di sant' Agostino*, Bari, Laterzo, 1980.

Pizzolato, L.F. *Le fondazioni dello stile delle* Confessioni *di Sant'Agostino*, Milan, Vita e Pensiero, 1972.

Portalié, E. "Augustin (Saint)," in *Dictionnaire de la théologie catholique*, vol. I, 2, Paris, 1931, cols. 2268-2472.

Schanz, M. *Geschichte der römischen Literatur.* iv. 2. *Die Literatur des 5 u. 6 Jahrhunderts*, von Schanz-Hosius-Krüger, (*Handbuch der Altertumswissenschaft*), Munich, 1920, 398-472.

3. Editions of the Confessions

Gibb, J. and Montgomery, W. *The Confessions of Augustine*, Cambridge, Cambridge University Press, 1908, 2nd ed., 1927. Introduction, Text and Notes.

Knöll, P. (1) in *Corpus Scriptorum Ecclesiasticorum Latinorum*, vol. 33, Vienna, 1898; (2) in *Bibliotheca Teubneriana*, B.G. Teubner, Leipzig, 1909; 2nd ed. revised by P.F. Skutella, 1934; ed. corr. H. Juergens & W. Schaub, Stuttgart, Teubner, 1969, 1981.

Labriolle, P. de. *Saint Augustin Confessions*, vol. I. i-viii, vol. II. ix-xiii, *Société d' Édition "Les Belles Lettres"*, Paris, 1925-1926. 5th ed., Paris, 1950. De Labriolle's text was the one used for the present English edition which appeared in 1931. Since then two very important new editions have appeared:

Oeuvres de saint Augustin, 2e Sér.: *Dieu et son oeuvre*, XIII & XIV: *Les Confessions*, texte de l'éd. Skutella M., Introd. et notes de Solignac A., trad. de Tréhorel E. et Bouissou G. Paris, Desclée de Brouwer, 1962.

Sancti Augustini Confessionum Libri xiii quos post Martinum Skutella iterum edidit Lucas Verheijen, O.S.A. *Corpus Christianorum, Series latina xxvii,* Brepols, Turnholt, 1981. See the series of articles by Verheijen, "Contributions à une édition critique améliorée des «Confessions» de s. Augustin", *Augustiniana* 20 (1970) 35-53 to *Augustiniana* 29 (1979) 87-96 for the rationale for this new edition, which contains an excellent Introduction on the manuscript tradition (pp. i-lxxix) and a Bibliography (pp. lxxxvii-xci). Variant readings which occur in this most recent *CCL* edition are noted on page 62 of this edition.

An important supplement to Verheijen's text is: *Catalogus verborum quae in operibus Sancti Augustini inveniuntur:* vol. VI. *Confessionum libri xiii,* Eindhoven, 1982.

Wolfschläger, K. und Koch, O. *St. Augustini Confessiones in Auswahl herausgegeben und erläutert,* 2 vols., Aschendorff, 2nd ed., Münster-in-Westphalia, 1927.

4. Translations of The Confessions
a. English

The 1931 edition of the present work selected the following translations:

Matthew, Sir Tobie. *Confessions,* London, 1620, 2nd. ed. Paris, 1638; revised and corrected by Dom Roger Hudleston, *The Confessions of St. Augustine, in the Translation of Sir Tobie Matthew,* London, Burns, Oates and Washbourne, 1923.

Pusey, E.B. *The Confessions of St. Augustine.* Library of the Fathers, 1-2, London, 1839, rp. with intro. by Fulton J. Sheen, New York, The Modern Library, Random House, 1949.

Bigg, Charles, *The Confessions of St. Augustine, Books i-ix,* London, Metheun, 1900.

Watts, W. *The Confessions of St. Augustine,* London, 1631, revised by W.H.D. Rouse, Loeb Classical Library, Cambridge, Mass., Harvard University Press, 1912, 2 vols.

The following additions may be made to this list of translations:

Bourke, Vernon J. *Saint Augustine Confessions. The Fathers of the Church*, vol. 21. New York, 1953.

Outler, A.C. *Augustine: Confessions and Enchiridion*, Philadelphia, Westminster Press, 1955.

Ryan, John K. tr. *The Confessions of St. Augustine. With an Introduction and Notes*, New York, Image Books, 1960.

Pine-Coffin, R.S. *Augustine, Confessions*, Penguin Books, 1961.

Sheed, F.J. *The Confessions of Saint Augustine, Books i-x*, New York, Sheed and Ward, 1942.

b. Non-English

See listings of translations in French, German, Italian, Dutch and Spanish in Bourke, Vernon, tr., xviii-xix; also in *Oeuvres de saint Augustine*, vol. 13, 243-245.

5. Miscellaneous

Arts, Sister Raphael, O.S.B. *The Syntax of the Confessions of St. Augustine*, Washington, Catholic University Press, 1927.

Boak, A.E.R. *A History of Rome to A.D. 565*, revised 6th ed. by W.G. Sinnigen, New York, Macmillan, 1977.

Bury, J.B. *A History of the Later Roman Empire (395 A.D.-565 A.D.)*, 2 vols., 2nd ed., London, Macmillan, 1923, rp. 1958.

Decret, F. *L'Afrique manichéenne (iv-v siècles) : Étude historique et doctrinale*, 2 vols., Paris, Études Augustiniennes, 1978.

Frend, W.H.C. *The Donatist Church*, Oxford, The Clarendon Press, 1952, rp.

Grant, R.M. *Augustus to Constantine*, New York, Harper and Rowe, 1971.

Hagendahl, H. *Latin Fathers and the Classics*, Göteborg, Elanders boktr. aktiebolag, 1958.

Kennedy, George. *The Art of Rhetoric in the Roman World, 300 B.C.-A.D. 300*, Princeton, N.J., Princeton University Press, 1972.

Labriolle, Pierre de. *Histoire de la littérature latine chrétienne,* 2nd ed., Paris, Société d'Edition "Les Belles Lettres", 1924, 519-562, and the English translation from the first French edition by Herbert Wilson under the title *History and Literature of Christianity from Tertullian to Boethius,* London, Kegan Paul, 1924, 389-422.

Laistner, M.L.W. *Christianity and Pagan Culture in the Later Roman Empire,* Ithaca, N.Y., Cornell University Press, 1951.

Marrou, Henri I. *A History of Education in Antiquity,* trans. by George Lamb, New York, Sheed and Ward, 1956, rp. 1964.

Monceaux, P. *Histoire de l'Afrique chrétienne depuis les origines jusqu' à l'invasion arabe,* Paris, E. Leroux, 1901.

Vogt, J. *The Decline of Rome: The Metamorphosis of Ancient Civilization,* tr. J. Sondheimer, New York, Praeger, 1967.

ABBREVIATIONS

A. = St. Augustine.

A-G. = Allen and Greenough's *New Latin Grammar.*

B. = Bennett's *Latin Grammar.*

C.E. = *The Catholic Encyclopedia.*

DeL. = De Labriolle's Translation of the *Confessions.* Cf. Bibliography 5.

De Labriolle = *The History and Literature of Christianity from Tertullian to Boethius.* Cf. Bibliography 5.

G-L. = Gildersleeve and Lodge's *Latin Grammar.*

G-M. = Gibb and Montgomery's edition of the *Confessions.* Cf. Bibliography 3.

W-K. = Wolfschläger and Koch's edition of the *Confessions.* Cf. Bibliography 3.

XI.　VARIANT READINGS
in the new *CCL* edition, ed. Verheijen, 1981

Present text Page, line		Present text Page, line	
67, 17	credunt	139, 109	nutabile aut uolubile
67, 19	inueniunt	142, 27	aberrabat, ille
68, 32	omnia et in uetustatem	145, 49	maris et diffidebam
68, 35	nutriens et perficiens	148, 88	gereret, et aduersus
69, 41	habet quidquam	148, 96	negotiorum hominum,
70, 2	meus, cui	150, 136	Tenebam enim
71, 32	ueresimilia	154, 3	quemadmodum me ex-
73, 55	ceteroque		emeris
76, 49	meus *(delete)*	156, 55	promeridiano
80, 2	et terram per eos unde	158, 87	deambulabat
80, 110	autem inuitus	158, 90	orta esset
84, 173	uanus est. Mihi tamen:	158, 92	nihilo
85, 185	sua, et qua non	159, 104	auertere a me
88, 220	deus meus, quod mihi	161, 4	Quid est hoc? Quid
89, 244	Quid autem		audisti?
90, 256	excellentissimo atque	162, 32	sed uelle fortiter
	optimo	164, 54	uanitatium
91, 267	sunt. Non	168, 39	comessationibus
92, 3	istuc	171, 16	humilitatis
101, 5	fames	174, 2	oportet
102, 18	mirabilis insania?	174, 5	pedo
102, 27	et gaudens lacrimat	174, 12	delictum non habebam.
107, 34	nondum		Quod enim et nutrie-
107, 37	amplexarem		batur
111, 21	domine, exaudisti	177, 45	est: ex illo
112, 41	trahere	177, 58	exiluit
120, 46	expectabant	179, 18	regimen unici tui
121, 66	inuicem uel simul	183, 104	Ponitis
	mori, qua	185, 134	feminae— quoniam tu
123, 12	odiosum	186, 147	in planctu
123, 14	grandi	186, 149	iuuenali uoce cordis
123, 16	quia non mihi	188, 198	balanion
126, 55	tu portabis *(delete)*	189, 202	dormiui et euigilaui
131, 71	coartare	189, 209	sopora
135, 44	quia hoc	189, 213	luctuque
135, 51	illa autem non?	192, 27	Superexultet
136, 68	rursus	192, 36	aromatis
138, 99	preces et tam		

THE CONFESSIONS OF ST. AUGUSTINE

Theater facade and Christian Oratory at side, where Monica and Augustine talked before her death. Ostia.

S. AURELI AUGUSTINI

CONFESSIONUM

LIBRI TREDECIM

LIBER PRIMUS

I. Preliminary Prayer

Thou hast Thyself implanted within me my desire to praise Thee, O Lord. Do Thou tell me the very method my praise to Thee should follow.

I. 1 Magnus es, domine, et laudabilis valde: 1 magna virtus tua et sapientiae tuae non est numerus.

I. Preliminary Prayer

1. Magnus: The word **confessio**, as used by A. to designate his book, connotes praise of God as well as accusation of self. The work, therefore, begins appropriately on the note of praise and more appropriately with words (from *Ps.* 144: 3; 146: 5) inspired by Him in Whose praise the *Confessions* were written. (On A.'s Scriptural borrowings, cf. §§ 105, 106.) A., with piety as well as philosophic insight, ascribes even his desire to praise God to God Himself and acknowledges his inability to praise God rightly without God's guidance. This guidance he finds in a sequence of thoughts (**Da mihi . . . laudabunt** eum) that is itself a subtle praise of God, since these thoughts at once are echoes of the inspired word of God, the source of his guidance, and recall the years of infidelity from which God had finally delivered him. A. resolves to begin his praise by calling upon the Lord, Whom he does not know fully, but in Whom, thanks to the sacrifice of the Cross and the offices of St. Ambrose, he believes fully.

The three elements of prayer—praise, petition, thanksgiving—are in this chapter. The entire first chapter —in fact, the first five chapters—is a prayer. It is thus a foretaste of a work that in its totality is a prayer, a confessio, a prayer of praise and

Et laudare te vult homo, aliqua portio creaturae tuae,
5 et homo circumferens mortalitatem suam, circumferens
testimonium peccati sui et testimonium, quia superbis
resistis.

Et tamen laudare te vult homo, aliqua portio creaturae
tuae.

10 Tu excitas, ut laudare te delectet, quia fecisti nos ad
te et inquietum est cor nostrum, donec requiescat in te.

---

thanksgiving rising from a profound
and subtle mind and a temperament
superlatively artistic.

No English translation could repro-
duce the lyric beauty of the opening
sentences—an effect achieved largely
by the liberal use of the figures of
repetition and elaborations thereof.
Cf. §§ 29–48. Together with the rhetorical questions employed, they are
an eloquent vehicle for the tenderness,
gratitude, and humility which fill the
author's heart; e.g.:

epanaphora—magnus . . . magna
. . . (with polyptoton)

anadiplosis —testimonium . . . testimonium . . .

geminatio —Et laudare te vult homo,
aliqua portio creaturae
tuae, . . . et tamen
laudare te vult homo,
aliqua portio creaturae
tuae . . .
—te . . . te . . . te . . . ad
te . . . in te . . . te . . .
te . . . te . . . te . . . te
. . . te? . . . te . . . te
. . . te . . . in te . . .
te (with occasional ana-
diplosis)
—invocare . . . invocare
. . .
—nesciens . . . nesciens
. . .

polyptoton — . . . invocare . . . invocat . . . invocaris

. . . ? . . . invocabunt
. . . ?
— . . . invenient . . .
invenientes . . .
— . . . invocans . . .
invocem . . .

repetitive paronomasia— . . . circumferens . . . circum-
ferens . . .

Figures of repetition and sound, or
suggestions of them, abound in devout
and reflective passages throughout
the *Confessions*, e.g., I, 19, 21, 24, 31;
II, 17, 18, etc.

1. Magnus . . . valde: cf. *Ps.* 144:
3, " Great is the Lord, and greatly
to be praised."

2. magna . . . numerus: cf. *Ps.*
146: 5, " Great is our Lord, and great
is His power: and of His wisdom there
is no number."

4. aliqua portio . . . tuae: " a part
(as he is) of Thy creation."

6. testimonium peccati sui: the
" testimony " of man's sin is his
mortality. Cf. *Rom.* 5: 12 ff., where
St. Paul writes of death as the consequence of Adam's Fall.

6. quia: cf. § 97.

6. superbis resistis: cf. *James* 4: 6,
" God resisteth the proud."

10. excitas ut . . . delectet: as the
object of **delectet**, sc. **hominem**. God
has placed in man a delight in praising
Him.

10. ad te: " for Thyself." Cf.
§ 86a, 2.

Da mihi, domine, scire et intellegere, utrum sit prius invocare te an laudare te et scire te prius sit an invocare te. Sed quis te invocat nesciens te? Aliud enim pro alio potest invocare nesciens. An potius invocaris, ut sciaris? Quomodo autem invocabunt, in quem non crediderunt? Aut quomodo credent sine praedicante? Et laudabunt dominum qui requirunt eum. Quaerentes enim invenient eum et invenientes laudabunt eum.

Quaeram te, domine, invocans te et invocem te credens in te: praedicatus enim es nobis. Invocat te, domine, fides mea, quam dedisti mihi, quam inspirasti mihi per humanitatem filii tui, per ministerium praedicatoris tui.

I praise Thee, O God, and am soon lost
in paradox, so inadequate is language to
Thy unspeakable attributes. And yet how
far worse is silence, when attempts to ex-
press Thee fall so short of Thy due?

---

12. **Da . . . intellegere:** cf. §89 b.

12. **utrum . . . sit: invocare . . . laudare** are subjects of **sit.**

14. **Aliud . . . pro alio:** "for he who is not acquainted with Thee can invoke another in Thy place." A. may be referring to the objects of his worship when he was a Manichaean; hence the neuter **Aliud.**

16. **Quomodo . . . praedicante:** cf. *Rom.* 10: 14, "How then shall they call on him, in whom they have not believed? . . . Or how shall they hear without a preacher?" (i.e., as I did not believe and did not hear, until after I had heard St. Ambrose.)

16. **in quem:** cf. § 88a, 3.

18. **Et laudabunt . . . eum:** cf. *Ps.* 21: 27, "and they shall praise the Lord that seek him."

19. **Quaerentes . . . laudabunt eum:** cf. *Matt.* 7: 7, "seek and you shall find."

21. **Quaeram:** note that **quaeram,** like **invocem,** is subjunctive, "Let me seek. . . ."

22. **in te:** cf. § 88a, 3.

23. **inspirasti mihi:** cf. § 82b.

23. **per humanitatem:** cf. § 86c, 1.

24. **ministerium praedicatoris: ministerium** is used here in its Christian sense of "office of preacher of Christ." The reference, in all probability, is to St. Ambrose, the chief instrument in A.'s conversion.

25 **IV. 4** Quid es ergo, deus meus?   Quid, rogo, nisi dominus
deus?   Quis enim dominus praeter dominum?
Aut quis deus praeter deum nostrum?

Summe, optime, potentissime, omnipotentissime, misericordissime et iustissime, secretissime et praesentissime,
30 pulcherrime et fortissime, stabilis et inconprehensibilis,
inmutabilis, mutans omnia, numquam novus, numquam
vetus, innovans omnia; in vetustatem perducens
superbos et nesciunt; semper agens, semper quietus, colligens et non egens, portans et implens et protegens,
35 creans et nutriens, perficiens, quaerens, cum nihil desit

---

25. deus meus: A., in imitation of the language of the Psalms, always employs **deus meus** in direct address instead of **mi deus.** W-K. Cf. § 80.

26. Quis . . . praeter deum nostrum: cf. *Ps.* 17: 32, " For who is God but the Lord? or who is God but our God? "

28. Summe, optime . . . muti sunt: a litany of praise adorned by paradox, asyndeton, and rhetorical question, the chapter also abounds in figures of repetition, sound, and parallelism; e.g.:
parison (with epanaphora)—**numquam novus, numquam vetus.**
—**semper agens, semper quietus.**
—**Reddis debita nulli debens, donas debita nihil perdens** (with alliteration and repetitive paronomasia).
repetitive paronomasia—**opera mutas nec mutas consilium** (with chiasmus).
—**aut quid dicit aliquis, cum de te dicit?**

28. omnipotentissime: the superlative of **omnipotens,** which in itself has superlative force, is illogical, but it is used here for rhetorical effect. It tries to express God's omnipotence in

language and echoes the ending of the preceding **potentissime.**

31. numquam . . . vetus: i.e., " new " and " old " are appropriate to temporal beings, not to the Eternal.

32. in . . . nesciunt: Cf. *Job* 9:5 (Old Version), in **vetustatem perducens montes et nesciunt.** A. thus interprets **montes** as referring to the proud.

33. semper . . . quietus: " In God there is no transition from **potentia** to **actus,** from possibility to actuality, but God is **actus purus,** therefore **semper agens.** God is no mere lifeless concept but is living power. Although the work of creation is completed, there is no inactivity or stagnation in God, but rather a manifold, interior divine life (the Trinity). Nevertheless, God is the highest and most perfect repose inasmuch as He is **actus purus,** in Whom the moment of unrest—the change from **potentia** to **actus**—is lacking." W-K.

34. portans . . . et protegens: sc. **omnia.** On portans, cf. *Hebr.* 1: 3, **portansque omnia verbo virtutis suae;** on implens, cf. *Jer.* 23: 24, **caelum et terram ego impleo;** on protegens, cf. *Ps.* 16: 8, **sub umbra alarum tuarum protege me.** W-K.

tibi. Amas nec aestuas, zelas et securus es, paenitet te
et non doles, irasceris et tranquillus es, opera mutas nec
mutas consilium; recipis quod invenis et numquam amisisti; numquam inops et gaudes lucris, numquam avarus
et usuras exigis. Supererogatur tibi, ut debeas, et quis 40
habet quicquam non tuum? Reddis debita nulli debens,
donas debita nihil perdens. Et quid diximus, deus meus,
vita mea, dulcedo mea sancta, aut quid dicit aliquis, cum
de te dicit? Et vae tacentibus de te, quoniam loquaces
muti sunt. 45

II. Infancy

*From Thee, O God, came all blessings of
my infancy, so that my parents and my
servants were but instruments of Thy
mercy.*

VI. 7 Sed tamen sine me loqui apud misericordiam

36. Amas nec aestuas: contrast between divine and human love, i.e., "You love, but not with passion."

36. zelas: i.e., God is jealous to possess us, but without perturbation, as becomes God. Cf. *Exod.* 20: 5, "I am the Lord thy God, mighty, jealous."

36. paenitet te: cf. *Gen.* 6: 6, "It repented him that he had made man on the earth."

37. opera . . . consilium: i.e., God's universe exhibits constant change, but God Himself is unchangeable.

38. recipis . . . amisisti: i.e., God can never lose anything which He has created, because no created being can become independent of God, its creator.

39. numquam . . . avarus: i.e., God is not poor, but He rejoices in the gain that comes from our using His gifts to us profitably; He is not avari-

cious, yet He demands that we give returns for His gifts to us.

40. Supererogatur . . . debeas: i.e., when one renders to God more than justice requires, God, as it were, becomes such a one's debtor. W-K.

40. quis habet . . . non tuum: cf. I *Cor.* 4: 7, "Or what hast thou that thou hast not received?"

41. Reddis . . . debens: i.e., God makes Himself a "debtor" to man by His promises, yet His indebtedness is, of course, only a gratuitous act of His divine love. W-K.

44. quoniam loquaces, etc.: i.e., God is so great that even the most eloquent in His praise are as if mute. On **vae tacentibus,** cf. § 82d.

II. Infancy

1. apud misericordiam tuam: "in the presence of Thy mercy"; i.e., "before Thee in Thy attribute of God of Mercy (and not of Justice, for instance)."

tuam, me terram et cinerem, sine tamen loqui, quoniam
ecce misericordia tua est-non homo, inrisor meus-cui loquor.
Et tu fortasse inrides me, sed conversus misereberis mei.
5 Quid enim est quod volo dicere, domine, nisi quia nescio,
unde venerim huc, in istam dico vitam mortalem an mortem vitalem? Nescio. Et susceperunt me consolationes
miserationum tuarum, sicut audivi a parentibus carnis
meae, ex quo et in qua me formasti in tempore: non enim
10 ego memini.

Exceperunt ergo me consolationes lactis humani, nec
mater mea vel nutrices meae sibi ubera implebant, sed tu
mihi per eas dabas alimentum infantiae secundum institutionem tuam et divitias usque ad fundum rerum dispositas.
15 Tu etiam mihi dabas nolle amplius, quam dabas, et nutri-
entibus me dare mihi velle quod eis dabas: dare enim mihi

---

2. terram et cinerem: cf. *Gen.* 18:
27, " I will speak to my Lord, whereas
I am dust and ashes."

2. quoniam . . . loquor: " for behold it is Thy mercy—not man, my
mocker—to which I speak "; i.e.,
man, who would be my mocker, were
I so to speak to him.

4. conversus: i.e., once Thou hast
turned to me and noted my speech-
lessness on the mystery of birth.

**5. nisi quia nescio, unde venerim
huc:** whether the individual human
soul is created by God or is trans-
mitted by parents to their offspring
through the process of generation was
a mooted question among churchmen
long before A.'s time. As early as
395 A. D. (and, therefore, before the
above words were written), in his
treatise *On Free Will* (III, 56), A. was
in suspense on the question. (Cf.
Letter 166, 7.) He was distressed
about it long after the *Confessions*
were finished, when the polemic of
Pelagius against the fact of original
sin inclined him to favor the generated

rather than the created soul. On **nisi
quia,** cf. § 98e.

**6. istam . . . vitam mortalem an
mortem vitalem:** cf. § 40. On **istam =
hanc,** cf. § 68c, 1.

**7. consolationes miserationum tu-
arum:** cf. *Ps.* 93: 19 and *Ps.* 68: 17.

9. ex . . . qua: i.e., ex quo (father);
in qua (mother). These relatives
have **parentibus** as their antecedent:
" from (the one of) whom and in (the
other of) whom."

9. in tempore: " at a certain time."

11. Exceperunt: " received."

12. sibi . . . implebant: " did fill
their own breasts." On **sibi,** cf.
§ 82d. On **nec . . . vel:** cf. § 94b.

13. institutionem: i.e., the divine
arrangement of the world.

13. secundum . . . dispositas: " according to Thy institution and Thy
riches, organized (as they are) down
to the very foundation of things."

15. dabas nolle: cf. § 89b.

16. dare . . . ex te: " for they were
willing to give to me because of that

per ordinatum affectum volebant quo abundabant ex te.
Nam bonum erat eis bonum meum ex eis, quod ex eis non,
sed per eas erat: ex te quippe bona omnia, deus, et ex deo
meo salus mihi universa. Quod animadverti postmodum 20
clamante te mihi per haec ipsa, quae tribuis intus et foris.
Nam tunc sugere noram, et adquiescere delectationibus,
flere autem offensiones carnis meae—nihil amplius.

8 Post et ridere coepi, dormiens primo, deinde vigilans.
Hoc enim de me mihi indicatum est et credidi quoniam sic 25
videmus alios infantes: nam ista mea non memini. Et ecce
paulatim sentiebam, ubi essem, et voluntates meas volebam
ostendere eis, per quos implerentur, et non poteram, quia
illae intus erant, foris autem illi nec ullo suo sensu valebant
introire in animam meam. Itaque iactabam et membra et 30
voces, signa similia voluntatibus meis, pauca quae poteram,
qualia poteram: non enim erant veri similia. Et cum mihi
non obtemperabatur vel non intellecto vel ne obesset, in-

---

foreordained affection, wherewith
they did abound from Thee."

18. Nam bonum . . . eas erat: "For
good *for* them was my good *from*
them, which was not (strictly speaking) *from* them, but *through* them ":
i. e., the blessing of nourishment which
he received from his mother and nurses
was a blessing to them in turn; yet
they were not the source, but the
instrument of this blessing.

20. Quod animadverti . . . foris:
" And this (i.e., the truth of the preceding sentence) I noted afterwards,
when Thou didst cry to me through
those very things which Thou dost
grant inwardly and outwardly (i.e.,
my interior and exterior faculties)."

22. sugere noram: cf. § 89b.

26. ista mea: " these my (actions
of the same sort)." On **ista = haec,**
cf. § 68c, 1.

29. illae: sc. **voluntates.**

29. illi: refers to per quos imple-

rentur. The child A. could not yet
express his desires through the medium
of language.

29. nec ullo suo sensu: " and not
by any sense of theirs."

29. valebant introire: cf. § 89b.

30. iactabam . . . voces: " I was
wont to toss about my limbs and my
cries "; i.e., " I was wont to toss
about my limbs and utter cries." On
the zeugma, cf. § 49.

31. signa similia: i.e., the signs
made by his movements and cries
were as vague as his desires. W-K.

32. non enim . . . veri similia:
" For they were not representative of
the truth." On the antimetathesis,
similia . . . similia, cf. § 32.

33. intellecto: construe with **mihi**
and render " either because I was not
understood."

**33. indignabar non subditis maio-
ribus et liberis non servientibus:** " I
became angry at my elders, not sub-

dignabar non subditis maioribus et liberis non servientibus
35 et me de illis flendo vindicabam. Tales esse infantes didici—
quos discere potui—et me talem fuisse magis mihi ipsi
indicaverunt nescientes quam scientes nutritores mei.

*With the mind which Thou gavest me I
learned how to speak.*

VIII. 13 Nonne ab infantia huc pergens veni in pueriti-
iam? Vel potius ipsa in me venit et successit infantiae?
40 Nec discessit illa: quo enim abiit? Et tamen iam non erat.
Non enim eram infans, qui non farer, sed iam puer loquens
eram. Et memini hoc, et unde loqui didiceram, post ad-
verti. Non enim docebant me maiores homines praebentes
mihi verba certo aliquo ordine doctrinae, sicut paulo post
45 litteras, sed ego ipse mente, quam dedisti mihi, deus meus,
cum gemitibus et vocibus variis et variis membrorum
motibus edere vellem sensa cordis mei, ut voluntati parere-
tur, nec valerem quae volebam omnia nec quibus volebam
omnibus. Prensabam memoria, cum ipsi appellabant rem
50 aliquam et cum secundum eam vocem corpus ad aliquid

---

ject to me, and at children not
humoring me"; or "I became angry
at my elders, who, not subject to me
and free, did not act as my slaves";
or "I became angry with my elders,
who were unsubmissive to me and in
their freedom would not serve me."
On chiastic order, cf. § 35.

35. de . . . vindicabam: cf. § 87d, 4.

36. ipsi: sc. **infantes** and take with **nescientes.**

38. ab infantia huc pergens: "pro-
ceeding from infancy up to the present
point"; i.e., "in the course of my
progress from infancy up to the present time."

39. ipsa: its antecedent is **pueritiam.**

40. illa: its antecedent is **infantiae.**

41. Non . . . infans . . . farer:
"For I was not an in-fans (one not
speaking), one who did not speak."
The clause **qui . . . farer** is a relative
clause of characteristic.

42. didiceram : cf. § 96.

44. certo . . . doctrinae "in any
fixed order of instruction."

45. ego ipse: sc. **me docebam.**

48. nec valerem: sc. **edere,** cf.
§ 89b.

49. Prensabam memoria: "I was
wont to seize with my memory." Another reading is **Pensabam memoria:**
"I thought the matter out with the
aid of my memory."

movebant: videbam et tenebam hoc ab eis vocari rem illam, quod sonabant, cum eam vellent ostendere. Hoc autem eos velle ex motu corporis aperiebatur tamquam verbis naturalibus omnium gentium, quae fiunt vultu et nutu oculorum ceterorumque membrorum actu et sonitu vocis 55 indicante affectionem animi in petendis, habendis, reiciendis fugiendisve rebus. Ita verba in variis sententiis locis suis posita et crebro audita quarum rerum signa essent paulatim colligebam measque iam voluntates edomito in eis signis ore per haec enuntiabam. 60

Sic cum his, inter quos eram, voluntatum enuntiandarum signa conmunicavi et vitae humanae procellosam societatem altius ingressus sum, pendens ex parentum auctoritate nutuque maiorum hominum.

III. BOYHOOD INFLUENCES

How I beseeched Thee, O God, against the
chastisements of schooldays and was mocked
by my parents for my unanswered prayers.
I feared the rod in my wretchedness and yet
played the truant, a laggard in my tasks as
my teachers in theirs.

---

51. tenebam hoc . . . ostendere: "I did remember that this thing was called by them that (sound) which they uttered whenever they wished to indicate this (thing)." For **vellent**, cf. §102a. **hoc . . . quod sonabant** is used predicatively after **vocari**.

52. Hoc . . . velle . . . aperiebatur: "That they meant this was revealed by the movement of the body." On instrumental **ex**, cf. § 87e, 1.

53. tamquam verbis naturalibus: in apposition with **motu:** "the natural words, as it were, of all peoples"; i.e., the universal language of signs, as the next clause explains.

56. affectionem animi: "the affections of the mind."

59. edomito . . . ore: "my mouth having been broken in in these signs"; i.e., "accustomed to these signs." On **in**, cf. § 88b, 3.

60. per haec: haec (sc. **signa**) = "sounds." On **per**, cf. § 86c, 1.

IX. 14 Deus, deus meus, quas ibi miserias expertus sum et ludificationes, quandoquidem recte mihi vivere puero id proponebatur, obtemperare monentibus, ut in hoc saeculo florerem et excellerem linguosis artibus ad honorem hominum et falsas divitias famulantibus! Inde in scholam datus sum, ut discerem litteras, in quibus quid utilitatis esset ignorabam miser. Et tamen, si segnis in discendo essem, vapulabam. Laudabatur enim hoc a maioribus, et multi ante nos vitam istam agentes praestruxerant aerumnosas vias, per quas transire cogebamur, multiplicato labore et dolore filiis Adam.

Invenimus autem, domine, homines rogantes te et didicimus ab eis, sentientes te, ut poteramus, esse magnum aliquem, qui posses etiam non adparens sensibus nostris exaudire nos et subvenire nobis. Nam puer coepi rogare te, auxilium et refugium meum, et in tuam invoca-

---

III. Boyhood Influences

1. ibi: i.e., the **vitae humanae procellosam societatem** of the preceding chapter.

2. recte . . . monentibus: "to me, a boy, it was proposed that this was to live rightly, (namely) to obey my advisers."

3. in hoc saeculo: "in this world" as opposed to Heaven and Eternity.

4. linguosis artibus: "linguacious arts"; a contemptuous reference to the rhetorical studies which were so large a part of ancient education. Conscious of the pagan origins of such studies and of their close association with worldly success, many churchmen came to denounce them, even though adept in them themselves. Cf. De Labriolle, 13ff.

4. ad . . . famulantibus: cf. § 86a, 3.

4. honorem . . . divitias: professors and practitioners of rhetoric under the Empire enjoyed an affluence and social standing not to be paralleled in other civilizations. Cf. Sandys, 236.

7. essem: Cf. § 102c.

10. vias: i.e., to knowledge.

11. filiis Adam: dative of disadvantage. Cf. *Eccles.* 40: 1, "Great labour is created for all men, and a heavy yoke is upon the children of Adam"; *Gen.* 3: 16–17; and *Jer.* 32: 19.

13. ut poteramus: "as (well as) we could."

13. magnum aliquem: "some great person."

16. auxilium et refugium meum: an echo from *Ps.* 93: 22 (*Old Version;* the *Vulgate* has **refugium . . . adiutorium**): "But the Lord is my refuge; and my God the help of my hope."

16. in tuam invocationem: cf. § 88a, 1.

tionem rumpebam nodos linguae meae et rogabam te parvus
non parvo affectu, ne in schola vapularem. Et cum me non
exaudiebas, quod non erat ad insipientiam mihi,
ridebantur a maioribus hominibus usque ab ipsis parentibus, 20
qui mihi accidere mali nihil volebant, plagae meae, magnum
tunc et grave malum meum.

15 Estne quisquam, domine, tam magnus animus, praegrandi affectu tibi cohaerens, estne, inquam, quisquam—
facit enim hoc quaedam etiam stoliditas—est ergo, qui 25
tibi pie cohaerendo ita sit affectus granditer, ut eculeos et
ungulas atque huiuscemodi varia tormenta, pro quibus
effugiendis tibi per universas terras cum timore magno
supplicatur, ita parvi aestimet—diligens eos, qui haec acer-
bissime formidant—quemadmodum parentes nostri ridebant 30
tormenta, quibus pueri a magistris affligebamur? Non
enim aut minus ea metuebamus aut minus te de his eva-
dendis deprecabamur, et peccabamus tamen minus scribendo
aut legendo aut cogitando de litteris, quam exigebatur a
nobis. 35

Non enim deerat, domine, memoria vel ingenium, quae
nos habere voluisti pro illa aetate satis, sed delectabat
ludere et vindicabatur in nos ab eis qui talia utique agebant.
Sed maiorum nugae negotia vocantur, puerorum autem

---

19. quod . . . ad insipientiam mihi:
Cf. *Ps.* 21:3, "and it shall not be reputed as folly in me." On the use of
ad here, cf. § 86a, 2.

20. ridebantur: its subject is plagae
meae below.

22. malum meum: "an evil for
me." malum is in apposition with
plagae.

23. Estne . . . tormenta: construe
Estne quisquam . . . qui sit affectus
ita granditer ut ita parvi aestimet
. . . quemadmodum parentes nostri
ridebant tormenta. . . . On the da-

tive with cohaerens, cf. § 82b. On
the final use of pro, cf. § 87h.

29. diligens eos . . . formidant:
"yet loving (as he does) those who
fear these instruments most keenly."

33. peccabamus . . . a nobis: construe peccabamus tamen scribendo
minus aut legendo (minus) aut cogitando de litteris (minus) quam (id
quod) exigebatur a nobis.

39. Sed maiorum . . . vocantur:
"But grownups' play is called business."

39. puerorum: predicate genitive,

40 talia cum sint, puniuntur a maioribus, et nemo miseratur
pueros vel illos vel utrosque. Nisi vero adprobat quisquam
bonus rerum arbiter vapulasse me, quia ludebam pila puer
et eo ludo inpediebar, quominus celeriter discerem litteras,
quibus maior deformius luderem. Aut aliud faciebat idem
45 ipse, a quo vapulabam, qui si in aliqua quaestiuncula a
condoctore suo victus esset, magis bile atque invidia tor-
queretur quam ego, cum in certamine pilae a conlusore meo
superabar?

*Despite parents and teachers I slighted my
studies, to be first in the games and attend
on the shows.*

X. 16 Et tamen peccabam, domine deus meus, ordinator
50 et creator rerum omnium naturalium, peccatorum autem
tantum ordinator, domine deus meus, peccabam faciendo
contra praecepta parentum et magistrorum illorum. Poteram enim postea bene uti litteris, quas volebant ut discerem, quocumque animo, illi mei. Non enim meliora
55 eligens inoboediens eram, sed amore ludendi, amans in
certaminibus superbas victorias et scalpi aures meas falsis
fabellis, quo prurirent ardentius, eadem curiositate magis

" and though such things are proper
to boys."
41. illos: i.e., the " grownups."
42. ludebam pila: ball-playing was
popular among schoolboys of the
time. For the various kinds of ball
played, cf. Preston and Dodge, 155–
156; Sandys, 203.
44. quibus . . . luderem: " with
the aid of which, as a man (**maior**), I
would play more improperly "; i.e.,
the " game " of rhetoric, with all the
tricky devices characteristic of its
practice.
44. idem ipse: i.e., the schoolmaster.
49. ordinator . . . tantum ordi-

nator: " the orderer and creator of all
things of nature, but of sins the
orderer merely "; i.e., God ordained
(or ordered) and then created all
things, but sin he merely ordered or
permitted; allowed it a place in the
divine order for the world, but did not
create it.
54. quocumque animo: " whatever
their purpose was."
54. illi mei: " these my (parents
and masters) "; subject of **volebant.**
55. amans . . . scalpi: " loving in
the contests the proud victories and
that my ears be tickled." On **amans**
with the infinitive, cf. § 89b.
57. eadem . . . emicante in spec-

magisque per oculos emicante in spectacula, ludos maiorum; quos tamen qui edunt, ea dignitate praediti excellunt, ut hoc paene omnes optent parvulis suis, quos tamen caedi 60 libenter patiuntur, si spectaculis talibus inpediantur ab studio, quo eos ad talia edenda cupiunt pervenire.

Vide ista, domine, misericorditer et libera nos iam invocantes te, libera etiam eos qui nondum te invocant, ut invocent te et liberes eos.   65

With Thy cross and Thy salt I was marked
from my birth and in boyhood illness did
cry for Thy grace, yet my mother's anxiety
deferred my baptism—and I fell into what
evil ways, O my God.

XI. 17 Audieram enim ego, adhuc puer, de vita aeterna promissa nobis per humilitatem domini dei nostri descendentis ad superbiam nostram et signabar iam signo crucis

---

tacula: "the same curiosity (i.e., which the stories had aroused) reaching out more and more through my eyes toward shows."

59. **quos** (i.e., **ludos**) . . . **excellunt:** "and yet those who give these (diversions) stand out through being endowed with this dignity, that . . ."; i.e., "yet those who give these diversions enjoy such honor and prestige."

60. **omnes:** i.e., parents.

62. **ad talia edenda:** sc. **spectacula.**

63. **Vide ista:** "look down upon these things." On **ista**=**haec**, cf. § 68c, 1.

63. **libera nos:** cf. *Ps.* 7: 2, "save me from all them that persecute me, and deliver me"; and *Ps.* 108: 21–22.

68. **signabar . . . condiebar . . .:** referring to the ceremonies of the Catechumenate. The Catechumenate —one of the two stages preliminary to Baptism—was a period of instruction and trial, and entrance to it was celebrated by certain rites. The signing with the cross and the application of salt—now features of the ceremony of formal Baptism of Infants—were two of these. One could be a catechumen as long as one wished. Although infant baptism had become widely established in Africa many years before A.'s time, St. Monnica, it seems, dreaded the loss of baptismal grace in her son more than the danger of his not receiving it finally. A.'s own career, as told by himself in the *Confessions*, explains its further postponement. Such tardiness was not uncommon in the Early Church. St. Gregory of Nazianzus and St. John Chrysostom, for instance, were born of Christian mothers and were baptized only in young manhood. Cf. C.E., III, s.v. *Catechumen*, pp. 430–432.

eius et condiebar eius sale iam inde ab utero matris meae,
70 quae multum speravit in te.

Vidisti, domine, cum adhuc puer essem et quodam die
pressu stomachi repente aestuarem paene moriturus, vidisti,
deus meus, quoniam custos meus iam eras, quo motu animi
et qua fide baptismum Christi tui, dei et domini mei,
75 flagitavi a pietate matris meae et matris omnium nostrum,
ecclesiae tuae.

Et conturbata mater carnis meae, quoniam et sempiter-
nam salutem meam carius parturiebat corde casto in fide
tua, iam curaret festinabunda, ut sacramentis salutaribus
80 initiarer et abluerer, te, domine Iesu, confitens in remissionem peccatorum, nisi statim recreatus essem.   Dilata est
itaque mundatio mea, quasi necesse esset, ut adhuc sordidarer, si viverem, quia videlicet post lavacrum illud maior
et periculosior in sordibus delictorum reatus foret.

---

70. speravit in te: on **in,** cf. § 88a,
3.   The phrase is Scriptural.

75. flagitavi: on the indicative, cf.
§ 96.

75. a pietate matris meae: cf. §§ 29,
83c.

77. quoniam . . . in fide tua: " for
she was in travail even with greater
love in her chaste heart for my eternal
salvation in Thy faith (than she was
for my birth into the flesh) "; or " for
in her faith in Thee she was in labor
of my eternal salvation in her chaste
heart even more fondly (than she was
in her womb of my flesh)."

79. sacramentis salutaribus: " saving rites "—explained by **initiarer** and
abluerer and **confitens in remissionem peccatorum.** A. frequently
used **sacramentum** in the sense of
" rite." The context compels that
meaning here and clearly refers to the
rites of Baptism. The ceremonies of
Baptism consisted and consist of
initiatory rites (**initiarer**) such as the
renunciation of the devil and the

confession of faith (**confitens,** etc.)
(and to-day, too, of the two catechumenate rites described by **signabar**
and **condiebar** above) and of the
ablution from sin (**abluerer**). Baptism and Confirmation in the Early
Church were generally given to adults
in immediate succession, the latter
usually being conferred by the bishop.
In the case of the dangerously ill and
those living at a distance from the
episcopal city, Baptism could be given
alone.   A. could have received it on
either score at the time.   He must
have been old enough to make his
own profession of faith, since he was
old enough to long for Baptism.   On
the ceremonies, cf. Cabrol-Leclercq,
art. *Baptême,* vol. 2, part 1, col.
251–346; *ibid.,* art. *Confirmation,* vol.
3, part 2, col. 2515–2544.   On **confitens in remissionem,** cf. § 88a, 1.

82. adhuc: cf. § 72.

**83. maior et periculosior . . . re-
atus:** i.e., since his previous falls
would have been forgiven by Baptism.

Ita iam credebam et illa et omnis domus, nisi pater solus, 85
qui tamen non evicit in me ius maternae pietatis, quominus
in Christum crederem, sicut ille nondum crediderat. Nam
illa satagebat, ut tu mihi pater esses, deus meus, potius
quam ille, et in hoc adiuvabas eam, ut superaret virum, cui
melior serviebat, quia et in hoc tibi utique id iubenti 90
serviebat.

18 Rogo te, deus meus—vellem scire, si tu etiam velles—
quo consilio dilatus sum, ne tunc baptizarer, utrum bono
meo mihi quasi laxata sint lora peccandi an non laxata sint.
Unde ergo etiam nunc de aliis atque aliis sonat undique in 95
auribus nostris: « Sine illum, faciat; nondum enim baptizatus est ». Et tamen in salute corporis non dicimus:
« Sine vulneretur amplius; nondum enim sanatus est. ».
Quanto ergo melius et cito sanarer et id ageretur mecum
meorum meaque diligentia, ut recepta salus animae meae 100
tuta esset tutela tua, qui dedisses eam.

Melius vero. Sed quot et quanti fluctus inpendere temp-

---

85. **illa:** Monnica.

86. **ius maternae pietatis:** the right
of his mother's piety is contrasted with
his pagan father's civil right (**patria
potestas**) to control the religion of his
son. On the right of **patria potestas**
here, cf. Greenidge, 18 ff.; Sandys,
304–305.

86. **quominus . . . crederem:** depends on the idea of prohibition in
evicit. Cf. A-G., § 558, b; G-L.,
§ 549. On in, cf. § 88a, 3.

87. **nondum crediderat:** Patricius
became a Christian only shortly before
his death.

90. **melior:** " although she was the
better (morally)."

93. **quo consilio dilatus sum:** " with
what purpose I was put off." Cf.
§ 96.

93. **bono meo:** dative of purpose.

94. **an non:** sc. **bono meo mihi:** " or

was it not for my good that they
were loosened for me."

95. **de aliis atque aliis:** " regarding this one and that one."

98. **vulneretur:** a substantive clause
developed from the volitive. It is not
necessary to supply **ut** in such clauses;
cf. B., § 295, 8.

99. **Quanto ergo . . . tua:** " How
much better, then, both would I have
been swiftly cured and (how much
better) would it have been with me, as
a result of my friends' and my own
diligence, that the health of my soul
had been brought back safe under
Thy protection " (i.e., through the
regenerative grace of Baptism).

100. **recepta:** construe as an adjective with **salus;** i.e., brought back
from the state of original (and perhaps
personal) sin to the state of Sanctify-
ing Grace.

tationum post pueritiam videbantur, noverat eos iam illa
mater et terram potius, unde postea formarer, quam ipsam
105 iam effigiem conmittere volebat.

My elders' blunder in forcing me to study
Thou madest occasion of profit to me.

XII. 19 In ipsa tamen pueritia, de qua mihi minus quam
de adulescentia metuebatur, non amabam litteras et me in
eas urgeri oderam; et urgebar tamen et bene mihi fiebat, nec
faciebam ego bene: non enim discerem, nisi cogerer. Nemo
110 enim invitus bene facit, etiamsi bonum est quod facit.
Nec qui me urgebant, bene faciebant, sed bene mihi fiebat
abs te, deus meus. / Illi enim non intuebantur, quo referrem
quod me discere cogebant praeterquam ad satiandas insatia-
biles cupiditates copiosae inopiae et ignominiosae gloriae.
115 Tu vero, c u i n u m e r a t i s u n t c a p i l l i n o s t r i, errore
omnium, qui mihi instabant ut discerem, utebaris ad utili-
tatem meam, meo autem, qui discere nolebam, utebaris ad
poenam meam, qua plecti non eram indignus, tantillus

---

103. **videbantur:** cf. § 96.

104. **et terram . . . volebat:** construe **et volebat conmittere terram,
unde postea formarer, (fluctibus)
potius quam conmittere ipsam iam
effigiem** (fluctibus).

104. **terram:** i.e., man minus the
life of grace that Baptism infuses;
translate " clay."

105. **effigiem:** the image of God,
the putting on of Christ, the sacra-
mental character of Baptism.

106. **de qua . . . metuebatur:** " in
connection with which there was less
fear for me than (there was fear for
me) in connection with (my) adolescence."

108. **urgeri oderam:** on the infinitive, cf. § 89f.

109. **non . . . discerem, nisi
cogerer:** on the tense, cf. § 78b.

112. **quo referrem . . . cogebant:**
" to what end I should put that which
they were forcing me to learn."

113. **satiandas . . . gloriae:** successive oxymora. Cf. § 40.

115. **cui numerati . . . nostri:** cf.
Matt. 10: 30, " But the very hairs of
your head are all numbered."

117. **meo:** sc. **errore.**

118. **plecti . . . indignus:** on the
infinitive, cf. § 89e.

118. **tantillus . . . peccator:** A. does
not try to excuse even the faults of
his early boyhood. By employing
tantus in opposition to **tantillus,** he
emphasizes the objective enormity of
sin.

puer et tantus peccator. Ita non de bene facientibus tu
bene faciebas mihi et de peccante me ipso iuste retribuebas 120
mihi. Iussisti enim et sic est, ut poena sua sibi sit omnis
inordinatus animus.

*My soul hated Greek and elementary
studies, and sought out the vanities of
literary invention.*

XIII. 20 Quid autem erat causae, cur graecas litteras
oderam, quibus puerulus imbuebar, ne nunc quidem mihi
satis exploratum est. Adamaveram enim latinas, non quas 125
primi magistri, sed quas docent qui grammatici vocantur.
Nam illas primas, ubi legere et scribere et numerare discitur,
non minus onerosas poenalesque habebam quam omnes
graecas. Unde tamen et hoc nisi de peccato et vanitate
vitae, qua caro eram et spiritus ambulans et non 130
revertens? Nam utique meliores, quia certiores, erant
primae illae litterae, quibus fiebat in me et factum est et
habeo illud, ut et legam, si quid scriptum invenio, et

119. non: construe with **facientibus**.

120. **mihi**: construe with both **facientibus** and **faciebas**.

123. **causae**: construe as partitive genitive with **Quid**.

123. **cur . . . oderam**: cf. § 96.

123. **graecas litteras**: i.e., early studies in Greek and whatever else of it was taught A. at the time.

125. **adamaveram**: on the tense, cf. § 78a.

126. **primi magistri . . . grammatici**: the **primi magistri**, as A. indicates here, taught **legere et scribere et numerare**. The **grammatici**, presiding at a higher stage of instruction, taught correctness of diction and aimed to inculcate an appreciation of literature. They thus drilled their pupils in prose composition, made them commit to memory long passages of poetry, and gave much effort to the elucidation of the poets. On the curriculum of the Roman school, cf. De Labriolle, 6 ff.; Sandys, 228–229; Gwynn, 82–100.

127. **illas primas**: sc. **litteras**, "those first elements."

127. **ubi . . . discitur**: on **ubi = quibus**, cf. § 73.

130. **caro . . . non revertens**: cf. *Ps.* 77: 39, "And he remembered that they are flesh: a wind that goeth and returneth not."

132. **litterae . . . scribam**: i.e.,

$$\left.\begin{array}{l}\text{fiebat . . .}\\\text{litterae, quibus et factum est}\\\text{et habeo}\end{array}\right\rbrace\text{illud.}$$

133. **ut et legam**: in apposition with **illud**, which is subject of **fiebat** and **factum est** and object of **habeo**.

scribam ipse, si quid volo, quam illae, quibus tenere cogebar
135 Aeneae nesciocuius errores, oblitus errorum meorum, et
plorare Didonem mortuam, quia se occidit ab amore, cum
interea me ipsum in his a te morientem, deus, vita mea,
siccis oculis ferrem miserrimus.

21 Quid enim miserius misero non miserante se ipsum et
140 flente Didonis mortem, quae fiebat amando Aenean, non
flente autem mortem suam, quae fiebat non amando te,
deus, lumen cordis mei et panis oris intus animae meae et
virtus maritans mentem meam et sinum cogitationis meae?

22 Sed nunc in anima mea clamet deus meus, et veritas
145 tua dicat mihi: non est ita, non est ita. Melior est prorsus
doctrina illa prior. Nam ecce paratior sum oblivisci errores
Aeneae atque omnia eius modi quam scribere et legere.
At enim vela pendent liminibus grammaticarum scholarum,

---

134. illae: sc. **litterae** and transl.
" readings," " lessons in literature,"
as opposed to the **litterae,** " rudiments," mentioned above.

134. tenere: sc. **memoria.**

135. nesciocuius: by this indifferent, almost chilly, adjective, A. again
professes his divorce from the pagan
studies of his formative years. Cf.
Conf. I, 9, 14, and *Conf.* III, 4, 7:
" librum cuiusdam Ciceronis."

135. errores . . . errorum: antimetathesis; cf. § 32.

136. plorare Didonem: the story
of Dido, the traditional queen of nearby Carthage, must have had a special
appeal for A. Cf. De Labriolle, 14.

137. in his: " in these things."

137. a te morientem: " dying apart
from Thee."

137. deus, vita mea: cf. *John* 14: 6,
" I am the way, the truth, and the
life."

139. miserius misero non miserante: paronomasia, cf. § 43.

141. mortem suam: " his own
death."

142. panis oris intus animae meae:
" bread of the mouth within of my
soul "; i.e., " bread of the interior
mouth of my soul." Cf. *John* 6: 35,
" I am the bread of life."

143. virtus maritans mentem:
" power that impregnates my mind."

148. vela pendent liminibus: the
pergula—in one of its forms a building
or room of a building opening on a
street and therefore useful in several
branches of commerce—was employed
frequently as a schoolroom. To protect the pupils from the sun and the
distractions of the street, curtains
(**vela**) were suspended over the entrance. A curtain was also hung
frequently before the shrine that
housed the image of some divinity, to
afford it, among other things, an
added air of mystery and to increase
the reverence of the beholder. A. here
sarcastically vents his disapproval of
the **grammatici** of his own youth by attributing to the **vela** of their schools
the dubious usages of the **vela** of pagan
shrines. As the curtains of a pagan

sed non illa magis honorem secreti quam tegimentum erroris significant. Non clament adversus me quos iam non timeo, 150 dum confiteor tibi quae vult anima mea, deus meus, et adquiesco in reprehensione malarum viarum mearum, ut diligam bonas vias tuas; non clament adversus me venditores grammaticae vel emptores, quia, si proponam eis interrogans, utrum verum sit quod Aenean aliquando 155 Carthaginem venisse poeta dicit, indoctiores nescire se respondebunt, doctiores autem etiam negabunt verum esse. At si quaeram, quibus litteris scribatur Aeneae nomen, omnes mihi, qui haec didicerunt, verum respondent secundum id pactum et placitum, quo inter se homines ista signa 160 firmarunt. Item si quaeram, quid horum maiore vitae huius incommodo quisque obliviscatur, legere et scribere

---

shrine do not so much afford added honor (honorem) to the false image it contains as they conceal the falseness (erroris) of the doctrine it represents, so the curtains employed by the grammatici do not so much afford added honor to their instruction as they conceal the falseness of it. On Latin schools and school buildings, cf. Sandys, 230–232. On the omission of the preposition with liminibus, cf. § 84a.

150. Non: cf. § 75e.

150. Non clament . . .: i.e., Let not the grammatici censure me now that I value the learning to read and to write above the vain tales which they taught me, for their own conduct is partially the cause of my preference. On the one hand, they are not unanimous as to the truth of Vergil's account of Aeneas' coming to Carthage; deny it, in fact, by their answers. On the other hand, they exhibit a suspicious unanimity as to the spelling of Aeneas' name. To

their pupil, therefore, looking back on the studies of his youth, the literary side seems an empty fiction, but the rudiments seem as truth itself.

153. venditores . . . emptores: many grammatici were avaricious. Some of them refused to use the vela referred to above so that the exposed schoolroom might attract the more clients from the passing crowd. Cf. Sandys, 231. There is an added thrust in the word emptores.

155. quod: introducing substantive clause used as subject of sit; translate, " the fact that."

159. verum . . . placitum, quo: "give the correct answer according to that pact and agreement, whereby."

161. quid horum . . . figmenta: " which one of these things, reading and writing or these fictions of the poets, anyone could forget with greater detriment to this life." Note that quid is used here for the pronoun utrum. Cf. § 69a.

an poetica illa figmenta, quis non videat, quid responsurus
sit, qui non est penitus oblitus sui?

165 Peccabam ergo puer, cum illa inania istis utilioribus
amore praeponebam vel potius ista oderam, illa amabam.
Iam vero unum et unum duo, duo et duo quattuor odiosa
cantio mihi erat et dulcissimum spectaculum vanitatis equus
ligneus plenus armatis et Troiae incendium a t q u e i p s i u s
170 u m b r a C r e u s a e.

> But the fictions of Homer could not delight
> me, compelled to learn them in a foreign
> tongue; yet compulsion, though a hindrance
> to facility in language, is a part of Thy
> saving restraint, O my God.

XIV. 23 Cur ergo graecam etiam grammaticam oderam
talia cantantem? Nam et Homerus peritus texere tales
fabellas et dulcissime vanus est et mihi tamen amarus erat
puero. Credo etiam graecis pueris Vergilius ita sit, cum
175 eum sic discere coguntur ut ego illum. Videlicet difficultas,
difficultas omnino ediscendae linguae peregrinae quasi felle
aspergebat omnes suavitates graecas fabulosarum narra-

---

165. **istis utilioribus:** on istis = his,
cf. § 68c, 1.

167. **odiosa cantio:** "insufferable
sing-song."

168. **spectaculum vanitatis:** cf.
§ 83b.

169. **atque ipsius umbra Creusae:**
exact quotation of Vergil, *Aeneid* 2,
772.

171. **graecam etiam grammaticam:**
"Greek literature even" (i.e., as well
as the rudiments).

172. **Homerus:** Homer, the most
widely used school-text among the
Greeks, was one of the first works
studied in the course in Greek given
in the Roman schools.

172. **peritus texere:** on the infinitive, cf. § 89e.

174. **Credo:** parenthetical.

174. **Vergilius:** Vergil, the most important Latin textbook in the schools
of the Empire, was one of the obvious
books for boys who were learning
Latin in Greek-speaking communities.

177. **graecas:** either a transferred
epithet and, therefore, to be taken as
if written **omnes suavitates grae-
carum fabulosarum narrationum,** or it
is an acknowledgment of the mature
A. that there are literary delights that
are peculiarly and exclusively Greek
and that these delights are minimized,
if not lost, for one not at home in the
Greek language.

tionum. Nulla enim verba illa noveram et saevis terroribus
ac poenis, ut nossem, instabatur mihi vehementer.

Nam et latina, aliquando infans, utique nulla noveram 180
et tamen advertendo didici sine ullo metu atque cruciatu
inter etiam blandimenta nutricum et ioca arridentium et
laetitias alludentium. Didici vero illa sine poenali onere
urgentium, cum me urgeret cor meum ad parienda concepta
sua, id quod non esset, nisi aliqua verba didicissem non a 185
docentibus, sed a loquentibus, in quorum et ego auribus
parturiebam quidquid sentiebam.

Hinc satis elucet maiorem habere vim ad discenda ista
liberam curiositatem quam meticulosam necessitatem. Sed
illius fluxum haec restringit legibus tuis, deus, legibus tuis 190

---

178. Nulla enim verba illa noveram:
as in the case of St. Thomas Aquinas
and of Shakespeare, A.'s knowledge of
Greek has been depreciated unduly.
It seems certain that he lacked the
facility of his fellow countryman,
Tertullian, and of many other third-
century North Africans in the language. It is known that his knowledge of it was something more than
rudimentary, that he could at least
read it with understanding. In this
passage and in *Conf.* I, 13, 20, above,
we must remember that A. is referring
to his schoolboy attitude towards
Greek. In fact, in *Conf.* I, 13, 20, he
finds that schoolboy aversion a mystery to his more mature self (**ne nunc
quidem mihi satis exploratum est**).
In two places he depreciates his
knowledge of Greek; cf. *Contra Litteras Petiliani* II, 38, 91, and *De
Trinitate* III, 1, 1. We may interpret the first, and perhaps the second,
depreciation as Ben Jonson's "little
Latin and less Greek" of Shakespeare
is sometimes interpreted, i.e., that the
author is making use of a standard of
Hellenic excellence much loftier than
what obtains among us. Something

less than a century before A.'s birth,
Greek was in wide use even as a ver-
nacular among the educated of the
province of Africa. This tradition
may have furnished the standard for
A.'s self-depreciation; cf. De Labriolle,
395–396, and 395, footnote 4. For
those who can obtain it, there is an
excellent summary of the subject of
A.'s knowledge of Greek in S. Angus,
*The Sources of the First Ten Books of
the De Civitate Dei of St. Augustine,*
Princeton, 1906.

180. latina . . . noveram: A.'s
native language was Punic, a Semitic
tongue, but it is clear from the context that Latin was also freely spoken
in the household of Patricius and
Monnica.

181. advertendo: sc. animum. The
use of **adverto** without **animum** in the
sense of "note," as here, is very
common in the Late writers.

184. ad parienda concepta sua:
"to bring forth its own thoughts."

185. id quod non esset: "that
which could not have happened."

186. in quorum . . . auribus: "in
whose hearing." Cf. § 88b, 1.

a magistrorum ferulis usque ad temptationes martyrum, valentibus legibus tuis miscere salubres amaritudines revocantes nos ad te a iucunditate pestifera, qua recessimus a te.

Whatever of use I learned as a boy, may all of it always serve Thee, O my God.

XV. 24 Exaudi, domine, deprecationem meam,
195 ne deficiat anima mea sub disciplina tua neque deficiam in confitendo tibi miserationes tuas, quibus eruisti me ab omnibus viis meis pessimis, ut dulcescas mihi super omnes seductiones, quas sequebar, et amem te validissime et amplexer manum tuam totis praecordiis meis et eruas me ab
200 omni temptatione usque in finem. Ecce enim tu, domine, rex meus et deus meus, tibi serviat quidquid utile puer didici; tibi serviat quod loquor et scribo et lego et numero, quoniam cum vana discerem, tu disciplinam dabas mihi et in eis vanis peccata delectationum mearum dimisisti
205 mihi. Didici enim in eis multa verba utilia; sed et in rebus non vanis disci possunt, et ea via tuta est, in qua pueri ambularent.

Thy gifts to me became occasion of pride in the empty declamations my masters assigned me. If only Thy praises had en-

---

192. **valentibus . . . miscere:** cf. § 89b.

192. **salubres amaritudines:** " salutary bitterness."

194. **Exaudi . . . deprecationem meam:** cf. *Ps.* 60: 2, "Hear, O God, my supplication."

195. **sub disclipina tua:** cf. § 88c.

195. **neque deficiam:** on neque for the usual Classical **neve,** cf. § 75b.

197. **super:** on super in sense of " more than," cf. § 88d, 3.

199. **et eruas . . . temptatione:** cf. *Ps.* 17: 30 (*Old Version*), **Quoniam a** te eruar a temptatione: the *Vulgate* has **Quoniam in te eripiar a tentatione,** " For by thee I shall be delivered from temptation."

200. **usque in finem:** cf. I *Cor.* 1: 8, " Who also will confirm you into the end without crime."

201. **rex meus et deus meus:** cf. *Ps.* 5: 3, " O my King and my God."

204. **in eis vanis:** construe with delectationum.

207. **ambularent:** " should walk." The subjunctive is potential.

*gaged my talents, I might have withstood
the applause for my excellence.*

XVII. **27** Sine me, deus meus, dicere aliquid et de ingenio
meo, munere tuo, in quibus a me deliramentis atterebatur.
Proponebatur enim mihi negotium animae meae satis in- 210
quietum praemio laudis et dedecoris vel plagarum metu,
ut dicerem verba Iunonis irascentis et dolentis, quod non
possit I t a l i a   T e u c r o r u m   a v e r t e r e   r e g e m, quae
numquam Iunonem dixisse audieram. Sed figmentorum
poeticorum vestigia errantes sequi cogebamur et tale 215
aliquid dicere solutis verbis, quale poeta dixisset versi-
bus: et ille dicebat laudabilius, in quo pro dignitate adum-
bratae personae irae ac doloris similior affectus eminebat
verbis sententias congruenter vestientibus.

---

208. ingenio: A. writes frankly of
his ability, but not proudly; for he
immediately acknowledges (**munere
tuo**) that God has given it to him.

209. in quibus . . . atterebatur: sc.
ingenium as subject. On the mood,
cf. § 96. On **in**, cf. § 88b, 4.

210. animae meae: construe as
dative of reference with **inquietum**.

211. praemio . . . metu: ablatives
of cause explaining **inquietum**.

212. dicerem verba Iunonis: two
kinds of declamation were practiced
in the rhetorical schools: the **suasoriae**, in which the declaimer, repre-
senting himself as some illustrious
person, discoursed on a subject suggested by that person's career;
and the **controversiae**, argumentative
pieces in imitation of the advocate's
practice in the courtroom. The
suasoriae, requiring less maturity,
came first in a youth's rhetorical
training. Of this kind was the task
here assigned to A. He was to im-
personate Juno, angry and sorrowful
at not being able to keep the King of

the Trojans from Italy. Cf. **Duff**,
23–41; Sandys, 233–235; Gwynn, 153–
179; C. S. Baldwin, *Ancient Rhetoric
and Poetic*, New York, 1924, 90 ff.

213. possit: we should ordinarily
expect **posset**. The present subjunctive is kept for vividness. Cf. § 78c.

213. Italia . . . regem: the words
occur in Vergil, *Aeneid* 1, 38.

214. figmentorum poeticorum: the
protest of *Conf.* I, 13, 21.

216. solutis verbis: "free words";
i.e., released from the laws of metric.
Hence, a technical name for prose.

217. laudabilius: "with the more
applause." The comparative rather
than the superlative is used here
because the applause evoked by the
successful declaimer is compared by
implication with the applause earned
by all the rest together.

217. in quo . . . eminebat: "in
whom the emotion of anger and of
sorrow, in accordance with the dignity
of the person represented, appeared
the more faithful."

220 Ut quid mihi illud, o vera vita, deus meus? Quid mihi
recitanti adclamabatur prae multis coaetaneis et conlec-
toribus meis? Nonne ecce illa omnia fumus et ventus?
Itane aliud non erat, ubi exerceretur ingenium et lingua
mea? Laudes tuae, domine, laudes tuae per scripturas
225 tuas suspenderent palmitem cordis mei, et non raperetur
per inania nugarum turpis praeda volatilibus. Non enim
uno modo sacrificatur transgressoribus angelis.

Of barbarisms of speech I grew more afraid
than of the envy and pride my training was
fostering.

XIX. 30 Horum ego puer morum in limine iacebam miser,
et huius harenae palaestra erat illa, ubi magis timebam
230 barbarismum facere quam cavebam, si facerem, non facientibus invidere.

Dico haec et confiteor tibi, deus meus, in quibus laudabar

---

220. Ut quid mihi illud: " Why was
that to me? " i.e., " Why did that
happen to me? " On **ut quid = cur,**
cf. § 74.

221. adclamabatur: impersonal; cf.
§ 77. On **prae,** cf. § 87g, 3.

222. illa . . . et ventus: cf. *Wis.* 5:
15, " For the hope of the wicked is as
dust which is blown away with the
wind . . . and a smoke that is scattered abroad by the wind."

223. ubi: = quo. Cf. § 73.

**224. Laudes tuae . . . per scripturas
tuas:** " Thy praises (distributed)
throughout Thy sacred writings."
The rigorism of A., thirteen years in the
Faith, when he wrote the above, is
protesting here against his one-time
complacency in his own verbal facility.
The Scriptures were not, of course,
a substitute for rhetoric in the education of a fourth-century youth.
Rather were the Classics alleged to be
a necessary propaedeutic to serious

Scriptural studies. A. here regards
his rhetorical studies solely as the
occasion of pride they had been to
him.

225. suspenderent: the subjunctive
is potential.

226. inania nugarum: cf. § 83a.

227. sacrificatur: impersonal.

227. transgressoribus angelis: who
transgressed through pride and to
whom, therefore, pride would be an
appropriate sacrifice. On **transgressor** as an adjective, cf. § 64.

228. Horum . . . in limine: " on
the threshold of these customs ";
i.e., " on the threshold of the school
where customs of this sort were the
rule."

230. cavebam: " I took care not."
Cf. § 89b.

230. si facerem: the subjunctive is
iterative, " if I ever made any." Cf.
G-L., § 567, note. Cf. § 102c.

ab eis, quibus placere tunc mihi erat honeste vivere. Non
enim videbam voraginem turpitudinis, in quam proiectus eram ab oculis tuis.   235

Nam in illis iam quid me foedius fuit, ubi etiam talibus
displicebam fallendo innumerabilibus mendaciis et paedagogum et magistros et parentes amore ludendi, studio
spectandi nugatoria et imitandi ludicra inquietudine? Furta
etiam faciebam de cellario parentum et de mensa, vel gula 240
imperitante vel ut haberem quod darem pueris, ludum
suum mihi, quo pariter utique delectabantur, tamen vendentibus. In quo etiam ludo fraudulentas victorias ipse
vana excellentiae cupiditate victus saepe aucupabar. Quid
enim tam nolebam pati atque atrociter, si deprehenderem, 245
arguebam, quam id quod aliis faciebam? Et, si deprehensus
arguerer, saevire magis quam cedere libebat.

Istane est innocentia puerilis? Non est, domine, non

---

233. quibus placere . . . vivere:
"to please whom then was to me to
live honorably." **placere** is the subject of **erat; vivere** is the predicate.

234. proiectus . . . ab oculis tuis:
cf. *Ps.* 30: 23, "I am cast away from
before Thy eyes."

236. illis: sc. **oculis.**

236. ubi: transl. "when."

236. talibus: "those like myself."

237. paedagogum: the slave or
freedman employed in prosperous
Roman families to supervise the manners and morals of boys from the
seventh to the sixteenth year was
called a **paedagogus.** The **paedagogus**
accompanied the boy under his charge
to the school and awaited him there.
Cf. Sandys, 330.

238. magistros: the **magistri,** as
opposed to the **paedagogi,** organized
schools of their own, to which they
tried to attract pupils.

239. ludicra: take either as neuter
plural object of **imitandi,** noting chi-

astic arrangement

    studio spectandi nugatoria
    imitandi ludicra inquietudine

or construe as adjective in the ablative, modifying **inquietudine.**

240. vel gula imperitante: on the
ablative absolute, cf. § 84c.

241. pueris . . . vendentibus: sc.
vendentibus after **pueris,** "to boys
(selling) me their own game—wherein
they, of course, equally delighted—
(but) selling it nevertheless." His
playmates loved their game, but they
loved A.'s bribes more.

244. excellentiae cupiditate: i.e.,
cupiditate excellendi.

244. Quid . . . faciebam: "For
what was I unwilling to endure and
what did I fiercely wrangle at, if I
discovered it (in others), other than
that which I did do to others?"

245. si deprehenderem: the subjunctive is iterative. Cf. note on **si
facerem,** line 230, above.

est, oro te, deus meus. Nam haec ipsa sunt, quae a
250 paedagogis et magistris, a nucibus et pilulis et passeribus,
ad praefectos et reges, aurum, praedia, mancipia, haec ipsa
omnino succedentibus maioribus aetatibus transeunt, sicuti
ferulis maiora supplicia succedunt.

Humilitatis ergo signum in statura pueritiae, rex noster,
255 probasti, cum aisti: t a l i u m e s t r e g n u m c a e l o r u m.

Thanks be to Thee for the gifts of my child-
hood, though used apart from Thee to my
later undoing.

XX. 31 Sed tamen, domine, tibi excellentissimo, optimo
conditori et rectori universitatis, d e o nostro g r a t i a s,
etiamsi me puerum tantum esse voluisses. Eram enim
etiam tunc, vivebam atque sentiebam meamque incolumi-

---

249. oro te: a polite parenthesis
meaning, " I pray Thee that I may
say it," like an English, " may it
please you," or " so please you."

**249. Nam haec ipsa . . . succe-
dunt:** " For these are the very things
(the incipient vices just alluded to)
which pass (**transeunt**) from tutors
and teachers, from nuts and balls and
birds to governors and kings, to gold,
estates, and slaves; even these very
acts, I say (**omnino**), pass to the succeeding, older periods of life, just as
heavier penalties succeed the canes ";
i.e., the bad tendencies of the child,
if uncorrected, grow into the monstrous vices and punishments at-
tendant upon maturity.

250. a nucibus . . . et passeribus:
on the various games played with
nuts, cf. Smith, Wayte, and Marindin,
II, s.v. **Nuces**, 247–248. On bird-
catching in antiquity, cf. *ibid*, I,
s.v. **Auceps**, 245.

254. Humilitatis . . . probasti:
" Therefore (only) the symbol of

humility, (as it is typified) in the
stature of childhood you approved."
The unusual position of **humilitatis**
compels the insertion of " only " in
the English translation. On the
hyperbaton, cf. § 39; i.e., the humility
and dependence which are expressed in
the undeveloped, weak bodies of
children earned Our Lord's approval,
not the pride which is found even in
children.

255. talium . . . caelorum: *Matt.*
19: 14, " For the kingdom of Heaven
is for such."

257. deo nostro gratias: the phrase
is Scriptural. Cf. II *Cor.* 2: 14, **Deo
autem gratias. gratias** is the object
of some form of the verb **dare** understood.

258. puerum . . . voluisses: i.e.,
even if God had not permitted him to
live beyond boyhood.

259. incolumitatem: construe as
object of **habebam. curae** is dative
of purpose or end.

tatem, vestigium secretissimae unitatis, ex qua eram, curae 260
habebam, custodiebam interiore sensu integritatem sensuum
meorum inque ipsis parvis parvarumque rerum cogita-
tionibus veritate delectabar.   Falli nolebam, memoria vigebam, locutione instruebar, amicitia mulcebar, fugiebam
dolorem, abiectionem, ignorantiam.   Quid in tali animante 265
non mirabile atque laudabile?   At ista omnia dei mei dona
sunt, non mihi ego dedi haec: et bona sunt et haec omnia
ego.   Bonus ergo est qui fecit me, et ipse est bonum meum
et illi exulto bonis omnibus, quibus etiam puer eram.

Hoc enim peccabam, quod non in ipso, sed in creaturis 270
eius me atque ceteris voluptates, sublimitates, veritates
quaerebam, atque ita inruebam in dolores, confusiones,
errores.   Gratias tibi, dulcedo mea et honor meus et fiducia
mea, deus meus, gratias tibi de donis tuis; sed tu mihi ea
serva.   Ita enim servabis me, et augebuntur et perficientur 275
quae dedisti mihi, et ero ipse tecum, quia et ut sim tu
dedisti mihi.

---

260. **unitatis:** i.e., the union of his father and mother, from which he took his being.   The following note from W-K. may make the passage clearer: " A. was filled with a strong consciousness of life (**vivebam atque sentiebam**) and a conscious care to preserve his ego, his personality, the image (**vestigium**) of the mysterious union (of father and mother) from which he had his origin (**ex qua eram**); therefore he watched over the integrity of his external senses with the clear-visioned eye of his intellect, and, while his childish thoughts might be insignificant in themselves and concerned with unimportant matters, of one thing he was always

clearly conscious: his soul sought repose in truth (**veritate delectabar**). Under all circumstances his inner being sought to penetrate to the essence of truth; this is the dominant trait in the nature of A."   Cf. § 25.

263. **memoria vigebam:** " I had a strong memory."

267. **et haec omnia ego:** " and all these (good things) was I."

269. **illi exulto:** " I exult to Him."

269. **quibus . . . eram:** take **quibus** as an ablative of means.

273. **Gratias tibi:** cf. note 257 above.

276. **quia . . . mihi:** construe **quia tu dedisti mihi et ut sim.** On **et,** cf. § 94a, 1.

LIBER SECUNDUS

IV. ADOLESCENCE

*Out of love for Thee I shall now recall the
bitter memories of my misspent youth.*

I. 1 Recordari volo transactas foeditates meas et carnales corruptiones animae meae, non quod eas amem, sed ut amem te, deus meus. Amore amoris tui facio istud, recolens vias meas nequissimas in amaritudine recogitationis meae,
5 ut tu dulcescas mihi, dulcedo non fallax, dulcedo felix et secura, et colligens me a dispersione, in qua frustatim discissus sum, dum ab uno te aversus in multa evanui. Exarsi enim aliquando satiari inferis in adulescentia et silvescere ausus sum variis et umbrosis amoribus, et con-
10 tabuit species mea et conputrui coram oculis tuis placens mihi et placere cupiens oculis hominum.

IV. Adolescence

4. amaritudine: recollections of his sinful youth still distress A.

5. dulcedo non fallax . . . secura: i.e., in his sins there had been a passing sweetness; in God alone has he found true and enduring sweetness.

6. et colligens: construe either with dulcedo non fallax (i.e., **tu . . . dulcedo non fallax . . . et colligens me a dispersione**, "sweetness that doth not fail and that draweth me (ever) from (that) moral disorganization)," or with **felix** and **secura**, "a sweetness happy and enduring and that (ever) draweth me away from (that) moral disorganization."

6. dispersione: "moral disorganization."

7. dum . . . evanui: "as long as, having turned from Thee (who art) the One, I disintegrated into many things"; i.e., having turned from Thee, the unifying principle of moral organization, I became completely disorganized morally, my moral self vanishing into a thousand follies.

8. Exarsi . . . satiari: cf. § 89b.

8. satiari inferis: "to get my fill of Hell"; i.e., "to get my fill of evil pleasures."

9. et contabuit species mea: cf. *Dan.* 10: 8, **sed et species mea immutata est in me:** "and the appearance of my countenance was changed in me."

10. coram oculis tuis: cf. § 87b.

*By my sixteenth year a slave of lust, Thou
didst alloy my pleasures with a saving
bitterness.*

II. 2 Et quid erat, quod me delectabat, nisi amare et
amari? Sed non tenebatur modus ab animo usque ad
animum, quatenus est luminosus limes amicitiae, sed exhala-
bantur nebulae de limosa concupiscentia carnis et scatebra 15
pubertatis et obnubilabant atque obfuscabant cor meum,
ut non discerneretur serenitas dilectionis a caligine libidinis.
Utrumque in confuso aestuabat et rapiebat inbecillam
aetatem per abrupta cupiditatum atque mersabat gurgite
flagitiorum. 20
Invaluerat super me ira tua, et nesciebam. Obsurdueram
stridore catenae mortalitatis meae, poena superbiae animae
meae, et ibam longius a te, et sinebas, et iactabar et effundebar et diffluebam et ebulliebam per fornicationes meas, et
tacebas. 25

---

13. tenebatur . . . amicitiae: " The
mean from soul to soul was not maintained—to what extent is the luminous
boundary of friendship "; more freely,
" The mean was not maintained
between soul and soul, within which
is the luminous boundary of friendship."
14. luminosus: i.e., " good,"
" proper," " righteous." This adjective exemplifies the usage found in
Early Christian Literature, as elsewhere, of expressing what is good in
terms of brightness and light and
what is bad in terms of darkness.
15. scatebra pubertatis: " bubbling
spring of adolescence."
18. Utrumque: i.e., the **serenitas
dilectionis** and **caligo libidinis** were
engaged in a confused and mingled
struggle.
19. mersabat gurgite: on omission
of the preposition, cf. § 84a.
21. Invaluerat super: the expression

is Scriptural; cf. IV *Kings,* 14: 10,
invaluisti super Edom: " Thou hast
. . . prevailed over Edom." Cf.
§ 88d, 1.
22. stridore catenae mortalitatis:
" because of the clanking of the chain
of my mortality "; i.e., we cannot
escape our mortality, i.e., our fallen
nature subject to death and always
capable of sin. We are joined to it
as if by a chain. This mortality had
become so insistent during my ado-
lescent years, it had pulled at the
chain which bound me so violently
that amid the clankings of the chain
I had become deaf to the voice of Thy
wrath.
22. poena: in apposition with **stridore**, i.e., the clanking of that chain
and the moral deafness it induced
were Thy punishment for the pride
of my mind.
25. tacebas: i.e., God, Who speaks
through the conscience. W-K.

O tardum gaudium meum! Tacebas tunc, et ego ibam
porro longe a te in plura et plura sterilia semina dolorum
superba deiectione et inquieta lassitudine.

4 Sed efferbui miser, sequens impetum fluxus mei relicto
30 te, et excessi omnia legitima tua nec evasi flagella tua: quis
enim hoc mortalium? Nam tu semper aderas misericorditer
saeviens, et amarissimis aspergens offensionibus omnes
illicitas iucunditates meas, ut ita quaererem sine offensione
iucundari et, ubi hoc possem, non invenirem quicquam
35 praeter te, domine, praeter te, qui fingis dolorem in
praecepto et percutis, ut sanes, et occidis nos, ne
moriamur abs te.

Ubi eram et quam longe exulabam a deliciis domus tuae
anno illo sexto decimo aetatis carnis meae, cum accepit in
40 me sceptrum—et totas manus ei dedi—vesania libidinis
licentiosae per dedecus humanum, inlicitae autem per leges
tuas? Non fuit cura meorum ruentem excipere me matri-
monio, sed cura fuit tantum, ut discerem sermonem facere
quam optimum et persuadere dictione.

---

26. **tardum:** A.'s regret for his be-
lated conversion.

28. **superba deiectione et inquieta
lassitudine:** cf. § 40.

29. **sequens impetum fluxus mei:**
" following the violence of my
stream "; i.e., " of my changing, uncertain nature." A., in *Sermon* 119,
3 (cited by G-M.) speaks of the
flumen carnis: noli sequi flumen
carnis. Caro quippe ista fluvius est;
non enim manet.

30. **quis . . . mortalium:** " for who
of mortals (could do) this? "

33. **quaererem . . . iucundari:** on
the infinitive, cf. § 89b.

34. **hoc possem:** the antecedent of
hoc is sine offensione iucundari.
With **possem,** sc. facere or a like
verb.

34. **non invenirem:** sc. ut from
above.

35. **qui fingis . . . in praecepto:**
cf. *Ps.* 93: 20, " who framest labour
in commandment "; i.e., " who commands suffering for his people."

36. **et percutis . . . ne moriamur:**
cf. *Deut.* 32: 39, " I will kill and I
will make to live: I will strike and I
will heal."

39. **cum accepit . . . tuas?:** vesania
is subject of accepit. Construe cum
vesania libidinis licentiosae per dedecus humanum (inlicitae autem per
leges tuas) accepit sceptrum in me, et
totas manus ei dedi. On the hyperbaton, vesania, cf. § 39. On per,
cf. § 86c, 2.

40. **totas manus ei dedi:** " I gave
my hands entire to it," i.e., " surrendered completely to it."

42. **meorum:** sc. parentum.

42. **excipere:** on the infinitive, cf.
§ 89c.

In that sixteenth year, returned from Ma-
daura, I tarried at home in a dangerous
leisure. Through the words of my mother
Thou Thyself didst forewarn me, but I
flouted her words and therefore Thy words,
my God.

III. 5 Et anno quidem illo intermissa erant studia mea, 45
dum mihi reducto a Madauris, in qua vicina urbe iam
coeperam litteraturae atque oratoriae percipiendae gratia
peregrinari, longinquioris apud Carthaginem peregrinationis
sumptus praeparabantur animositate magis quam opibus
patris, municipis Thagastensis admodum tenuis.   50

Cui narro haec?   Neque enim tibi, deus meus: sed apud
te narro haec generi meo, generi humano—quantulacumque

---

46. mihi reducto: construe with **praeparabantur.**

46. Madauris: Madauri or Madaura (to-day Mdaourouch) is situated about twenty miles south of A.'s native village, Thagaste (to-day Souk-Ahras). Birthplace of the Latin writer, Apuleius, 200 years before, and situated in a rich, well-watered valley, Madaura was still locally important in the arts and sciences and still predominantly pagan when A. went there to school. Such an atmosphere was spiritually most unfortunate for the youthful A. He may even have been perverted to paganism there, as W-K. infer, from a reproachful passage in a letter written by a teacher of Madaura to A. later, viz., **a secta nostra deviasti.** On the use of the preposition **a,** cf. § 87a, 1.

48. apud Carthaginem: = Carthagine. Cf. § 86b.

50. municipis: a citizen of the municipium of Thagaste, A.'s father enjoyed the civic rights of a Roman citizen. Cf. Arnold, 246; Sandys, 366–368; 371–379.

50. admodum tenuis: i.e., modest, but not poor. Patricius was a member of the municipal curia (i.e., the local senate), an office that presupposed the possession of some wealth. But the cost of maintaining A. in the relatively distant and certainly expensive Carthage called for considerable foresight on Patricius' part; compelled, in fact, the interruption of A.'s training for a year while the necessary funds were being assembled. The members of the curia in each municipality were made responsible for the local share of the imperial taxes. These were so heavy in the fourth century that Patricius may more than once have been embarrassed by them.

52. quantulacumque ex particula: a phrase used adjectivally to describe a supplied **genus** and adverbially to describe **incidere.** The whole clause **quantulacumque . . . litteras** is a qualifying afterthought to **generi humano,** " to the human race—of however small a part (the race) can come upon my pages "; i.e., " to the human race—(that is) in however small a part (the race) can come upon my pages."

ex particula incidere potest in istas meas litteras. Et ut
quid hoc? Ut videlicet ego et quisquis haec legit cogitemus,
55 de quam profundo clamandum sit ad te. Et quid propius
auribus tuis, si cor confitens et vita ex fide est?

Quis enim non extollebat laudibus tunc hominem, patrem
meum, quod ultra vires rei familiaris suae impenderet filio,
quidquid etiam longe peregrinanti studiorum causa opus
60 esset? Multorum enim civium longe opulentiorum nullum
tale negotium pro liberis erat, cum interea non satageret
idem pater, qualis crescerem tibi aut quam castus essem,
dummodo essem disertus vel desertus potius a cultura tua,
deus, qui es unus verus et bonus dominus agri tui, cordis mei.
65 6 Sed ubi sexto illo et decimo anno interposito otio ex
necessitate domestica feriatus ab omni schola cum parentibus esse coepi, excesserunt caput meum vepres libidinum,
et nulla erat eradicans manus.

7 Ei mihi! Et audeo dicere tacuisse te, deus meus, cum
70 irem abs te longius? Itane tu tacebas tunc mihi? Et
cuius erant nisi tua verba illa per matrem meam, fidelem
tuam, quae cantasti in aures meas? Nec inde quicquam

---

53. Et ut quid hoc?: " And why
(do I write) this? " On **ut quid** =
quid, cf. § 74.

55. de quam profundo: " from
how (great) depths." Cf. *Ps.* 129:
1: **De profundis clamavi ad te,
Domine**, " Out of the depths I have
cried to thee, O Lord."

55. Et quid . . . ex fide est: " And
what (is) nearer to Thy ears, if a
heart is penitent and life is according
to faith "; i.e., " What is dearer to
Thy ears than a penitent heart, etc."
Cf. *Rom.* I: 17, **Iustus autem ex fide
vivit**, " The just man liveth by faith."

61. non satageret . . . pater: A. is
very grateful to his father for the
sacrifices which he had made for him,
but he would seem to be censuring him
for lack of interest in his son's spiritual
welfare.

62. qualis . . . tibi: " of what sort
I was growing up to Thee "; i.e.,
" with what sort of character, in Thy
sight, I was growing up." On the
dative, cf. § 82d.

63. disertus vel desertus: parechesis. Cf. § 42.

63. cultura tua, deus: cf. I *Cor.*
3: 9, " you are God's husbandry."
On **a**, cf. § 87a, 2.

65. ex necessitate domestica: " because of lack of money at home."

67. excesserunt . . . libidinum: cf.
Ps. 37: 5, " For my iniquities are gone
over my head."

descendit in cor, ut facerem illud. Volebat enim illa, et
secreto memini ut monuerit cum sollicitudine ingenti, ne
fornicarer maximeque ne adulterarem cuiusquam uxorem. 75
Qui mihi monitus muliebres videbantur, quibus obtemperare erubescerem. Illi autem tui erant, et nesciebam et
te tacere putabam atque illam loqui, per quam mihi tu non
tacebas, et in illa contemnebaris a me, a me, filio eius, filio
ancillae tuae, servo tuo. Sed nesciebam et praeceps 80
ibam tanta caecitate, ut inter coaetaneos meos puderet
me minoris dedecoris, quoniam audiebam eos iactantes
flagitia sua et tanto gloriantes magis, quanto magis turpes
essent, et libebat facere non solum libidine facti verum etiam
laudis. Quid dignum est vituperatione nisi vitium? Ego 85
ne vituperarer, vitiosior fiebam, et ubi non suberat, quo
admisso aequarer perditis, fingebam me fecisse quod non
feceram, ne viderer abiectior, quo eram innocentior, et ne
vilior haberer, quo eram castior.

In enjoyment of the malice of the act alone,
I joined with my playmates in a pear tree
robbery.

IV. 9 Furtum certe punit lex tua, domine, et lex scripta 90
in cordibus hominum, quam ne ipsa quidem delet iniquitas:

73. illud: its antecedent is **quicquam.**
73. illa: Monnica.
74. secreto: construe with **monuerit.**
**76. quibus obtemperare erubes-
cerem:** " to obey which I should have
blushed."   On the infinitive, cf. § 89b.
77. Illi: the antecedent is **monitus.**
79. in illa . . . a me: cf. I *Thess.*
4: 8, " Therefore he that despiseth
these things, despiseth not man, but
God."
79. filio . . . servo tuo: cf. *Ps.*
115: 16, " I am thy servant, and the
son of thy handmaid."

81. puderet . . . dedecoris: i.e., A.
was ashamed that his evil actions
were not so wicked as those of his
companions.
85. vituperatione . . . vitium
. . . vituperarer, vitiosior: On paronomasia, cf. § 43.
86. et ubi . . . perditis: " and when
there was not (a crime) at hand, by
which, having been committed, I
might equal my depraved (companions)."
88. abiectior: sc. **eo.**
90. lex scripta . . . hominum: i.e..
the Natural Law expressing itself
through the conscience.

quis enim fur aequo animo furem patitur? Nec copiosus adactum inopia. Et ego furtum facere volui et feci nulla conpulsus egestate nisi penuria et fastidio iustitiae et sagina
95 iniquitatis. Nam id furatus sum, quod mihi abundabat et multo melius, nec ea re volebam frui, quam furto appetebam, sed ipso furto et peccato.

Arbor erat pirus in vicinia nostrae vineae pomis onusta nec forma nec sapore inlecebrosis. Ad hanc excutiendam
100 atque asportandam nequissimi adulescentuli perreximus nocte intempesta, quousque ludum de pestilentiae more in areis produxeramus, et abstulimus inde onera ingentia non ad nostras epulas, sed vel proicienda porcis, etiamsi aliquid inde comedimus, dum tamen fieret a nobis quod eo liberet,
105 quo non liceret.

What did I love in that pear tree theft,
except the base joy of joining in evil?

VIII. 16 Q u e m   f r u c t u m habui miser aliquando i n
h i s, quae nunc recolens erubesco, maxime in illo furto, in quo ipsum furtum amavi, nihil aliud, cum et ipsum esset

---

92. **Nec:** = ne . . . quidem here. Cf. § 75a.

92. **Nec copiosus** . . . **inopia:** i.e., Nec copiosus (furem) adactum inopia (patitur).

94. **penuria** . . . **iustitiae:** " by (my) want of and distaste for justice."

95. **mihi abundabat:** on the dative, cf. § 82d.

95. **et multo melius:** " and (which was) much better "; i.e., of much better quality.

101. **de pestilentiae more:** " in accordance with the custom of our unwholesomeness "; i.e., " in accordance with our unwholesome custom." Cf. §§ 29, 83b.

102. **abstulimus inde onera** . . .

proicienda: on the use of the gerundive, cf. § 90b.

103. **etiamsi** . . . **non liceret:** " although we ate some of it (inde), in order, however, that that might be done by us which pleased us for this reason (namely)—that it was forbidden "; i.e., " in order that we might do that which pleased us for just one reason, namely, that it was forbidden."

104. **dum:** on the use of dum here, cf. § 99c.

104. **eo** . . . **quo** = " for the reason that." Cf. § 98c.

106. **Quem fructum** . . . **erubesco:** cf. *Rom.* 6: 21, " What fruit, therefore, had you then in those things, of which you are now ashamed? "

108. **esset:** sc. furtum as subject.

nihil et eo ipso ego miserior? Et tamen solus id non fecissem—sic recordor animum tunc meum—solus omnino 110 id non fecissem. Ergo amavi ibi etiam consortium eorum, cum quibus id feci. Non ergo nihil aliud quam furtum amavi; immo vero nihil aliud, quia et illud nihil est.

Quid est re vera? Quis est, qui doceat me, nisi qui inluminat cor meum et discernit umbras eius? Quid est, 115 quod mihi venit in mentem quaerere et discutere et considerare, quia si tunc amarem poma illa, quae furatus sum, et eis frui cuperem, possem etiam solus, si satis esset, conmittere illam iniquitatem, qua pervenirem ad voluptatem meam, nec confricatione consciorum animorum accenderem 120 pruritum cupiditatis meae? Sed quoniam in illis pomis voluptas mihi non erat, ea erat in ipso facinore, quam faciebat consortium simul peccantium.

---

111. consortium eorum: A.'s remarks on the "gang spirit" in him reveal again the keen psychologist.

112. cum quibus: cf. § 87c.

113. illud: its antecedent is consortium.

114. qui inluminat cor meum: cf. *Eccles.* 2: 10, "Ye that fear the Lord, love him, and your hearts shall be enlightened."

116. quaerere: on the infinitive with venit in mentem, cf. § 89c.

117. quia . . . possem: cf. § 97.

118. si satis esset: "if this were enough."

120. nec: connects possem and accenderem, which are in the same construction.

120. confricatione . . . animorum: "by the interfriction of guilty minds"; i.e., "by the strong incentive arising from conscious association in evil."

123. consortium simul peccantium: "the company of those sinning together (with me)."

LIBER TERTIUS

V. To Carthage

*To Carthage, with all its corruption, I came
and sought out an object for my depraved
desires.*

I. 1 Veni Carthaginem, et circumstrepebat me undique
sartago flagitiosorum amorum.   Nondum amabam et amare
amabam et secretiore indigentia oderam me minus indigentem.   Quaerebam quid amarem, amans amare, et oderam

---

V. To Carthage

1. **Veni Carthaginem:** Carthage, the
metropolis of the Diocese of Africa,
the capital of the province of Africa
Proconsularis, great Mediterranean
seaport, and one of the first cities of
all the Roman Empire, must have
impressed profoundly, with its cos-
mopolitan variety, the eager and ob-
servant youth fresh from Thagaste
and Madaura.   But the Bishop of
Hippo, writing of his Carthage days
after the lapse of twenty-five years,
ignores his other experiences to con-
centrate on the larger facts of his
spiritual development.   In *Conf.* V,
8, 15, he is also strangely silent about
the details of his journey to Rome,
and in *Conf.* V, 9, 16, of his first impressions of the panorama of the
world's capital.

The position of the phrase, **Veni
Carthaginem**, first in the chapter and
first in the book, suggests the importance which the author, in the interpretation of his life, attaches to his
time at Carthage.   Carthage was a
turning-point in his religious experiences.   The prayerful purpose of the

Confessions explains in part the brevity
and abruptness of the phrase.   The
word **Carthago** had a world of meaning
for the penitent A., all the more
felt because unelaborated.

1. **circumstrepebat . . . sartago:**
" there hummed about me on every
hand a kettle."   Carthage had a
reputation for immorality even beyond that of contemporary cities.

1. **Carthaginem . . . sartago:** parechesis.   Note also in this passage
amare amabam, paronomasia, and
indigentia . . . indigentem, paronomasia.   Cf. §§ 42, 43.

2. **amare amabam:** on amo with the
infinitive, cf. § 89b.

3. **secretiore indigentia . . . indigentem:** " because of a deeper want
(i.e., his unconscious longing for God)
I hated myself (as) longing less (to
love than I thought I should) "; i.e.,
because my real hunger—longing for
Thee, my God—was so concealed from
me, I thought in my blindness that
my soul's unrest was unsatisfied profane love alone and I was therefore
violently angry with myself because I
did not discover a stronger urge in me
to profane love.

securitatem et viam sine muscipulis, quoniam famis mihi 5
erat intus ab interiore cibo, te ipso, deus meus, et ea fame
non esuriebam, sed eram sine desiderio alimentorum incor-
ruptibilium, non quia plenus eis eram, sed quo inanior,
fastidiosior. Et ideo non bene valebat anima mea et
ulcerosa proiciebat se foras, miserabiliter scalpi avida con- 10
tactu sensibilium. Sed si non haberent animam, non utique
amarentur.

What is the lure of tragic stage-plays, such
as then intrigued and corrupted my soul?

II. 2 Rapiebant me spectacula theatrica plena imaginibus
miseriarum mearum et fomitibus ignis mei. Quid est, quod
ibi homo vult dolere cum spectat luctuosa et tragica, quae 15

---

5. quoniam . . . cibo . . . esurie-
bam: "for there was a hunger to me
within from a lack of (or, as regards)
the interior food, Thyself, my God,
and with this hunger I felt not hungry." A.'s hunger was basically a
hunger for the interior food which is
God.

8. sed quo inanior, fastidiosior:
"but the more empty (I was of
them), the more disgusted (I felt
towards them)." As G-M. points
out, this is an accurate metaphor from
hunger-nausea.

10. (anima) ulcerosa . . . foras:
"(my soul), full of ulcers, was casting itself without"; i.e., my soul,
full of corruption from my base desires, was now seeking to leave its
proper sphere of spiritual aspiration
(was casting itself without its true
self) in order to have part in sensual
pleasures. Cf. *Job* 2: 7-8. On *et
ideo*, cf. § 95a.

10. scalpi avida: "itching to be
scratched." Cf. § 89e.

11. Sed si non haberent animam:
A. means that material things must

have some active power of attraction
which impels our souls to desire them.

13. plena . . . ignis mei: plays
then presented—whether tragedy,
comedy, mime, or pantomime—dealt
almost exclusively with immoral
love themes.

**14. Quid est, quod ibi homo vult
dolere . . .:** A. raises here the important question of the nature of the
pleasure derived from witnessing
dramatic performances, particularly
tragedies. He seems to incline here
to Plato's unfavorable opinion of
drama. Thus Plato, in his *Republic*
(10, 606 A), states that the natural
hunger for sorrow and weeping, which
is kept under control in our own
calamities, is satisfied and delighted
by the poets. "Poetry feeds and
waters the passions instead of starving
them." To-day, following Aristotle
rather than Plato in this, we are more
kindly towards the drama. For a
discussion of this subject, cf. S. H.
Butcher, *Aristotle's Theory of Poetry
and Fine Art*, 2nd ed., pp. 236-295.
London, 1898.

tamen pati ipse nollet?   Et tamen pati vult ex eis dolorem
spectator et dolor ipse est voluptas eius.   Quid est nisi
miserabilis insania?   Nam eo magis eis movetur quisque,
quo minus a talibus affectibus sanus est, quamquam, cum
20 ipse patitur, miseria, cum aliis compatitur, misericordia dici
solet.   Sed qualis tandem misericordia in rebus fictis et
scenicis?   Non enim ad subveniendum provocatur auditor,
sed tantum ad dolendum invitatur et auctori earum imag-
inum amplius favet, cum amplius dolet.   Et si calamitates
25 illae hominum vel antiquae vel falsae sic agantur, ut qui
spectat non doleat, abscedit inde fastidiens et reprehendens;
si autem doleat, manet intentus et gaudens.

> *Sinking to the depths of sinful indulgence*
> *and swollen with pride over achievements in*
> *school, I yet was less proud than the*
> *"Overturners," whose company I sought,*
> *though abhorring their deeds.*

III. 5 Et circumvolabat super me fidelis a longe misericordia tua.   In quantas iniquitates distabui et sacrilegam
30 curiositatem secutus sum, ut deserentem te deduceret me

---

19. a talibus affectibus sanus: on a
with **sanus,** cf. § 87a, 3.

20. miseria: predicate of **dici solet**
to be supplied.

21. misericordia: cf. the interesting
definition of **misericordia** given by A.
in his *De Moribus Ecclesiae Catholicae*
27, 53 (cited by G-M.): **Quis ignoret
ex eo appellatam esse misericordiam,
quod miserum cor faciat condolentis
alieno malo?**

25. antiquae vel falsae: " of olden
times or purely imagined."

27. si . . . doleat: cf. § 102c.

27. manet: " stays to the end."

28. fidelis: " genuine "; i.e., genuine, effective mercy and not the

spurious ineffective substitute felt by
spectators of sad scenes in the theatre.
The hyperbaton formed by the position of **fidelis** suggests the translation
" truly genuine " here.   Cf. § 39.

28. a longe: " from afar "; i.e.,
" far above," in this context.   God's
mercy is represented as hovering over
A. but at a great distance because of
A.'s spiritual estrangement at the
time.   On **a** with the adverb, cf.
§ 87a, 4.

29. sacrilegam: sc. **quantam** before
sacrilegam.

30. deduceret: sc. **sacrilega curiositas** as subject.

ad ima infida et circumventoria obsequia daemoniorum,
quibus immolabam facta mea mala, et in omnibus flagellabas
me!

6 Habebant et illa studia, quae honesta vocabantur,
ductum suum intuentem fora litigiosa, ut excellerem in eis, 35
hoc laudabilior, quo fraudulentior. Tanta est caecitas
hominum de caecitate etiam gloriantium! Et maior iam
eram in schola rhetoris et gaudebam superbe et tumebam
tyfo, quamquam longe sedatior, domine, tu scis, et remotus
omnino ab eversionibus, quas faciebant eversores—hoc enim 40

---

31. ad ima infida: "to the depths of faithlessness "; i.e., either of moral faithlessness or of infidelity.

31. circumventoria ... daemoniorum: " (to) the deceitful service of daemons." We cannot determine whether this context refers to a formal participation in pagan rites or to moral delinquencies alone. It may conceivably refer to both. The " daemons " here may be a metaphor for his immoralities. The notorious licentiousness of pagan rites at Carthage suggests that A. may have been lured into taking a part in them. The vagueness of the passage is appropriate to a work that is first of all prayerful. What is vague to us was known in all details to God and the penitent A.

32. quibus . . . facta mea: cf. *Deut.* 32: 17, " They sacrificed to devils and not to God."

34. Habebant ... litigiosa: " Moreover, these studies, which were called honorable, had their bent fixed upon the litigious fora "; i.e., " were conducted with an eye towards lawsuits in the forum." For an account of these studies, cf. Gwynn, 82–92.

36. hoc laudabilior, quo fraudulentior: an elaboration of his protests against ancient Education in *Conf.* I, 9, 14; I, 14, 23; I, 17, 27; I, 18, 28;

I, 19, 30. Rhetoric, with a bad name among its critics reaching back to the schools of the Greek sophists in the fifth century B.C., deserved, in the schools of A.'s youth, A.'s blunt stricture against it here. The more artful and successful the defense of an unjust cause, the greater glory redounding to the schoolboy protagonist.

37. maior . . . in schola: " leader," " head."

38. schola rhetoris: the rhetorical school was the most important educational institution under the Empire. For an account, cf. Duff, 31–41.

38. tumebam tyfo: " I was swollen with vanity."

39. quamquam: cf. § 76b.

39. longe sedatior: " much more restrained (than others)."

39. remotus . . . ab: " removed from "; i.e., " having no connection or part in."

40. eversores: " He (i.e., A.) was disgusted, for instance, by the wild follies of a set of undisciplined students who styled themselves ' wreckers ' (**eversores**) like the Mohawks of seventeenth-century London, who amused themselves by annoying freshmen, insulting strangers, and making themselves a nuisance generally. A. had acquaintances among

nomen scaevum et diabolicum velut insigne urbanitatis
est—inter quos vivebam pudore inpudenti, quia talis non
eram: et cum eis eram et amicitiis eorum delectabar aliquando, a quorum semper factis abhorrebam, hoc est ab
45 eversionibus, quibus proterve insectabantur ignotorum
verecundiam, quam proturbarent gratis inludendo atque
inde pascendo malivolas laetitias suas. Nihil est illo actu
similius actibus daemoniorum. Quid itaque verius quam
eversores vocarentur, eversi plane prius ipsi atque perversi
50 deridentibus eos et seducentibus fallacibus occulte spiritibus
in eo ipso, quo alios inridere amant et fallere?

VI. The Hortensius of Cicero

And then, having come upon Cicero's
Hortensius, I began consciously to long for
Thyself, O my God.

IV. 7 Inter hos ego inbecilla tunc aetate discebam libros
eloquentiae, in qua eminere cupiebam fine damnabili et

---

this crew, but he was not one of them,
nor had he any wish to emulate their
senseless behavior. He possessed
qualities which lifted him far above
their level. . . ." Ottley, 10–11.

42. pudore inpudenti: note the
oxymoron, "in shameless shame"; i.e.,
"shameless," because he associated
with such fellows, but "shame," because (as the **quia** clause explains) he
was not one of them in their characteristic escapades. Cf. § 40.

45. ignotorum: " freshmen."

46. inludendo . . . pascendo: perhaps best taken as datives of purpose
or of the end for which, after **proturbarent.** The use of an accusative
object after the dative of the gerund,
as here with **pascendo,** is rare and is
not found in Class. Latin. Cf.
G-L., § 429, note 2.

49. eversi . . .: construe **eversi
. . . atque perversi fallacibus spiritibus, occulte deridentibus eos et
seducentibus in eo ipso. . . .**

**49. eversores . . . eversi . . . per-
versi:** note the paronomasia. Cf.
§ 43.

50. spiritibus: on the dative of
agent, cf. § 82e.

51. in eo ipso: " in that very
thing, wherein." On **in,** cf. § 88b, 4.

51. inridere amant: cf. § 89b.

VI. The Hortensius of Cicero

1. hos: i.e., the **eversores.**

1. inbecilla . . . aetate: A. was
nineteen. On **tunc,** cf. § 71.

1. libros eloquentiae: along with
the orations of Cicero, his philo-

ventoso per gaudia vanitatis humanae, et usitato iam
discendi ordine perveneram in librum cuiusdam Ciceronis,
cuius linguam fere omnes mirantur, pectus non ita.   Sed 5
liber ille ipsius exhortationem continet ad philosophiam et
vocatur Hortensius.

Ille vero liber mutavit affectum meum et ad te ipsum,
domine, mutavit preces meas et vota ac desideria mea fecit
alia.   Viluit mihi repente omnis vana spes et inmortalitatem 10
sapientiae concupiscebam aestu cordis incredibili et surgere
coeperam, ut ad te redirem.   Non enim ad acuendam
linguam—quod videbar emere maternis mercedibus, cum
agerem annum aetatis undevicensimum iam defuncto patre

---

sophical works were studied for their
style rather than for their content.

3. per gaudia: per = " on account
of "; cf. § 86c, 2.

3. usitato . . . ordine: "in the
ordinary course of study."

4 cuiusdam: by this depreciatory
adjective, A. again professes his estrangement from pagan studies (cf.
Conf. I, 13, 20), and yet Cicero's name
was as familiar to students of the Empire as is Shakespeare's to the modern
student.

**5. linguam . . . pectus non ita:
pectus** = "heart." A., trained in
rhetoric, could admire the style of the
great Roman master, Cicero, although
he was not blind, of course, to defects
of his character appreciated then as
well as to-day.

7. Hortensius: a dialogue in two
books, of which only a few fragments
are extant and these mostly in A.'s
own works. In it Cicero defends the
study of philosophy against the
strictures of the orator Hortensius;
insists upon its superiority over the
study of oratory, which Hortensius is
defending, and praises it as the intellectual pursuit most efficacious for
happiness. The fragments of the

Hortensius, scattered at wide intervals
through A.'s theological writings, bear
witness to the esteem in which he held
it even in his maturity.

8. ad te ipsum: construe with
mutavit preces meas.

10. Viluit mihi: cf. § 82d.

10. inmortalitatem sapientiae: =
inmortalem sapientiam. On the genitive, cf. §§ 29, 83c.

11. aestu cordis incredibili: "with
an unbelievable yearning of heart."

11. surgere coeperam: probably an
echo from *Luke*, 15: 18, where the
Prodigal Son says: "**surgam, et ibo
ad patrem meum**"; "I will arise, and
I will go to my father."

12. ad acuendam linguam: for pre-
paring himself to be a rhetor.

13. (id) quod videbar emere: the
clause is in apposition with **ad acuendam linguam.**

13. maternis mercedibus: i.e., with
the funds supplied by his mother.

14. defuncto patre: A.'s mere passing reference to the death of his
father is curious. In *Conf.* IX, 9,
19–22, we learn that Patricius became
a Christian only a short time before
his death and that he was not a very
amiable character.

15 ante biennium—non ergo ad acuendam linguam referebam illum librum neque mihi locutionem, sed quod loquebatur persuaserat.

8 Quomodo ardebam, deus meus, quomodo ardebam revolare a terrenis ad te, et nesciebam quid ageres mecum!
20 Apud te est enim sapientia. Amor autem sapientiae nomen graecum habet philosophiam, quo me accendebant illae litterae. Sunt qui seducant per philosophiam, magno et blando et honesto nomine colorantes et fucantes errores suos, et prope omnes, qui ex illis et supra temporibus tales
25 erant, notantur in eo libro et demonstrantur, et manifestatur ibi salutifera illa admonitio spiritus tui per servum tuum bonum et pium: videte, ne quis vos decipiat per philosophiam et inanem seductionem secundum traditionem hominum, secundum ele-
30 menta huius mundi et non secundum Christum, quia in ipso inhabitat omnis plenitudo divinitatis corporaliter.

Et ego illo tempore, scis tu, lumen cordis mei, quoniam

---

15. non ergo . . . persuaserat: " not, therefore, for sharpening my tongue did I use that book, and it had not persuaded its style to me, but that which it was saying"; i.e., ". . . and it had impressed on me not its style but its subject matter." A. tells us above that he had come upon the *Hortensius* in the ordinary course of rhetorical studies at the time (**usitato iam discendi ordine**). In thus going beyond the mere form of the dialogue to its thought, A. reveals his superiority to both his masters and his fellow pupils in penetration and power of reflection.

18. ardebam revolare: on the infinitive, cf. § 89b.

20. Apud . . . sapientia: cf. *Job* 12: 13, " With him is wisdom and strength."

20. Amor . . . sapientiae . . . philosophiam: " But ' love of wisdom ' has the Greek name ' philosophy ' "; i.e., " ' love of wisdom,' is called "philosophy ' in Greek."

21. quo: referring to **amor**.

22. illae litterae: i.e., the *Hortensius*.

22. magno . . . nomine: construe with **colorantes**.

24. ex illis . . . temporibus: " of those (i.e., Cicero's) and earlier times."

27. videte . . . corporaliter: *Col.* 2: 8–9: " Beware lest any man cheat you by philosophy, and vain deceit; according to the tradition of men, according to the elements of this world, and not according to Christ. For in him dwelleth all the fullness of the Godhead corporeally."

necdum mihi haec apostolica nota erant, hoc tamen solo
delectabar in illa exhortatione, quod non illam aut illam 35
sectam, sed ipsam quaecumque esset sapientiam ut diligerem
et quaererem et adséquerer et tenerem atque amplexarer
fortiter, excitabar sermone illo et accendebar et ardebam,
et hoc solum me in tanta flagrantia refrangebat, quod
nomen Christi non erat ibi, quoniam hoc nomen secun- 40
dum misericordiam tuam, domine, hoc nomen
salvatoris mei, fili tui, in ipso adhuc lacte matris tenerum
cor meum pie biberat et alte retinebat, et quidquid sine
hoc nomine fuisset, quamvis litteratum et expolitum et
veridicum, non me totum rapiebat.   45

---

34. necdum: = nondum. Cf. § 75c.

34. tamen: tamen refers more to
the preceding paragraph than to its
own. A. uses **tamen** here to contrast
his general condemnation of pagan
philosophy in the preceding paragraph (**sunt qui seducant . . .**),
representative of his attitude after
he had been converted and was writing
the *Confessions*, with his enjoyment
of one phase (**hoc . . . solo . . . quod**)
of the *Hortensius* at the time he first
read the work. The **quoniam . . .
erant** clause explains why he delighted
in the *Hortensius* in his Carthage
days, viz., because he knew not yet
the writings of St. Paul.

35. illa exhortatione: i.e., the *Hortensius*.

35. quod non illam . . . ardebam:
construe quod illo sermone excitabar
et . . . ut diligerem . . . fortiter
non illam aut illam sectam, sed
ipsam sapientiam, quaecumque esset.

36. sectam: a " school " of philosophy. Cicero was an eclectic in
philosophy. He drew what he
thought was best from various sys-
tems.

36. diligerem . . . amplexarer:
note the rhetorical effect produced by

amplification and polysyndeton. Cf.
§ 46.

39. quod nomen Christi: this need
for the " name of Christ " was
a gift from his mother, St. Monnica.
Impressed on him in his earliest years,
it endured throughout the time of his
spiritual wandering. The presence
of the Holy Name in the Manichaean
system may have urged on his conversion to Manichaeism. Still later,
he turned from the Academics because they were " without the saving
name of Christ" (cf. *Conf.* V, 14, 25),
to become a Christian catechumen in
earnest.

A.'s statement here contradicts only
superficially his other references to his
state of soul at this time. His love
of Christ's name was an echo from
his childhood, half-forgotten amid
the pleasures of Carthage, but it
immediately asserted itself, once the
Hortensius took A. beyond the things
of the moment.

40. secundum misericordiam tuam:
cf. *Ps.* 24: 7, " According to thy
mercy, remember thou me."

42. adhuc: " even." Cf. § 72.

43. quidquid . . . fuisset: on the
subjunctive, cf. § 102b.

> *But missing Thy Name in Cicero's Hor-*
> *tensius, I turned to a study of the Holy*
> *Scriptures.*

V. 9 Itaque institui animum intendere in scripturas
sanctas et videre, quales essent. Et ecce video rem non
conpertam superbis neque nudatam pueris, sed incessu
humilem, successu excelsam et velatam mysteriis, et non
50 eram ego talis, ut intrare in eam possem aut inclinare
cervicem ad eius gressus. Non enim sicut modo loquor,
ita sensi, cum adtendi ad illam scripturam, sed visa est mihi
indigna, quam Tullianae dignitati conpararem. Tumor
enim meus refugiebat modum eius et acies mea non pene-
55 trabat interiora eius. Verum tamen illa erat, quae cresceret
cum parvulis, sed ego dedignabar esse parvulus et turgidus
fastu mihi grandis videbar.

---

46. Itaque: A., under the influence
of the *Hortensius*, now began to
examine the Scriptures, but it is significant of how distant he was from
the ideals of his childhood and of how
thoroughly he was steeped in the
rhetoric of the time that he found
them so repugnant. Unlike his masters and fellow students, he could go
beyond the style of the *Hortensius*
to its thought, but the plainness of
the Scriptures was a barrier to his
mind. Note how A.'s attitude here
towards his earlier repugnance accords
with the view of the Christian human-
ists of antiquity that pagan classics
were a propaedeutic to the Scriptures.
Cf. De Labriolle, 25–28.

**47. rem non conpertam . . . ex-
celsam:** " a thing not disclosed to the
proud nor revealed to children, but
as to entrance, lowly; as to progress,
lofty "; i.e., " low as one enters, but

becoming lofty, progressively, as one
advances." The metaphor seems to
be that of a building with a very low
entrance, through which one passes to
an interior of constantly increasing
magnificence.

51. Non enim . . . scripturam:
" For not as I now so speak did I so
feel when I (first) turned seriously to
that Scripture."

52. ad illam scripturam: on the bald
Latin versions of the Scriptures which
preceded St. Jerome's work and to
which A. must refer here, cf. De
Labriolle, 43–49. Cf. also §§ 59,
105.

53. quam . . . conpararem: on the
comparative clause without *ut*, cf.
A-G., § 535c.

53. Tullianae dignitati: " the stateliness of Tully " (Cicero).

56. dedignabar esse: cf. § 89b.

VII. THE MANICHEE

But in my pride of language I turned from Thy Scriptures, and became a disciple of the Manichees.

VI. 10 Itaque incidi in homines superbe delirantes, carnales nimis et loquaces, in quorum ore laquei diaboli et viscum confectum conmixtione syllabarum nominis tui et domini Iesu Christi et paracleti consolatoris nostri spiritus sancti. Haec nomina non recedebant de ore eorum, sed 5 tenus sono et strepitu linguae; ceterum cor inane veri. Et

---

VII. The Manichee

1. Itaque incidi: of Manichaeism it is sufficient for the present passage to recall that its founder, Mani, was born at Babylon at about the beginning of the third century; that about fifty years before the time of A.'s perversion, it had begun to spread in the West, particularly in Roman Africa. Purporting to represent the best of contemporary religious thought, it was a heresy compounded of elements primarily Babylonian and Persian which appropriated certain Christian ideas in its progress (cf. **conmixtione syllabarum . . . spiritus sancti** in the present chapter). As it grew in the West it posed as the better and more complete Christianity. It went to great pains to impress the cultured with its scientific method, its freedom of investigation, its criticism of the Scriptures. The promises of light, wisdom, and enfranchisement thus held out were just suited to A.'s intellectual state at the time; blown up, as he was, with scholastic success, thirsting for truth, disappointed with the Scriptures, impatient of authority, and yet still stamped, however faintly, by the Christian associations of his youngest days. The doctrine that sin was a merely physical, and not a moral, evil may have been a further argument to him amid the pleasures of Carthage. That he clung to this sect for nine years was a mystery to his later self. On Manichaeism, cf. Burkitt, *The Religion of the Manichees*, Cambridge, 1925; C.E., IX, pp. 591–596.

1. superbe delirantes: " doting in their pride."

2. in quorum ore laquei: sc. sunt or **erant.** The word **laqueus,** "snare," is used among the Ecclesiastical writers in the sense of " the snare of sin," " the snare of temptation," as here.

3. viscum: " birdlime," used here in sense of " birdlime of error," i.e., " allurement of heretical teaching."

3. conmixtione syllabarum . . . spiritus sancti: cf. note 1 above.

5. non recedebant de ore: cf. *Josue* I: 8, " Let not the book of this law depart from thy mouth."

6. tenus sono: " as far as sound ";
i.e., " they were only sound." In Class. Latin, **tenus** is postpositive. Cf. A-G., § 435; G-L., § 417, 14.

dicebant: « veritas et veritas » et multum eam dicebant
mihi, et nusquam erat in eis, sed falsa loquebantur non de
te tantum, qui vere veritas es, sed etiam de istis elementis
10 huius mundi, creatura tua, de quibus etiam vera dicentes
philosophos transgredi debui prae amore tuo, mi pater
summe bone, pulchritudo pulchrorum omnium.
O veritas, veritas, quam intime etiam tum medullae
animi mei suspirabant tibi, cum te illi sonarent mihi fre-
15 quenter et multipliciter voce sola et libris multis et ingenti-
bus!

My mother ceased not to bewail my apos-
tasy, until calmed by a dream which Thou
sent her, my God. Through nine full years
I clung to my error, but her prayers of hope
went up daily to Thee.

XI. 19 Et misisti manum tuam ex alto et de hac profunda
caligine eruisti animam meam, cum pro me fleret
ad te mea mater, fidelis tua, amplius quam flent matres
20 corporea funera. Videbat enim illa mortem meam ex fide

---

7. **" veritas et veritas ":** the Manichaeans had the word " truth " constantly on their lips.

9. **elementis huius mundi:** in the
fantastic cosmology of the Manichaeans, the world arose from the
invasion of the eternal kingdom of
light by wicked demons from the
eternal kingdom of darkness.

11. **transgredi debui:** " I should
have passed by "; i.e., later (cf.
Conf. V, 3, 3, and V, 6, 11) A. turned
from the tenets of the Manichaeans
regarding the universe in an effort
to find solid truth in the Neoplatonic
philosophers, but even then he was
not prepared to go further and examine the teachings of the Christian
faith. On causal **prae,** cf. § 87g, 2.

12. **pulchritudo pulchrorum omnium:** cf. §§ 43, 83a.

14. **suspirabant tibi:** cf. § 82b.

14. **te . . . sonarent:** " sounded
Thy name." On the subjunctive, cf.
§ 102a.

17. **misisti . . . ex alto:** cf. *Ps.*
143: 7, " Put forth thy hand from
on high."

18. **eruisti animam meam:** cf. *Ps.*
85: 13, " and thou hast delivered my
soul."

18. **fleret ad te:** on ad, cf. § 86a,
3.

20. **corporea funera:** " bodily
deaths."

20. **ex fide et spiritu:** on the hendiadys, cf. § 38. On **ex,** cf. § 87e, 1.

et spiritu, quem habebat ex te, et exaudisti eam, domine.
Exaudisti eam nec despexisti lacrimas eius, cum profluentes
rigarent terram sub oculis eius in omni loco orationis eius:
exaudisti eam. Nam unde illud somnium, quo eam con-
solatus es, ut vivere mecum cederet et habere mecum 25
eandem mensam in domo? Quod nolle coeperat aversans et
detestans blasphemias erroris mei. Vidit enim se stantem
in quadam regula lignea et venientem ad se iuvenem
splendidum hilarem atque arridentem sibi, cum illa esset
maerens et maerore confecta. Qui cum causas ab ea 30
quaesisset maestitiae suae cotidianarumque lacrimarum—
docendi, ut adsolet, non discendi gratia—atque illa respon-
disset perditionem meam se plangere, iussisse illum, quo
secura esset, atque admonuisse, ut adtenderet et videret,
ubi esset illa, ibi esse et me. Quod illa ubi adtendit, vidit 35
me iuxta se in eadem regula stantem.

Unde hoc, nisi quia erant aures tuae ad cor eius, o tu
bone omnipotens, qui sic curas unumquemque nostrum,
tamquam solum cures, et sic omnes, tamquam singulos?

---

23. **in omni loco orationis eius:** "in every place of her prayer"; i.e., "wherever she prayed."

24. **exaudisti eam:** by repeating the phrase twice, A. tries to convey to God something of his sense of gratitude. Cf. § 37.

25. **vivere . . . cederet:** cf. § 89b.

26. **Quod nolle coeperat:** "And this she had begun to be unwilling (to do)." After completing his studies at Carthage, A. returned to Thagaste, where for a time, according to his *Contra Academicos* II, 2, 3, he lived with his friend, Romanianus. It would seem that Monnica, outraged at her son's apostasy, refused him her house until after the dream related here.

28. **regula:** "rule," and here, "the rule of faith." In *Conf.* VIII, 12, 30, A., just converted, speaks of him-self as now **stans in ea regula fidei, in qua me ante tot annos ei** (i.e., Monnica) **revelaveras.**

32. **ut adsolet:** "as is wont to be done (in such cases)."

33. **iussisse illum:** after **vidit** of preceding sentence.

33. **quo:** = ut. On the use of such a substantive clause after **iubeo,** cf. § 99b.

34. **adtenderet et videret:** cf. *Lament.* 1: 12, "O all ye that pass by the way, attend, and see."

37. **Unde hoc:** sc. somnium.

37. **nisi quia:** cf. § 98e.

37. **aures tuae ad cor eius:** "Thy ears were (inclined) to her heart." Cf. *Ps.* 10: 17, "thy ear hath heard the preparation of their heart."

39. **tamquam solum cures:** "as if you were caring but for him alone."

40   **20** Unde illud etiam, quod cum mihi narrasset ipsum visum et ego ad id detrahere conarer, ut illa se potius non desperaret futuram esse quod eram, continuo sine aliqua haesitatione: "Non" inquit "non enim mihi dictum est: ubi ille, ibi et tu, sed: ubi tu, ibi et ille."

45   Confiteor tibi, domine, recordationem meam, quantum recolo—quod saepe non tacui—amplius me isto per matrem vigilantem responso tuo, quod tam vicina interpretationis falsitate turbata non est et tam cito vidit quod videndum fuit—quod ego certe, antequam dixisset, non videram—

50   etiam tum fuisse conmotum quam ipso somnio, quo feminae piae gaudium tanto post futurum ad consolationem tunc praesentis sollicitudinis tanto ante praedictum est.

    Nam novem ferme anni secuti sunt, quibus ego in illo limo profundi ac tenebris falsitatis, cum saepe surgere

55   conarer et gravius alliderer, volutatus sum, cum tamen illa vidua, casta, pia et sobria, quales amas, iam quidem spe alacrior, sed fletu et gemitu non segnior, non desineret horis omnibus orationum suarum de me plangere ad te, et intra-

---

40. Unde illud . . . haesitatione . . . (respondit): "Whence this too, the fact that when she had told me that vision and I was trying to make it mean (lit., bring it down to this) that she should not despair that she would be (one day) what I was, promptly, without any hesitation, she replied."

40. ipsum: = hunc or illum. Cf. § 68d, 1.

46. quod saepe non tacui: translate, " and I have often said this."

46. amplius . . . somnio: construe me amplius etiam tum fuisse conmotum isto responso tuo per matrem vigilantem quam ipso somnio.

47. vicina . . . falsitate: " (my) specious falsity of interpretation "

= " my specious, false interpretation." Cf. §§ 29, 83c.

50. quo feminae . . . praedictum est: " by which the joy of that holy woman, to be realized (futurum) so long afterwards, was foretold to her so long before for the consolation of her distress then present."

53. in illo limo profundi: cf. *Ps.* 68: 3, " I stick fast in the mire of the deep."

54. saepe surgere conarer: i.e., from Manichaeism.

56. vidua . . . quales amas: a state of peculiar honor in the Early Church. quales is plural because A. is thinking of the class of viduae.

58. intrabant . . . preces eius: cf. *Ps.* 87: 3, " Let my prayer come in before thee."

bant in conspectum tuum preces eius, et me tamen
dimittebas adhuc volvi et involvi illa caligine.   60

A Bishop, himself once a Manichee heretic,
assured my mother of my final conversion.

XII. 21 Et dedisti alterum responsum interim, quod
recolo. Nam et multa praetereo, propter quod propero ad
ea quae me magis urguent confiteri tibi, et multa non
memini.

Dedisti ergo alterum per sacerdotem tuum, quendam 65
episcopum nutritum in ecclesia et exercitatum in libris tuis.
Quem cum illa femina rogasset, ut dignaretur mecum conloqui et refellere errores meos et dedocere me mala ac docere
bona—faciebat enim hoc, quos forte idoneos invenisset—
noluit ille, prudenter sane, quantum sensi postea. Respon- 70
dit enim me adhuc esse indocilem, eo quod inflatus essem
novitate haeresis illius et nonnullis quaestiunculis iam
multos inperitos exagitassem, sicut illa indicaverat ei.
"Sed" inquit "sine illum ibi. Tantum roga pro eo dominum: ipse legendo reperiet, quis ille sit error et quanta 75
inpietas." Simul etiam narravit se quoque parvulum a
seducta matre sua datum fuisse manichaeis, et omnes paene
non legisse tantum verum etiam scriptitasse libros eorum
sibique adparuisse, nullo contra disputante et convincente,

---

60. dimittebas . . . volvi: cf. § 89f.
61. alterum: sc. responsum.
62. propter quod: = propterea
quod. Cf. § 98d.
63. urguent confiteri: cf. § 89ff.
66. nutritum in ecclesia: a Manichee in youth, the bishop had turned
to Christianity so early in life that
he could be said to have been "reared
in the church."
67. dignaretur . . . conloqui: cf.
§ 89b.

69. quos . . . invenisset: = si quos.
The subjunctive is iterative. Cf.
§ 102b.
71. eo quod: = quod. Cf. § 98b.
72. nonnullis quaestiunculis: "with
all manner of trifling questions."
74. sine: from sino.
77. seducta matre: i.e., she had
joined the Manichaeans.
77. omnes: construe with libros.
78. scriptitasse: " had often cop-
ied."

80 quam esset illa secta fugienda: itaque fugisse. Quae cum
ille dixisset atque illa nollet adquiescere, sed instaret magis
deprecando et ubertim flendo, ut me videret et mecum
dissereret, ille iam substomachans taedio: "Vade" inquit
"a me; ita vivas, fieri non potest, ut filius istarum lacri-
85 marum pereat."

Quod illa ita se accepisse inter conloquia sua mecum
saepe recordabatur, ac si de caelo sonuisset.

LIBER QUARTUS

*In open pursuit of applause and pleasures,
in secret purgation from their physical
stain, my companions and I spent these
nine years together; seducing, and seduced
by, each other in turn.*

I. 1 Per idem tempus annorum novem, ab undevicesimo
anno aetatis meae usque ad duodetricensimum, seduceba-
90 mur et seducebamus; falsi atque fallentes in variis cupidi-

---

80. **quam esset . . . fugienda:** indirect question with **adparuisse.**

84. **ita vivas:** " as true as you live."
The subjunctive is optative. Cf.
A-G., § 441; G-L., § 262.

86. **Quod . . . recordabatur:** "And
this she was wont often to recall."

87. **sonuisset:** impersonal; i.e., " as
if these words had sounded from
heaven."

88. **idem:** i.e., he is treating here of
the same period of his life as above
in *Conf.* III, 6, 10 and III, 11, 19–
20, and 12, 21. Cf. particularly *Conf.*
III, 11, 20, **nam novem ferme
anni . . . .**

89. **seducebamur:** i.e., A. and his
fellow converts to Manichaeism from
among the professional class. The
first person plural throughout this
passage must be interpreted in the
light of the last sentence of the
paragraph (**Et sectabar . . . cum
amicis meis . . . deceptis**).

90. **falsi atque fallentes:** " de-
ceived and deceiving."

90. **cupiditatibus:** under this word,
A. groups all the aberrations of these
nine years from the severe moral
standards of his later life as a Christian: his ambitions as rhetor, his sinful
pleasures, and his activities as a
Manichaean " hearer."

tatibus; et palam per doctrinas quas liberales vocant, occulte
autem falso nomine religionis; hic superbi, ibi superstitiosi,
ubique vani; hac popularis gloriae sectantes inanitatem
usque ad theatricos plausus et contentiosa carmina et
agonem coronarum faenearum et spectaculorum nugas et 95
intemperantiam libidinum, illac autem purgari nos ab istis
sordibus expetentes, cum eis, qui appellarentur electi et

---

91. palam . . . occulte: the Manichaeans had earned the first of many imperial proscriptions under Diocletian, about a century before A. wrote these lines. In A.'s youth they were under the ban of the Church as well. "In public," therefore, A. and his fellow students were being "seduced, etc." by the empty vanities of literary and rhetorical contests and "were seducing, etc." by teaching the so-called liberal arts to others; "in secret" they were "being seduced, etc." by their progressive entanglement in Manichaean doctrines and practices and "were seducing, etc." by their sustained bad example to one another in pursuing a specious religion. A.'s use of **seducebamur** and **falsi** . . . is not mere attempt at rhetorical paronomasia. Manichaeism was still virulent and aggressive when he wrote the *Confessions*. (It disappeared as a sect only in the sixth century.)

91. per . . . liberales vocant: "through (our teaching of) the so-called liberal arts," i.e., primarily literature and rhetoric, but including such studies as music, mathematics, and especially philosophy. Cf. Gwynn, 82–100; C. E., I, s.v. "Arts, The Seven Liberal," pp. 760–765. On **per**, cf. § 86c, 1.

93. vani: an implied zeugma meaning both "empty" and "proud." Cf. § 49.

93. hac . . . illac: "on the one

hand" (**palam**) . . . "on the other hand" (**occulte**).

94. usque ad theatricos plausus: "even to the applause of the theater." Victory in rhetorical and literary contests gave the rhetor a fame and prestige unparalleled in modern civilization.

94. contentiosa carmina: "poetical competitions."

95. agonem coronarum faenearum: "contest for crowns of grass." Such garlands were frequently given as prizes.

95. spectaculorum nugas et intemperantiam libidinum: cf. § 83c.

96. purgari . . . expetentes: on the infinitive, cf. § 89f.

97. electi . . . afferremus escas: the Manichaeans were divided into the "Elect," who had renounced the use of flesh and wine and the state of marriage, and the "Hearers," who were excused from such rigors, but were held, among other duties, to provide food for the "Elect." A., like most Manichaeans, never passed beyond the condition of "Hearer." It seems that when the "Hearers" bore food to the "Elect," they were cleansed by a ceremony connected with the consumption of the food from what the Manichaeans believed to be sin. Sins, according to them, were physical contacts of whatever kind with the world, itself wholly evil in their eyes, because it had been created by the "Principle of Dark-

sancti, afferremus escas, de quibus nobis in officina aqualiculi sui fabricarent angelos et deos, per quos liberaremur.
100 Et sectabar ista atque faciebam cum amicis meis per me ac
mecum deceptis.

In my teaching of rhetoric and keeping a
mistress I yet showed traces of faith in Thee.

II. 2 Docebam in illis annis artem rhetoricam et victoriosam loquacitatem victus cupiditate vendebam.   Malebam
tamen, domine, tu scis, bonos habere discipulos, sicut

ness." The pleasures and ambitions referred to by A. in **hac popularis . . . libidinum** above—moral evils to Christians—were certainly, but at the same time merely, physical evils to the Manichaeans. Cf. *Conf.* III, 6, 10 and p. 109, note 1.

98. de quibus: = **ex quibus.** Cf. § 87d, 2.

98. in officina aqualiculi: "in the workshop of their own paunches." The word usually denotes "a small vessel"; occasionally, as here, it is used contemptuously to mean "bel-ly," "paunch." The allusion here is undoubtedly an effective polemical thrust.

99. angelos et deos: according to the Manichaean belief (as stated in *Conf.* III, 10, 18), the "Elect," on eating the food prepared for them by the "Hearers," breathed forth angels and gods, i.e., particles of the "Principle of Light."

102. in illis annis: i.e., during his Manichaean years. As a matter of fact, A. began his professional career as a teacher not of rhetoric but of grammar, and in his native Thagaste in 374. But within a year he had exchanged grammar for rhetoric and Thagaste for the larger field of Carthage. For the next eight years, 375-383, he was thus engaged at Carthage and it is to these eight years

that the events in this chapter refer. Later in this book (*Conf.* IV, 4, 5 ff.) his words are to be associated with his earlier and briefer professional days in his native village, but in both places he was a Manichaean, and in describing his state of soul he prefers the topical to a rigidly chronological treatment.   On temporal **in**, cf. § 88b, 2.

102. victoriosam loquacitatem . . . vendebam: again A. is somewhat disparaging of his one-time profession. The rhetors did teach for fees (**vendebam**), an art which emphasized victory (**victoriosam**) above all things else, and many of the devices which they taught their pupils to this end deserved, when stripped of their trickery, the designation **loquacitatem.** A.'s several references to rhetoric and rhetors are alike depreciatory. Cf. *Conf.* I, 17, 27; III, 3, 6; IV, 1, 1; IX, 4, 7; 5, 13.

103. cupiditate: a reference to the avarice of the typical rhetor, who, in addition to his income from the state, exacted as much compensation as he could from his pupils. From the next sentence it is obvious that **cupiditate** in the strict sense of avarice does not apply to A. He is emphasizing rather his need to earn sufficient funds to support a manner of living which he later thought luxurious.

appellantur boni, et eos sine dolo docebam dolos, non quibus 105
contra caput innocentis agerent, sed aliquando pro capite
nocentis. Et, deus, vidisti de longinquo lapsantem in
lubrico et in multo fumo scintillantem fidem meam, quam
exhibebam in illo magisterio diligentibus v a n i t a t e m et
quaerentibus m e n d a c i u m, socius eorum.   110

In illis annis unam habebam non eo quod legitimum
vocatur coniugio cognitam, sed quam indagaverat vagus
ardor inops prudentiae, sed unam tamen, ei quoque servans
tori fidem.

VIII. Death of a Friend

*Deeply attached to a boyhood playmate, I
led him away from allegiance to Thee and
when he had died in a deathbed repentance,
I had tears; not Thyself, in his stead, O my
God.*

IV. 7 In illis annis, quo primum tempore in municipio,

---

105. boni: i.e., " good " students, not necessarily students of good moral character. A. finds some consolation for his Carthage days from his anxiety to train his students well; a conscientiousness not characteristic of rhetors as a class.

105. eos: refers to **discipulos.**

105. dolos: the artifices and tricks of rhetoric. On **dolo . . . dolos,** cf. §§ 32, 45.

107. in lubrico: " on slippery ground."

108. in multo fumo . . . meam: cf. *Matt.* 12: 30, **et linum fumigans non extinguet,** " and smoking flax he shall not extinguish."

108. fidem meam . . . exhibebam: A. consoles himself in that he preserved some traces of Christian rectitude in teaching an art that had become immoral in practice.

109. diligentibus vanitatem et quaerentibus mendacium: cf. *Ps.* 4: 3,

" why do you love vanity, and seek after lying? "

111. unam . . .: construe **habebam unam non cognitam eo coniugio quod legitimum vocatur sed quam. . . .** He refers to his union with an unknown woman who became the mother of his son Adeodatus. This union lasted thirteen years. The moral depravity of his time is brought out strikingly by the implication (**sed unam tantum**) that such faithfulness to a single mistress was quite exceptional.

113. ardor: " passion."

VIII. Death of a Friend

1. In illis annis: again, as at the beginning of *Conf.* IV, 1, 1, and midway in *Conf.* IV, 2, 2, A. makes a general reference to his nine years as a Manichaean.

1. quo primum tempore . . .

quo natus sum, docere coeperam, conparaveram amicum
societate studiorum nimis carum, coaevum mihi et conflorentem flore adulescentiae. Mecum puer creverat et
5 pariter in scholam ieramus pariterque luseramus. Sed
nondum erat sic amicus, quamquam ne tunc quidem sic,
uti est vera amicitia, quia non est vera, nisi cum eam tu
agglutinas inter haerentes tibi caritate diffusa in cordibus nostris per spiritum sanctum, qui datus
10 est nobis. Sed tamen dulcis erat nimis, cocta fervore
parilium studiorum. Nam et a fide vera, quam non germanitus et penitus adulescens tenebat deflexeram eum in
superstitiosas fabellas et perniciosas, propter quas me
plangebat mater. Mecum iam errabat in animo ille homo,
15 et non poterat anima mea sine illo. Et ecce tu inminens
dorso fugitivorum tuorum, deus ultionum et fons
misericordiarum simul, qui convertis nos ad te miris modis,
ecce abstulisti hominem de hac vita, cum vix explevisset

---

coeperam: " what time I first began
to teach." The clause is in apposition
with **illis annis** and specifies to what
period of the nine years he is referring,
i.e., to his brief sojourn in 374 at
Thagaste, teaching grammar, before
his return to Carthage as a professor
of rhetoric.

3. conflorentem flore: note the
paronomasia, § 43.

**5. Sed nondum . . . qui datus est
nobis:** " But not yet (i.e., in boyhood) was he such a friend (as he
afterwards became); although not
even then (i.e., at that later time)
(was our friendship) such as true
friendship is, because (friendship) is
not true except when Thou dost solder
it between those cleaving to Thee by
the charity of God poured forth ' in
our hearts, by the Holy Ghost, who is
given to us.' " Cf. *Conf.* II, 2, 2,

quatenus est luminosus limes amicitiae, and *Rom.* 5: 5.

10. cocta fervore: " ripened by the
heat," or, because of **agglutinas** above
and because **coctus** is also used of
bricks hardened in the sun, it may be
translated " strengthened," " made
fast."

11. parilium studiorum: " like
tastes," " like enthusiasms."

13. superstitiosas fabellas: i.e., the
teachings of Manichaeism.

**13. propter quas . . . plangebat
mater:** cf. *Conf.* III, 11, 19.

15. tu inminens . . . tuorum: " Thou
close upon the back(s) of Thy fugi-
tives," i.e., " of those fleeing from
Thee."

16. deus ultionum: cf. *Ps.* 93: 1,
Deus ultionum Dominus: " The
Lord is the God to whom revenge
belongeth." On the genitive, cf.
§ 83d.

annum in amicitia mea, suavi mihi super omnes suavitates
illius vitae meae.   20

8 Quis laudes tuas enumerat unus in se uno, quas
expertus est? Quid tunc fecisti, deus meus, et quam
investigabilis abyssus iudiciorum tuorum? Cum enim
laboraret ille febribus, iacuit diu sine sensu in sudore letali
et, cum desperaretur, baptizatus est nesciens, me non   25
curante et praesumente id retinere potius animam eius
quod a me acceperat, non quod in nescientis corpore fiebat.
Longe autem aliter erat. Nam recreatus est et salvus
factus, statimque, ut primo cum eo loqui potui—potui autem
mox ut ille potuit, quando non discedebam et nimis pende- 30
bamus ex invicem—temtavi apud illum inridere, tamquam
et illo inrisuro mecum baptismum, quem acceperat mente
atque sensu absentissimus. Sed tamen iam se accepisse

---

19. super omnes suavitates: on
super, cf. § 88d, 3.

21. Quis laudes tuas enumerat: cf.
Ps. 105: 2, " Who shall declare the
powers of the Lord? who shall set
forth all his praises? "

21. Quis . . . expertus est: " What
one person declares Thy praises in
himself alone, those which he has
felt," i.e., what one person can render
adequately the praises due Thee, even
in the occasions for such praise as he
has found in his own experience of
Thee. Construe **laudes tuas** with
in se uno. quas expertus est is an
afterthought in apposition with and
limiting **laudes tuas.**

**22. quam investigabilis abyssus
. . . tuorum:** cf. *Ps.* 35: 7, " thy
judgments are a great deep," and
Rom. 11: 33, " How incomprehensible
are his judgments, and how unsearchable his ways! "

25. nesciens: " while unconscious "
—on the assumption that the unconscious person, if conscious of the im-

minence of death, would certainly
desire Baptism. On the practice of
postponing Baptism, cf. *Conf.* I, 11,
17–18 and p. 77, note 68.

**25. me . . . praesumente . . .
fiebat:** " I not objecting and taking it
for granted that his soul retained
rather what it had received from me
(i.e., doctrines of Manichaeism), not
what was being done (i.e., Baptism)
on the body of him not knowing (of
it)."

30. mox ut: = ut primum. Cf.
§ 101a.

31. ex invicem: " upon each other."
Cf. § 67.

31. temtavi . . . inridere: on infinitive, cf. § 89b.

**31. tamquam et illo inrisuro . . .
baptismum:** " as if he also would
laugh with me at the Baptism." On
the future participle in an ablative
absolute, cf. §84c.

33. absentissimus: a rhetorical
rather than logical superlative. Cf.
Conf. I, 4, 4, omnipotentissime.

didicerat. At ille ita me exhorruit ut inimicum admonuit-
35 que mirabili et repentina libertate, ut, si amicus esse vellem,
talia sibi dicere desinerem. Ego autem stupefactus atque
turbatus distuli omnes motus meos, ut convalesceret prius
essetque idoneus viribus valetudinis, cum quo agere possem
quod vellem. Sed ille abreptus dementiae meae, ut apud
40 te servaretur consolationi meae: post paucos dies me absente
repetitur febribus et defungitur.

9 Quo dolore contenebratum est cor meum, et quidquid
aspiciebam mors erat. Et erat mihi patria supplicium et
paterna domus mira infelicitas, et quidquid cum illo con-
45 municaveram, sine illo in cruciatum inmanem verterat.
Expetebant eum undique oculi mei, et non dabatur; et
oderam omnia, quod non haberent eum, nec mihi iam dicere
poterant: "Ecce veniet," sicut cum viveret, quando absens
erat. Factus eram ipse mihi magna quaestio et interroga-
50 bam animam meam, quare tristis esset et quare conturbaret
me valde, et nihil noverat respondere mihi. Et si dicebam:
"Spera in deum," iuste non obtemperabat, quia verior erat

---

35. mirabili: because A. suddenly discovers that he has lost his dominance over the mind of his friend.

37. motus meos: though distressed, A. represses his natural desire to correct his friend, until the latter be his old self again.

38. viribus valetudinis: = viribus validis. Cf. §§ 29, 83b.

38. cum quo: A. was confident of recovering his dominance, once his friend recovered his health. The latter's independence, meanwhile, A. thought the resultant of bodily weakness and the experience of near-death. On **cum quo** for **quocum,** cf. § 87c.

39. dementiae meae: dative of separation. Cf. § 82d.

42. Quo dolore contenebratum est cor meum: cf. *Lament.* 5: 17, "There-

fore is our heart sorrowful; therefore are our eyes become dim."

49. Factus eram . . . magna quaestio: "I (myself) became a great enigma to myself"; i.e., on account of excessive grief.

50. quare tristis esset et quare conturbaret me valde: cf. *Ps.* 41: 6, 12, "Why art thou sad, O my soul? and why dost thou trouble me?" "Why art thou cast down, O my soul? and why dost thou disquiet me?"

51. noverat respondere: on the infinitive, cf. § 89b.

52. "Spera in deum:" cf. *Ps.* 41: 6. "Hope in God." On **in,** cf. § 88a, 3.

52. obtemperabat amiserat iubebatur } sc. **anima mea.**

et melior homo, quem carissimum amiserat, quam phantasma, in quod sperare iubebatur. Solus fletus erat dulcis
mihi et successerat amico meo i n d e l i c i i s animi mei.   55

> *Wedded to earth and heedless of Thee;*
> *weary of living, and yet fearful of death;*
> *in bitter tears only I found some release,*
> *expecting that all men soon would die.*

VI. 11 Quid autem ista loquor? Non enim tempus
quaerendi nunc est, sed confitendi tibi. Miser eram, et
miser est omnis animus vinctus amicitia rerum mortalium
et dilaniatur, cum eas amittit, et tunc sentit miseriam, qua
miser est et antequam amittat eas. Sic ego eram illo   60
tempore et flebam amarissime et requiescebam i n a m a r i -
t u d i n e . Ita miser eram et habebam cariorem illo amico
meo vitam ipsam miseram. Nam quamvis eam mutare
vellem, nollem tamen amittere magis quam illum et nescio
an vellem vel pro illo, sicut de Oreste et Pylade traditur, si 65
non fingitur, qui vellent pro invicem simul mori, quia morte

---

53. **phantasma:** as a consolation
for his grief-stricken soul, he was
bidding it to hope in God, but his
faith in God had become so weak
(thanks to the vague concepts of
Manichaeism) and his love for his
departed friend was still so strong
that in trying to substitute God and
his promises of eternity for the loss
of his earthly friend, God and eternity
became a nebulous phantasm in comparison with the crushing reality of
his grief.

55. **in deliciis animi mei:** cf. *Ps.*
138: 11, **et nox illuminatio mea in
deliciis meis,** " and night shall be my
light in my pleasures."

56. **ista:** refers to his discussion of
the consolations of weeping, *Conf.* IV,
5, 10, omitted here.

56. **Non enim tempus quaerendi**
nunc est: " For now is not the time
for questioning."

60. **et antequam: et = etiam.** Cf.
§ 94a.

61. **requiescebam in amaritudine:**
cf. *Job.* 3: 20, **Quare misero data est
lux, et vita his qui in amaritudine
animae sunt:** " Why is light given to
him that is in misery, and life to them
that are in bitterness of soul? "

64. **amittere:** sc. **eam** as object.

64. **et nescio an vellem vel pro illo:**
" and I do not know whether I should
have wished (to lose it) even for him."

65. **Oreste et Pylade:** like the
story of Damon and Pythias, the
story of the intense love of Orestes
and Pylades was widely known among
the Greeks and Romans.

66. **pro invicem:** " for each other."
Cf. § 67.

peius eis erat non simul vivere. Sed in me nescio quis
affectus nimis huic contrarius ortus erat et taedium vivendi
erat in me gravissimum et moriendi metus. Credo, quo
70 magis illum amabam, hoc magis mortem, quae mihi eum
abstulerat, tamquam atrocissimam inimicam oderam et
timebam et eam repente consumpturam omnes homines
putabam, quia illum potuit. Sic eram omnino, memini.

IX. CARTHAGE ONCE MORE

*In the vague God of Mani having found no
escape; in all earthly contacts recalling but
death; unable to break from the prison of
self; from the haunts of my friend to
Carthage I fled.*

VII. 12 O dementiam nescientem diligere homines humaniter! O stultum hominem inmoderate humana patien-
tem! Quod ego tunc eram. Itaque aestuabam, suspirabam, flebam, turbabar, nec requies erat nec consilium.
5 Portabam enim concisam et cruentam animam meam
inpatientem portari a me, et ubi eam ponerem non inveniebam. Non in amoenis nemoribus, non in ludis atque
cantibus nec in suave olentibus locis nec in conviviis
apparatis nec in voluptate cubilis et lecti, non denique in
10 libris atque carminibus adquiescebat. Horrebant omnia et

---

68. **nimis huic contrarius:** " quite
different from this (of theirs)."

IX. Carthage Once More

1. **O dementiam . . .:** on the accusative, cf. A-G., § 397, d; G-L.,
§ 343, 1.
1. **homines humaniter . . . hominem . . . humana:** note the paronomasia. Cf. § 43.
1. **humaniter:** " humanwise," i.e.,

in a manner consistent with the passing character of all human relation-
ships and especially of man's mortality.
2. **humana:** " human things," i.e.,
the lot of man.
3. **aestuabam:** " I raved " (as in a
fever).
6. **inpatientem portari:** cf. § 89e.
9. **in voluptate cubilis et lecti:** i.e.,
in the pleasures of sensual enjoyment.

ipsa lux, et quidquid non erat quod ille erat, inprobum et taediosum erat praeter gemitum et lacrimas; nam in eis solis aliquantula requies. Ubi autem inde auferebatur anima mea, onerabat me grandis sarcina miseriae.

Ad te, domine, levanda erat et curanda, sciebam, 15 sed nec volebam nec valebam, eo magis, quod mihi non eras aliquid solidum et firmum, cum de te cogitabam. Non enim tu eras, sed vanum phantasma et error meus erat deus meus. Si conabar eam ibi ponere, ut requiesceret, per inane labebatur et iterum ruebat super me, et ego mihi 20 remanseram infelix locus, ubi nec esse possem nec inde recedere. Quo enim cor meum fugeret a corde meo? Quo a me ipso fugerem? Quo non me sequerer?

Et tamen fugi de patria. Minus enim eum quaerebant oculi mei, ubi videre non solebant, atque a Thagastensi 25 oppido veni Carthaginem.

---

11. quidquid non . . . ille erat: "whatever was not what he was"; i.e., "everything which was not he."

13. Ubi: temporal.

13. inde: i.e., from **gemitus** and **lacrimae.**

15. Ad te, domine, levanda erat: cf. *Ps.* 24: 1, " To thee, O Lord, have I lifted up my soul."

16. nec volebam nec valebam: note the parechesis. Cf. § 42.

16. quod mihi . . . solidum et firmum: cf. *Conf.* IV, 4, 9, quam phantasma in quod sperare iubebatur and p. 121, note 53. The Manichaean concept of God was too vague and shadowy for the grief-stricken A., hungry for consolation.

17. Non enim tu eras: " For Thou (i.e., as I know Thee with the eyes of full faith) were not (the object of my thought)."

19. ibi: refers to **vanum phantasma.**

19. per inane: " through the void."

21. remanseram: cf. § 78a.

22. Quo enim . . . fugerem: The soul naturally seeks release from self in time of profound sorrow, turning to God and human friends. A.'s soul, however, was so shocked by this disruption of a human friendship by death that he became deranged temporarily on the subject of mortality, was reminded of it in all his human contacts, and thus was deprived of consolation from human sources. But in reaching out for the divine, he had only the nebulous God of the Manichees as a source, and thus had to fall back upon, or rather could not escape from, himself.

24. fugi de patria: on de, cf. § 87d, 1.

24. Minus . . . solebant: " For my eyes were not looking for him (i.e., my friend) where they were not accustomed to see him."

25. a Thagastensi . . . Carthaginem: we learn from the *Contra Academicos,*

> *But slowly my sorrow gave way to old pleas-*
> *ures, to the moral immunities of Manichee*
> *friends, but though my soul itched for their*
> *freedom in action, in the joys of pure*
> *friendship it was still more consoled.*

VIII. 13 Non vacant tempora nec otiose volvuntur per
sensus nostros: faciunt in animo mira opera. Ecce veniebant et praeteribant de die in diem et veniendo et
30 praetereundo inserebant mihi spes alias et alias memorias
et paulatim resarciebant me pristinis generibus delectationum, quibus cedebat dolor meus ille; sed succedebant
non quidem dolores alii, causae tamen aliorum dolorum.
Nam unde me facillime et in intima dolor ille penetraverat,
35 nisi quia fuderam in harenam animam meam diligendo
moriturum acsi non moriturum?
Maxime quippe me reparabant atque recreabant aliorum
amicorum solacia, cum quibus amabam quod pro te amabam, et hoc erat ingens fabula et longum mendacium, cuius

---

II, 2, 2, that at this time (376 A.D.)
he suddenly left Thagaste, without
informing anyone of his plans except
his friend Romanianus, with whom he
had taken up his abode after his
estrangement from his mother. Cf.
Conf. III, 11, 19 and p. 111, note 26.
Romanianus gave him the money
necessary for his journey and estab-
lishment in Carthage. Some time
later, Monnica joined her son in that
city.

27. Non vacant tempora: " Time is
not idle." Where our idiom calls for
the singular in this sense, Latin may
use the plural.

29. de die in diem: cf. *Ps.* 60: 9,
" that I may pay my vows from day
to day."

31. resarciebant me: " filled me
again," or " restored me."

33. causae . . . dolorum: i.e., his
old pleasures, which had been inter-
rupted temporarily by his bereave-
ment.

34. unde: " why."

34. in intima: " to my innermost
(parts) "; i.e., " to my innermost and
deepest self which should have been
reserved for God alone."

35. nisi quia: cf. § 98e.

35. harenam: metaphor for the
instability of those objects upon which
A. was lavishing his affections in his
Manichaean years.

36. acsi: = quasi. cf. § 76a.

38. pro te: " in place of Thee ";
i.e., Manichaeism and the worldly
atmosphere and practices of Manichaean and Carthaginian society, with
the consoling sophistries that excused
worldly conduct.

adulterina confricatione corrumpebatur mens nostra pru- 40
riens in auribus. Sed illa mihi fabula non moriebatur, si
quis amicorum meorum moreretur. Alia erant, quae in
eis amplius capiebant animum, conloqui et conridere et
vicissim benivole obsequi, simul legere libros dulciloquos,
simul nugari et simul honestari, dissentire interdum sine 45
odio tamquam ipse homo secum atque ipsa rarissima
dissensione condire consensiones plurimas, docere aliquid
invicem aut discere ab invicem, desiderare absentes cum
molestia, suscipere venientes cum laetitia: his atque huius
modi signis a corde amantium et redamantium procedenti- 50
bus per os, per linguam, per oculos et mille motus gratissimos
quasi fomitibus conflare animos et ex pluribus unum facere.
 XVI. 31 O domine deus noster, i n v e l a m e n t o a l a r u m

---

40. pruriens in auribus: cf. II *Tim.*
4: 3, coacervabunt sibi magistros,
prurientes auribus: " they will heap
to themselves teachers, having itching ears." The Manichaean doctrine
that sin was a physical, not a moral,
evil; the consequent emancipation
from moral scruples; the living of this
doctrine and the enjoyment of this
emancipation by his Manichaean
friends, so in harmony with the atmosphere of pagan Carthage, must
have been a comfort and encouragement to the stricken A. Cut off from
the consolations of Christianity by
his deviation from the path that led
to full faith and Baptism, only worldly
consolations were available and A.'s
soul fairly itched in its eagerness to
take in the doctrine that gave a philosophical sanction to such consolations.
 42. moreretur: cf. § 102c. the experience of his friend's mortality
should have called him from the
sophistries of Manichaeism.
 42. Alia erant . . . facere: note the
delightful picture of the joys of friendship.

43. conloqui et conridere . . .
conflare . . . facere: all infinitives in
the passage are in apposition with
Alia. Cf. § 89a.
 44. vicissim benivole obsequi: " to
be kindly deferential to one another."
Cf. § 67.
 45. dissentire . . . dissensione
. . . consensiones: note the paronomasia. Cf. § 43.
 48. invicem . . . ab invicem: cf.
§ 67.
 52. quasi fomitibus conflare animos: " to fuse our minds by (such)
kindling material, as it were."
 52. ex pluribus unum: " one out of
many."
 53. in . . . speremus: cf. § 88a, 3.
 53. velamento alarum . . . protege
nos: cf. *Ps.* 16: 8, Sub umbra alarum
tuarum protege me, " Protect me
under the shadow of thy wings ";
Ps. 62: 8, et in velamento alarum
exultabo, " and I will rejoice under
the covert of thy wings "; *Ps.* 35: 8,
Filii autem hominum in tegmine
alarum tuarum sperabunt, " But the

tuarum speremus, et protege nos et porta nos. Tu
55 portabis, tu portabis et parvulos et usque ad canos
tu portabis, quoniam firmitas nostra, quando tu es, tunc est
firmitas; cum autem nostra est, infirmitas est. Vivit apud
te semper bonum nostrum, et quia inde aversi sumus,
perversi sumus. Revertamur iam, domine, ut non ever-
60 tamur, quia vivit apud te sine ullo defectu bonum nostrum,
quod tu ipse es, et non timemus, ne non sit quo redeamus,
quia nos inde ruimus; nobis autem absentibus non ruit
domus nostra, aeternitas tua.

LIBER QUINTUS

X. Faustus

*In my twenty-ninth year came Faustus to
Carthage, a Manichee bishop reputed most
wise.*

III. 3 Proloquar in conspectu dei mei annum illum un-
detricesimum aetatis meae.

Iam venerat Carthaginem quidam manichaeorum episco-

children of men shall put their trust
under the covert of thy wings."
54. **Tu portabis, tu portabis:** anadiplosis. Cf. § 31.
55. **et usque ad canos tu portabis:**
cf. *Is.* 46: 4, " Even to your old age
I am the same, and to your grey hairs
I will carry you."
58. **aversi . . . perversi . . . Revertamur . . . evertamur:** cf. § 43.
59. **ut non:** = ne. Cf. § 75f.
61. **quod tu ipse es:** " which (good)
art Thou Thyself."
61. **non timemus . . . aeternitas
tua:** i.e., if we neglect our earthly
homes for any length of time, they

fall into ruin; but the eternal home of
the soul—heaven—remains imperish-
able forever.
61. **ne non:** cf. A-G, § 564; G-L.,
§ 550, 2.

X. Faustus

1. **in conspectu dei:** " in the sight
of God," " before God." A common
Scriptural phrase; cf. e.g., *Ps.* 67: 4.
Cf. § 88b, 1.
3. **episcopus:** the Manichaean hi-
erarchical organization resembled in
many respects that of the Roman
Catholic Church.

pus, Faustus nomine, magnus laqueus diaboli, et
multi inplicabantur in eo per inlecebram suaviloquentiae. 5
Quam ego iam tametsi laudabam, discernebam tamen a
veritate rerum, quarum discendarum avidus eram, nec
quali vasculo sermonis, sed quid mihi scientiae comedendum
adponeret nominatus apud eos ille Faustus intuebar. Fama
enim de illo praelocuta mihi erat, quod esset honestarum 10
omnium doctrinarum peritissimus et adprime disciplinis
liberalibus eruditus.

Et quoniam multa philosophorum legeram memoriaeque
mandata retinebam, ex eis quaedam conparabam illis
manichaeorum longis fabulis, et mihi probabiliora ista 15

---

4. Faustus: the intellectual luminary of the Western Manichees at the time; a native of Milevis in Numidia; a man of such great reputation that A., sometime after he had concluded his *Confessions*, found it necessary to write a *Contra Faustum*, in 33 books, in refutation of a work of Faustus which had meanwhile appeared. Cf. C.E., IX, s.v. *Manichaeism*, p. 595.

4. laqueus diaboli: cf. I *Tim.* 3: 7, " lest he fall into reproach and the snare of the devil."

5. in eo: note that A. keeps up the figure of Faustus as being a snare.

6. discernebam: sc. quam as object.

7. quarum: refers strictly to **rerum,** showing that **a veritate rerum = a veris rebus.** Cf. §§ 29, 83c.

7. nec . . . intuebar: " and not in what vessel of discourse, but what knowledge . . . Faustus was setting before me to partake of did I look to." On the gerundive construction here, cf. § 90b.

9. Fama . . . quod esset: on the **quod** clause, cf. § 97.

10. honestarum omnium doctri-
narum: i.e., all those studies which formed the basis of a broad and varied education, among which the liberal arts proper (**disciplinis liberalibus**) were considered the most important. Cf. *Conf.* IV, 1, 1 and p. 115, note 91. Gwynn, 82–100; C. E., I, s.v. *Arts, The Seven Liberal*, pp. 760–765.

13. philosophorum: under this term, A., following the custom of antiquity, includes not only philosophers in our modern sense, but also (and particularly in this passage) investigators in and writers on the natural sciences. He probably has in mind here the astronomical works of Ptolemy and his interpreters. The Manichaean imaginings (**longis fabulis**) on the origin of the world, for instance, suffered by contrast with the empirically founded theories of the astronomers, and A. was consequently anxious about a question so fundamental to the Manichaean system. Cf. *Conf.* V, 7, 12, below.

13. memoriaeque mandata retinebam: "(them) committed to memory I retained "; i.e., " I still had them in my memory."

videbantur, quae dixerunt illi, qui tantum potuerunt
valere, ut possent aestimare saeculum, quamquam eius dominum minime invenerint.

*To him had I looked for release from my
doubts, but I found in his wisdom words
only, my God.*

VI. 10 Et per annos ferme ipsos novem, quibus eos
20 animo vagabundus audivi, nimis extento desiderio venturum
expectabam istum Faustum. Ceteri enim eorum, in quos
forte incurrissem, qui talium rerum quaestionibus a me
obiectis deficiebant, illum mihi promittebant, cuius adventu
conlatoque conloquio facillime mihi haec et si qua forte
25 maiora quaererem enodatissime expedirentur.

Ergo ubi venit, expertus sum hominem gratum et iucun-
dum verbis et ea ipsa, quae illi solent dicere, multo suavius
garrientem.

11 Igitur aviditas mea, qua illum tanto tempore expec-
30 taveram hominem, delectabatur quidem motu affectuque
disputantis et verbis congruentibus atque ad vestiendas
sententias facile occurrentibus. Delectabar autem et cum
multis vel etiam prae multis laudabam ac ferebam; sed

---

16. illi: i.e., the philosophers.
16. qui tantum . . . invenerint: cf.
Wis. 13, 9, " For if they were able to
know so much as to make judgment of
the world: how did they not more
easily find out the Lord thereof? "
19. per annos ferme ipsos novem:
on ipsos = eosdem, cf. § 68d, 2.
19. eos: i.e., the Manichees.
21. Ceteri: i.e., all the other
Manichees except Faustus.
21. in quos . . . incurrissem: on
the subjunctive, cf. § 102b.
24. conlatoque conloquio: on the
ablative absolute, cf. § 84c.

24. haec et si qua . . . quaererem:
' these and if I should ask, perchance,
any more difficult (**maiora**) things'';
i.e., " these questions and any more
difficult ones that I might ask."
29. tanto tempore: on the ablative
of duration of time, cf. § 84b.
30. affectu: " animation."
31. verbis . . . occurrentibus: " and
with words appropriate and coming
(to him) easily for clothing his
thoughts."
33. multis: i.e., of his admirers.
On **prae**, cf. § 87g, 3.

moleste habebam, quod in coetu audientium non sinerer
ingerere illi et partiri cum eo curas quaestionum mearum 35
conferendo familiariter et accipiendo ac reddendo sermonem.
Quod ubi potui et aures eius cum familiaribus meis eoque
tempore occupare coepi, quo non dedeceret alternis disserere,
et protuli quaedam, quae me movebant, expertus sum prius
hominem expertem liberalium disciplinarum nisi gram- 40
maticae atque eius ipsius usitato modo. Et quia legerat
aliquas Tullianas orationes et paucissimos Senecae libros
et nonnulla poetarum et suae sectae si qua volumina latine
atque conposite conscripta erant, et quia aderat cotidiana
sermocinandi exercitatio, inde suppetebat eloquium, quod 45
fiebat acceptius magisque seductorium moderamine ingenii
et quodam lepore naturali.

Itane est, ut recolo, domine deus meus, arbiter conscien-
tiae meae? Coram te cor meum et recordatio mea, qui me
tunc agebas abdito secreto providentiae tuae et inhonestos 50

---

35. ingerere: " bring before, " "submit to." Construe with **curas** below.
35. curas quaestionum mearum:
" the cares of my problems," " the
problems which were worrying me."
**36. accipiendo ac reddendo ser-
monem:** " by listening to discourse
and replying (**reddendo**) (in turn)."
37. Quod ubi potui: cf.
37. et aures . . . disserere: " and
when, with my friends, I began to
busy his ears, and at such a time that
it was not improper to enter into
mutual discussion with him."
38. dedeceret: subjunctive of characteristic.
38. alternis: sc. vicibus " by alternate changes," " alternately," " by
turns."
39. expertus sum . . . expertem:
paronomasia. Cf. § 43.
**40. nisi grammaticae . . . usitato
modo:** i.e., his knowledge even of

grammar and literature was only the
superficial sort characteristic of the
contemporary rhetor.
42. Senecae: L. Annaeus Seneca
(circa 4 B.C.–65 A.D.), Stoic philosopher and poet. His works, written
in a brilliant, sententious style, exercised a great influence in the Middle
Ages and after, as well as in antiquity.
Because of the loftiness of many of
his moral sayings, he was much admired by the Latin Fathers and was
considered by some of them almost a
Christian. Cf. Duff, 196–278.
43. suae sectae: i.e., the Manichaeans.
45. inde suppetebat eloquium:
"through this an eloquence was furnished him."
46. moderamine ingenii: " by his
control of his talent."
49. Coram te: cf. § 87b.
50. agebas: " direct," " lead."

errores meos iam c o n v e r t e b a s a n t e f a c i e m meam,
ut viderem et odissem.

And thus, though attracted by Faustus' de-
meanor and a mutual regard for rhetorical
art, I began to withdraw from Manichaeism,
Thyself directing in secret, my God.

VII. 12 Nam posteaquam ille mihi inperitus earum ar-
tium, quibus eum excellere putaveram, satis apparuit,
55 desperare coepi posse mihi eum illa, quae me movebant,
aperire atque dissolvere; quorum quidem ignarus posset
veritatem tenere pietatis, sed si manichaeus non esset.
Libri quippe eorum pleni sunt longissimis fabulis de caelo
et sideribus et sole et luna: quae mihi eum—quod utique
60 cupiebam—conlatis numerorum rationibus, quas alibi ego
legeram, utrum potius ita essent, ut Manichaei libris
continebantur, an certe vel par etiam inde ratio redderetur,
subtiliter explicare posse iam non arbitrabar.

---

51. convertebas ante faciem: cf.
Ps. 49: 21, " I will reprove thee and
set before thy face."

**56. quorum quidem . . . manichaeus
non esset:** " and though ignorant of
these things, he could, of course, have
possessed true piety, but only if he
had not been a Manichaean "; i.e.,
piety can be mere liking for religious
exercises and assiduity in practicing
them. But true piety implies, in addition, the practice of the moral virtues. Since the fundamental tenets
of Manichaeism absolved its followers
from moral responsibility, zeal for the
liturgical practices of Manichaeism
on the part of either the simple or the
skeptical ran counter to that cultivation of the virtues which is a necessary mark of true piety. Manichaean

" piety " was an obstacle to the acquisition of true piety.

57. veritatem . . . pietatis: = veram
pietatem. Cf. §§ 29, 83c.

58. fabulis de caelo: i.e., the
elaborate Manichaean cosmology. Cf.
Conf. V, 3, 3, **illis Manichaeorum
longis fabulis.**

59. quae mihi eum: construe with
subtiliter . . . arbitrabar.

60. conlatis numerorum rationibus:
" having compared the computations
of astronomy."

60. alibi: i.e., the works of the
philosophers and astronomers.

62. an . . . redderetur: " or
whether indeed an even equal explanation (i.e., to that of the astronomers)
also could be given from their books
(inde)." On **inde,** cf. § 73.

Quae tamen ubi consideranda et discutienda protuli, modeste sane ille nec ausus est subire ipsam sarcinam. 65 Noverat enim se ista non nosse nec eum puduit confiteri. Non erat de talibus, quales multos loquaces passus eram, conantes ea me docere et dicentes nihil. Iste vero c o r habebat, etsi n o n r e c t u m ad te, nec tamen nimis incautum ad se ipsum. Non usquequaque inperitus erat 70 inperitiae suae et noluit se temere disputando in ea coartari, unde nec exitus ei ullus nec facilis esset reditus: etiam hinc mihi amplius placuit. Pulchrior est enim temperantia confitentis animi quam illa, quae nosse cupiebam. Et eum in omnibus difficilioribus et subtilioribus quaestionibus talem 75 inveniebam.

13 Refracto itaque studio, quod intenderam in Manichaei litteras, magisque desperans de ceteris eorum doctoribus, quando in multis, quae me movebant, ita ille nominatus apparuit, coepi cum eo pro studio eius agere vitam, quo 80 ipse flagrabat in eas litteras, quas tunc iam rhetor Cartha-

---

64. consideranda . . . protuli: on the gerundive, cf. § 90b.

65. ipsam: = eam or illam. Cf. § 68d, 1.

66. ista: = illa. Cf. § 68c, 2.

68. Iste: = Ille. Cf. § 68c, 2.

68. cor . . . non rectum ad te: cf. *Ps.* 77: 37, " But their heart was not right with him," and *Acts* 8: 21, " For thy heart is not right in the sight of God." Cf. also § 86a, 1.

69. nec . . . nimis incautum . . . ipsum: " and not too unwary towards himself "; i.e., " and not too uncritical towards himself."

71. in ea: sc. inperitia.

72. hinc: " for this reason " (i.e., that he was so frank in avowing his ignorance).

77. Refracto . . . studio . . . magis- que desperans: on the ablative absolute, cf. § 84c.

78. doctoribus: i.e., the other official magistri or teachers of Manichaeism.

79. in multis: " as regards the many (problems)."

79. quae me movebant: cf. *Conf.* V, 6, 11; V, 7, 12.

79. ita . . . apparuit: " appeared thus "; i.e., as quite incapable of solving my problems.

79. ille nominatus: cf. *Conf.* V, 3, 3, nominatus apud eos ille Faustus.

80. coepi . . . docebam: " I began to associate (agere vitam) with him in consequence of (pro) his enthusiasm —wherewith he himself was inflamed —for those (branches of) letters which I, already a rhetor, was teaching youths of Carthage."

ginis adulescentes docebam, et legere cum eo sive quae ille
audita desideraret sive quae ipse tali ingenio apta existima-
rem. Ceterum conatus omnis meus, quo proficere in illa
85 secta statueram, illo homine cognito prorsus intercidit, non
ut ab eis omnino separarer, sed, quasi melius quicquam
non inveniens, eo, quo iam quoquo modo inrueram, contentus interim esse decreveram, nisi aliquid forte, quod
magis eligendum esset, eluceret.
90   Ita ille Faustus, qui multis l a q u e u s m o r t i s extitit,
meum quo captus eram relaxare iam coeperat nec volens
nec sciens. Manus enim tuae, deus meus, in abdito providentiae tuae non deserebant animam meam, et de sanguine
cordis matris meae per lacrimas eius diebus et noctibus
95 pro me sacrificabatur tibi, et egisti mecum m i r i s m o d i s.
Tu illud egisti, deus meus. Nam a d o m i n o g r e s s u s
h o m i n i s d i r i g u n t u r, e t v i a m e i u s v o l e t. Aut
quae procuratio salutis praeter manum tuam reficientem
quae fecisti?

XI. To Rome

And thus, grown impatient of the pranks
of my pupils, deceiving my mother and
ignoring her prayers, I journeyed to Rome,
under Thy secret guidance, in quest of more
orderly pupils, my God.

VIII. 14 Egisti ergo mecum, ut mihi persuaderetur Romam pergere et potius ibi docere quod docebam Carthagini.

Et hoc unde mihi persuasum est, non praeteribo confiteri tibi, quoniam et in his altissimi tui recessus et praesentissima 5 in nos misericordia tua cogitanda et praedicanda est.

Non ideo Romam pergere volui, quod maiores quaestus maiorque mihi dignitas ab amicis, qui hoc suadebant, promittebatur—quamquam et ista ducebant animum tunc meum—sed illa erat causa maxima et paene sola, quod 10 audiebam quietius ibi studere adulescentes et ordinatiore disciplinae coercitione sedari, ne in eius scholam, quo magistro non utuntur, passim et proterve inruant, nec eos admitti omnino, nisi ille permiserit. Contra apud Carthaginem foeda est et intemperans licentia scholasticorum: 15 inrumpunt inpudenter et prope furiosa fronte perturbant

XI. To Rome

2. **Carthagini:** locative. The form Carthagine is more common.

4. **confiteri:** on the infinitive, cf. § 89b.

5. **in his:** "in these (circumstances)."

5. **altissimi tui recessus . . . misericordia tua:** "Thy deepest secrecies (i.e., the depths of Thy secrets) and Thy most ready mercy towards us." Note the antithetical thought in **recessus** and **praesentissima.**

6. **cogitanda est:** the verb agrees with the nearest of its subjects.

11. **ordinatiore . . . coercitione:** at Rome unruly activities of students were checked to some extent by the magistrates.

12. **in eius . . . quo magistro non utuntur:** "into the school of him whom they did not have as a teacher."

13. **inruant:** on the sequence, cf. § 78c.

14. **apud Carthaginem:** = Carthagine: cf. § 86b.

16. **inrumpunt:** note the vividness gained by the historical present.

ordinem, quem quisque discipulis ad proficiendum insti-
tuerit. Multa iniuriosa faciunt mira hebetudine et punienda legibus, nisi consuetudo patrona sit, hoc miseriores eos
20 ostendens, quo iam quasi liceat faciunt, quod per tuam
aeternam legem numquam licebit, et inpune se facere
arbitrantur, cum ipsa faciendi caecitate puniantur et inconparabiliter patiantur peiora, quam faciunt.

Ergo quos mores cum studerem meos esse nolui, eos cum
25 docerem cogebar perpeti alienos, et ideo placebat ire, ubi
talia non fieri omnes qui noverant indicabant. Verum
autem tu, spes mea et portio mea in terra viven-
tium, ad mutandum terrarum locum pro salute animae
meae et Carthagini stimulos, quibus inde avellerer, ad-
30 movebas, et Romae inlecebras, quibus adtraherer, propone-
bas mihi per homines, qui diligunt vitam mortuam, hinc
insana facientes, inde vana pollicentes, et ad corrigendos
gressus meos utebaris occulte et illorum et mea per-
versitate. Nam et qui perturbabant otium meum, foeda
35 rabie caeci erant, et qui invitabant ad aliud, terram sapiebant, ego autem, qui detestabar hic veram miseriam, illic
falsam felicitatem appetebam.

---

19. nisi consuetudo patrona sit:
"were not custom their protectress."
The apodosis is in the gerundive
punienda.

22. caecitate: i.e., since they are
unconscious of God's omnipresence
and justice.

23. peiora: i.e., since the injury
they do to others is physical, while
the injury they do themselves is
moral.

24. quos mores . . . alienos: "what
manners, when I was a student, I was
unwilling to be mine; these, when I
was a teacher, I was forced to endure
(as the manners) of others."

**27. spes mea . . . in terra viven-
tium:** cf. *Ps.* 141: 6, " Thou art my

hope, my portion in the land of the
living."

28. terrarum locum: " (my) place
of abode." On the genitive, cf. § 83b.

29. Carthagini . . . appetebam:
note the antithetical parallelisms.

29. stimulos: construe with **ad-
movebas.**

33. gressus meos: cf. *Ps.* 39: 3,
" And he set my feet upon a rock, and
directed my steps."

35. aliud: " something else "; i.e.,
another situation.

35. terram sapiebant: " savored of
earth "; i.e., " were earthly-minded."
Cf. *Philip.* 3: 19, " Whose end is
destruction, . . . who mind earthly
things."

15 Sed quare hinc abirem et illuc irem, tu sciebas, deus,
nec indicabas mihi nec matri, quae me profectum atrociter
planxit et usque ad mare secuta est.   Sed fefelli eam vio- 40
lenter me tenentem, ut aut revocaret aut mecum pergeret,
et finxi me amicum nolle deserere, donec vento facto
navigaret. Et mentitus sum matri, et illi matri, et evasi,
quia et hoc dimisisti mihi misericorditer servans me ab
aquis maris plenum exsecrandis sordibus usque ad aquam 45
gratiae tuae, qua me abluto siccarentur flumina maternorum
oculorum, quibus pro me cotidie tibi rigabat terram sub
vultu suo.
   Et tamen recusanti sine me redire vix persuasi, ut in
loco, qui proximus nostrae navi erat, memoria beati Cypri- 50
ani, maneret ea nocte.   Sed ea nocte clanculo ego profectus
sum, illa autem mansit orando et flendo.
   Et quid a te petebat, deus meus, tantis lacrimis, nisi ut
navigare me non sineres?   Sed tu alte consulens et exaudiens
cardinem desiderii eius non curasti quod tunc petebat, ut 55
me faceres quod semper petebat.
   Flavit ventus et implevit vela nostra et litus subtraxit
aspectibus nostris, in quo mane illa insaniebat dolore et

---

43. navigaret: sc. amicus as subject. To conceal his real purpose, A.
pretends that he is at the shore to see
a friend off on a voyage.
   43. Et mentitus . . . evasi . . .
sub vulto suo: " And I lied to my
mother even to such a (illi) mother,
and I escaped (i.e., the fatalities of
the sea, or merely, " I escaped from
her presence ") because Thou for-
gavest even this, mercifully preserving
me, though full of abominable un-
cleannesses, from the waters of the
sea even to the water of Thy grace
(i.e., Baptism), whereby, I having
been washed, the rivers of my mother's
tears might be dried, with which
daily to Thee in my behalf she did wet

the earth beneath her countenance."
   50. memoria: a memorial chapel or
oratory in the vicinity of Carthage and
near the seashore. It was the first
church raised in or near the city in
honor of St. Cyprian, her great bishop,
who had suffered martyrdom about a
century and a quarter (258) before the
events here recorded. For a sketch
of St. Cyprian, cf. C. E., IV, s.v.
Cyprian of Carthage, 583–589; and
De Labriolle, 132–168.
   52. orando et flendo: cf. § 91b, 1.
   53. nisi ut: " except that," cf.
§ 100b.
   55. quod: sc. id.
   57. subtraxit aspectibus nostris:
on the dative, cf. § 82d.

querellis et gemitu implebat aures tuas contemnentis ista,
60 cum et me cupiditatibus meis raperes ad finiendas ipsas
cupiditates et illius carnale desiderium iusto dolorum flagello
vapularet. Amabat enim secum praesentiam meam more
matrum, sed multis multo amplius, et nesciebat, quid tu
illi gaudiorum facturus esses de absentia mea. Nesciebat,
65 ideo flebat et eiulabat atque illis cruciatibus arguebatur in
ea reliquiarium Evae, cum gemitu quaerens quod cum
gemitu pepererat. Et tamen post accusationem fallaciarum
et crudelitatis meae conversa rursum ad deprecandum te
pro me abiit ad solita, et ego Romam.

And Thy Providence made me fall sick of a
fever, while the prayers of my mother
ascended to Thee, and her prayers Thou
didst hear in Thy own foreordaining that
one day my soul should also be cured.

70 **IX.** **16** Et ecce excipior ibi flagello aegritudinis corporalis

59. querellis . . . vapularet: i.e.,
A.'s longing to go to Rome was an
unconscious but necessary stage in his
progress towards Milan and St. Ambrose and Baptism, and Monnica's
longing that A. stay with her was an
unconscious opposition to God's
providence, perfectly natural in a
mother, but somewhat selfish and
lacking that calm faith in God's
providence which the perfection of
faith demands in such a trial. Monnica, therefore, like all the daughters
of Eve, suffers according to the
measure of her imperfection.
59. ista: i.e., such complaints on her
part.
**60. cupiditatibus . . . ad finiendas
ipsas cupiditates:** note the oxymoron.
Cf. § 40.
63. multis: sc. **matribus,** ablative of
comparison.

63. nesciebat . . . Nesciebat: geminatio. Cf. § 37.
65. illis cruciatibus . . . pepererat:
" by these tortures was the remnant
of Eve made manifest in her; with
groaning seeking what with groaning
she had brought forth." The allusion
is to *Gen.* 3: 16. On **in,** cf. § 88b, 3.
66. quaerens: construe with the
subject of **eiulabat.**
69. et ego Romam: the reticence of
A. on the details of so momentous a
voyage is in keeping with the spiritual
purpose of his autobiography. Cf.
Conf. III, 1, 1, **Veni Carthaginem.**
70. ibi: a strange abruptness on the
part of a provincial, from whom we
could expect, even in a spiritual biography, a record of the impressions
made on him by the capital of the
Empire.
70. flagello: i.e., as a punishment

et ibam iam ad inferos portans omnia mala, quae
conmiseram et in te et in me et in alios, multa et gravia
super originalis peccati vinculum, quo omnes in Adam
morimur. Non enim quicquam eorum mihi donaveras in
Christo, nec solverat ille in cruce sua inimicitias, quas 75
tecum contraxeram peccatis meis. Quomodo enim eas
solveret in cruce phantasmatis, quod de illo credideram?
Quam ergo falsa mihi videbatur mors carnis eius, tam vera
erat animae meae, et quam vera erat mors carnis eius, tam
falsa vita animae meae, quae id non credebat.   80

Et ingravescentibus febribus iam ibam et peribam. Quo
enim irem, si hinc tunc abirem, nisi in ignem atque
tormenta digna factis meis in veritate ordinis tui? Et hoc
illa nesciebat et tamen pro me orabat absens. Tu autem
ubique praesens ubi erat exaudiebas eam et ubi eram 85

for his sinful life and particularly for
his recent conduct towards his mother.

71. **ibam iam ad inferos**: for the
expression, cf. *Job* 7: 9, " so he that
shall go down to hell shall not come
up."

73. **super . . . vinculum**: on **super**,
cf. § 88d, 2.

73. **omnes in Adam morimur**: cf.
I *Cor.* 15: 22, " And as in Adam all die,
so also in Christ all shall be made
alive."

74. **eorum**: sc. **malorum.**

75. **nec solverat . . . inimicitias**: cf.
Eph. 2: 16, " and might reconcile
both to God in one body by the cross,
killing the enmities in himself." A.,
as he states below, did not yet believe
that it was Christ who had died upon
the Cross. Therefore, he had no
claim to the grace of absolution, a
first condition of which is the believing
that Christ suffered and died for our
sins. On **in**, cf. § 88b, 4.

76. **Quomodo . . . credideram**:
" For how could He have canceled

them (i.e., *inimicitias*) on the cross
of a phantom—which I had believed
of Him? " To the Manichees Christ
was a divine being who appeared on
earth, but not in a human body. The
victim of the Crucifixion was an evil
spirit (**phantasma**) in disguise, mis-
taken by the Jews for Christ. "How
could He have canceled these enmities by that cross, when, according
to my belief at that time, there had
been suspended only a phantom of
Him? "

78. **Quam ergo . . . credebat**: i.e.,
my own spiritual death was directly
in proportion to my disbelief in
Christ's death.

82. **irem . . . abirem**: present rather
than past contrary-to-fact for vividness. Cf. § 78b.

82. **nisi in ignem**: cf. *Matt.* 25: 41,
" Depart from me, you cursed, into
everlasting fire."

83. **in veritate ordinis**: " in the
truth of (Thy) dispensation." On **in**,
cf. § 88b, 3.

84. **illa**: i.e., Monnica.

miserebaris mei, ut recuperarem salutem corporis adhuc
insanus corde sacrilego.

Neque enim desiderabam in illo tanto periculo baptismum
tuum et melior eram puer, quo illum de materna pietate
90 flagitavi, sicut iam recordatus atque confessus sum. Sed
in dedecus meum creveram et consilia medicinae tuae
demens irridebam, qui non me sivisti talem bis mori. Quo
vulnere si feriretur cor matris, numquam sanaretur. Non
enim satis eloquor, quid erga me habebat animi et quanto
95 maiore sollicitudine me parturiebat spiritu, quam carne
pepererat.

17 Non itaque video, quomodo sanaretur, si mea talis
illa mors transverberasset viscera dilectionis eius. Et ubi
essent tantae preces, tam crebrae sine intermissione? Nus-
100 quam nisi ad te. An vero tu, deus misericordiarum,
sperneres cor c o n t r i t u m et h u m i l i a t u m viduae

---

89. quo: construe as ablative of
degree of difference with melior.

89. de materna pietate: = de pia
matre. Cf. § 29.

90. iam recordatus: cf. Conf. I, 11,
17.

91. in dedecus . . . creveram: cf.
§ 88a, 2.

91. medicinae: in the Fathers,
terms from the field of medicine are
often employed metaphorically to
signify the operations of grace in
curing the soul. For the allusion
here, cf. Conf. IV, 4, 8, where he
derides his friend's piety.

92. talem bis mori: i.e., to die in the
body as well as in the soul.

93. vulnere: i.e., I dying unbaptized.

93. feriretur . . . sanaretur: cf.
note 82 above.

94. quanto maiore . . . parturiebat: cf. Conf. I, 11, 17, quoniam . . .
carius parturiebat . . . On the mood
habebat and parturiebat, cf. § 96.

97. talis illa mors: "that kind of
death"; i. e., unbaptized.

98. viscera dilectionis eius: "the
vitals of her love." For the form of
expression, cf. Philip. 2: 1; Col. 3:
12.

98. Et ubi essent tantae preces
. . . ad te: "And where (in the case
of my dying unbaptized) would have
been (essent) such mighty prayers ";
i.e., even if the precise request made
be not granted, the prayer is not fruit-
less. God hears it and compensates
in other ways in accordance with
His providence. Cf. C.E., XII, s.v.
Prayer, subdivision, Effect of Prayer,
346.

100. ad te: "before Thee." Cf.
§ 86a, 1.

100. deus misericordiarum: on the
genitive, cf. § 83d.

101. sperneres: "would you have
spurned " (i.e., in a case much worse
than my own, seeing that my mother
was so persistent and devout in her
supplications.)

101. cor contritum et humiliatum:
cf. Ps. 50: 19, " A sacrifice to God is

castae ac sobriae, frequentantis elemosynas, obsequentis atque servientis sanctis tuis, nullum diem praetermittentis oblationem ad altare tuum, bis die, mane et vespere, ad ecclesiam tuam sine ulla intermissione venientis, non ad 105 vanas fabulas et aniles loquacitates, sed ut te audiret in tuis sermonibus et tu illam in suis orationibus? Huiusne tu lacrimas, quibus non a te aurum et argentum petebat nec aliquod mutabile aut volubile bonum, sed salutem animae filii sui, tu, cuius munere talis erat, contemneres et repelleres 110 ab auxilio tuo? Nequaquam, domine, immo vero aderas et exaudiebas et faciebas ordine, quo praedestinaveras esse faciendum. Absit, ut tu falleres eam in illis visionibus et responsis tuis, quae iam conmemoravi et quae non conmemoravi, quae illa fideli pectore tenebat et semper orans 115 tamquam chirografa tua ingerebat tibi. Dignaris enim, quoniam in saeculum misericordia tua, eis quibus omnia debita dimittis, etiam promissionibus debitor fieri.

In Rome I was cheated by dishonest pupils.

XII. 22 Sedulo ergo agere coeperam, propter quod veneram, ut docerem Romae artem rhetoricam, et prius domi 120 congregare aliquos, quibus et per quos innotescere coeperam.

---

an afflicted spirit: a contrite and humble heart, O God, thou wilt not despise."
103. sanctis tuis: "Thy saints," "Thy consecrated ones," i.e., the clergy.
104. bis die: cf. § 84b.
110. tu, cuius munere talis erat: "Thou, by Whose grace she was such," i.e., prayerful. We cannot even pray without the initial and supporting grace of God.
113. Absit, ut: cf. § 100a.
114. iam conmemoravi: cf. *Conf.* III, 11, 19–20; 12, 21.

115. et semper orans . . . ingerebat tibi: "and which, always praying, she was wont to urge upon Thee, as it were, Thy signed pledges."
116. Dignaris . . . fieri: on the infinitive, cf. § 89b.
117. in saeculum misericordia tua: cf. *Ps.* 117: 1, "Give praise to the Lord, for he is good: for his mercy endureth forever."
117. eis quibus . . . promissionibus: "to become a debtor by your promises to those to whom" . . .
119. agere: sc. id as object.

Et ecce cognosco alia Romae fieri, quae non patiebar in Africa. Nam re vera illas eversiones a perditis adulescentibus ibi non fieri manifestatum est mihi: "Sed subito" 125 inquiunt "ne mercedem magistro reddant, conspirant multi adulescentes et transferunt se ad alium, desertores fidei et quibus prae pecuniae caritate iustitia vilis est."

Oderat etiam istos cor meum quamvis non p e r f e c t o o d i o. Quod enim ab eis passurus eram, magis oderam 130 fortasse quam eo, quod cuilibet inlicita faciebant.

XII. To MILAN AND St. AMBROSE

And therefore, accepting appointment to Milan, near Thy servant, Ambrose, I thus came to live.

XIII. 23 Itaque posteaquam missum est a Mediolanio Romam ad praefectum urbis, ut illi civitati rhetoricae magister provideretur inpertita etiam evectione publica,

---

126. fidei: "of (their) promise."

127. prae . . . caritate: on **prae,** cf. § 87g, 2.

128. perfecto odio: i.e., hatred proper to a person leading the life of perfection. His hatred was imperfect because he did not distinguish between the malice of their acts, the proper object of "perfect" hatred, and their persons. Cf. *Ps.* 138: 22, "I have hated them with a perfect hatred."

XII. To Milan and St. Ambrose

1. posteaquam missum est: "After (a request) had been sent." Cf. § 77.

1. Mediolanio: from 296 the ordinary residence of the Western emperors.

2. praefectum urbis: " Praefect of the City (of Rome)," one of the high-est offices in the Empire. Cf. **praefectus tunc Symmachus** below. Q. Aurelius Symmachus, as his **nomen** suggests, was a member of one of the most illustrious Roman families, generally eminent because of his wealth, culture, and oratorical gifts; tenacious leader of the dying paganism; companion of St. Ambrose in their youth and now his opponent in the struggle between paganism and Christianity. He was **Praefectus Urbis** from about the year 384. On the duties of the **Praefectus Urbis,** cf. Sandys, 295–297; Abbott, 224, 281. On Symmachus, cf. Smith and Wace, s.v. *Symmachus* (3) IV, 749–751.

3. inpertita . . . evectione publica: " a post-warrant also being furnished "; i.e., the right of traveling in the carriage of the Imperial Post.

ego ipse ambivi per eos ipsos manichaeis vanitatibus ebrios
—quibus ut carerem ibam, sed utrique nesciebamus—ut 5
dictione proposita me probatum praefectus tunc Symmachus
mitteret.

Et veni Mediolanium ad Ambrosium episcopum, in
optimis notum orbi terrae, pium cultorem tuum, cuius tunc
eloquia strenue ministrabant adipem frumenti tui et laeti- 10
tiam olei et sobriam vini ebrietatem populo tuo. Ad eum
autem ducebar abs te nesciens, ut per eum ad te sciens
ducerer.

---

4. per eos ipsos . . . ebrios: i.e.,
the Manichaean community at Rome,
among whom, as a newcomer to the
city and a member of the prescribed
sect, A. lived.

5. utrique: i.e., myself and the
Manichaean devotees just mentioned.

**6. dictione proposita . . . proba-
tum:** " having been proven by a trial-
theme that had been set (by him)."
A. had to give proof of his attainments
in rhetoric by composing a discourse
on a theme proposed by Symmachus,
himself one of the most celebrated
orators of the time. A., consistently
with the spiritual character of his
autobiography, says nothing of the
severity of the test or of the skill
implied in his having passed it successfully.

6. praefectus tunc: on tunc, cf.
§ 71.

8. Ambrosium: descendant of the
Aurelii, one of the first of ancient
Roman families; son of a politically
eminent father; one of the four
Western doctors of the Church; distinguished as an orator, an adminis-
trator, and for his knowledge of Greek,
in a century when Greek was becoming
rare in the West; governor of Aemilia
and Liguria, 372-374; elected Bishop of
Milan through popular acclaim in 374,
while still only a catechumen; one of
the chief figures in the political and ec-

clesiastical life of his time and one of
the great patristic influences on the
Middle Ages. He had been a bishop
eight years when Augustine came to
Milan and was in the midst of a
struggle with the dying but still influential paganism. A. could not
have escaped knowing of the struggle,
yet, in keeping with the character of
his biography, he makes no mention
of it in the *Confessions*. Cf. De
Labriolle, 264-286; De Labriolle,
The Life and Times of St. Ambrose,
translated by Herbert Wilson, St.
Louis, 1928; E. K. Rand, *Founders of
the Middle Ages,* Cambridge, 1928, 69-
101.

9. notum orbi terrae: " known
to all the world (as being) among
(its) choicest men."

10. adipem frumenti tui: cf. *Ps.* 80:
17, " And he fed them with the fat of
wheat."

10. laetitiam olei: cf. *Ps.* 44: 8,
" therefore God, thy God, hath
anointed thee with the oil of glad-
ness."

11. sobriam vini ebrietatem: a
phrase borrowed from St. Ambrose's
hymn, *Splendor Paternae Gloriae,*
lines 23-24, " sober intoxication of
wine "; i.e., not intoxicated with the
wine of the grape, but intoxicated
with the wine of the spirit of God.
For the thought, cf. *Eph.* 5: 18.

Suscepit me paterne ille h o m o d e i et peregrinationem
15 meam satis episcopaliter dilexit.

Et eum amare coepi, primo quidem non tamquam doc-
torem veri, quod in ecclesia tua prorsus desperabam, sed
tamquam hominem benignum in me. Et studiose audiebam disputantem in populo, non intentione, qua debui, sed
20 quasi explorans eius facundiam, utrum conveniret famae
suae an maior minorve proflueret, quam praedicabatur, et
verbis eius suspendebar intentus, rerum autem incuriosus
et contemptor adstabam et delectabar suavitate sermonis,
quamquam eruditioris, minus tamen hilarescentis atque
25 mulcentis, quam Fausti erat, quod attinet ad dicendi
modum. Ceterum rerum ipsarum nulla conparatio: nam ille
per manichaeas fallacias aberrabat, iste autem saluberrime
docebat salutem.

Sed l o n g e est a p e c c a t o r i b u s s a l u s; qualis ego
30 tunc aderam. Et tamen propinquabam sensim et nesciens.

XIII. HESITATIONS

*Attracted at first by his language alone, the
doctrine of Ambrose I grew to respect.*

XIV. 24 Cum enim non satagerem discere quae dicebat,
sed tantum quemadmodum dicebat audire—ea mihi quippe

" And be not drunk with wine, wherein is luxury; but be ye filled with the
holy Spirit."

14. homo dei: cf. IV *Kings* 1: 9.

15. satis episcopaliter: " quite as a
bishop (should)."

17. quod: relative. Its antecedent
is **veri.**

18. benignum in me: on **in,** cf.
§ 88a, 4.

22. verbis eius suspendebar: " I
hung upon his words."

22. rerum: " the subject matter."
" content." On the genitive with
incuriosus, cf. § 83e.

25. Fausti: sc. sermo.

27. iste: = hic. Cf. § 68c, 1.

27. saluberrime . . . salutem:
paronomasia. Cf. § 43.

29. longe est a peccatoribus salus:
cf. *Ps.* 118: 155, " Salvation is far
from sinners; because they have not
sought thy justifications."

XIII. Hesitations

2. quemadmodum dicebat: on the
indicative, cf. § 96.

2. ea . . . inanis cura: note the
striking hyperbaton. Cf. §39.

iam desperanti ad te viam patere homini inanis cura remanserat—veniebant in animum meum simul cum verbis, quae
diligebam, res etiam, quas neglegebam. Neque enim ea 5
dirimere poteram. Et dum cor aperirem ad excipiendum,
quam diserte diceret, pariter intrabat et quam vere diceret,
gradatim quidem.

Nam primo etiam ipsa defendi posse mihi iam coeperunt
videri et fidem catholicam, pro qua nihil posse dici adversus 10
oppugnantes manichaeos putaveram, iam non inpudenter
asseri existimabam, maxime audito uno atque altero et
saepius aenigmate soluto de scriptis veteribus, ubi, cum ad
litteram acciperem, occidebar. Spiritaliter itaque plerisque
illorum librorum locis expositis iam reprehendebam despera- 15
tionem meam illam dumtaxat, qua credideram legem et
prophetas detestantibus atque irridentibus resisti omnino
non posse.

Nec tamen iam ideo mihi catholicam viam tenendam esse
sentiebam, quia et ipsa poterat habere doctos adsertores 20
suos, qui copiose et non absurde obiecta refellerent, nec
ideo iam damnandum illud, quod tenebam, quia defensionis
partes aequabantur. Ita enim catholica, non mihi victa,
videbatur ut nondum etiam victrix appareret.

---

6. dum . . . aperirem: for the subjunctive, cf. § 101b.

7. et: = etiam. Cf. § 94a.

9. ipsa: i.e., the things he was saying. On ipsa = ea or illa, cf. § 68d, 1.

9. defendi posse . . . videri: "began
to seem to be able to be defended."

12. maxime audito . . . occidebar:
"especially (did I conclude that the
Catholic faith could be maintained
without temerity) after I heard explained, even rather often, one and
another obscurity of the Old Testament (scriptis veteribus) (obscure
passages) wherein I was slain when
I interpreted according to the let-

ter." On the mood of acciperem,
cf. § 102a.

14. occidebar: cf. II Cor. 3: 6,
" For the letter killeth; but the spirit
quickeneth."

16. legem et prophetas: construe
as objects of detestantibus and irridentibus.

20. et ipsa: = etiam ipsa (via).

22. damnandum (esse): construe
with sentiebam.

22. illud: i.e., Manichaeism.

22. defensionis partes: " the side
of the defense "; i.e., the Catholic side.

23. Ita . . . appareret: " For the
Catholic (Church), although not con-

25   25 Tunc vero fortiter intendi animum, si quo modo
possem certis aliquibus documentis manichaeos convincere
falsitatis.   Quod si possem spiritalem substantiam cogitare,
statim machinamenta illa omnia solverentur et abicerentur
ex animo meo: sed non poteram.   Verum tamen de ipso
30 mundi huius corpore omnique natura, quam sensus carnis
attingeret, multo probabiliora plerosque sensisse philosophos
magis magisque considerans atque comparans iudicabam.
      Itaque Academicorum more, sicut existimantur, dubitans
de omnibus atque inter omnia fluctuans manichaeos quidem
35 relinquendos esse decrevi, non arbitrans eo ipso tempore
dubitationis meae in illa secta mihi permanendum esse, cui
iam nonnullos philosophos praeponebam: quibus tamen
philosophis, quod sine salutari nomine Christi essent,
curationem languoris animae meae conmittere omnino
40 recusabam.
      Statui ergo tamdiu esse catechumenus in catholica ecclesia

---

quered in my opinion (**mihi**), was so
regarded (by me) that she did not yet
appear as victor." With **catholica** sc.
ecclesia, or **via** from the preceding
sentence.

      27. Quod si possem . . . cogitare:
" But if I could have conceived of a
spiritual substance." From long ha-
bituation, A.'s thought was still
wedded to materialistic principles,
which led him back to dualism—to
the Manichaean opposition between
the divine realm of light and dark,
depraved matter.   On the imperfect
subjunctives **possem . . . solverentur,**
cf. § 78b.

      31. philosophos: cf. *Conf.* V, 3, 3
and p. 127, note 13.

      33. Academicorum: A. refers here
to the skeptical doctrines characteristic of the Middle Academy and in
part of the New Academy.

      33. sicut existimantur: " as they
are thought (to do) "—a qualifying

statement.   As a matter of fact, the
Academics were not of a piece in their
skepticism regarding the attainment
of complete knowledge.   While the
Middle Academy was dominated by
this skeptical attitude, the New
Academy marked a return, in many
of its members, to the more positive
epistemology of Plato.

      38. salutari nomine Christi: cf.
Conf. III, 4, 8, wherein he tells us
that the *Hortensius*, despite its appeal, could not dominate his soul
because **nomen Christi non erat ibi.**

      41. catechumenus: i.e., A. formally
resumes the catechumenate.   Cf.
Conf. I, 11, 17–18.   His earliest
spiritual training, which had remained
in some faint fashion with him, now
asserts itself under the combined and
cumulative influence of Ambrose and
Catholic life at Milan, disillusionment
relative to Manichaeism, and the in-
sufficiency of the Academics.

mihi a parentibus commendata, donec aliquid certi eluceret, quo cursum dirigerem.

LIBER SEXTUS

And now that my mother had come up to Milan and learned of my leaving the Manichee sect, she doubled her prayers, resorting to Ambrose, through whom she believed I should soon turn to Thee.

I. 1 Spes mea a iuventute mea, ubi mihi eras et quo recesseras? An vero non tu feceras me et discreveras 45 me a quadrupedibus et volatilibus caeli sapientiorem me feceras? Et ambulabam per tenebras et lubricum et quaerebam te foris a me et non inveniebam deum cordis mei; et veneram in profundum maris. Et diffidebam et desperabam de inventione veri. 50

Iam venerat ad me mater pietate fortis, terra marique me sequens et in periculis omnibus de te secura. Nam et per marina discrimina ipsos nautas consolabatur—a quibus rudes abyssi viatores, cum perturbantur, consolari solent—pollicens eis perventionem cum salute, quia hoc ei tu per 55 visum pollicitus eras.

---

44. Spes mea a iuventute mea: cf. *Ps.* 70: 5, " For thou art my patience, O Lord: my hope, O Lord, from my youth."

45. quo recesseras: cf. *Ps.* 10: 1, " Why, O Lord, hast thou retired afar off? "

45. discreveras . . . me feceras: for the thought, cf. *Job* 35: 11.

47. Et ambulabam per tenebras et lubricum: cf. *Ps.* 34: 6, " Let their way become dark and slippery."

48. foris a me: cf. § 87f.

48. deum cordis mei: cf. *Ps.* 72: 26, ". . . thou art the God of my heart, . . ."

49. in profundum maris: cf. *Ps.* 67: 23, " I will turn them into the depth of the sea."

52. de te secura: " safe from Thee "; i.e., " deriving her safety from Thee."

Et invenit me periclitantem quidem graviter desperatione
indagandae veritatis, sed tamen ei cum indicassem non me
quidem iam esse manichaeum, sed neque catholicum
60 christianum, non, quasi inopinatum aliquid audierit, exiluit
laetitia, cum iam secura fieret ex ea parte miseriae meae, in
qua me tamquam mortuum, sed resuscitandum tibi flebat
et feretro cogitationis offerebat, ut diceres filio viduae:
iuvenis, tibi dico, surge, et revivesceret et inciperet
65 loqui et traderes illum matri suae.   Nulla ergo turbulenta
exultatione trepidavit cor eius, cum audisset ex tanta parte
iam factum, quod tibi cotidie plangebat ut fieret, veritatem
me nondum adeptum, sed falsitati iam ereptum: immo vero
quia certa erat et quod restabat te daturum, qui totum
70 promiseras, placidissime et pectore pleno fiduciae respondit
mihi credere se in Christo, quod priusquam de hac vita
emigraret, me visura esset fidelem catholicum.   Et hoc

---

58. ei cum indicassem: ei is placed
before its proper clause.

61. cum iam secura . . . viduae:
" since she had already become assured as to this part of my misery
(i.e., my being a Manichee), in which
she was bewailing me as one dead but
(as one) destined to be revived by
Thee and she was offering (me) (to
Thee) on the bier of her thought that
Thou mightest say to the son of the
widow. . . ."   The spiritual state of
A. weighed down upon St. Monnica's
thoughts so that it was the chief
burden which her thought supported.
Therefore, in praying to God for the
spiritual resurrection of her spiritually
dead son, her thought was displaying
him in spiritual death to the mercy of
God even as the bier in the Gospel
supported and displayed the son of
the widow of Naim in physical death
to the mercy of Christ.   Cf. *Luke* 7:
11 ff.

61. ex ea parte miseriae meae:

i.e., she had been reassured of his
return to the Faith in which she had
instructed him as a child by the
dream recorded in *Conf.* III, 11, 20.
One great step in that return she
heard of now, but she was prepared
for it through nine years of expectancy.

62. resuscitandum tibi flebat: cf.
§ 90a.

63. feretro: take as local ablative.
Cf. § 84a.

64. iuvenis . . . surge: *Luke* 7: 14,
" Young man, I say to thee, arise."

64. revivesceret: sc. **ut.**

68. adeptum . . . ereptum: infinitives (sc. **esse**) in apposition with
(id) **factum** (esse) **quod.** . . .

69. et quod: = etiam id quod.
Construe with **daturum.**

69. qui totum promiseras: cf. note
61 above.

71. in Christo: cf. § 88a, 3.

71. quod . . . visura esset: for the
quod clause in place of the infinitive
with subject accusative, cf. § 97.

quidem mihi. Tibi autem, fons misericordiarum, preces et lacrimas densiores, ut accelerares adiutorium tuum et inluminares t e n e b r a s m e a s, et studiosius ad ecclesiam 75 currere et in Ambrosi ora suspendi, ad fontem s a l i e n t i s a q u a e i n v i t a m a e t e r n a m. Diligebat autem illum virum s i c u t a n g e l u m d e i, quod per illum cognoverat me interim ad illam ancipitem fluctuationem iam esse perductum, per quam transiturum me ab aegritudine ad 80 sanitatem intercurrente artiore periculo quasi per accessionem, quam criticam medici vocant, certa praesumebat.

In vain did I seek to find Ambrose with leisure sufficient to hear of the state of my soul, but hearing him preach from Thy Scriptures on Sundays, I came more and more to esteem them, my God.

III. 3 Nec iam ingemescebam orando, ut subvenires mihi, sed ad quaerendum intentus et ad disserendum inquietus erat animus meus, ipsumque Ambrosium felicem 85

---

73. . . . mihi. Tibi . . .: sc. some form of **dico**, with **Monnica** as subject.

74. **accelerares adiutorium tuum:** cf. *Ps.* 69: 2, " O God, come to my assistance. . . ."

75. **inluminares tenebras meas:** cf. *Ps.* 17: 29, " . . .; O my God, enlighten my darkness."

76. **currere . . . suspendi:** historical infinitives. Sc. **Monnica** as subject.

76. **ad fontem . . . aeternam:** cf. *John* 4: 14, " But the water that I will give him, shall become in him a fountain of water, springing up into life everlasting." **ad fontem** is in apposition with **in Ambrosi ora. suspendi:** Render " as to a fountain. . . ." On **in**, cf. § 88a, 3.

78. **sicut angelum dei:** cf. *Gal.* 4: 14, " You despised not, nor rejected: but received me as an angel of God, even as Christ Jesus."

80. **transiturum:** construe with **praesumebat.**

80. **per quam . . . intercurrente . . . vocant:** " through which I would pass from sickness to health, (with a period of) deeper peril intervening, through the paroxysm, as it were, which physicians call the critical one "; i.e., the " crisis."

82. **certa:** sc. **Monnica.**

83. **Nec iam:** " And not yet "; i.e., not yet did A. perceive that the solution of his difficulties lay in fervent prayer.

83. **orando:** cf. § 91b, 1.

quendam hominem secundum saeculum opinabar, quem sic
tantae potestates honorarent: caelibatus tantum eius mihi
laboriosus videbatur. Quid autem ille spei gereret, adversus ipsius excellentiae temtamenta quid luctaminis habe-
90 ret quidve solaminis in adversis, et occultum os eius, quod
erat in corde eius, quam sapida gaudia de pane tuo ruminaret, nec conicere noveram nec expertus eram.

Nec ille sciebat aestus meos nec foveam periculi mei.
Non enim quaerere ab eo poteram quod volebam, sicut
95 volebam, secludentibus me ab eius aure atque ore catervis
negotiosorum hominum, quorum infirmitatibus serviebat:
cum quibus quando non erat, quod perexiguum temporis
erat, aut corpus reficiebat necessariis sustentaculis aut
lectione animum.

100 Sed cum legebat, oculi ducebantur per paginas et cor
intellectum rimabatur, vox autem et lingua quiescebant.
Saepe, cum adessemus—non enim vetabatur quisquam
ingredi aut ei venienti nuntiari mos erat—sic eum
legentem vidimus tacite et aliter numquam, sedentesque
105 in diuturno silentio (quis enim tam intento esse oneri
auderet?) discedebamus et coniectabamus eum parvo ipso
tempore, quod reparandae menti suae nanciscebatur, feriatum ab strepitu causarum alienarum nolle in aliud avocari
et cavere fortasse, ne auditore suspenso et intento, si qua

---

90. et occultum os eius: construe
as subject of **ruminaret.**

92. nec conicere noveram: on the
infinitive with **novi,** cf. § 89b.

96. quorum . . . serviebat: on the
crowded life and manifold duties of a
fourth-century bishop, cf. De Labriolle, 264.

**101. vox autem et lingua quies-
cebant:** to A. this was something
remarkable, since the ancient custom
of reading aloud was still the vogue.
On this custom, cf. Norden, I, 6, and
especially *Nachträge,* 1–3, and Josef

Balogh, *Voces Paginarum,* in *Phi-
lologus,* vol. LXXXII (1927), 84 ff.
and 202 ff.

103. ei: construe with **nuntiari.**

105. tam intento esse oneri: "to
be for a burden to one so intent."

107. reparandae menti suae: = **ad
reparandam mentem suam.** Cf.
§ 90c.

108. in aliud: "to other (employment) (than that of study)."

109. ne . . . legeret: "lest his
auditor having become intent and

obscurius posuisset ille quem legeret, etiam exponere esset 110
necesse aut de aliquibus difficilioribus dissertare quaestionibus atque huic operi temporibus inpensis minus quam
vellet voluminum evolveret, quamquam et causa servandae
vocis, quae illi facillime obtundebatur, poterat esse iustior
tacite legendi. Quolibet tamen animo id ageret, bono 115
utique ille vir agebat.

4 Sed certe mihi nulla dabatur copia sciscitandi quae
cupiebam de tam sancto oraculo tuo, pectore illius, nisi cum
aliquid breviter esset audiendum. Æstus autem illi mei
otiosum eum valde, cui refunderentur, requirebant nec 120
unquam inveniebant. Et eum quidem in populo v e r b u m
v e r i t a t i s r e c t e t r a c t a n t e m omni die dominico
audiebam, et magis magisque mihi confirmabatur omnes
versutarum calumniarum nodos, quos illi deceptores nostri
adversus divinos libros innectebant, posse dissolvi. 125

And though I forgot not my recent delusion,
I refused an assent that implied aught of
faith.

IV. 6 Gaudebam etiam, quod vetera scripta legis et pro-
phetarum iam non illo oculo mihi legenda proponerentur,

eager, if that (author) whom he was
reading had stated some things in a
manner somewhat obscure. . . .''
 112. atque . . . evolveret: sc. ne
from above, '' and lest, if time were
spent on such a task, he would read
(evolveret) fewer volumes than he
wished.'' The fact that the ancient
book was in the form of a roll explains
the use of **evolvere** in the sense of
'' to read.''
 114. iustior: construe with **causa.**
 115. Quolibet . . . ageret: on quilibet = quicumque, cf. § 69b. The

subjunctive here is probably iterative.
Cf. § 102b.
 115. bono: sc. **animo.**
 120. cui refunderentur: '' into
whom they might be poured.'' On
the dative, cf. § 82b.
 121. verbum veritatis recte trac-
tantem: cf. II *Tim.* 2: 15, '' . . . a
workman that needeth not to be
ashamed, rightly handling the word
of truth.''
 124. deceptores nostri: i.e., the
Manichees.
 127. legenda proponerentur: on
the gerundive, cf. § 90b.

quo antea videbantur absurda, cum arguebam tamquam
ita sentientes sanctos tuos; verum autem non ita sentiebant.
130 Et tamquam regulam diligentissime conmendaret, saepe
in popularibus sermonibus suis dicentem Ambrosium laetus
audiebam: littera occidit, spiritus autem vivificat, cum ea, quae ad litteram perversitatem docere
videbantur, remoto mystico velamento spiritaliter aperiret,
135 non dicens quod me offenderet, quamvis ea diceret, quae
utrum vera essent adhuc ignorarem. Tenebam cor meum
ab omni adsensione timens praecipitium et suspendio magis
necabar. Volebam enim eorum quae non viderem ita me
certum fieri, ut certus essem, quod septem et tria decem
140 sint. Neque enim tam insanus eram, ut ne hoc quidem
putarem posse conprehendi, sed sicut hoc, ita cetera cupiebam sive corporalia, quae coram sensibus meis non adessent,
sive spiritalia, de quibus cogitare nisi corporaliter nesciebam.

Et sanari credendo poteram, ut purgatior acies mentis
145 meae dirigeretur aliquo modo in veritatem tuam semper
manentem et ex nullo deficientem; sed, sicut evenire assolet,

---

130. Et tamquam . . . audiebam:
construe **Et laetus audiebam Am-**
brosium saepe in popularibus ser-
monibus suis dicentem, tamquam
. . . .

130. tamquam . . . conmendaret:
" as though he were most urgently
commending it as a rule."

132. littera . . . vivificat: II *Cor.*
3: 6, " For the letter killeth, but the
spirit quickeneth."

136. Tenebam . . . adsensione . . .
suspendio . . . necabar: " I was keeping my heart from all assent, fearing
the precipice and I was the more
being killed by suspense." adsensione suggests its homonym ad-
scensione. Hence the presence of
timens praecipitium in the context;
i.e., " I kept my heart from all

ascent, fearing precipitation, and was
being killed the more by the sus-
pension."

138. eorum . . . certum: on the
genitive, cf. § 83e.

139. certus essem: potential subjunctive.

139. quod . . . sint: instead of
the accusative and infinitive. Cf.
§ 97.

140. hoc: i.e., the proposition that
7 + 3 = 10.

141. cupiebam: sc. **comprehendere.**

142. coram sensibus meis: on
coram, cf. § 87b.

145. in veritatem tuam semper
manentem: cf. *Ps.* 116: 2, " . . . and
the truth of the Lord remaineth forever."

ut malum medicum expertus etiam bono timeat se conmittere, ita erat valetudo animae meae, quae utique nisi
credendo sanari non poterat et, ne falsa crederet, curari
recusabat, resistens manibus tuis, qui medicamenta fidei 150
confecisti et sparsisti super morbos orbis terrarum et
tantam illis auctoritatem tribuisti.

*Two friends from my country had joined
me at Milan and together we sighed for
release from our plight.*

X. 17 Nebridius etiam, qui relicta patria vicina Carthagini
atque ipsa Carthagine, ubi frequentissimus erat, relicto
paterno rure optimo, relicta domo et non secutura matre 155
nullam ob aliam causam Mediolanium venerat, nisi ut
mecum viveret in flagrantissimo studio veritatis atque
sapientiae, pariter suspirabat pariterque fluctuabat beatae
vitae inquisitor ardens et quaestionum difficillimarum scrutator acerrimus.   Et erant ora trium egentium et inopiam 160
suam sibimet invicem anhelantium et ad te expectantium,

---

147. medicum: the figure of the physician, good and bad, is a favorite metaphor among ancient writers, both pagan and Christian.

148. valetudo animae meae: "the state of health of my soul."

153. Nebridius: construe as subject of suspirabat . . . fluctuabat below.

153. etiam: i.e., in addition to one Alypius from A.'s native town, Thagaste. Alypius had studied under A. there and afterwards at Carthage. He had preceded A. to Rome as a student of law, had formed a close friendship with him there, and had accompanied him to Milan, where he was following in some fashion his profession and, even as A., was disturbed spiritually meanwhile.

155. relicta ... non secutura matre: "having left a mother not inclined to follow him." A grateful allusion, by way of contrast, to Monnica, who bravely had made the difficult journey from Africa and was now with A. in Milan. Cf. *Conf.* VI, 1, 1.

156. nisi ut . . . viveret: on **nisi ut,** cf. § 100b.

160. trium egentium: i.e., Alypius, Nebridius, and A.

161. sibimet invicem: on this form of expressing reciprocal relation, cf. § 67.

161. ad te expectantium: "waiting for Thee," i.e., "with eyes turned expectantly to Thee." On **ad,** cf. § 86a, 3.

ut dares eis escam in tempore oportuno. Et in
omni amaritudine, quae nostros saeculares actus de misericordia tua sequebatur, intuentibus nobis finem, cur ea
165 pateremur, occurrebant tenebrae, et aversabamur gementes
et dicebamus: "Quamdiu haec?" Et hoc crebro dicebamus
et dicentes non relinquebamus ea, quia non elucebat certum
aliquid, quod illis relictis adprehenderemus.

But still I did cling to sensible pleasures,
as if in them somewhere lurked spiritual
rest.

XI. 18 Et ego maxime mirabar satagens et recolens,
170 quam longum tempus esset ab undevicesimo anno aetatis
meae, quo fervere coeperam studio sapientiae; disponens,
ea inventa, relinquere omnes vanarum cupiditatum spes
inanes et insanias mendaces. Et ecce iam tricenariam
aetatem gerebam in eodem luto haesitans aviditate fruendi
175 praesentibus fugientibus et dissipantibus me, dum dico:
"Cras inveniam; ecce manifestum apparebit, et tenebo;
ecce Faustus veniet et exponet omnia. . . ."
20 Cum haec dicebam et alternabant hi venti et inpelle-
bant huc atque illuc cor meum, transibant tempora, et

---

162. dares . . . oportuno: cf. *Ps.*
144: 15, " The eyes of all hope in
thee, O Lord: and thou givest them
meat in due season."
163. de misericordia tua: " in accordance with Thy mercy."
164. intuentibus nobis finem: " us
seeking out the purpose." Construe
as dative with occurrebant.
164. ea: i.e., the ideas and opinions
we then held, or our strivings at the
time.
169. satagens et recolens: " anxious and reflecting." Hendiadys for
" anxiously reflecting." Cf. § 38.
171. quo: A. refers to what followed on his study of Cicero's *Hortensius.* Cf. *Conf.* III, 4, 7–8.

171. disponens . . . relinquere: on
the infinitive, cf. § 89b.
172. ea: sc. sapientia.
172. omnes vanarum cupiditatum
spes inanes: on the genitive, cf. § 83b.
175. praesentibus ... me: " present
things fleeting and dispersing me."
For the expression, cf. *Conf.* II, 1, 1.
177. Faustus: i.e., Faustus, the final
hope of A. for intellectual security
among the Manichees (cf. *Conf.* V,
3, 3; 6, 10–11) is used by him now as
a symbol for the instrument of release from his present doubts.
178. hi venti: i.e., the winds of
doubt and uncertainty and contrary
desires.

tardabam converti ad dominum et differebam de 180
die in diem vivere in te et non differebam cotidie
in memet ipso mori: amans beatam vitam timebam illam
in sede sua et ab ea fugiens quaerebam eam. Putabam
enim me miserum fore nimis, si feminae privarer amplexibus,
et medicinam misericordiae tuae ad eandem infirmitatem 185
sanandam non cogitabam, quia expertus non eram, et
propriarum virium credebam esse continentiam, quarum
mihi non eram conscius, cum tam stultus essem, ut nescirem,
sicut scriptum est, neminem posse esse continentem, nisi
tu dederis. Utique dares, si gemitu interno pulsarem aures 190
tuas et fide solida in te iactarem curam meam.

LIBER OCTAVUS

XIV. The Life of St. Anthony

*At length I did learn of the Hermit of
Egypt, and the two high officials his Life
turned to Thee.*

VI. 13 Et de vinculo quidem desiderii concubitus, quo

---

180. tardabam converti ad dominum: cf. *Eccles.* 5: 8, " Delay not to be converted to the Lord." On the infinitive, cf. § 89b.

180. differebam de die in diem: cf. *Eccles.* 5: 8, " and defer it not from day to day." On the infinitive with **differo**, cf. § 89b.

182. in memet ipso mori: i.e., by keeping up his old manner of life in a vain quest for happiness.

183. in sede sua: " in its (proper) abode "; i.e., in God, not in the pleasures of this world.

186. expertus non eram: sc. **misericordiam tuam.**

187. propriarum virium . . . esse: " to be of one's own powers "; i.e.,

" was in one's own powers."

187. quarum mihi non eram conscius: " of which I was not conscious to myself "; i.e., " which I did not feel that I possessed."

189. scriptum est: a stereotyped expression among Christian writers for introducing Scriptural quotations.

189. neminem posse . . . dederis: cf. *Wis.* 8: 21, " And as I knew that I could not otherwise be continent, except God gave it. . . ."

XIV. The Life of St. Anthony

1. de vinculo . . . concubitus: " from the bond of desire for sensual pleasure."

1. quo artissimo: sc. **vinculo.**

artissimo tenebar, et saecularium negotiorum servitute quemadmodum exemeris, narrabo et confitebor nomini tuo, domine, adiutor meus et redemptor
5 meus.

Agebam solita crescente anxitudine et cotidie suspirabam tibi, frequentabam ecclesiam tuam, quantum vacabat ab eis negotiis, sub quorum pondere gemebam. Mecum erat Alypius otiosus ab opere iuris peritorum post assessionem
10 tertiam, expectans quibus iterum consilia venderet, sicut ego vendebam dicendi facultatem, si qua docendo praestari potest. Nebridius autem amicitiae nostrae cesserat, ut omnium nostrum familiarissimo Verecundo, Mediolanensi et civi et grammatico, subdoceret, vehementer desideranti
15 et familiaritatis iure flagitanti de numero nostro fidele adiutorium, quo indigebat nimis. Non itaque Nebridium cupiditas conmodorum eo traxit—maiora enim posset, si vellet, de litteris agere—sed officio benivolentiae petitionem nostram contemnere noluit amicus dulcissimus et mitissi-
20 mus. Agebat autem illud prudentissime cavens innotescere personis secundum hoc saeculum maioribus, devitans

---

2. **servitute:** sc. **de.**

3. **confitebor nomini tuo, domine:** cf. *Ps.* 53: 8, " and (I) will give praise, O God, to thy name."

4. **adiutor meus et redemptor meus:** cf. *Ps.* 18: 15, " O Lord, my helper and redeemer."

8. **eis negotiis:** i.e., his work as a professor of rhetoric.

9. **post assessionem tertiam:** " after (his) third assession "; i.e., after he had been assessor for the third time. Roman magistrates were not necessarily skilled in the law, since the judicial was only one phase of their official activity. The practice therefore grew up in the Republic, and was continued under the Empire, of having a body of legal consultants (**iuris**

peritorum) sit in attendance (**assessores**) with the magistrates at judicial processes. Cf. Abbott, 411.

11. **qua:** sc. **facultas.**

13. **Verecundo:** owner of an estate at Cassiciacum near Milan, to which A. and his companions retired later on, in the period between his conversion and baptism.

17. **maiora . . . agere:** " derive greater (returns). . . ."

18. **officio benivolentiae:** cf. § 83b.

20. **illud:** i.e., the office of assistant teacher.

20. **cavens innotescere:** on the infinitive with **caveo,** cf. § 89b.

21. **secundum hoc saeculum:** cf. *Eph.* 2: 2, " according to the course of this world."

in eis omnem inquietudinem animi, quem volebat habere
liberum et quam multis posset horis feriatum ad quaerendum aliquid vel legendum vel audiendum de sapientia.

14 Quodam igitur die—non recolo causam, qua erat 25
absens Nebridius—cum ecce ad nos domum venit ad me et
Alypium Ponticianus quidam, civis noster, in quantum
Afer, praeclare in palatio militans, nescio quid a nobis
volebat. Et consedimus, ut conloqueremur. Et forte
supra mensam lusoriam, quae ante nos erat, adtendit 30
codicem: tulit, aperuit, invenit apostolum Paulum, inopinate
sane; putaverat enim aliquid de libris, quorum professio
me conterebat. Tum vero arridens meque intuens gratulatorie miratus est, quod eas et solas prae oculis meis
litteras repente conperisset. Christianus quippe et fidelis 35
erat et saepe tibi, deo nostro, prosternebatur in ecclesia
crebris et diuturnis orationibus. Cui ego cum indicassem
illis me scripturis curam maximam inpendere, ortus est
sermo, ipso narrante, de Antonio Aegyptio monacho, cuius

22. in eis: "in these things "; i.e.,
"under these circumstances " or "by
these measures."
22. quem volebat . . . feriatum:
"which he wished to have free and
at leisure. . . ."
23. quam multis posset horis: "for
as many hours as possible." On the
ablative of duration of time and on
the positive in place of the superlative
here, cf. §§ 84b, 70. The subjunctive
is potential.
27. Ponticianus: subject of venit,
when we should expect it to be subject
of the main verb volebat. The Confessions seems to be the only source for
his biography.
27. in quantum Afer: "in so far as
he was an African." On in quantum,
cf. § 88a, 5.
28. praeclare . . . militans: "serv-
ing in a high capacity at Court." In
the Later Latin, militare comes to be

used of civil as well as of military
functions.
31. codicem: on this form of the
ancient book, cf. Sandys, 238.
32. aliquid de libris: "something
of books "; i.e., "something in the
way of books " or "some book or
other." The neuter pronoun suggests
vagueness. On de, cf. § 87d, 3.
39. Antonio: the *Vita Antonii*
had been composed in Greek, probably by St. Athanasius, around 357.
It had been translated into Latin by
Evagrius of Antioch some time before
388 and is in all probability the version
described here. St. Anthony, who
flourished in Egypt in the second half
of the third century, is generally re-
cognized as the founder of that organized Christian asceticism which we
call monasticism. Cf. C. E., Vol. I,
s.v. *Anthony*, 553–555; Campbell, J.
M., *The Greek Fathers*, New York,

40 nomen excellenter clarebat apud servos tuos, nos autem
usque in illam horam latebat. Quod ille ubi conperit,
inmoratus est in eo sermone insinuans tantum virum
ignorantibus et admirans eandem nostram ignorantiam.
Stupebamus autem audientes tam recenti memoria et prope
45 nostris temporibus testatissima mirabilia tua in fide
recta et catholica ecclesia. Omnes mirabamur, et nos,
quia tam magna erant, et ille, quia inaudita nobis erant.

15 Inde sermo eius devolutus est ad monasteriorum
greges et mores suaveolentiae tuae et ubera deserta heremi,
50 quorum nos nihil sciebamus. Et erat monasterium Medio-
lanii plenum bonis fratribus extra urbis moenia sub Ambrosio nutritore, et non noveramus. Pertendebat ille et
loquebatur adhuc, et nos intenti tacebamus. Unde incidit,
ut diceret nescio quando se et tres alios contubernales suos—
55 nimirum apud Treveros, cum imperator pomeridiano circen-
sium spectaculo teneretur—exisse deambulatum in hortos
muris contiguos atque illic, ut forte combinati spatia-
bantur, unum secum seorsum et alios duos itidem seorsum
pariterque digressos; sed illos vagabundos inruisse in quan-
60 dam casam, ubi habitabant quidam servi tui spiritu

Longmans, Green and Co., 1929, 53–
58.

42. in eo sermone: " in this discussion "; i.e., in this part of his discussion.

45. mirabilia tua: for the expression, cf. *Ps.* 144: 5, " and (they)
shall tell thy wondrous works."

49. mores suaveolentiae tuae: " the
customs of Thy sweet odor "; i.e.,
the holiness of the ascetic life of the
monks, a sweet odor, so to speak, of
the Divine Life.

54. nescio quando: " I do not know
when "; i.e., " at one time or other."

55. apud Treveros: i.e., " at
Trèves," on the right bank of the
Moselle. Founded as a Roman town,
probably by Augustus, and raised to

the dignity of a **colonia** by Claudius,
it had been from the time of Diocletian
a center of imperial authority, being
the focal point of frontier adminis-
tration in the West, the headquarters
of the Western Caesar, and necessarily
the frequent residence of the emperor
amid the frontier problems of the de-
clining Empire. On **apud,** cf. § 86b.

56. deambulatum: supine. Cf. §93.

58. unum secum . . . digressos:
i.e., having formed two groups of
two, they separated, walking in different directions.

59. illos: refers to **alios duos.**

**60. spiritu pauperes . . . regnum
caelorum:** cf. *Matt.* 5: 3, " Blessed
are the poor in spirit; for theirs is the
kingdom of heaven."

pauperes, qualium est regnum caelorum, et in-
venisse ibi codicem, in quo scripta erat vita Antonii.
Quam legere coepit unus eorum et mirari et accendi et inter
legendum meditari arripere talem vitam et relicta militia
saeculari servire tibi. Erant autem ex eis, quos dicunt 65
agentes in rebus. Tum subito repletus amore sancto et
sobrio pudore iratus sibi coniecit oculos in amicum et ait
illi: "Dic, quaeso te, omnibus istis laboribus nostris quo
ambimus pervenire? Quid quaerimus? Cuius rei causa
militamus? Maiorne esse poterit spes nostra in palatio, 70
quam ut amici imperatoris simus? Et ibi quid non fragile
plenumque periculis? Et per quot pericula pervenitur ad
grandius periculum? Et quando istuc erit? Amicus autem
dei, si voluero, ecce nunc fio."

Dixit hoc et turbidus parturitione novae vitae reddidit 75
oculos paginis: et legebat et mutabatur intus, ubi tu videbas,
et exuebatur mundo mens eius, ut mox apparuit. Namque
dum legit et volvit fluctus cordis sui, infremuit aliquando et
discrevit decrevitque meliora iamque tuus ait amico suo:
"Ego iam abrupi me ab illa spe nostra et deo servire statui 80
et hoc ex hac hora, in hoc loco aggredior. Te si piget

---

63. et . . . et . . . et . . . et: note
the effect of the polysyndeton; cf.
§ 46.

63. inter legendum: on inter with
the gerund, cf. § 91a.

66. agentes in rebus: " special
agents." A numerous and privileged
class of imperial officials employed by
the later emperors. They were attached to the palace under the authority of the Master of Offices and were
used in various roles, e.g., imperial
messengers and secret police. Cf.
Pauly-Wissowa, Real-Encyclopädie der
classischen Altertumswissenschaft, vol.
1, Stuttgart, 1894, s.v. Agentes in
rebus, 776–780.

69. ambimus pervenire: on the infinitive, cf. § 89b.

71. amici imperatoris: " Friends of

Caesar." A small circle inaugurated
by Augustus and recruited from the
senatorial and equestrian classes; on
terms of intimacy with the emperor;
consulted on matters of state, and
enjoying special privileges and honors.
Cf. Bury, 22, and Greenidge, 357–358.

76. intus, ubi tu videbas: for the
thought, cf. Matt. 6: 18.

79. discrevit decrevitque: note the
parechesis. Cf. § 42.

79. iamque tuus: " and (as if) already Thine."

81. aggredior: the present is used in
in place of the future to emphasize
the immediate execution of the resolve. Note the similar use of the
present infinitive adhaerere below.

81. piget imitari: on the infinitive,
cf. § 89d.

imitari, noli adversari." Respondit ille adhaerere se socium
tantae mercedis tantaeque militiae. Et ambo iam tui
aedificabant turrem sumptu idoneo relinquendi omnia sua
85 et sequendi te.

Tum Ponticianus et qui cum eo per alias horti partes
deambulabant, quaerentes eos devenerunt in eundem locum
et invenientes admonuerunt, ut redirent, quod iam declinas-
set dies. At illi narrato placito et proposito suo—quoque
90 modo in eis talis voluntas orta est atque firmata—petiverunt
ne sibi molesti essent, si adiungi recusarent. Isti autem
nihil mutati a pristinis fleverunt se tamen, ut dicebat, atque
illis pie congratulati sunt et conmendaverunt se orationibus
eorum et trahentes cor in terra abierunt in palatium, illi
95 autem affigentes cor caelo manserunt in casa.

Et habebant ambo sponsas: quae posteaquam hoc
audierunt, dicaverunt etiam ipsae virginitatem tibi.

Though straightway pursuaded and filled
with compunction, I still did not make
full surrender to Thee.

VII. 16 Narrabat haec Ponticianus. Tu autem, domine,
inter verba eius retorquebas me ad me ipsum, auferens me
100 a dorso meo, ubi me posueram, dum nollem me adtendere,

---

84. **aedificabant turrem:** for the
thought, cf. *Luke* 14: 28–30.

84. **sumptu idoneo relinquendi:** " at
the cost (alone) appropriate of aban-
doning."

86. **qui:** i.e., his comrade. Occasionally a subject in the singular to
which is attached an ablative with
cum, governs a plural verb by synesis.
Cf. A-G., § 317, note.

89. **narrato placito . . . quoque
modo:** on the ablative absolute, cf.
§ 84c.

89. **quoque modo . . . orta est:**
on the indicative here, cf. § 96.

91. **adiungi:** used in a middle sense,
" to join themselves (to them)." Cf.
§ 77.

91. **Isti:** i.e., Ponticianus and his
friend. On isti = **hi,** cf. § 68c, 1.

94. **trahentes cor in terra:** " trailing
their hearts on the earth "; i.e., " with
their minds attached to earthly
things."

100. **dum nollem:** on the subjunctive with **dum** in the sense of " while "
or " because," cf. § 98f.

et constituebas me ante faciem meam, ut viderem, quam
turpis essem, quam distortus et sordidus, maculosus et
ulcerosus. Et videbam et horrebam, et quo a me fugerem
non erat. Et si conabar a me avertere aspectum, narrabat
ille quod narrabat, et tu me rursus opponebas mihi et 105
inpingebas me in oculos meos, ut invenirem iniquitatem
meam et odissem. Noveram eam, sed dissimulabam et
cohibebam et obliviscebar.

17 Tunc vero quanto ardentius amabam illos, de quibus
audiebam salubres affectus, quod se totos tibi sanandos 110
dederant, tanto exsecrabilius me conparatum eis oderam,
quoniam multi mei anni mecum effluxerant—forte duodecim
anni—ex quo ab undevicensimo anno aetatis meae lecto
Ciceronis Hortensio excitatus eram studio sapientiae et
differebam contemta felicitate terrena ad eam investigandam 115
vacare, cuius non inventio, sed vel sola inquisitio iam
praeponenda erat etiam inventis thesauris regnisque gentium et ad nutum circumfluentibus corporis voluptatibus.
At ego adulescens miser valde, miser in exordio ipsius
adulescentiae, etiam petieram a te castitatem et dixeram :120
"Da mihi castitatem et continentiam, sed noli modo."
Timebam enim, ne me cito exaudires et cito sanares a
morbo concupiscentiae, quem malebam expleri quam

---

105. ille: i.e., Ponticianus.
106. ut invenirem . . . odissem: cf.
Ps. 35: 3, " that his iniquity may be
found unto hatred."
109. illos: i.e., the two friends of
Ponticianus mentioned above.
113. ex quo: sc. tempore. Cf.
§ 87e, 2.
113. lecto . . . Hortensio: cf. *Conf.*
III, 4, 7.
115. differebam . . . vacare: " and
I kept deferring, having (first) con-
temned earthly happiness, to have
leisure for investigating it (i.e., true
wisdom) "; i.e., " and I kept deferring

to despise earthly happiness that
thereby I might have leisure to investigate it (i.e., true wisdom)."
On the infinitive with **differre,** cf.
§ 89b.
115. eam: refers to **sapientiam** as
its antecedent.
**116. cuius non inventio . . . prae-
ponenda erat:** " of which not the
finding but the seeking alone should
have been preferred to."
119. miser valde, miser: anadiplosis. Cf. § 31.
121. noli: sc. **dare.**

exstingui. Et ieram per vias pravas superstitione
125 sacrilega non quidem certus in ea, sed quasi praeponens eam
ceteris, quae non pie quaerebam, sed inimice oppugnabam.

18 Et putaveram me propterea differre de die in diem
contemta spe saeculi te solum sequi, quia non mihi apparebat certum aliquid, quo dirigerem cursum meum. Et
130 venerat dies, quo nudarer mihi et increparet in me conscientia mea: "Ubi est lingua? Nempe tu dicebas propter
incertum verum nolle te abicere sarcinam vanitatis. Ecce
iam certum est, et illa te adhuc premit umerisque liberioribus
pinnas recipiunt, qui neque ita in quaerendo adtriti sunt
135 nec decennio et amplius ista meditati."

Ita rodebar intus et confundebar pudore horribili vehementer, cum Ponticianus talia loqueretur. Terminato
autem sermone et causa, qua venerat, abiit ille, et ego ad
me. Quae non in me dixi? Quibus sententiarum verber-
140 ibus non flagellavi animam meam, ut sequeretur me conan-
tem post te ire? Et renitebatur, recusabat et non se

---

124. **per vias pravas:** for the expression, cf. *Eccles.* 2: 16, "Woe to
them . . . that have forsaken the right
ways, and have gone aside into
crooked ways."

124. **superstitione sacrilega:** i.e.,
Manichaeism.

125. **non quidem certus in ea:** A.
tells us in his *De Vita Beata* I, 4, that
he had not surrendered himself completely to Manichaeism because of intellectual difficulties. (De L., I,
190, footnote 1.) The Faustus epi-
sode (*Conf.* V, 3, 3 ff.) agrees with
this.

126. **ceteris:** "to other things";
i.e., to all other teachings.

127. **differre de die in diem:** cf.
Eccles. 5: 8, "and defer it not from
day to day." On the infinitive after
differre, cf. § 89b.

129. **Et venerat dies:** i.e., of Ponticianus' recital. A. now discovers

that moral impediments were playing
a part in what he had supposed were
purely intellectual difficulties.

131. **propter incertum verum:** "on
account of the uncertain truth";
i.e., "on account of the truth being
uncertain."

133. **illa:** sc. sarcina vanitatis.

133. **umerisque . . . recipiunt, qui:**
"and with freer shoulders (through
having cast aside the **sarcina vanitatis**) they receive wings, who. . . ." In
pinnas recipiunt there is possibly an
allusion to Plato's *Phaedrus*, 249.
Those souls receive their wings the
sooner, whose owners are sincere
lovers of wisdom.

135. **decennio:** on the ablative of
duration of time, cf. § 84b.

138. **et ego ad me:** sc. abii.

141. **post te ire:** i.e., "to follow
Thee." The expression is Biblical.
Cf. § 86d.

excusabat. Consumpta erant et convicta argumenta omnia: remanserat muta trepidatio et quasi mortem reformidabat restringi a fluxu consuetudinis, quo tabescebat in
mortem.   145

XV. In the Garden

In anguish of spirit I rushed to the garden,
distraught at my will's hesitation, my God.

VIII. 19 Tum in illa grandi rixa interioris domus meae,
quam fortiter excitaveram cum anima mea in cubiculo
nostro, corde meo, tam vultu quam mente turbatus invado
Alypium, exclamo: "Quid patimur? Quid est hoc, quod
audisti? Surgunt indocti et caelum rapiunt, et nos cum   5
doctrinis nostris sine corde ecce ubi volutamur in carne
et sanguine! An quia praecesserunt, pudet sequi et non
pudet nec saltem sequi?"
    Dixi nescio qua talia, et abripuit me ab illo aestus meus,
cum taceret attonitus me intuens. Neque enim solita 10
sonabam. Plus loquebantur animum meum frons, genae,
oculi, color, modus vocis quam verba, quae promebam.
    Hortulus quidam erat hospitii nostri, quo nos utebamur
sicut tota domo: nam hospes ibi non habitabat, dominus

---

143. **remanserat:** on the tense, cf.
§ 78a.
143. **et quasi mortem reformidabat
. . . restringi:** " and it feared to be
kept back as if (it were fearing)
death."
144. **in mortem:** i.e., spiritual
death.

XV. In the Garden

5. **caelum rapiunt:** cf. *Matt.* 11: 12,
" the kingdom of heaven suffereth
violence, and the violent bear it
away."
5. **nos cum doctrinis . . . sanguine:**

construe **nos** after **ubi.** The prolep-
sis helps to emphasize A.'s deep
humiliation.
6. **sine corde:** " without heart ";
i.e., without the warmth of faith.
7. **pudet:** sc. **nos.** On **nec saltem**
= ne . . . quidem, cf. § 75d.
10. **Neque enim solita sonabam:**
" I did not voice my customary
(sounds) "; i.e., " I did not speak as
usual."
11. **loquebantur animum meum:**
" bespoke my mind "; i.e., bespoke
what was passing within me.

15 domus. Illuc me abstulerat tumultus pectoris, ubi nemo
impediret ardentem litem, quam mecum aggressus eram,
donec exiret, qua tu sciebas, ego autem non; sed tantum
insaniebam salubriter et moriebar vitaliter, gnarus, quid
mali essem, et ignarus, quid boni post paululum futurus
20 essem.
Abscessi ergo in hortum et Alypius pedem post pedem.
Neque enim secretum meum non erat, ubi ille aderat. Aut
quando me sic affectum desereret?
Sedimus quantum potuimus remoti ab aedibus. Ego
25 fremebam spiritu indignans indignatione turbulentissima,
quod non irem in placitum et pactum tecum, deus meus, in
quod eundum esse omnia ossa mea clamabant et in
caelum tollebant laudibus. Et non illuc ibatur navibus
aut quadrigis aut pedibus, quantum saltem de domo in
30 eum locum ieram, ubi sedebamus. Nam non solum ire
verum etiam pervenire illuc nihil erat aliud quam velle ire,
sed fortiter et integre, non semisauciam hac atque hac
versare et iactare voluntatem parte adsurgente cum alia
parte cadente luctantem.

---

16. **impediret:** the clause is characteristic; hence the subjunctive.

17. **donec exiret ... sciebas:** "until it should issue in which way Thou knewest."

18. **insaniebam ... vitaliter:** oxymoron; cf. § 40. "I was healthily insane and was dying after a living manner"; i.e., "I was mad with a distress that was healthy for my soul and was dying to the life according to this world in a manner that meant my living according to God."

21. **pedem post pedem:** sc. secutus est or the like.

22. **Neque ... aderat:** "For not even when he was near was my secret not (a secret)."

26. **quod non irem ... et pactum tecum:** cf. *Ezech.* 16: 8, "and I en-

tered into a covenant with thee, saith the Lord God."

27. **eundum esse:** sc. mihi.

27. **omnia ossa mea clamabant:** cf. *Ps.* 34: 10, "All my bones shall say."

27. **et in caelum tollebant:** sc. quod (pactum tecum).

28. **illuc:** i.e., in pactum tecum.

29. **quantum ... ubi sedebamus:** "even as far as I had gone from the house to that place where we were sitting."

32. **sed fortiter et integre:** sc. ire.

33. **voluntatem:** construe as object of versare et iactare.

33. **parte adsurgente ... luctantem:** "struggling, while one part is advancing, with the other that is falling back."

Though twelve years' indulgence kept pull-
ing me backward, Thy grace had begun to
prevail in my soul.

XI. 25 Sic aegrotabam et excruciabar accusans memet 35
ipsum solito acerbius nimis ac volvens et versans me in
vinculo meo, donec abrumperetur totum, quo iam exiguo
tenebar. Sed tenebar tamen. Et instabas tu in occultis
meis, domine, severa misericordia flagella ingeminans
timoris et pudoris, ne rursus cessarem et non abrumperetur 40
id ipsum exiguum et tenue, quod remanserat, et revalesceret
iterum et me robustius alligaret.
   Dicebam enim apud me intus: "Ecce modo fiat, modo
fiat," et cum verbo iam ibam in placitum. Iam paene
faciebam, et non faciebam, nec relabebar tamen in pristina, 45
sed de proximo stabam et respirabam. Et item conabar et
paulo minus ibi eram et paulo minus, iam iamque adtingebam et tenebam: et non ibi eram nec adtingebam nec
tenebam, haesitans mori morti et vitae vivere, plusque in
me valebat deterius inolitum, quam melius insolitum, 50
punctumque ipsum temporis, quo aliud futurus eram, quanto propius admovebatur, tanto ampliorem incutiebat horrorem; sed non recutiebat retro nec avertebat, sed suspendebat.

---

36. **solito:** ablative of comparison.
40. **timoris et pudoris:** construe with **flagella.**
41. **id ipsum . . . tenue:** sc. **vinculum.**
44. **et cum verbo . . . in placitum:** "and with the word I was already moving towards decision."
46. **de proximo stabam:** "I stood very near"; i.e., but little removed from it.
47. **paulo minus ibi eram:** "I was by a little (paulo) not (minus) there."
49. **haesitans mori . . . vivere:** on the infinitive with **haesitans,** cf. § 89b. On **morti,** cf. § 82d.

49. **plusque in me valebat . . . insolitum:** "and the ingrown worse prevailed in me more than the unwonted better"; i.e., "and the worse that had (long) grown (in me) was stronger in me than the better, (so) unaccustomed (to me)."
51. **punctumque ipsum . . . horrorem:** "and the nearer the very point of time, wherein I was to be something else, approached, the greater terror it struck in me." On **admovebatur,** cf. § 77.
53. **recutiebat . . . suspendebat:** sc. **punctum ipsum temporis** as subject.

26 Retinebant nugae nugarum et vanitates vanitantium,
55 antiquae amicae meae, et succutiebant vestem meam
carneam et submurmurabant: "Dimittisne nos?" et "a
momento isto non erimus tecum ultra in aeternum" et
"a momento isto non tibi licebit hoc et illud ultra in
aeternum." Et quae suggerebant in eo, quod dixi "hoc
60 et illud," quae suggerebant, deus meus? Avertat ab anima
servi tui misericordia tua! Quas sordes suggerebant, quae
dedecora! Et audiebam eas iam longe minus quam
dimidius, non tamquam libere contradicentes eundo in
obviam, sed velut a dorso mussitantes et discedentem quasi
65 furtim vellicantes, ut respicerem. Retardabant tamen
cunctantem me abripere atque excutere ab eis et transilire
quo vocabar, cum diceret mihi consuetudo violenta:
"Putasne sine istis poteris?"

27 Sed iam tepidissime hoc dicebat. Aperiebatur enim
70 ab ea parte, qua intenderam faciem et quo transire trepida-
bam, casta dignitas continentiae, serena et non dissolute
hilaris, honeste blandiens, ut venirem neque dubitarem, et
extendens ad me suscipiendum et amplectendum pias
manus plenas gregibus bonorum exemplorum. Ibi tot
75 pueri et puellae, ibi iuventus multa et omnis aetas et graves

---

54. vanitates vanitantium: cf. *Eccles.* 1: 2, "Vanitas vanitatum," "vanity of vanities." **vanitantium** is neuter plural. On the genitive, cf. § 83a.

55. amicae meae, et succutiebant . . .: note the vividness given by personification.

59. Et quae suggerebant . . . "hoc et illud": "and what things they suggesting in that which I have called "this and that"?

59. suggerebant . . . suggerebant: geminatio. Cf. § 37.

60. Avertat: sc. **quae** from above as object.

63. in obviam: cf. § 88a, 5.

63. non tamquam . . . mussitantes: "not, as it were, openly contradicting (me) by opposing me face to face, but murmuring behind my back, so to speak."

68. Putasne . . . poteris?: "Will you be able (to live) without these things, do you think?" **putasne** is parenthetical.

69. dicebat: sc. **consuetudo** as subject.

69. Aperiebatur: its subject is **casta dignitas continentiae** below.

75. iuventus multa: "a numerous youth."

viduae et virgines anus, et in omnibus ipsa continentia
nequaquam sterilis, sed fecunda mater filiorum gaudiorum
de marito te, domine.

Et inridebat me inrisione hortatoria, quasi diceret: "Tu
non poteris, quod isti, quod istae? An vero isti et istae in 80
se ipsis possunt ac non in domino deo suo? Dominus deus
eorum me dedit eis. Quid in te stas et non stas? Proice
te in eum, noli metuere; non se subtrahet, ut cadas: proice
te securus, excipiet et sanabit te." Et erubescebam nimis,
quia illarum nugarum murmura adhuc audiebam, et 85
cunctabundus pendebam. Et rursus illa, quasi diceret:
"Obsurdesce adversus inmunda illa membra tua super
terram, ut mortificentur. Narrant tibi delectationes,
sed non sicut lex domini dei tui." Ista controversia
in corde meo non nisi de me ipso adversus me ipsum. At 90
Alypius affixus lateri meo inusitati motus mei exitum tacitus
opperiebatur.

---

76. et in omnibus . . . domine:
"and in all was continence herself
not at all sterile, but the fruitful
mother of the children of joys (sent)
from Thee, her Spouse, O Lord."
For the thought sterilis . . . mater,
cf. Ps. 112: 9.

79. inridebat . . . inrisione: paronomasia. Cf. § 43.

80. isti . . . istae: the men and
women mentioned above. Sc. facere
potuerunt. Cf. § 68c, 2.

80. in se ipsis: "in themselves
(alone)," i.e., "of themselves," "by
their own powers." On in, cf. § 88b, 3.

82. Quid in te stas et non stas:
"Why in Thyself dost Thou stand
and (yet) not stand?"

83. eum: i.e., dominum.

87. membra tua, . . . mortificentur:
cf. Col. 3: 5, "mortify therefore your
members which are upon the earth."
On super = in with the ablative, cf.
§ 88d, 1.

88. Narrant tibi . . . dei tui: cf.
Ps. 118: 85, "The wicked have told
me fables, but not as thy law."

90. non nisi: "(was) not unless";
i.e., "was entirely."

XVI. The Voice in the Garden

Until in my sorrow Thy grace overtook me,
through the voice of a child and the words
of St. Paul.

XII. 28 Ubi vero a fundo arcano alta consideratio traxit
et congessit totam miseriam meam in conspectu cordis
mei, oborta est procella ingens ferens ingentem imbrem
lacrimarum. Et ut totum effunderem cum vocibus suis,
5 surrexi ab Alypio—solitudo mihi ad negotium flendi aptior
suggerebatur—et secessi remotius, quam ut posset mihi
onerosa esse etiam eius praesentia.

Sic tunc eram, et ille sensit: nescio quid enim, puto,
dixeram, in quo apparebat sonus vocis meae iam fletu
10 gravidus, et sic surrexeram. Mansit ergo ille ubi sedebamus
nimie stupens. Ego sub quadam fici arbore stravi me
nescio quomodo et dimisi habenas lacrimis, et proruperunt
flumina oculorum meorum, acceptabile sacrificium tuum,
et non quidem his verbis, sed in hac sententia multa dixi
15 tibi: "Et tu, domine, usquequo? Usquequo,
domine, irasceris in finem? Ne memor fueris
iniquitatum nostrarum antiquarum." Sentiebam enim eis me teneri. Iactabam voces miserabiles:

XVI. The Voice in the Garden

1. **a fundo arcano:** sc. "of my
soul."

2. **in conspectu:** for the expression,
cf., e.g., *Ps.* 22: 5, **Parasti in conspectu
meo mensam,** "Thou hast prepared
a table before me." Cf. also § 88b, 1.

4. **ut totum (imbrem) effunderem
. . . suis:** "that I might pour out the
whole tempest with its sounds";
i.e., sounds suitable to a tempest.

9. **in quo:** "in (the utterance of)
which." On **in,** cf. § 88b, 4.

11. **fici arbore:** on the genitive, cf.
§ 83b.

13. **acceptabile sacrificium tuum:**
cf. *Ps.* 50: 19, "A sacrifice to God is
an afflicted spirit."

14. **in hac sententia:** cf. § 88b, 5.

15. **Et tu, domine, usquequo?:** cf.
Ps. 6: 4, "but thou, O Lord, how
long? "

15. **Usquequo . . . in finem?:** cf. *Ps.*
78: 5, "How long, O Lord, wilt thou
be angry forever?"

16. **Ne memor . . . antiquarum:**
cf. *Ps.* 78: 8, "Remember not our
former iniquities."

18. **eis:** sc. **iniquitatibus.**

"Quamdiu, quamdiu, cras et cras"?   Quare non modo?
Quare non hac hora finis turpitudinis meae?"   20

29 Dicebam haec et flebam amarissima contritione cordis
mei. Et ecce audio vocem de vicina domo cum cantu
dicentis et crebro repetentis—quasi pueri an puellae, nescio
—"Tolle, lege; tolle, lege." Statimque mutato vultu in-
tentissimus cogitare coepi, utrumnam solerent pueri in   25
aliquo genere ludendi cantitare tale aliquid, nec occurrebat
omnino audisse me uspiam repressoque impetu lacrimarum
surrexi nihil aliud interpretans divinitus mihi iuberi, nisi
ut aperirem codicem et legerem quod primum caput
invenissem. Audieram enim de Antonio, quod ex evan-   30
gelica lectione, cui forte supervenerat, admonitus fuerit,
tamquam sibi diceretur quod legebatur: v a d e, v e n d e
o m n i a, q u a e h a b e s, d a p a u p e r i b u s et h a b e b i s
t h e s a u r u m i n c a e l i s; e t v e n i, s e q u e r e m e, e t t a l i
oraculo confestim ad te esse conversum.   35

    Itaque concitus redii in eum locum, ubi sedebat Alypius:
ibi enim posueram codicem apostoli, cum inde surrexeram.

---

22. cum cantu dicentis . . . nescio: " with the singing tone of one
saying and frequently repeating, as
it were, whether boy or girl I know
not."
    25. utrumnam: cf. § 96.
    28. nihil aliud: construe as subject
of iuberi.
    28. nisi ut: cf. § 100b.
    29. codicem: cf. Conf. VIII, 6,
14 and p. 55, note 31.
    29. primum caput: assimilated into
the relative clause. Construe as object of legerem.
    30. Audieram . . . quod . . . ad-
monitus fuerit: on the quod clause
for the accusative and the infinitive,
cf. § 97. On the sequence, cf. § 78c.
    30. Antonio: cf. Conf. VIII, 6, 14.

    30. ex evangelica lectione, . . .
supervenerat: " through (lit., from)
a reading of the Gospel, at which
perchance he had been present."
    32. vade, vende . . . sequere me:
Matt. 19: 21, " go sell what thou
hast, and give to the poor, and thou
shalt have treasure in heaven; and
come, follow me." On instrumental
ex, cf. § 87e, 1.
    34. et . . . esse conversum: sc. An-
tonium and construe with audieram
above. Note that A. in the indirect
discourse here employs the non-
Classical quod clause and the Classical infinitive with subject accusative
after the same verb audieram, and
connects the two constructions as
equivalents by et.

Arripui, aperui et legi in silentio capitulum, quo primum
coniecti sunt oculi mei: non in comisationibus et
40 ebrietatibus, non in cubilibus et inpudici-
tiis, non in contentione et aemulatione, sed
induite dominum Iesum Christum et carnis
providentiam ne feceritis in concupiscentiis.
Nec ultra volui legere nec opus erat. Statim quippe cum
45 fine huiusce sententiae quasi luce securitatis infusa cordi
meo omnes dubitationis tenebrae diffugerunt.
30 Tum interiecto aut digito aut nescio quo alio signo
codicem clausi et tranquillo iam vultu indicavi Alypio.
At ille quid in se ageretur—quod ego nesciebam—sic
50 indicavit. Petit videre quid legissem: ostendi, et adtendit
etiam ultra quam ego legeram. Et ignorabam quid
sequeretur. Sequebatur vero: infirmum autem vero
in fide recipite. Quod ille ad se rettulit mihique
aperuit. Sed tali admonitione firmatus est placitoque ac
55 proposito bono et congruentissimo suis moribus, quibus a

---

38. in silentio: it was customary to read aloud. Cf. *Conf.* VI, 3, 3 and p. 148, note 101.

38. quo primum . . . oculi mei: the practice of consulting the **sortes**, so prevalent in the later paganism, crept into Christianity relative to the Bible and became widespread enough to earn several condemnations by fourth-century councils. Cf. C.E., V, s.v. *Divination*, pp. 48–49.

39. non in comisationibus . . . concupiscentiis: cf. *Rom.* 13: 13–14, " . . . not in rioting and drunkenness, not in chambering and impurities, not in contention and envy: But put ye on the Lord Jesus Christ, and make not provision for the flesh in its concupiscences."

45. cordi meo: = **in cor meum.** On the dative, cf. § 82b.

48. indicavi: sc. "my whole experience."

50. Petit videre: on the infinitive, cf. § 89b.

51. quid sequeretur: i.e., in the text of St. Paul.

52. infirmum autem . . . recipite: cf. *Rom.* 14: 1, " Now him that is weak in faith, take unto you."

54. placitoque ac proposito: construe as ablative of means with **coniunctus est.**

55. congruentissimo . . . distabat: " most agreeable to his character, in which from me he did differ very much for the better now for a long time." On **in melius,** cf. § 88a, 5.

me in melius iam olim valde longeque distabat, sine ulla
turbulenta cunctatione coniunctus est. Inde ad matrem ingredimur, indicamus: gaudet. Nar-
ramus quemadmodum gestum sit: exultat et triumphat; et
benedicebat tibi, qui potens es ultra quam peti- 60
mus aut intellegimus facere, quia tanto amplius sibi
a te concessum de me videbat, quam petere solebat miserabil-
ibus flebilibusque gemitibus. Convertisti enim me ad te, ut
nec uxorem quaererem nec aliquam spem saeculi huius,
stans in ea regula fidei, in qua me ante tot annos ei reve- 65
laveras, et convertisti luctum eius in gaudium
multo uberius, quam voluerat, et multo carius atque
castius, quam de nepotibus carnis meae requirebat.

LIBER NONUS

XVII. Cassiciacum

*I retired with my friends to a house in the
country, to draw close to Thee through
study and prayer.*

IV. 7 Et venit dies, quo etiam actu solverer a pro-

---

57. **coniunctus est:** sc. **mihi.**

58. **indicamus:** cf. note 48.

60. **qui potens . . . facere:** cf.
Eph. 3: 20, " Now to him who is
able to do all things more abundantly
than we desire or understand."

64. **uxorem quaererem:** St. Monnica's hopes for A.'s conversion from
his sinful life had included legitimate
wedlock. Cf. § 9.

65. **stans in ea regula . . . revelaveras:** cf. *Conf.* III, 11, 19.

65. **ante tot annos:** twelve years
before.

66. **convertisti . . . in gaudium:**

cf. *Ps.* 29: 12, " Thou hast turned
for me my mourning into joy."

67. **carius atque castius:** sc. **gaudium.**

68. **de nepotibus carnis meae:**
" from grandchildren (born) of my
flesh." If A. had been married, as
St. Monnica in her hopes for his conversion had been praying, his children
would have been a joy, but they could
not have equaled the joy that now
was hers.

XVII. Cassiciacum

1. **venit dies . . . a professione
rhetorica:** in *Conf.* IX, 2, 2, A. de-

fessione rhetorica, unde iam cogitatu solutus eram. Et
factum est, eruisti linguam meam, unde iam erueras cor
meum, et benedicebam tibi gaudens profectus in villam
5 cum meis omnibus.

Ibi quid egerim in litteris iam quidem servientibus tibi,
sed adhuc superbiae scholam tamquam in pausatione anhelantibus testantur libri disputati cum praesentibus et
cum ipso me solo coram te; quae autem cum absente
10 Nebridio, testantur epistulae.

Et quando mihi sufficiat tempus conmemorandi omnia
magna erga nos beneficia tua in illo tempore praesertim ad
alia maiora properanti? Revocat enim me recordatio mea,
et dulce mihi fit, domine, confiteri tibi, quibus internis me

---

clares his intention of quietly resigning
his professorship of rhetoric at the
beginning of the **Vindemiales Feriae,**
the Vintage Holidays, which extended
from August 22 to October 15. A
serious ailment in his throat and
lungs, but particularly the conviction
that the profession of rhetoric was
incompatible with his new choice of
life, urged this decision upon him.

2. unde iam cogitatu solutus eram:
i.e., by his new sympathies so at
variance with rhetoric as then practiced. On **unde = a qua,** cf. § 73.

4. in villam . . . omnibus: i.e., to
the villa of his friend Verecundus at
Cassiciacum near Milan. " The little
company included his mother Monnica, his brother Navigius and his
son Adeodatus; his two cousins Las-
tidianus and Rusticus, his friend
Alypius, his pupils Licentius, son of
Romanianus, and Trygetius, a Tha-
gastan." G-M.

**7. sed adhuc superbiae . . .
anhelantibus:** " but still exhaling, as
it were, the school of pride, during
the period of rest "; i.e., just as the
athlete, in the period of rest after the
conflict, shows by his heavy breathing

the severity of the struggle he has
endured, so A., after his conversion,
shows by the ostentatious style of the
works he was then composing, the
struggle he had had against the pomp
of this world.

7. superbiae scholam: i.e., rhetoric
as then practiced tended to instill
false pride in its devotees, hence
" school of pride."

8. libri disputati cum praesentibus:
i.e., the books which grew out of the
discussions with his associates at
Cassiciacum: *Contra Academicos, De
Beata Vita,* and *De Ordine.* Cf. De
Labriolle, 402.

**9. (libri disputati) cum ipso me
solo:** i.e., A.'s *Soliloquia,* composed
during this time.

10. testantur epistulae: in the
Benedictine edition of A.'s letters,
Nos. 3, 4, 7, and 9–14 are addressed
to Nebridius, and Nos. 5, 6, and 8
are from Nebridius to A. We have
only a fraction of a copious corre-
spondence.

12. in illo tempore: cf. §§ 88b, 2.

13. properanti: construe with **mihi**
above.

stimulis perdomueris et quemadmodum me conplanaveris 15
humiliatis montibus et collibus cogitationum mearum et
tortuosa mea direxeris et aspera lenieris quoque modo ipsum
etiam Alypium, fratrem cordis mei, subegeris nomini
unigeniti tui, d o m i n i e t s a l v a t o r i s n o s t r i I e s u
C h r i s t i, quod primo dedignabatur inseri litteris nostris. 20
Magis enim eas volebat redolere gymnasiorum c e d r o s,
quas iam contrivit d o m i n u s, quam salubres herbas
ecclesiasticas adversas serpentibus.

8 Quas tibi, deus meus, voces dedi, cum legerem psalmos
David, cantica fidelia, sonos pietatis excludentes turgidum 25
spiritum, rudis in germano amore tuo, catechumenus in
villa cum catechumeno Alypio feriatus, matre, adhaerente
nobis muliebri habitu, virili fide, anili securitate, materna
caritate, christiana pietate! Quas tibi voces dabam in
psalmis illis et quomodo in te inflammabar ex eis et accende- 30

**15. quemadmodum me conplana-
veris . . . lenieris:** cf. *Is.* 40: 4, " and
every mountain and hill shall be
made low, and the crooked shall
become straight, and the rough ways
plain."

19. domini . . . Iesu Christi: cf.
II *Peter* 18, " and the knowledge of
our Lord and Saviour Jesus Christ."

**20. quod . . . dedignabatur inseri
litteris:** the antecedent of **quod** is
nomini above. On the infinitive
with **dedignor,** cf. § 89f. On the
dative **litteris,** cf. § 82b.

21. Magis enim . . . cedros: " For
he rather wished that they (i.e., my
writings) be redolent of the cedars of
the schools "; i.e., reflect the preten-
tious heights of philosophy and rhetoric.

22. quas iam contrivit dominus: cf.
Ps. 28: 5, " The voice of the Lord
breaketh the cedars; yea, the Lord
shall break the cedars of Libanus."

23. adversas serpentibus: "(giving
protection) against the serpents ";

i.e., against the Powers of Evil. The
serpent, who traditionally allures
through pride and who comes so un-
obtrusively that only the lowly
bushes can detect him, i.e., only those
persons not lifted up to the cedar-like
heights of pagan culture.

24. cum legerem psalmos: the
fact that nearly four hundred quotations or echoes from the Psalms are
found in the thirteen books of the
Confessions alone indicates how fond
of and familiar with these songs A.
became.

25. sonos pietatis: on the genitive,
cf. § 83b.

26. catechumenus: on the catechumenate, cf. *Conf.* I, 11, 17 and p.
77, note 68.

28. muliebri habitu, virili fide:
" with the dress of a woman, (but)
with the faith of a man."

29. Quas tibi voces: note the effect
of the repetition.

30. accendebar . . . recitare: on the
infinitive, cf. § 89b.

bar eos recitare, si possem, toto orbe terrarum adversus
tyfum generis humani! Et tamen toto orbe cantantur, et
non est qui se abscondat a calore tuo. Quam
vehementi et acri dolore indignabar manichaeis et miserabar
35 eos rursus, quod illa sacramenta, illa medicamenta nescirent
et insani essent adversus antidotum, quo sani esse potuis-
sent!

12 Quando recordabor omnia dierum illorum feriatorum?
Sed nec oblitus sum nec silebo flagelli tui asperitatem et
40 misericordiae tuae mirabilem celeritatem.

Dolore dentium tunc excruciabas me, et cum in tantum
ingravesceret, ut non valerem loqui, ascendit in cor meum
admonere omnes meos, qui aderant, ut deprecarentur te
pro me, deum salutis omnimodae. Et scripsi hoc in cera
45 et dedi, ut eis legeretur. Mox ut genua supplici affectu
fiximus, fugit dolor ille. Sed quis dolor? Aut quomodo
fugit? Expavi, fateor, domine meus et deus meus: nihil
enim tale ab ineunte aetate expertus fueram. Et insinuati
sunt mihi in profundo nutus tui et gaudens in fide laudavi
50 nomen tuum, et ea fides me securum esse non sinebat de
praeteritis peccatis meis, quae mihi per baptismum tuum
remissa nondum erant.

---

33. non est qui . . . a calore tuo:
cf. *Ps.* 18:7, "and there is no one who
can hide himself from his heat."

35. illa sacramenta: " those mys-
teries "; i.e., the Psalms in their mys-
tical character.

36. insani . . . sani: paronomasia.
Cf. § 43.

38. dierum . . . feriatorum: cf.
p. 169, note 1 above.

42. valerem loqui: on the infinitive,
cf. § 89b.

**42. ascendit in cor meum ad-
monere:** cf. *Jer.* 32: 35, " neither
entered it into my heart." On the
infinitive, cf. § 89c.

44. cera: on the use of waxed

writing tablets among the Ancients'
cf. Sandys, 238.

45. eis: dative of agent. Cf. § 82e.

45. Mox ut: = Classical **ut primum.**
Cf. § 101a.

46. quis dolor?: " what (kind of a)
pain (was it)? "

47. domine meus et deus meus:
cf. *John* 20: 28, " Thomas answered
and said to him: My Lord, and my
God."

48. insinuati sunt . . . nutus tui:
" Thy will forced itself into me in the
very depths (of my heart)." On
mihi, cf. § 82b.

49. gaudens in fide: on **in,** cf.
§ 88b, 3.

I began and abandoned the Book of Isaias,
being not yet adept in Thy language, my
God.

V. 13 Renuntiavi peractis vindemialibus, ut scholasticis
suis Mediolanenses venditorem verborum alium providerent,
quod et tibi ego servire delegissem et illi professioni prae 55
difficultate spirandi ac dolore pectoris non sufficerem.

Et insinuavi per litteras antistiti tuo, viro sancto Ambrosio, pristinos errores meos et praesens votum meum, ut
moneret, quid mihi potissimum de libris tuis legendum
esset, quo percipiendae tantae gratiae paratior aptiorque 60
fierem. At ille iussit Esaiam prophetam, credo, quod
prae ceteris evangelii vocationisque gentium sit praenuntiator apertior. Verum tamen ego, primam huius lectionem
non intellegens totumque talem arbitrans, distuli repetendum exercitatior in dominico eloquio.

---

53. **peractis vindemialibus:** cf. *Conf.*
IX, 4, 7 and p. 169, note 1.
54. **venditorem verborum:** A. is
disparaging the rhetorical teachers of
his time here, as always in the *Confessions.* Cf. *Conf.* III, 3, 5–6, p. 103,
note 36; IV, 2, 2 and p. 116, note 102.
55. **servire delegissem:** on the
infinitive, cf. § 89b.
55. **prae difficultate . . . pectoris:**
Conf. IX, 4, 7 and p. 169, note 1.
59. **quid . . . de libris:** on de, cf.
§ 87d, 3.
60. **percipiendae tantae gratiae:** =
ad percipiendam tantam gratiam. Cf.
§ 90c.

62. **prae ceteris:** on **prae,** cf.
§ 87g, 3.
63. **primam . . . lectionem non intellegens:** "not understanding my
first reading of him " (sc. Isaias).
64. **totumque talem arbitrans:** "and
thinking that the whole (would be)
such (reading)."
64. **distuli repetendum exercitatior:** " I postponed it to be repeated,
more versed "; i.e., " I postponed it
in order to take it up again when more
versed." **repetendum** takes its gen-
der from **totum.** On the gerundive,
cf. § 90b.

XVIII. Baptism

Then Alypius and I, with the son of my
sin, were baptized at Milan, and at length
were at peace.

VI. 14 Inde ubi tempus advenit, quo me nomen dare
oporteret, relicto rure Mediolanium remeavimus.

Placuit et Alypio renasci in te mecum iam induto humilitate sacramentis tuis congrua et fortissimo domitori corporis
5 usque ad Italicum solum glaciale nudo pede obterendum
insolito ausu.—Adiunximus etiam nobis puerum Adeodatum ex me natum carnaliter de peccato meo. Tu bene
feceras eum. Annorum erat ferme quindecim et ingenio
praeveniebat multos graves et doctos viros. Munera tua
10 tibi confiteor, domine deus meus, creator omnium et multum
potens reformare nostra deformia: nam ego in illo puero
praeter delictum nihil habebam. Quod enim enutriebatur

XVIII. Baptism

1. nomen dare: " submit my
name " (i.e., as a candidate for Baptism). The preparation for Baptism
consisted of a series of instructions
and examinations during the Lenten
season. The assemblies held for this
purpose were called scrutinies. " At
the first scrutiny the elect gave in
their names, which were inscribed in
a register." Cf. Duchesne, *Christian
Worship, Its Origin and Evolution,*
London, 1903, pp. 298–299.
2. rure: i.e., Cassiciacum.
3. renasci in te: i.e., through Baptism.
3. induto humilitate: " having
clothed himself with humility." Cf.
Col. 3: 12, " Put ye on therefore . . .
humility, modesty, patience."

5. usque ad . . . obterendum:
" even to the extent of treading upon."
5. nudo pede: i.e., as a severe form
of penance.
6. Adeodatum: son of A. and an
unnamed African woman, with whom
he had lived loyally, but, according
to his own words, illicitly, from his
first years at Carthage until after his
return to the catechumenate at
Milan—in all, over thirteen years.
She had then returned to Africa leaving her highly-endowed son with A.
7. Tu bene feceras eum: " Thou
(on Thy part) hadst fashioned him
well," had endowed him with excellent talents.
**11. potens reformare nostra de-
formia:** note the paronomasia. On
the infinitive with potens, cf. § 89e.
12. Quod: " as to the fact that."

a nobis in disciplina tua, tu inspiraveras nobis, nullus alius: munera tua tibi confiteor.

Est liber noster, qui inscribitur *de Magistro*. Ipse ibi 15 mecum loquitur. Tu scis illius esse sensa omnia, quae inseruntur ibi ex persona conlocutoris mei, cum esset in annis sedecim. Multa eius alia mirabiliora expertus sum. Horrori mihi erat illud ingenium: et quis praeter te talium miraculorum opifex? 20

Cito de terra abstulisti vitam eius, et securior eum recordor non timens quicquam pueritiae nec adulescentiae nec omnino homini illi.

Sociavimus eum coaevum nobis in gratia tua, educandum in disciplina tua: et baptizati sumus et fugit a nobis sollici- 25 tudo vitae praeteritae.

Nec satiabar illis diebus dulcitudine mirabili, considerare altitudinem consilii tui super salutem generis humani. Quantum flevi in hymnis et canticis tuis, suave sonantis ecclesiae tuae vocibus conmotus acriter! Voces illae influe- 30 bant auribus meis et eliquabatur veritas in cor meum et

---

13. inspiraveras nobis: " hadst inspired (this) in us." Cf. § 82b.
14. munera tua . . . confiteor: repetition for emphasis. Cf. § 37.
15. de Magistro: this little dialogue was written by A. in 389, about two years after his Baptism.
15. Ipse: i.e., Adeodatus.
16. illius esse: " are his own."
17. ex persona: " under the name of."
19. Horrori: " Awe."
21. Cito: in 390 at the latest.
22. pueritiae . . . adulescentiae . . . homini: datives of reference.
22. nec omnino homini illi: " nor at all for him (as a) man "; i.e., susceptible to the temptations of an adult.
24. coaevum . . . in gratia tua: A.

and his son were baptized at the same time.
24. educandum: on the gerundive with socio, cf. § 90b.
25. fugit . . . sollicitudo vitae praeteritae: because the sins of their past life had been remitted by Baptism.
27. dulcitudine mirabili, considerare: " with wonderful sweetness of considering." The infinitive further explains dulcitudine. Cf. § 89a.
28. altitudinem consilii tui: cf. *Rom.* 11: 33, " O the depth of the riches of the wisdom and of the knowledge of God."
28. super: = " concerning." Cf. § 88d, 4.
31. auribus meis: = in auris meas. On the dative, cf. § 82b.

exaestuabat inde affectus pietatis, et currebant lacrimae, et bene mihi erat cum eis.

The hymns of that season recall a great marvel which rescued Thy people, but not me, O God.

VII. 15 Non longe coeperat Mediolanensis ecclesia genus
35 hoc consolationis et exhortationis celebrare magno studio fratrum concinentium vocibus et cordibus. Nimirum annus erat aut non multo amplius, cum Iustina, Valentiniani regis pueri mater, hominem tuum Ambrosium persequeretur haeresis suae causa, qua fuerat seducta ab Arrianis. Excu-
40 babat pia plebs in ecclesia mori parata cum episcopo suo,

---

32. affectus pietatis: on the genitive, cf. § 83b.

33. bene mihi erat cum eis: i.e., "it was good for me to weep."

36. fratrum concinentium . . . et cordibus: St. Ambrose had introduced not long before the practice, already familiar in the Orient, of the antiphonal singing of psalms and hymns.

36. Nimirum annus erat: A. was baptized at Easter, 387. The outbreak mentioned here occurred during Easter Week of the preceding year. Ambrose had been consecrated Bishop of Milan in 374 and the four-year-old Valentinian II had come to the throne in 375, on the sudden death of his orthodox father, Valentinian I. His unorthodox and Arian mother, Justina, thus put in control of affairs, was abetted by Arian heretics at Court in the efforts which she immediately inaugurated to strengthen the Arian heresy in the West. Thus, she had come into a long and losing conflict with Bishop Ambrose. During the early part of 385, Ambrose was summoned before the Imperial Court and was requested to give over the Basilica to the Arians, who had no place of public worship in Milan. He refused. The Empress spent the rest of the year trying to persuade or to force Ambrose. Finally, in Holy Week of 386, she ordered him to leave the city. Ambrose, however, proceeded with services in the Basilica as usual and was thus besieged, together with a congregation, during the succeeding Easter Week. Many of the besieging troops finally joined in the singing from within the walls and the Empress was thereby worsted. Cf. C. E., I, s.v. *Ambrose, Saint*, p. 385; and for a more detailed account, De Labriolle, *Life and Times of St. Ambrose*, New York, 1928, pp. 39–65. On the Ambrosian Basilica at Milan, cf. C. E., I, s.v. *Ambrosian Basilica*, pp. 388–389.

39. Excubabat: the siege lasted for several days.

40. plebs: "the Christian People," "the Faithful People of God," as so often in Ecclesiastical Latin.

40. mori parata: on the infinitive, cf. § 89e.

servo tuo. Ibi mater mea, ancilla tua, sollicitudinis et vigiliarum primas tenens, orationibus vivebat. Nos adhuc frigidi a calore spiritus tui excitabamur tamen civitate adtonita atque turbata. Tunc hymni et psalmi ut canerentur secundum morem orientalium partium, ne populus 45 maeroris taedio contabesceret, institutum est: et ex illo in hodiernum retentum multis iam ac paene omnibus gregibus tuis et per cetera orbis imitantibus.

16 Tunc memorato antistiti tuo per visum aperuisti quo loco laterent martyrum corpora Protasi et Gervasi, 50 quae per tot annos incorrupta in thesauro secreti tui reconderas, unde oportune promeres ad cohercendam rabiem femineam, sed regiam. Cum enim propalata et effossa digno cum honore transferrentur ad Ambrosianam basilicam, non solum quos inmundi vexabant spiritus confessis eisdem 55 daemonibus sanabantur, verum etiam quidam plures annos caecus civis civitatique notissimus, cum populi tumultuante laetitia causam quaesisset atque audisset, exilivit eoque se ut duceret suum ducem rogavit. Quo perductus inpetravit admitti, ut sudario tangeret feretrum pretiosae in con- 60

---

41. sollicitudinis . . . primas (partes) tenens: "having a chief role in solicitude and watches."

42. adhuc frigidi . . . spiritus tui: "still cold (away) from the heat of Thy spirit"; i.e., not yet warmed by the heat of Thy Spirit.

44. Tunc hymni et psalmi: cf. note 36 above. On the development of hymnology, cf. C. E., VII, s.v. *Hymnody and Hymnology*, pp. 596–601. For the part of St. Ambrose in, cf. C. E., I, s.v. *Ambrosian Hymnography*, pp. 392–393, and De Labriolle, 285.

46. ex illo: sc. tempore. Cf. § 87e, 2. On in hodiernum, cf. § 88a, 5.

47. retentum (est): sc. this new custom.

47. multis . . . gregibus: dative of agent. Cf. § 82e.

48. per cetera orbis: = per ceterum orbem. On the genitive, cf. § 83a.

50. corpora Protasi et Gervasi: cf. C. E., VI, s.v. *Gervasius and Protasius*, p. 537.

52. rabiem femineam, sed regiam: i.e., of the Empress Justina.

53. propalata et effossa: sc. corpora.

55. confessis eisdem daemonibus: on the ablative absolute, cf. § 84c.

58. eoque se . . . rogavit: "and asked his guide to lead him thither."

59. inpetravit admitti: on the infinitive, cf. § 89f.

60. pretiosae in conspectu . . . tuorum: cf. *Ps.* 115: 15, "Precious

spectu tuo mortis sanctorum tuorum. Quod ubi
fecit atque admovit oculis, confestim aperti sunt. Inde
fama discurrens, inde laudes tuae ferventes, lucentes, inde
illius inimicae animus etsi ad credendi sanitatem non
65 applicatus, a persequendi tamen furore conpressus est.

Gratias tibi, deus meus! Unde et quo · duxisti
recordationem meam, ut haec etiam confiterer tibi, quae
magna oblitus praeterieram? Et tamen tunc, cum ita
flagraret odor unguentorum tuorum, non curre-
70 bamus post te; ideo plus flebam inter cantica hymnorum
tuorum olim suspirans tibi et tandem respirans, quantum
patet aura in domo faenea.

XIX. The Death of St. Monnica

Returning to Carthage to serve Thee the
better, at Ostia my mother departed this life.
My Confessions must pass over much that
concerns me, but not the life nor the death
of this servant of Thine.

VIII. 17 Qui habitare facis unanimes in domo,

in the sight of the Lord is the death
of his saints."

62. admovit oculis: sc. sudarium.

**62. Inde fama discurrens . . .
ferventes: sc.** some verb like **ortae
sunt.**

64. illius inimicae: i.e., Justina.

66. Gratias tibi, deus meus: cf.
Luke 18: 11, " O God, I give thee
thanks." The ellipsis of the verb is
common here.

67. quae magna: " which, great (as
they are)."

69. odor unguentorum . . . post te:
cf. *Cant.* 1: 3, " We will run after
thee to the odour of thy ointments."
On **post,** cf. § 86d.

71. olim suspirans . . . respirans

. . . **faenea:** " once breathing out
after Thee and at length breathing
(Thee) in, in so far as air has space in a
' house of grass ' "; i.e., " once
sighing after Thee and at length receiving Thee, as far as the human
body can." For **domus faenea** =
body, cf. *Is.* 40: 6, " All flesh is grass,"
and II *Cor.* 5: 1, " if our earthly
house of this habitation be dissolved." On **tibi,** cf. § 82b.

XIX. The Death of St. Monnica

1. Qui habitare facis . . . in domo:
cf. *Ps.* 67: 7, " God who maketh men
of one manner to dwell in a house."
On the infinitive with **facio,** cf. § 89f.

consociasti nobis et Evodium iuvenem ex nostro municipio.
Qui cum agens in rebus militaret, prior nobis ad te conversus
est et baptizatus et relicta militia saeculari accinctus in tua.
Simul eramus, simul habitaturi placito sancto.   5

Quaerebamus, quisnam locus nos utilius haberet servientes
tibi: pariter remeabamus in Africam.   Et cum apud Ostia
Tiberina essemus, mater defuncta est.

Multa praetereo, quia multum festino.   Accipe confessiones meas et gratiarum actiones, deus meus, de rebus   10
innumerabilibus, etiam in silentio.   Sed non praeteribo
quidquid mihi anima parturit de illa famula tua, quae me
parturivit et carne, ut in hanc temporalem, et corde, ut in
aeternam lucem nascerer.   Non eius, sed tua dicam dona
in eam.   Neque enim se ipsa fecerat aut educaverat se   15
ipsam: tu creasti eam, nec pater nec mater sciebat, qualis
ex eis fieret.   Et erudivit eam in timore tuo virga
Christi tui, regimen unici filii tui in domo fideli, bono
membro ecclesiae tuae.

Nec tantam erga suam disciplinam diligentiam matris   20

---

2. **Evodium**: Later, Bishop of
Uzala, near Utica in North Africa.
He remained a lifelong friend and
correspondent of A. Cf. Smith and
Wace, II, s.v. *Evodius* (3), 429–430.

2. **nostro municipio**: i.e., Thagaste.

3. **agens in rebus**: cf. *Conf.* VIII,
6, 13–15 and p. 157, note 66.

4. **relicta militia . . . in tua**: " and
having abandoned worldly service,
girded himself in Thine."

5. **simul habitaturi**: " intending to
dwell together."

7. **apud Ostia Tiberina**: = Ostiis
Tiberinis: cf. § 86b.

12. **quidquid mihi . . . nascerer**:
" whatever my soul brings forth about
that servant of Thine, who brought
me forth both in her flesh, that I
might be born to this temporal light
and in her heart, (that I might be

born) to the eternal light." Cf. *Conf.*
I, 11, 17: **Et conturbata mater . . .
parturiebat corde.**

15. **in eam**: " to her."

15. **Neque . . . aut**: = neque . . .
neque; cf. § 94b, 2.

16. **qualis ex eis fieret**: " what
kind of child would be born of them."

17. **in timore tuo**: cf. *Ps.* 5: 8, " I
will worship towards thy holy
temple. in thy fear."

17. **virga Christi tui**: " the rod of
Thy Christ "; i.e., the discipline and
training that conscientious Christianity imposes.

18. **in domo fideli**: the parents of
Monnica and their servants were
staunch Catholics.

20. **Nec tantam . . . praedicabat
quantam**: " And she did not praise

praedicabat quantam famulae cuiusdam decrepitae, quae patrem eius infantem portaverat, sicut dorso grandiuscularum puellarum parvuli portari solent. Cuius rei gratia et propter senectam ac mores optimos in domo christiana
25 satis a dominis honorabatur. Unde etiam curam dominicarum filiarum conmissam diligenter gerebat et erat in eis cohercendis, cum opus esset, sancta severitate vehemens atque in docendis sobria prudentia.

Nam eas praeter illas horas, quibus ad mensam parentum
30 moderatissime alebantur, etiamsi exardescerent siti, nec aquam bibere sinebat praecavens consuetudinem malam et addens verbum sanum: « Modo aquam bibitis, quia in potestate vinum non habetis; cum autem ad maritos veneritis, factae dominae apothecarum et cellariorum, aqua
35 sordebit, sed mos potandi praevalebit ». Hac ratione praecipiendi et auctoritate imperandi frenabat aviditatem tenerioris aetatis et ipsam puellarum sitim formabat ad honestum modum, ut iam non liberet quod non deceret.

18 Et subrepserat tamen, sicut mihi filio famula tua
40 narrabat, subrepserat ei vinulentia. Nam cum de more tanquam puella sobria iuberetur a parentibus de cupa vinum depromere, submisso poculo, qua desuper patet, priusquam in lagunculam funderet merum, primoribus labris

so much the care of her mother as that of. . . ."

22. eius: i.e., Monnica's.

22. sicut dorso . . . portari solent: the custom still continues in certain parts of North Africa.

25. dominicarum: i.e., of her master and mistress.

27. cum opus esset: the subjunctive is iterative. Cf. § 102a.

28. sobria prudentia: construe as ablative of quality with the subject of erat.

34. factae dominae: " having become mistresses."

38. ut iam non liberet: " so that

no longer was (that) pleasing (to them)."

39. famula tua: i.e., Monnica.

41. tanquam puella sobria: " as if (she were) a sober girl "; i.e., " because she was thought to be a sober girl."

42. submisso poculo, qua desuper patet: " after having put under the cup, where there is an opening (patet) from overhead "; i.e., " after having lowered the cup (into the cask) through the opening in its top."

43. primoribus . . . exiguum: " used to take in a little with the tips of her lips "; i.e., " used to take a sip."

sorbebat exiguum, quia non poterat amplius sensu recusante.
Non enim ulla temulenta cupidine faciebat hoc, sed qui- 45
busdam superfluentibus aetatis excessibus, qui ludicris
motibus ebulliunt et in puerilibus animis maiorum pondere
premi solent.
Itaque ad illud modicum cotidiana modica addendo—
quoniam qui modica spernit, paulatim decidit 50
—in eam consuetudinem lapsa erat, ut prope iam plenos
mero caliculos inhianter hauriret.
Ubi tunc sagax anus et vehemens illa prohibitio? Numquid valebat aliquid adversus latentem morbum, nisi tua
medicina, domine, vigilaret super nos? Absente patre et 55
matre et nutritoribus tu praesens, qui creasti, qui vocas,
qui etiam per praepositos homines boni aliquid agis ad
animarum salutem.
Quid tunc egisti, deus meus? unde curasti? unde sanasti?
nonne protulisti durum et acutum ex altera anima convicium 60
tamquam medicinale ferrum ex occultis provisionibus tuis
et uno ictu putredinem illam praecidisti?
Ancilla enim, cum qua solebat accedere ad cupam, litigans
cum domina minore, ut fit, sola cum sola, obiecit hoc crimen
amarissima insultatione vocans meribibulam. Quo illa 65

---

44. **poterat amplius:** sc. **bibere** or
sorbere.
44. **sensu recusante:** " her desire
(or her sense of taste) refusing
(more)."
45. **sed quibusdam . . . ebulliunt:** " but because of the over-
flowing aberrations of (that) age, as
it were, which express themselves
(lit., bubble forth) in absurd actions."
47. **maiorum pondere:** " by the
firmness (or authority) of elders."
50. **qui modica . . . decidit** (The
Vulgate has **decidet**): cf. *Eccles.* 19:
1, " and he that contemneth small
things, shall fall by little and little."
54. **tua medicina:** i.e., Thy grace.

55. **vigilaret super nos:** vigilaret
super is Scriptural. Cf. *Jer.* 31: 28,
" and as I have watched over them,
to pluck up, . . . so will I watch over
them, to build up." On **super,** cf.
also § 88d, 1.
56. **tu praesens:** sc. **eras.**
56. **creasti . . . vocas:** sc. **nos** as
object.
62. **putredinem illam:** i.e., Monnica's evil habit.
64. **domina minore (natu):** " her
young (lit., younger) mistress."
65. **vocans meribibulam (eam):**
" calling her a winebibbess." The
word occurs only here in ancient Latin
literature.

stimulo percussa respexit foeditatem suam confestimque
damnavit atque exuit.

Sicut amici adulantes pervertunt, sic inimici litigantes
plerumque corrigunt.

70   X. 23 Impendente autem die, quo ex hac vita erat
exitura—quem diem tu noveras, ignorantibus nobis—provenerat, ut credo, procurante te occultis tuis modis, ut
ego et ipsa soli staremus incumbentes ad quandam fenestram, unde hortus intra domum, quae nos habebat, pros-
75 pectabatur, illic apud Ostia Tiberina, ubi remoti a turbis
post longi itineris laborem instaurabamus nos navigationi.
Conloquebamur ergo soli valde dulciter et praeterita
obliviscentes in ea quae ante sunt extenti
quaerebamus inter nos apud praesentem veritatem, quod
80 tu es, qualis futura esset vita aeterna sanctorum, quam
nec oculus vidit nec auris audivit nec in cor
hominis ascendit. Sed inhiabamus ore cordis in
superna fluenta fontis tui, fontis vitae, qui est

---

71. provenerat: impersonal. Its
subject is the substantive clause **ut
ego . . . staremus.**
73. incumbentes ad: "leaning
upon."
**74. unde hortus . . . prospectaba-
tur:** "whence the garden within the
house which held us was seen";
i.e., "whence there was a view of the
garden within the house in which
we were staying." A. and his
mother were resting, apparently, at
an opening or window in a room
bordering on the peristyle, a garden
or court within the Graeco-Roman
house. Cf. Sandys, 219–221.
75. apud Ostia Tiberina: = Ostiis
Tiberinis; cf. § 86b.
76. post longi . . . laborem: from
Milan to Rome and from Rome to
Ostia.
76. navigationi: dative of purpose.
Cf. § 82c.

**77. praeterita obliviscentes . . .
extenti:** cf. *Philipp.* 3: 13, "But one
thing I do, forgetting the things that
are behind, and stretching forth
myself to those that are before."
**79. apud praesentem . . . (id)
quod tu es:** "before the present
Truth, that which Thou art"; i.e.,
"in the presence of the Truth, which
Thou art."
81. nec oculus . . . ascendit: I *Cor.*
2: 9, "But as it is written: That eye
hath not seen, nor ear heard, neither
hath it entered into the heart of man."
**82. Sed inhiabamus . . . fontis
tui:** "But we did gape with the
mouth of our heart for the supernal
streams of Thy fountain"; i.e., "we
thirsted for. . . ."
83. fontis vitae, qui est apud te:
cf. *Ps.* 35: 10, "For with thee is the
fountain of life."

apud te, ut inde pro captu nostro aspersi quoquo modo
rem tantam cogitaremus.   85

26 Dicebam talia, etsi non isto modo et his verbis,
tamen, domine, tu scis, quod illo die, cum talia loqueremur
et mundus iste nobis inter verba vilesceret cum omnibus
delectationibus suis, tunc ait illa: « Fili, quantum ad me
adtinet, nulla re iam delector in hac vita. Quid hic faciam 90
adhuc et cur hic sim, nescio, iam consumpta spe huius
saeculi. Unum erat, propter quod in hac vita aliquantum
inmorari cupiebam, ut te christianum catholicum viderem,
priusquam morerer. Cumulatius hoc mihi deus meus
praestitit, ut te etiam contemta felicitate terrena servum 95
eius videam. Quid hic facio? "

XI. 27 Ad haec ei quid responderim, non satis recolo,
cum interea vix intra quinque dies aut non multo amplius
decubuit febribus. Et cum aegrotaret, quodam die defectum animae passa est et paululum subtracta a praesentibus. 100
Nos concurrimus, sed cito reddita est sensui et aspexit
astantes me et fratrem meum et ait nobis quasi quaerenti
similis: « Ubi eram? » Deinde nos intuens maerore atto-
nitos: « Ponetis hic » inquit « matrem vestram ». Ego

---

84. **inde:** sc. fonte tuo.

86. **Dicebam talia . . . his verbis:**
in the omitted portion of the present
chapter, A. gives an account, in very
philosophical language, of the ecstasy
which he and Monnica experienced
in their conversation on the **vita
aeterna sanctorum** mentioned above.
Hence, he felt that it was necessary
to state here that his mother and he
did not discuss the subject in the
philosophical manner of the omitted
passage.

87. **scis, quod . . . tunc ait illa:**
on the **quod** clause for the infinitive
with subject accusative, cf. § 97.

88. **inter verba:** i.e., " during our
conversation."

91. **adhuc:** cf. § 72.

93. **ut . . . morerer:** substantive
clause in apposition with **unum.**

95. **contemta felicitate terrena:**
A. had informed Monnica of his intention of devoting himself entirely
to the service of God. Cf. *Conf.*
VIII, 12, 30, **Inde ad matrem ingredimur, indicamus.**

97. **Ad haec:** " As regards these
things."

99. **defectum animae passa est:**
" suffered the failing of her mind ";
i.e., lapsed into unconsciousness.

102. **quasi quaerenti similis:** " like,
as it were, to a person seeking (something)."

104. **Ponetis:** the future here has
the force of an imperative. Cf.
A-G., § 449, 2, b.

105 silebam et fletum frenabam. Frater autem meus quiddam locutus est, quo eam non peregre, sed in patria defungi tamquam felicius optaret. Quo audito illa vultu anxio reverberans eum oculis, quod talia saperet, atque inde me intuens: « Vide » ait « quid dicit ». Et mox ambobus: 110 « Ponite » inquit « hoc corpus ubicumque: nihil vos eius cura conturbet; tantum illud vos rogo, ut ad domini altare memineritis mei, ubiubi fueritis ». Cumque hanc sententiam verbis quibus poterat explicasset, conticuit et ingravescente morbo exercebatur.

115 28 Ego vero cogitans dona tua, deus invisibilis, quae immittis in corda fidelium tuorum, et proveniunt inde fruges admirabiles, gaudebam et gratias tibi agebam recolens, quod noveram, quanta cura semper aestuasset de sepulchro, quod sibi providerat et praeparaverat iuxta 120 corpus viri sui. Quia enim valde concorditer vixerant, id etiam volebat—ut est animus humanus minus capax divinorum—adiungi ad illam felicitatem et conmemorari ab hominibus, concessum sibi esse post transmarinam peregrinationem, ut coniuncta terra amborum coniugum terra 125 tegeretur.

---

106. **quo . . . optaret:** "whereby he hoped that . . ."; i.e., "whereby he expressed the hope that. . . ."

107. **vultu anxio:** construe with **illa.**

109. **quid dicit:** on the indicative, cf. § 96.

111. **ut ad domini . . . mei:** "that you remember me at the altar of the Lord," by prayer at God's altar.

115. **deus invisibilis:** for the expression, cf. *Col.* 1: 15, "Who is the image of the invisible God."

116. **et (quae) proveniunt . . . admirabiles:** "and (which) come forth thence (as) wonderful fruits."

117. **gratias tibi agebam:** cf. *Col.* 1: 3, "We give thanks to God."

120. **id:** construe as subject of the infinitives **adiungi** and **conmemorari.**

121. **ut est . . . divinorum:** "as the human heart is less capacious of divine things"; i.e., "to such a degree is the human heart unresponsive to divine things."

123. **concessum sibi . . . ut . . . tegeretur:** in apposition with **id** above.

124. **coniuncta terra:** "with joined earth"; i.e., with the same earth.

124. **terra . . . terra:** polyptoton and antimetathesis. Cf. §§ 32, 45.

Quando autem ista inanitas plenitudine bonitatis tuae coeperat in eius corde non esse, nesciebam et laetabar admirans, quod sic mihi apparuisset, quamquam et in illo sermone nostro ad fenestram, cum dixit: « Iam quid hic facio? » non apparuit desiderare in patria mori. Audivi 130 etiam postea, quod iam, cum Ostiis essemus, cum quibusdam amicis meis materna fiducia conloquebatur quodam die de contemtu vitae huius et bono mortis, ubi ipse non aderam, illisque stupentibus virtutem feminae—quam tu dederas ei —quaerentibusque utrum non formidaret tam longe a sua 135 civitate corpus relinquere: « Nihil » inquit « longe est deo, neque timendum est, ne ille non agnoscat in fine saeculi, unde me resuscitet ».

Ergo die nono aegritudinis suae, quinquagesimo et sexto anno aetatis suae, tricesimo et tertio aetatis meae, anima 140 illa religiosa et pia corpore soluta est.

> *Though I kept at her death a calm outward demeanor, in secret I wept in an agony of grief. I grieved that I grieved and ask others to grieve that I showed such a weakness and want of deep faith.*

XII. 29 Premebam oculos eius, et confluebat in praecordia mea maestitudo ingens et transfluebat in lacrimas, ibidemque oculi mei violento animi imperio resorbebant fontem suum usque ad siccitatem, et in tali luctamine valde 145 male mihi erat. Tum vero, ubi efflavit extremum, puer

---

126. **Quando . . . coeperat:** on the mood, cf. § 96.

129. **ad fenestram:** cf. *Conf.* IX, 10, 23.

130. **Audivi, . . . quod . . . conloquebatur:** on the quod clause in place of accusative and infinitive, cf. § 97.

135. **formidaret . . . relinquere:** on the infinitive, cf. § 89b.

136. **deo:** dative of reference.

144. **resorbebant fontem suum:** "repressed their flow."

145. **valde male mihi erat:** "it was very ill with me."

146. **extremum:** take as adverb or sc. **spiritum.**

Adeodatus exclamavit in planctum atque ab omnibus nobis
cohercitus tacuit. Hoc modo etiam meum quiddam puerile,
quod labebatur in fletus, iuvenali voce, voce cordis, coherce-
150 batur et tacebat. Neque enim decere arbitrabamur funus
illud questibus lacrimosis gemitibusque celebrare, quia his
plerumque solet deplorari quaedam miseria morientium aut
quasi omnimoda extinctio. At illa nec misere moriebatur
nec omnino moriebatur. Hoc et documentis morum eius
155 et f i d e n o n f i c t a rationibusque certis tenebamus.

30 Quid erat ergo, quod intus mihi graviter dolebat, nisi
ex consuetudine simul vivendi dulcissima et carissima
repente dirrupta vulnus recens? Gratulabar quidem testi-
monio eius, quod in ea ipsa ultima aegritudine obsequiis
160 meis interblandiens appellabat me pium et conmemorabat
grandi dilectionis affectu numquam se audisse ex ore meo
iaculatum in se durum aut contumeliosum sonum.

Sed tamen quid tale, deus meus, qui fecisti nos, quid
conparabile habebat honor a me delatus illi et servitus ab
165 illa mihi? Quoniam itaque deserebar tam magno eius
solacio, sauciabatur anima mea et quasi dilaniabatur vita,
quae una facta erat ex mea et illius.

---

147. exclamavit in planctum: on
in, cf. § 88a, 2.

**148. meum quiddam . . . in
fletus:** "something childish in me,
which was slipping away into tears."

151. his: i.e., questibus and gemitibus.

**152. quaedam miseria . . . ex-
tinctio:** "the miserable lot, so to
speak (quaedam), of those dying or,
as it were, their complete annihilation." Such lamentation befitted the
pagans, who either did not believe,
or believed only vaguely, in a life to
come.

155. fide non ficta: I *Tim.* 1: 5,
" and an unfeigned faith."

156. nisi . . . recens: construe

nisi vulnus recens ex consuetudine
. . . dirrupta.

159. eius: i.e., Monnica.

159. obsequiis meis interblandiens:
" in giving me a caress for my at-
tentions."

161. grandi dilectionis affectu: on
the genitive, cf. § 83b.

**163. quid tale, . . . conparabile
. . . ab illa mihi:** " what such, . . .
what comparable had the respect
rendered by me to her and the slavery
endured by her for me "; i.e., " what
likeness was there, . . . what comparison was there between the respect, etc."

166. quasi: construe with vita,
" my life, as it were."

167. ex mea et illius: sc. vita.

31 Cohibito ergo a fletu illo puero psalterium arripuit
Evodius et cantare coepit psalmum. Cui respondebamus
omnis domus: misericordiam et iudicium cantabo 170
tibi, domine. Audito autem quid ageretur, convene-
runt multi fratres ac religiosae feminae, et de more illis,
quorum officium erat, funus curantibus ego in parte, ubi
decenter poteram, cum eis, qui me non deserendum esse
censebant, quod erat tempori congruum disputabam eoque 175
fomento veritatis mitigabam cruciatum tibi notum illis
ignorantibus et intente audientibus et sine sensu doloris
me esse arbitrantibus. At ego in auribus tuis, ubi eorum
nullus audiebat, increpabam mollitiam affectus mei et
constringebam fluxum maeroris, cedebatque mihi paululum: 180
rursusque impetu suo ferebatur non usque ad eruptionem
lacrimarum nec usque ad vultus mutationem, sed ego
sciebam, quid corde premerem. Et quia mihi vehementer
displicebat tantum in me posse haec humana, quae ordine
debito et sorte conditionis nostrae accidere necesse est, alio 185
dolore dolebam dolorem meum et duplici tristitia macerabar.

---

168. illo puero: i.e., Adeodatus.
169. Evodius: cf. *Conf.* IX, 8,
17–18 and p. 179, note 2.
169. Cui respondebamus . . . domus: cf. *Conf.* IX, 7, 15–16 and p.
176, note 36; p. 177, note 44.
170. misericordiam . . . cantabo
tibi, domine: cf. *Ps.* 100: 1, " Mercy
and judgment I will sing to thee,
O Lord."
171. Audito autem quid ageretur:
a substantive clause plus a participle, to form an ablative absolute,
is a very rare construction in Class.
Latin. Cf. A-G., § 419b.
172. fratres: " brethren," i.e., fellow Christians.
172. de more: construe with curantibus.
173. in parte: sc. domus.

175. quod erat disputabam: " I
discoursed on what was suitable to
the occasion."
176. illis . . . arbitrantibus: ablative
absolute.
178. in auribus tuis: " in Thy
ears "; i.e., " in Thy hearing." Cf.
§ 88b, 1.
180. cedebat . . . ferebatur: sc.
fluxus maeroris as subject.
183. corde: = in corde. Cf. § 84a.
184. tantum in me . . . humana:
construe haec humana in me posse
tantum.
185. alio dolore . . . dolorem
meum: " I grieved over my grief
with another grief." Paronomasia.
Cf. § 43. A. regretted that he displayed so little faith in thus being
disturbed over Monnica's passing.

32 Cum ecce corpus elatum est, imus, redimus sine
lacrimis.   Nam neque in eis precibus, quas tibi fudimus,
cum offerretur pro ea sacrificium pretii nostri iam iuxta
190 sepulchrum posito cadavere, priusquam deponeretur, sicut
illic fieri solet, nec in eis ergo precibus flevi, sed toto die
graviter in occulto maestus eram et mente turbata rogabam
te, ut poteram, quo sanares dolorem meum, nec faciebas,
credo, conmendans memoriae meae vel hoc uno documento
195 omnis consuetudinis vinculum etiam adversus mentem quae
iam non fallaci verbo pascitur.   Visum etiam mihi est, ut
irem lavatum, quod audieram inde balneis nomen inditum,
quia Graeci βαλανεῖον dixerint, quod anxietatem pellat ex
animo.   Ecce et hoc confiteor misericordiae tuae, p a t e r

---

187. **imus, redimus:** asyndeton; cf.
§ 34.
188. **neque in eis precibus** . . .
nec in eis ergo precibus: note effect
of repetition. Cf. § 37.
189. **sacrificium pretii nostri:** " the
sacrifice of our redemption "; i.e.,
" the Eucharistic Sacrifice," the Mass.
On the offering of the Holy Sacrifice
as one of the essential funeral rites in
the Early Church, cf. C. E., III, s.v.
Burial, pp. 76–77.   Monnica's body
was removed to Rome in 1430 by
Pope Martin V; cf. C.E., I, s.v.
Monica (*sic*), pp. 482–483.
190. **sicut illic fieri solet:** " as is
wont to be done there "; i.e., in and
near Rome.   A. implies that in Africa
it was not customary to offer the
Holy Sacrifice at the grave.
191. **toto die:** on the ablative of
duration, cf. § 84b.
193. **ut poteram:** " as (best) I
could."
193. **quo sanares:** = ut sanares.
On quo here, cf. § 99b.
194. **conmendans** . . . **mentem:**
"commending to my memory surely by
this one proof the (power of the) bond
of all custom even against the mind ";
i.e., God permitted A. to suffer his

deep grief in order to impress upon
him the power of habit even upon
those who already enjoy the consolations and benefits of the Word of
Truth (**mentem, quae iam non fallaci verbo pascitur**).
196. **Visum** . . . **est, ut irem:** on
the ut clause, cf. § 99a.
197. **lavatum:** supine.   Cf. § 93.
197. **quod audieram** . . . **ex animo:**
" because I had heard that baths had
been given their name for this reason
(inde): that the Greeks say βαλανεῖον
because (the bath) drives sorrow
from the mind."   A. follows a popular etymology according to which
βαλανεῖον was derived from the verb
βάλλω, " I drive," " cast out," and
ἀνία, " grief," " sorrow."   The true
etymological meaning of the word
would seem to be " that which flows
or drips."   Cf. E. Boisacq, *Dictionnaire étymologique de la langue
grecque*, 2nd ed., 1923, Heidelberg and
Paris.
199. **confiteor** . . . **quoniam lavi**
. . . **eram:** on the quoniam clause in
place of the accusative and the infinitive in indirect discourse, cf. § 97.
199. **pater orfanorum:** cf. *Ps.* 67:

orfanorum, quoniam lavi et talis eram, qualis prius- 200
quam lavissem. Neque enim exudavit de corde meo
maeroris amaritudo. Deinde dormivi, evigilavi, et non
parva ex parte mitigatum inveni dolorem meum atque, ut
eram in lecto meo solus, recordatus sum veridicos versus
Ambrosii tui: tu es enim,   205

> Deus, creator omnium
> Polique rector vestiens
> Diem decoro lumine,
> Noctem soporis gratia,
> Artus solutos ut quies   210
> Reddat laboris usui
> Mentesque fessas allevet
> Luctusque solvat anxios.

33 Atque inde paulatim reducebam in pristinum sensum
ancillam tuam conversationemque eius piam in te et sancte 215
in nos blandam atque morigeram, qua subito destitutus
sum, et libuit flere in conspectu tuo de illa et pro illa,
de me et pro me. Et dimisi lacrimas quas continebam ut
effluerent quantum vellent, substernens eas cordi meo: et
requievit in eis, quoniam ibi erant aures tuae, non cuius- 220
quam hominis superbe interpretantis ploratum meum.

6, " who is the father of orphans and
the judge of widows."
   200. qualis (eram) . . . **lavissem:**
the subjunctive is probably due to
the fact that **priusquam lavissem** is
a subordinate clause in indirect discourse after **confiteor.**
   206. Deus, creator omnium . . .:
the first two stanzas of St. Ambrose's beautiful evening hymn. For
the meter, cf. A-G, § 618a (2); *ibid.*,
§ 619c. Cf. A. S. Walpole, *Early
Latin Hymns, With Introduction and
Notes*, Cambridge, 1922, 44–49, for a
commentary on this hymn.

   209. Noctem soporis gratia: sc.
vestiens.
   210. Artus solutos ut quies: construe **ut quies artus solutos.** . . .
   214. reducebam . . . **ancillam
tuam:** " I brought back Thy handmaid to my former thought"; i.e.,
" I recalled my former thoughts of
Thy handmaid." (Watts.)
   219. substernens eas cordi meo:
" strewing them (as a bed) for my
heart." G-M.
   220. requievit: sc. **cor meum** as
subject.
   220. non cuiusquam hominis: the

Et nunc, domine, confiteor tibi in litteris. Legat qui volet et interpretetur ut volet et si peccatum invenerit, flevisse me matrem exigua parte horae, matrem oculis meis 225 interim mortuam, quae me multos annos fleverat, ut oculis tuis viverem, non inrideat, sed potius, si est grandi caritate, pro peccatis meis fleat ipse ad te, patrem omnium fratrum Christi tui.

XX. Prayer for St. Monnica

Have mercy on her who had mercy on others, and inspire my readers to pray for her soul.

XIII. 34 Ego autem iam sanato corde ab illo vulnere, in quo poterat redargui carnalis affectus, fundo tibi, deus noster, pro illa famula tua longe aliud lacrimarum genus, quod manat de concusso spiritu consideratione periculorum 5 omnis animae, quae in Adam moritur. Quamquam illa in Christo vivificata etiam nondum a carne resoluta sic vixerit, ut laudetur nomen tuum in fide moribusque eius, non tamen audeo dicere, ex quo eam per baptismum regenerasti, nullum verbum exisse ab ore eius contra praeceptum tuum.

---

genitive depends upon **aures** to be supplied from the **aures** above.

222. Et nunc, domine . . .: considered one of the most beautiful passages in the *Confessions*.

224. exigua parte horae: on the ablative of duration of time, cf. § 84b.

224. matrem oculis . . . mortuam: "my mother dead for a time to my eyes." On the dative, cf. § 82d.

225. ut oculis tuis viverem: "that I might live for Thy eyes"; i.e., "that I might live for Thee, (O God)." On the dative, cf. § 82d.

226. non inrideat: on **non** for **ne**, cf. § 75e. Roman traditions in A.'s time disapproved of the open display of grief.

XX. Prayer for St. Monnica

2. carnalis affectus: genitive of the charge with **redargui**.

5. quae in Adam moritur: cf. I *Cor.* 15: 22, " And as in Adam all die, so also in Christ all shall be made alive."

5. Quamquam . . . vixerit: on quamquam with the subjunctive, cf. § 104.

5. in Christo vivificata: cf. I *Cor.* 15: 22.

6. etiam nondum . . . resoluta: construe with **illa**.

8. ex quo: sc. **tempore**. Cf. § 87e, 2.

9. nullum verbum . . . contra praeceptum tuum: for the thought,

Et dictum est a veritate, filio tuo: si quis dixerit fra- 10
tri suo «fatue» reus erit gehennae ignis: et vae
etiam laudabili vitae hominum, si remota misericordia
discutias eam! Quia vero non exquiris delicta vehementer,
fiducialiter speramus aliquem apud te locum. Quisquis
autem tibi enumerat vera merita sua, quid tibi enumerat 15
nisi munera tua? O si cognoscant se homines homines
et qui gloriatur, in domino glorietur!

35 Ego itaque, laus mea et vita mea, deus cordis
mei, sepositis paulisper bonis eius actibus, pro quibus
tibi gaudens gratias ago, nunc pro peccatis matris meae 20
deprecor te; exaudi me per medicinam vulnerum nos-
trorum, quae pependit in ligno et sedens ad dexteram
tuam te interpellat pro nobis. Scio misericorditer
operatam et ex corde dimisisse debita debitoribus
suis: dimitte illi et tu debita sua, si qua etiam contraxit per 25

---

cf. *Matt.* 12: 36, "But I say unto
you that every idle word that men
shall speak, they shall render an account for it in the day of judgment."
 10. veritate: antonomasia. Cf. § 33.
 **10. si quis dixerit . . . gehennae
ignis:** cf. *Matt.* 5: 22, "And whoso-
ever shall say (to his brother), Thou
fool, shall be in danger of hell fire."
 **11. et vae etiam . . . discutias
eam:** for the thought, cf. *Ps.* 142: 2,
"And enter not into judgment with
thy servant: for in thy sight no man
living shall be justified," and *Ps.*
129: 3, "If thou, O Lord, wilt mark
iniquities: Lord, who shall stand it?"
On dative with vae, cf. § 82d.
 16. O si cognoscant . . . homines:
"O if men would know that they are
(but) men." The use of si to introduce a wish is poetic in Class.
Latin; cf. A-G., § 442a. For a possible Scriptural source, cf. *Ps.* 9: 21,
"that the Gentiles may know themselves to be but men."

17. qui gloriatur . . . glorietur:
cf. II *Cor.* 10: 17, "But he that
glorieth, let him glory in the Lord."
 18. laus mea: cf. *Ps.* 117: 14,
"The Lord is my strength and my
praise."
 18. deus cordis mei: cf. *Ps.* 72:
26, "thou art the God of my heart."
 21. exaudi me: cf. *Ps.* 68: 14, "In
the multitude of thy mercy hear me,
in the truth of thy salvation."
 **21. per medicinam vulnerum no-
strorum:** i.e., through Christ. On
antonomasia, cf. § 33.
 **22. ad dexteram tuam . . . pro
nobis:** cf. *Rom.* 8: 34, "who is at the
right hand of God, who also maketh
intercession for us."
 24. operatam (esse): sc. **matrem
meam** as subject.
 **24. dimisisse debita debitoribus
suis:** cf. *Matt.* 6: 12, "and forgive us
our debts, as we also forgive our debt-
ors."

tot annos post aquam salutis. Dimitte, domine, dimitte,
obsecro, ne intres cum ea in iudicium. Superexaltet misericordia iudicio, quoniam eloquia
tua vera sunt et promisisti misericordiam misericordibus.
30 Quod ut essent, tu dedisti eis, qui misereberis, cui
misertus eris, et misericordiam praestabis,
cui misericors fueris.

36 Et, credo, iam feceris quod te rogo, sed voluntaria
oris mei adproba, domine. Namque illa immi-
35 nente die resolutionis suae non cogitavit suum corpus
sumptuose contegi aut condiri aromatibus aut monumentum
electum concupivit aut curavit sepulchrum patrium: non
ista mandavit nobis, sed tantummodo memoriam sui ad
altare tuum fieri desideravit, cui nullius diei praetermissione
40 servierat, unde sciret dispensari victimam sanctam, qua
deletum est chirografum, quod erat contrarium

---

26. post aquam salutis: i.e., Baptism. On the thought, cf. *Conf.* V, 8, 15, ad aquam gratiae tuae.

27. ne intres . . . in iudicium: cf. *Ps.* 142: 2.

27. Superexaltet (*Vulgate*, superexaltat) misericordia iudicio: cf. *James* 2: 13, " and mercy exalteth itself above judgment."

29. promisisti . . . misericordibus: cf. *Matt.* 5: 7, " Blessed are the merciful: for they shall obtain mercy."

30. Quod ut essent, tu dedisti eis: " and that they (i.e., the merciful) should be this (quod) (i.e., merciful), thou hast granted them."

30. misereberis . . . fueris: cf. *Rom.* 9: 15, " For he saith to Moses ' I will have mercy on whom I will have mercy; and I will shew mercy to whom I will shew mercy.' " On the dative with mis+rior, cf. § 82a.

33. iam feceris: " Thou wilt have already done."

33. voluntaria oris mei . . . domine: cf. *Ps.* 118: 108, " The free

offerings of my mouth make acceptable, O Lord."

35. die resolutionis suae: cf. II *Tim.* 4: 6, " and the time of my dissolution is at hand."

35. non cogitavit . . . contegi: " she did not think of her body being sumptuously covered."

37. aut curavit sepulchrum patrium: cf. *Conf.* IX, 11, 28.

38. memoriam sui ad altare tuum: cf. *Conf.* IX, 11, 27, ut ad domini altare memineritis mei.

39. cui: refers to altare as antecedent.

39. nullius diei praetermissione: cf. *Conf.* V, 9, 17, nullum diem praetermittentis oblationem ad altare tuum.

40. unde sciret: " because from it she knew "; relative clause of characteristic expressing cause.

41. chirografum . . . contrarium nobis: cf. *Col.* 2: 14, " Blotting out the handwriting of the decree that

n o b i s, qua triumphatus est hostis conputans delicta nostra et quaerens, quid obiciat, et nihil inveniens in illo in quo vincimus. Quis ei refundet innocentem sanguinem? Quis ei restituet pretium, quo nos emit, ut nos auferat ei? 45 Ad cuius pretii nostri sacramentum ligavit ancilla tua animam suam vinculo fidei. Nemo a protectione tua dirrumpat eam. Non se interponat nec vi nec insidiis leo et draco: neque enim respondebit illa nihil se debere, ne convincatur et obtineatur ab accusatore callido, sed respon- 50 debit dimissa debita sua ab eo, cui nemo reddet, quod pro nobis non debens reddidit.

37 Sit ergo in pace cum viro, ante quem nulli et post quem nulli nupta est, cui servivit f r u c t u m tibi afferens cum t o l e r a n t i a, ut eum quoque lucraretur tibi. Et 55

---

was against us, which was contrary to us."

42. qua: sc. **victima.**

42. hostis: i.e., Satan. For the thought, cf. *Apoc.* 12: 10, " Now is come salvation . . . and the power of his Christ: because the accuser of our brethren is cast forth, who accused them before our God day and night."

43. et nihil inveniens in illo: cf. *John* 14: 30, " For the prince of this world cometh, and in me he hath not anything."

44. innocentem sanguinem: cf. *Matt.* 27: 4, " I have sinned in betraying innocent blood."

45. auferat ei: ei refers to **hostis** above for its antecedent.

46. Ad cuius pretii nostri sacramentum: " And to the mystery of this (cuius) redemption of ours "; i.e., " to the mystery of this, our redemption."

47. Nemo . . . dirrumpat eam: for a possible Scriptural source, cf. *John* 10: 28-29.

48. Non se interponat: on **non** for **ne** in a prohibition, cf. § 75e.

48. leo et draco: cf. *Ps.* 90: 13, " and thou shalt trample under foot the lion and the dragon."

49. neque enim . . . callido: " and indeed she will not answer that she owes nothing, lest she be convicted and be obtained by the crafty accuser."

50. sed respondebit . . . reddidit: " but she will reply that her debts have been acquitted by Him to Whom no one repays what He Who Owes Nothing paid for us." Cf. § 33.

53. ante quem . . . nupta est: widows who did not remarry were honored in the Early Church. Cf. I *Tim.* 5: 9.

54. fructum . . . tolerantia: cf. *Luke* 8: 15, " . . . hearing the word, keep it, and bring forth fruit in patience."

55. ut eum . . . tibi: cf. 1 *Peter* 3: 1, " In like manner, also, let wives be subject to their husbands: that if any believe not the word, they may be won without the word, by the conversation (= manner of life) of the wives."

inspira, domine meus, deus meus, inspira servis tuis,
fratribus meis, filiis tuis, dominis meis, quibus et corde
et voce et litteris servio, ut quotquot haec legerint, meminerint ad altare tuum Monnicae, famulae tuae, cum Patricio,
60 quondam eius coniuge, per quorum carnem introduxisti
me in hanc vitam, quemadmodum nescio. Meminerint
cum affectu pio parentum meorum in hac luce transitoria
et fratrum meorum sub te patre in matre catholica et
civium meorum in aeterna Hierusalem, cui suspirat pere-
65 grinatio populi tui ab exitu usque ad reditum, ut quod a me
illa poposcit extremum uberius ei praestetur in multorum
orationibus per confessiones quam per orationes meas.

---

56. inspira servis tuis: on the dative, cf. § 82b.

57. quibus et corde . . . servio: " whom I serve by (all the love of) my heart and by my voice (i.e., by my preaching) and by my writings." W-K.

59. Monnicae: St. Monnica is mentioned by name in the *Confessions* here only.

63. fratrum . . . civium: fratrum and **civium** " both refer to Patricius and Monnica, who, while his parents in this transitory life, are also his

' brethren ' as children of the ' Catholic mother ' and his fellow-citizens in the heavenly city." G-M.

64. cui suspirat . . . populi tui: " for which the pilgrimage of Thy people sighs." A. refers to the Christian conception of our life here below as from beginning to end a pilgrimage preliminary to our proper abode in Heaven. On the dative, cf. § 82b.

66. illa: i.e., **Monnica.**

67. per orationes meas: " through my prayers (alone)."

VOCABULARY

Abbreviations Used in Vocabulary

a..........active	loc.......locative
abl.......ablative	m.........masculine
absol......absolutely	n.........neuter
acc.......accusative	neg.......negative
adj.......adjective	num......numeral
adv.......adverb	part......participle, participial
c.........common gender	pass......passive
cf.........compare	pers......personal or person
comp.....comparative	pl........plural
conj......conjunction	pos.......positive
dat.......dative	poss......possessive
def.......defective	p.p.......perfect passive participle
dem......demonstrative	prep......preposition
dep......deponent	pres......present
dim......diminutive	pron......pronoun
distr......distributive	reflex.....reflexive
f.........feminine	rel.......relative
fig.......figuratively	sc.........supply
gen.......genitive	sing......singular
imper.....imperative	subj......subjunctive
impers....impersonal or imperson-	subst.....substantive
ally	sup......supine
indecl.....indeclinable	superl....superlative
indef.....indefinite	v.........verb
inf.......infinitive	v.a.......transitive verb
interj.....interjection	v.n.......intransitive verb
interrog...interrogative	voc.......vocative
irr.......irregular	1, 2, 3, 4, with verbs..1st, 2nd, 3rd,
lit.......literally	or 4th conjugation

VOCABULARY

A

a (**ab, abs**), *prep. with abl.*, *with words or ideas expressing separation*, from, away from; *Conf.* II, 2, 4, **abs te**, away from Thee; *of place*, at, on, from; *of cause*, from, because of; *of time*, after, from, since; **iam inde ab**, even from; *of agency*, by; *of relation*, in regard to; *Conf.* III, 1, 1, **ab interiore cibo**, with respect to . . . ; **ab invicem**, from one another; *Conf.* VIII, 11, 27, **ab ea parte**, on this side

abditus, -a, -um, *part. adj.*, concealed, hidden; *n.*, **abditum, -i**, *as subst.*, secret

abeo, -ire, -ivi, -itum, *irr. v.n.*, go away, depart

aberro, 1.*v.n.*, wander, go astray

abhorreo, -ere, -ui, 2.*v.n.*, shrink back from, abhor, be averse to

abicio, -ere, -ieci, -iectum, 3.*v.a.*, cast out, cast aside

abiectio, -onis, *f.*, dejection, dejectedness

abiectus, -a, -um, *part. adj.*, despicable, unprincipled, low

abluo, -ere, -lui, -lutum, 3.*v.a.*, wash, wash away, cleanse

abripio, -ere, -ripui, -reptum, 3.*v.a.*, tear away, snatch away

abrumpo, -ere, -rupi, -ruptum, 3.*v.a.*, break off, sever

abruptum, -i, *n.*, precipice

abscedo, -ere, -cessi, -cessum, 3.*v.n.*, go away, depart

abscondo, -ere, -condi, -conditum, 3.*v.a.*, conceal, hide

absens, -ntis, *part. adj.*, absent

absentia, -ae, *f.*, absence

absum, abesse, afui, afuturus, *irr. v.n.*, be away, be absent; *Conf.* V, 9, 17, **Absit**, far be (*the thought*) from me

absurde, *adv.*, absurdly, illogically

absurdus, -a, um, *adj.*, absurd

abundo, 1.*v.n.*, abound in, overflow with, be in abundance

abyssus, -i, *f.*, abyss, bottomless deep; the sea

ac, *see* **atque**

Academici, -orum, *m.pl.*, the Academics, *adherents of the Academy or Platonic school of philosophy*

accedo, -ere, -cessi, -cessum, 3.*v.n.*, go to, approach

accelero, 1.*v.a.*, hasten

accendo, -ere, -cendi, -censum, 3.*v.a.*, inflame, excite, provoke, set on fire

acceptabilis, -e, *adj.*, acceptable

acceptus, -a, -um, *part. adj.*, acceptable, agreeable

accessio, -onis, *f.*, *of disease*, attack, paroxysm

accido, -ere, -cidi, *no sup.*, 3.*v.n.*, happen, befall, occur

accingo, -ere, -cinxi, -cinctum, 3.*v.a.*,

gird on; *in pass. with middle sense,* arm one's self, gird one's self

accipio, -ere, -cepi, -ceptum, 3.*v.a.,* take, receive, learn, hear

accusatio, -onis, *f.,* accusation

accusator, -oris, *m.,* accuser

accuso, 1.*v.a.,* accuse

acer, -cris, -cre, *adj.,* subtle, penetrating

acerbe, *adv.,* bitterly

acies, -ei, *f.,* glance, look; acuteness of mind

acriter, *adv.,* strongly, deeply

acsi, *conj. and adv.,* as if

actio, -onis, f., action; *with* **gratiarum,** giving of thanks

actus, -us, *m.,* action, motion, act; *Conf.* IX, 4, 7, **actu,** in fact

acuo, -ere, -ui, -utum, 3.*v.a.,* sharpen; make more fluent

acutus, -a, -um, *adj.,* sharp

ad, *prep. with acc.,* to, towards; *of place,* near to, in vicinity of, at, before, in the presence of; *of purpose,* for, for the purpose of; *of manner,* according to; **ad litteram,** according to the letter, literally

Adam, *indecl., m.,* Adam

adamo, 1.*v.a.,* love earnestly, take pleasure in

adclamo, 1.*v.a.,* applaud, acclaim; *used impers., Conf.* I, 17, 27

addo, -ere, -didi, -ditum, 3.*v.a.,* say in addition, add

Adeodatus, -i, *m.,* Adeodatus, *son of St. Augustine*

adeps, adipis, *c.,* fat

adhaereo, -ere, -haesi, -haesum, 2.*v.n.,* cleave to, stick to, be closely associated with

adhuc, *adv.,* until now, hitherto, as yet, still, more, even

adigo, -ere, -egi, -actum, 3.*v.a.,* force, compel

adipiscor, adipisci, adeptus sum, 3.*v.dep.,* arrive at, reach, obtain

adiungo, -ere, -iunxi, -iunctum, 3.*v.a.,* join; *pass. with middle sense,* join one's self to

adiutor, -oris, *m.,* helper

adiutorium, -ii, *n.,* help, aid

adiuvo, 1.*v.a.,* help, aid

admirabilis, -e, *adj.,* wonderful

admiror, 1.*v.dep.,* wonder at, marvel at

admitto, -ere, -misi, -missum, 3.*v.a.,* admit; *of crime,* perpetrate, commit

admodum, *adv.,* quite, very, in a large measure

admoneo, -ere, -monui, -monitum, 2.*v.a.,* urge, exhort, admonish

admonitio, -onis, *f.,* admonition

admoveo, -ere, -movi, -motum, 2.*v.a.,* move; move up; *pass. with middle sense (of time),* draw near; *of a good,* apply

adpareo, -ere, -ui, -itum, 2.*v.n.,* appear; *frequently impers.,* it is clear, it is manifest

adpono, -ere, -posui, -positum, 3.*v.a.,* put *or* place before

adprehendo, -ere, -prehendi, -prehensum, 3.*v.a.,* seize, lay hold upon

adprime, *adv.,* first of all, especially

adprobo, 1.*v.a.,* approve, receive with favor, make acceptable

adquiesco, -ere, -quievi, -quietum, 3.*v.n.,* rest, repose; *with dat.,* find comfort in, be satisfied with; *with*

in, find rest in; acquiesce, be satisfied

adsensio, -onis, *f.*, assent

adsequor, -sequi, -secutus sum, 3.*v.n.dep.*, gain, obtain

adsertor, -oris, *m.*, defender

adsolet, -ere, 2.*v.semidep.impers.*, it is customary; *especially in phrase* **ut adsolet,** as is wont to happen, as is customary, as is usual

adsto, -are, -stiti, *no sup.*, 1.*v.n.*, stand near, be present, be

adsum, -esse, -fui, -futurus, *irr.v.n.*, be present, be at hand

adsurgo, -ere, -surrexi, -surrectum, 3.*v.n.*, rise up, rise

adtendo, -ere, -tendi, -tentum, 3.*v.a.*, *with or without* **animum,** direct the attention towards, apply the mind to, observe, mark

adtero, *see* **attero**

adtineo, *see* **attineo**

adtingo, -ere, -tigi, -tactum, 3.*v.a.*, touch, reach

adtonitus, *see* **attonitus**

adtraho, -ere, -traxi, -tractum, 3.*v.a.*, attract

adulans, -ntis, *part. adj.*, flattering, fawning

adulescens, -ntis, *m.*, a youth, young man

adulescentia, -ae, *f.*, youth, young manhood

adulescentulus, -i, *m.*, a youth, a very young man

adulterinus, -a, -um, *adj.*, adulterous, impure

adultero, 1.*v.a.*, commit adultery with, defile

adumbratus, -a, -um, *part. adj.*, represented, characterized

advenio, -ire, -veni, -ventum, 4.*v.n.*, come, come near

adventus, -us, *m.*, arrival, coming

adversor, 1.*v.dep.*, oppose, resist

adversus, *prep. with acc.*, against

adversus, -a, -um, *adj.*, adverse; *n. pl. as subst.*, adverse things, adversity

adverto, -ere, -verti, -versum, 3.*v.a.*, = **animadverto,** observe, note

aedes, -ium, *f. pl.*, house

aedifico, 1.*v.a.*, build

aegritudo, -inis, *f.*, sickness, illness

aegroto, -are, -avi, -atum, 1.*v.n.*, be ill, be sick

Aegyptius, -ii, *m.*, an Egyptian

aemulatio, -onis, *f.*, envy

Aeneas, -ae, *m.*, Aeneas, *a Trojan prince, hero of Vergil's Aeneid*

aenigma, -atis, *n.*, obscure passage, crux

aequo, 1.*v.a.*, equal, compare to, make equal; *in pass., Conf.* V, 14, 24, be equal

aequus, -a, -um, *adj.*, fair, just; quiet, contented; **aequo animo,** patiently, with resignation, calmly

aerumnosus, -a, -um, *adj.*, full of hardship, painful

aestimo, 1.*v.a.*, value, estimate, judge

aestuo, 1.*v.n.*, *lit.* boil, seethe; *fig.* boil, seethe (*with passion*), be excited, be concerned, rave, burn, be violently ill

aestus, -us, *m.*, glow, ardor; *Conf.* VI, 3, 3, deep agitation of mind, deep anxiety, mental anguish

aetas, -tatis, *f.*, age

aeternitas, -tatis, *f.*, eternity

aeternus, -a, -um, *adj.*, eternal; **in aeternum,** forever

Afer, Afri, *m.*, an African
affectio, -onis, *f.*, disposition, affection
affectus, -us, *m.*, disposition, affection, love, passion, feeling, animation
affectus, -a, -um, *part. adj.*, affected, disposed
affero, -ferre, attuli, allatum, *irr.v.a.*, bring, carry to
afficio, -ere, -feci, -fectum, 3.*v.a.*, affect, influence
affigo, -ere, -fixi, -fictum, 3.*v.a.*, affix, attach to
affixus, -a, -um, *part. adj.*, joined to, close to
affligo, -ere, -ixi, -ictum, 3.*v.a.*, afflict
Africa, -ae, *f.*, Africa
ager, agri, *m.*, field
agglutino, 1.*v.a.*, cement, solder
aggredior, -gredi, -gressus sum, 3.*v.dep.*, begin
agnosco, -ere, -novi, -notum, 3.*v.a.*, recognize, know
ago, -ere, -egi, actum, 3.*v.a.*, lead, do, act, perform; *with* **cum,** urge something on a person, persuade, argue with, deal with, talk with; *of time,* pass, live, spend; *Conf.* VIII, 6, 13, **maiora . . . agere,** derive greater returns; *pres. part. m. as subst.,* **agens in rebus,** an imperial agent
agon, -onis, *m.*, contest
aio, *v.def.*, say; *2nd pers. sing. perf.,* **aisti,** *Conf.* I, 19, 30
ala, -ae, *f.*, wing
alacer, -cris, -cre, *adj.*, eager, happy, cheerful
alibi, *adv.*, elsewhere

alienus, -a, -um, *adj.*, belonging *or* relating to another
alimentum, -i, *n.*, food, nourishment
aliquando, *adv.*, once, once upon a time, formerly, in those days, sometimes, finally, at last
aliquantulus, -a, -um, *adj.*, little, small
aliquantum, *adv. of time,* a little while, some time more
aliqui, -qua, -quod, *indef. adj. and pron.,* some, any
aliquis, -qua, -quid, *indef. pron.,* some one, any one
aliter, *adv.*, otherwise, in another way
alius, -a, -ud, *pron. adj.*, other, another, different
allevo, 1.*v.a.*, lighten, comfort
allido, -ere, -lisi, -lisum, 3.*v.a.*, dash down, strike down
alligo, 1.*v.a.*, bind
alludo, -ere, -lusi, -lusum, 3.*v.a.*, play with, sport with, jest with
alo, alere, alui, altum, 3.*v.a.*, nourish, feed
altare, -is, *n.*, altar
alte, *adv.*, deeply
alter, -tera, -terum, *pron. adj.*, the other (*of two*), another, the second
alterno, 1.*v.n.*, change; *of winds,* blow one way and then another
alternus, -a, -um, *adj.*, by turns, alternate
altitudo, -inis, *f.*, depth
altum, -i, *n.*, height, depth; **ex alto,** from on high
altus, -a, -um, *adj.*, deep
Alypius, -ii, *m.*, Alypius, *a young friend of Augustine*

amare, *adv.*, bitterly
amaritudo, -dinis, *f.*, bitterness
amarus, -a, -um, *adj.*, bitter, unpleasant
ambio, -ire, -ivi, (-ii), -itum, 4.*v.n.* and *a.*, solicit, apply (*for a position*), strive, seek
ambo, -ae, -o, *adj.*, both
Ambrosianus, -a, um, *adj.*, Ambrosian, pertaining to Ambrose
Ambrosius, -ii, *m.*, Ambrose
ambulo, 1.*v.n.*, walk, go; *Conf.* I, 13, 20, pass away
amica, -ae, *f.*, a friend
amicitia, -ae, *f.*, friendship
amicus, -i, *m.*, a friend
amitto, -ere, -misi, -missum, 3.*v.a.*, lose
amo, 1.*v.a.*, love, delight in, desire
amoenus, -a, -um, *adj.*, pleasant, delightful
amor, -oris, *m.*, love, desire, passion
amplector, -plecti, -plexus sum, 3.*v.dep.*, embrace
amplexor, -ari, -atus sum, 1.*v.dep.*, embrace
amplexus, -us, *m.*, embrace
amplius, *comp. adv.*, more, longer, further
amplus, -a, -um, *adj.*, large, great
an, *conj.*; *in disjunctive interrog. statements, introducing the second member*, whether, or, or rather (*see* utrum); *also used with second member when interrog. particle is omitted in first member, as in Conf.* I, 6, 7; *sometimes used to introduce direct questions, in which case it is often not to be translated*
anceps, ancipitis, *adj.*, uncertain

ancilla, -ae, *f.*, a female servant, handmaid
angelus, -i, *m.*, an angel
anhelo, 1.*v.a.*, breathe out, exhale
anilis, -e, *adj.*, of *or* belonging to an old woman
anima, -ae, *f.*, soul
animadverto, -ere, -verti, -versum 3.*v.a.*, give attention, note, observe
animans, -ntis, *pres. part. used as subst.*, *m.*, *f.*, *and n.*, a living being, creature
animositas, -tatis, *f.*, ambition
animus, -i, *m.*, mind, disposition, heart, soul; purpose, intention
annus, -i, *m.*, year
ante, *as adv.*, before, first, ago; *as prep. with acc.*, *of place or time*, before; ante biennium, two years before
antea, *adv.*, before
antequam, *adv.*, before
antidotum, -i, *n.*, an antidote
antiquus, -a, -um, *adj.*, old, of olden times, ancient
antistes, -stitis, *m.*, a bishop
Antonius, -ii, *m.* Anthony (*of Egypt*)
anus, -us, *f.*, an old woman; *Conf.* VIII, 11, 27, virgines anus, aged virgins
anxietas, -tatis, *f.*, grief
anxitudo, -inis, *f.*, anxiety
anxius, -a, -um, *adj.*, anxious, causing trouble *or* anguish
aperio, -ire, -ui, -tum, 4.*v.a.*, open, reveal, make known, explain
apertus, -a, -um, *part. adj.*, clear
apostolicus, -a, -um, *adj.*, of *or* belonging to an apostle, apostolic
apostolus, -i, *m.*, apostle

apotheca, -ae, *f.*, storeroom

apparatus, -a, -um, *part. adj.*, sumptuous, splendid

appareo, *see* adpareo

appello, 1.*v.a.*, call, name

appeto, -ere, -petivi, (-ii), -petitum, 3.*v.a.*, desire, seek

applico, 1.*v.a.*, turn, direct towards

aptus, -a, -um, *adj.*, fit, suitable, apt

apud, *prep. with acc.*, with, by, at, before, in the presence of

aqua, -ae, *f.*, water

aqualiculus, -i, *m.*, stomach, paunch

arbiter, -tri, *m.*, judge, arbiter

arbitror, 1.*v.dep.*, think, be of opinion

arbor, -oris, *f.*, tree; arbor fici, fig tree

arcanus, -a, -um, *adj.*, hidden, secret

ardens, -ntis, *part. adj.*, ardent, eager

ardenter, *adv.*, violently, hotly, ardently

ardeo, -ere, arsi, -arsum, 2.*v.n.*, burn, be strongly affected, desire ardently

ardor, -oris, *m.*, ardor, passion

area, -ae, *f.*, square, playground

argentum, -i, *n.*, silver

argumentum, -i, *n.*, argument, proof

arguo, -ere, -ui, -utum, 3.*v.a.*, accuse, charge, blame; make manifest, make known

armatus, -a, -um, *part. adj.*, armed; *m. pl. as subst.*, armed men

aroma, -atis, *n.*, spice

Arriani, -orum, *m. pl.*, the followers of Arius, the Arians

arrideo, -ere, -risi, -risum, 2.*v.n.*, laugh with, laugh at, smile at, smile upon

arripio, -ere, -ripui, -reptum, 3.*v.a.*, take up, embrace

ars, artis, *f.*, art, skill; *in pl.*, pursuits, studies, the (*liberal*) arts

artus, -a, -um, *adj.*, serious, deep; close, tight

artus, -us, *m.*, *usually pl.*, limbs

ascendo, -ere, -scendi, -scensum, 3.*v.n.*, go up, enter

aspectus, -us, *m.*, gaze, look, view

asper, -era, -erum, *adj.*, rough; *n. pl. as subst.*, *Conf.* IX, 4, 7, rough ways

aspergo, -ere, -spersi, -spersum, 3.*v.a.*, sprinkle, mingle with

asperitas, -tatis, *f.*, harshness, severity

aspicio, -ere, -spexi, -spectum, 3.*v.a.*, look at, behold

asporto, 1.*v.a.*, rob, plunder

assero, -ere, -serui, -sertum, 3.*v.a.*, claim, assert, maintain

assessio, -onis, *f.*, assession

assolet, *see* adsolet

asto, *see* adsto

at, *conj.*, but yet, and again, but, now, at least; at enim, but certainly, but indeed

atque (*before consonants*, ac), *conj.*, and, and also; ac si, just as if

atrociter, *adv.*, harshly, savagely, bitterly

atrox, -ocis, *adj.*, savage, cruel, terrible

attero, -ere, -trivi, -tritum, 3.*v.a.*, waste, trifle away, wear down, wear away

attineo, -ere, -tinui, -tentum, 2.*v.a.*, hold near; *v.n.*, pertain, concern, *only in 3rd person;* **quod (quantum)** **attinet ad,** as regards, in respect to, *Conf.* V, 13, 23 *and Conf.* IX, 10, 26

attingo, -ere, -tigi, -tactum, 3.*v.a.,* touch, reach to

attonitus, -a, -um, *part. adj.,* astonished, amazed, terrified

auctor, -oris, *m.,* author

auctoritas, -tatis, *f.,* authority, power; *of medicine,* efficacy

aucupor, 1.*v.dep.,* strive for, seek to catch

audeo, -ere, ausus sum, 2.*v.semidep.,* dare

audio, -ire, -ivi, -itum, 4.*v.a.,* hear, learn

auditor, -oris, *m.,* hearer, auditor

aufero, -ferre, abstuli, ablatum, *irr.v.a.,* snatch away, pull away, take away, carry away, steal

augeo, -ere, auxi, auctum, 2.*v.a.,* increase

aura, -ae, *f.,* air

auris, -is, *f.,* the ear

aurum, -i, *n.,* gold

ausus, -us, *m.,* act of daring

aut, *conj., introducing an alternative, usually exclusive,* or, or else; **aut . . . aut,** either . . . or

autem, *conj., introducing an antithesis or a transition, but usually with some idea of contrast,* but, on the contrary, again, furthermore

auxilium, -ii, *n.,* help, aid

avarus, -a, -um, *adj.,* avaricious

avello, -ere, -velli, *and* **-vulsi, -vulsum,** 3.*v.a.,* drive away

aversor, 1.*v.dep.,* turn away, shun, avoid

averto, -ere, -ti, -sum, 3.*v.a.,* turn away, avert; *p.p. as adj.,* turned away, withdrawn from

aviditas, -tatis, *f.,* eagerness, desire, avidity, greediness

avidus, -a, -um, *adj.,* longing, eager

avoco, 1.*v.a.,* call away, divert

B

balneum, -i, *n.,* bath

baptismum (*and* **-us), -i,** *n.* (*and m.*), Baptism

baptizo, 1.*v.a.,* baptize

barbarismus, -i, *m.,* a barbarism

basilica, -ae, *f.,* basilica

beatus, -a, -um, *adj.,* blessed, happy

bene, *adv.,* well; *comp.,* **melius;** *superl.,* **optime**

benedico, -ere, -dixi, -dictum, 3.*v.n.,* bless

beneficium, -ii, *n.,* benefit

benevole, *adv.,* kindly

benevolentia, -ae, *f.,* good will, kindness

benignus, -a, -um, *adj.,* kind, benevolent

benivole, *see* **benevole**

benivolentia, *see* **benevolentia**

bibo, -ere, bibi, *no sup.,* 3.*v.a.,* drink, drink in

biennium, -ii, *n.,* period of two years, two years

bilis, -is, *f.,* gall, bile; *fig.,* anger

bis, *adv.,* twice

blandimentum, -i, *n., usually pl.,* flattering words, blandishments

blandior, -iri, -itus sum, 4.*v.dep.,* attract, invite

blandus, -a, -um, *adj.,* flattering, alluring, kind

blasphemia, -ae, *f.,* blasphemy

bonitas, -tatis, *f.,* goodness

bonum, -i, *n.*, a good

bonus, -a, -um, *adj.*, good, noble, virtuous, rich; *comp.*, melior, *superl.*, optimus; *n. pl. comp.* meliora *as subst.*, better things, a better course

breviter, *adv.*, briefly

C

cadaver, -eris, *n.*, corpse

cado, -ere, cecidi, casum, 3.*v.n.*, fall

caecitas, -tatis, *f.*, blindness

caecus, -a, -um, *adj.*, blind

caedo, -ere, caesi, caesum, 3.*v.a.*, strike, beat

caelibatus, -us, *m.*, celibacy

caelum, -i, *n.*, heaven, Heaven; *also in m.pl.*, caeli, -orum, the heavens, Heaven

calamitas, -tatis, *f.*, calamity, misfortune

caliculus, -i, *m.*, a cup

caligo, -inis, *f.*, mist, darkness

callidus, -a, -um, *adj.*, crafty

calor, -oris, *m.*, heat

calumnia, -ae, *f.*, calumny

cani, -orum (*sc.* capilli), *m.pl.*, grey hair

cano, -ere, cecini, cantum, 3.*v.a.*, sing

canticum, -i, *n.*, song

cantio, -onis, *f.*, song; *Conf.* I, 13, 22, sing-song

cantito, 1.*v.a.*, sing repeatedly

canto, 1.*v.a.*, chant, sing of, sing, repeat

cantus, -us, *m.*, song, singing, singing tone

capax, -acis, *adj.*, capacious; susceptible, fit

capillus, -i, *m.*, a hair

capio, -ere, cepi, captum, 3.*v.a.*, take, occupy

capitulum, -i, *n.*, chapter

captus, -us, *m.*, capacity

caput, capitis, *n.*, head; life; chapter

cardo, -inis, *m.*, a hinge; the chief *or* cardinal point

care, *adv.*, dearly

careo, -ere, -ui, -iturus, 2.*v.n.*, be without, dispense with

caritas, -tatis, *f.*, love, charity

carmen, -inis, *n.*, song, poem, poetry

carnalis, -e, *adj.*, of the flesh, carnal

carnaliter, *adv.*, carnally

carneus, -a, -um, *adj.*, fleshly, carnal

caro, carnis, *f.*, flesh; the body, the flesh, *as opposed to the soul*

Carthago, -inis, *f.*, Carthage, *the metropolis of North Africa in Augustine's time, and one of the most famous cities of the ancient world*

carus, -a, -um, *adj.*, dear

casa, -ae, *f.*, hut

castitas, -tatis, *f.*, chastity

castus, -a, -um, *adj.*, chaste, pure

catechumenus, -i, *m.*, a catechumen

catena, -ae, *f.*, a chain

caterva, -ae, *f.*, crowd, throng

catholicus, -a, -um, *adj.*, Catholic; *as subst. m.*, Catholicus, -i, a Catholic

causa, -ae, *f.*, cause, reason; affair, concern; *abl.*, causa, *with gen.*, on account of, for the sake of

caveo, -ere, cavi, cautum, 2.*v.n. and a.*, take care, guard against

-ce, *inseparable strengthening demonstrative particle joined to adverbs and pronouns*

cedo, ere, cessi, cessum, 3.*v.n.*,

yield, submit; concede, grant, permit

cedrus, -i, *f.*, the cedar

celebro, 1.*v.a.*, celebrate, practice, solemnize

celeritas, -tatis, *f.*, speed, swiftness

celeriter, *adv.*, quickly, speedily

cellarium, -ii, *n.*, pantry, cellar, storeroom

censeo, -ere, censui, censum, 2.*v.a.*, be of an opinion, think

cera, -ae, *f.*, wax; a writing tablet coated with wax

certamen, -inis, *n.*, contest

certe, *adv.*, certainly, surely

certus, -a, -um, *adj.*, certain, fixed

cervix, -icis, *f.*, the neck

cesso, -are, -avi, -atum, 1.*v.n.*, hold back, delay, stop

ceterum, *adv.*, for the rest, otherwise, but

ceterus, -a, -um, *adj.*, *usually in pl.*, the other, rest, remainder

chirographum, -i, *n.*, that which is written with one's own hand, a handwriting; a signed pledge, a bond

Christianus, -i, *m.*, a Christian

Christus, -i, *m.*, Christ

cibus, -i, *m.*, food

Cicero, -onis, *m.*, Cicero

cinis, -eris, *m.*, ashes

circenses, -ium, (*sc.* ludi), *m. pl.*, the contests, games of the circus

circumfero, -ferre, -tuli, -latum, *irr.v.a.*, carry round

circumfluo, -ere, -fluxi, *no sup.*, 3.*v.n.*, flow about, be present in abundance

circumstrepo, -ere, *no perf.*, -strepi-

tum, 3.*v.a.*, hum about, make a noise about

circumventorius, -a, -um, *adj.*, deceitful, fraudulent

circumvolo, 1.*v.a. and n.*, fly around, hover around

cito, *adv.*, quickly

civis, -is, *m.*, citizen

civitas, -tatis, *f.*, city

clamo, 1.*v.n. and a.*, cry, cry out, call

clanculo, *adv.*, secretly

clareo, -ere, 2.*v.n.*, shine; be distinguished

claudo, -ere, clausi, clausum, 3.*v.a.*, close

coaetaneus, -a, -um, *adj.*, of the same age

coaevus, -a, -um, *adj.*, of the same age

coarto, 1.*v.a.*, compress; *pass. with middle sense*, get one's self into tight quarters *or* into difficulty

coctus, -a, -um, *part. adj.*, ripened; strengthened, made fast

codex, -icis, *m.*, a codex, book

coepi, coepisse, coeptum, *def.v.a. and n.*, begin

coetus, -us, *m.*, gathering, assembly, circle

cogitatio, -onis, *f.*, thought, the faculty of thought

cogitatus, -us, *m.*, thought

cogito, 1.*v.a.*, think of, consider, reflect

cognosco, -ere, -novi, -nitum, 3.*v.a.*, become acquainted with, know, acknowledge

cogo, -ere, coegi, coactum, 3.*v.a.*, force, compel

cohaereo, -ere, -haesi, -haesum, 2.*v.n.*, cling to, cleave to

coherceo, -ere, -ui, -itum, 2.*v.a.*,
check, restrain

cohercitio, -onis, *f.*, restraint, coercion

cohibeo, -ere, -ui, -itum, 2.*v.a.*,
hold in check, check, stop; *Conf.*
VIII, 7, 16, keep (*from sight*)

colligo, -ere, -legi, -lectum, 3.*v.a.*,
collect, gather; *Conf.* II, 1, 1, colligens me, gathering me together

collis, -is, *m.*, hill

color, -oris, *m.*, color, complexion

coloro, 1.*v.a.*, color

combinatus, -a, -um, *part. adj.*,
united in pairs, two by two

comedo, -ere, -edi, -esum, 3.*v.a.*, eat

comisatio, -onis, *f.*, reveling, rioting

commemoro, *see* conmemoro

commodum, -i, *n.*, advantage, profit,
gain

commoveo, -ere, -movi, -motum,
2.*v.a.*, move, affect

comparo, *see* conparo

compatior, -pati, -passus sum,
3.*v.dep.*, sympathize with

compello, -ere, -puli, -pulsum, 3.*v.a.*,
compel, force

comperio, -ire, -peri, -pertum, 4.*v.a.*,
find, find out, learn; *p.p.* compertus *as adj.*, disclosed, revealed

conatus, -us, *m.*, attempt, striving

concedo, -ere, -cessi, -cessum,
3.*v.n. and a.*, grant, give

concepta, -orum, *p.p. as subst. in
n.pl.*, thoughts

concino, -ere, -cinui, *no sup.* 3.*v.n.*,
sing together, sing harmoniously

concio, -ire, -ivi, -itum, 4.*v.a.*,
arouse, excite, move

concisus, -a, -um, *part. adj.*, lacerated, rent, broken

concorditer, *adv.*, harmoniously,
amicably

concubitus, -us, *m.*, sensual pleasure

concupiscentia, -ae, *f.*, concupiscence

concupisco, -ere, -pivi, (-pii), -pitum,
3.*v.a.*, desire eagerly, covet

concurro, -ere, -curri, -cursum,
3.*v.n.*, run, rush

concutio, -ere, -cussi, -cussum,
3.*v.a.*, shake, disturb, trouble

condio, -ire, -ivi, (-ii), -itum, 4.*v.a.*,
season, embalm

conditio, -onis, *f.*, condition, state

conditor, -oris, *m.*, creator

condoctor, -oris, *m.*, fellow teacher

confectus, -a, -um, *part. adj.*, worn
out, overcome

confero, -ferre, -tuli, -latum, *irr.v.a.*,
bring together, join, discuss; *with*
conloquium, enter upon, engage
in; compare

confessio, -onis, *f.*, confession

confestim, *adv.*, immediately

conficio, -ere, -feci, -fectum, 3.*v.a.*,
make, complete, prepare; *with*
ex, make . . . out of

confirmo, 1.*v.a.*, confirm, prove

confiteor, -eri, -fessus sum, 2.*v.dep.*,
confess; acknowledge, give glory
to

conflo, 1.*v.a.*, fuse

conflorens, -ntis, *part.adj.*, flourishing together

confluo, -ere, -fluxi, *no sup.*, 3.*v.n.*,
flow

confricatio, -onis, *f.*, friction, interfriction

confundo, -ere, -fudi, -fusum, 3.*v.a.*,
confuse, confound, trouble

confusio, -onis, *f.*, confusion

confusus, -a, -um, *part.adj.*, con-

fused, disordered; *n.sing. as subst.*
in phrase in **confuso**, in confusion,
in a confused manner

congero, -ere, -gessi, -gestum, 3.*v.a.*,
collect, heap together

congratulor, 1.*v.dep.*, wish joy, congratulate

congrego, 1.*v.a.*, bring together,
gather

congruens, -ntis, *part.adj.*, appropriate, suitable, in accordance
with

congruenter, *adv.*, suitably, appropriately

congruus, -a, -um, *adj.*, suitable, in
accordance with

conicio, -ere, -ieci, -iectum, 3.*v.a.*
cast, direct; guess, conjecture

coniecto, -are, -avi, -atum, 1.*v.a.*,
conclude, conjecture

coniugium, -ii, *n.*, marriage

coniungo, -ere, -iunxi, -iunctum,
3.*v.a.*, join, unite; *pass. with middle sense*, join one's self to

coniux, -iugis, *f. and m.*, wife,
husband; *pl.*, husband and wife

conlector, -oris, *m.*, fellow student

conlocutor, -oris, *m.*, interlocutor

conloquium, -ii, *n.*, talk, conversation, conference, discourse

conloquor, -loqui, -locutus sum,
3.*v.dep.*, speak, converse with, talk

conlusor, -oris, *m.*, playmate

conmemoro, 1.*v.a.*, mention

conmendo, 1.*v.a.*, recommend, commend

conmitto, -ere, -misi, -missum,
3.*v.a.*, give up, commit to, entrust; *of crime*, commit

conmixtio, -onis, *f.*, a mixing,
mingling, mixture

conmodum, *see* **commodum**

conmoveo, *see* **commoveo**

conmunico, 1.*v.a.*, communicate

conor, 1.*v.dep.*, attempt, try

conparabilis, -e, *adj.*, comparable

conparatio, -onis, *f.*, comparison

conparo, 1.*v.a.*, compare

conparo, 1.*v.a.*, obtain, gain

conpello, *see* **compello**

conperio, *see* **comperio**

conplano, 1.*v.a.*, level *or* make plane

conposite, *adv.*, in an orderly *or*
skillful manner, ornately

conprehendo, -ere, -hendi, -hensum,
3.*v.a.*, comprehend, understand

conprimo, -ere, -pressi, -pressum,
3.*v.a.*, repress, check, restrain

conputo, 1.*v.a.*, compute, reckon up

conputresco, -ere, -putrui, *no sup.*,
3.*v.n.*, putrefy, become wholly
putrid

conrideo, -ere, -risi, -risum, 2.*v.n.*,
laugh together

conscientia, -ae, *f.*, conscience

conscius, -a, -um, *adj.*, conscious,
conscious to one's self; conscious
of guilt, guilty

conscribo, -ere, -scripsi, -scriptum,
3.*v.a.*, write, compose

consensio, -onis, *f.*, agreement,
unanimity

consideratio, -onis, *f.*, meditation,
thought, consideration

considero, 1.*v.a.*, consider

consido, -ere, -sedi, -sessum, 3.*v.n.*,
sit down

consilium, -ii, *n.*, plan, design, purpose, counsel, resolution

consocio, 1.*v.a.*, associate with

consolatio, -onis, *f.*, consolation

consolator, -oris, *m.*, comforter

consolor, 1.*v.dep.*, *pass.* *Conf.* VI, 1, 1, console

consortium, -ii, *n.*, company, fellowship, society

conspectus, -us, *m.*, sight, presence; in conspectu tuo (*also* in conspectum tuum), in Thy sight, *i.e.* before Thee

conspiro, 1.*v.n.*, unite, form a plot

constituo, -ere, -stitui, -stitutum, 3.*v.a.*, put, place, set

constringo, -ere, -strinxi, -strictum, 3.*v.a.*, restrain, suppress

consuetudo, -inis, *f.*, custom

consulo, -ere, -sului, -sultum, 3.*v.a. and n.*, take counsel, deliberate, take thought for

consumo, -ere, -sumpsi, -sumptum, 3.*v.a.*, consume, exhaust, destroy

contabesco, -ere, -tabui, *no sup.*, 3.*v.n.*, wither away, waste away, weaken

contactus, -us, *m.*, touch, contact

contego, -ere, -texi, -tectum, 3.*v.a.*, cover

contemno, -ere, -tempsi, -temtum, 3.*v.a.*, despise, make little of, reject

contemptor, -oris, *m.*, scorner, despiser

contemptus, (*and* contemtus), -us, *m.*, contempt

contenebro, 1.*v.a.*, darken

contentio, -onis, *f.*, contention

contentiosus, -a, -um, *adj.*, of *or* belonging to a contest *or* competition

contentus, -a, -um, *part. adj.*, content, satisfied

contero, -ere, -trivi, -tritum, 3.*v.a.*, wear away, wear down, break

conticesco, -ere, -ticui, *no sup.*, 3.*v.n.*, become silent

contiguus, -a, -um, *adj.*, contiguous, near

continens, -ntis, *part.adj.*, continent

continentia, -ae, *f.*, continence

contineo, -ere, -tinui, -tentum, 2.*v.a.*, contain, hold back

continuo, *adv.*, immediately, at once

contra, *as adv.*, in opposition, on the other hand; *as prep. with acc.*, against, contrary to

contradico, -ere, -dixi, -dictum, 3.*v.n.*, gainsay, oppose

contraho, -ere, -traxi, -tractum, 3.*v.a.*, form, contract

contrarius, -a, -um, *adj.*, opposite, opposed, contrary

contritio, -onis, *f.*, grief, contrition

contritus, -a, -um, *part. adj.*, contrite

controversia, -ae, *f.*, debate, discussion

contubernalis, -is, *m.*, comrade, companion

contumeliosus, -a, -um, *adj.*, abusive, reproachful

conturbo, 1.*v.a.*, disturb, trouble

convalesco, -ere, -valui, *no sup.*, 3.*v.n.*, recover from sickness, get well

convenio, -ire, -veni, -ventum 4.*v.n.*, come together; fit, be in agreement with

conversatio, -onis, *f.*, conversation; manner of life, life

converto, -ere, -verti, -versum, 3.*v.a.*, turn, set before; *fig.*, alter, change, convert

convicium, -ii, *n.*, insult, reproach

convinco, -ere, -vici, -victum, 3.*v.a.*,

overcome, refute, convince, prove, convict

convivium, -ii, *n.*, feast, banquet

copia, -ae, *f.*, opportunity

copiose, *adv.*, copiously, fully, at length

copiosus, -a, -um, *adj.*, copious, abounding, plentiful, wealthy

cor, cordis, *n.*, the heart; *fig.*, heart, soul (*both in a moral and an intellectual sense*)

coram, *adv.*, and *prep. with abl.*, before, in the presence of

corona, -ae, *f.*, crown, garland

corporalis, -e, *adj.*, relating to the body, corporeal

corporaliter, *adv.*, corporally, in a corporal manner

corporeus, -a, -um, *adj.*, of *or* belonging to the body, corporeal, bodily

corpus, -oris, *n.*, body; structure

corrigo, -ere, -rexi, -rectum, 3.*v.a.*, set right, correct

corrumpo, -ere, -rupi, -ruptum, 3.*v.a.*, corrupt

corruptio, -onis, *f.*, corruption

cotidianus, -a, -um, *adj.*, daily

cotidie, *adv.*, daily

cras, *adv.*, tomorrow

creator, -oris, *m.*, creator

creatura, -ae, *f.*, creation, creature

creber, -bra, -brum, *adj.*, numerous, frequent

crebro, *adv.*, frequently, often

credo, -ere, -didi, -ditum, 3.*v.a.*, believe, trust, put faith in; **credere in Deum,** to believe in God; *parenthetically,* **credo,** I believe, I imagine

creo, 1.*v.a.*, create

cresco, -ere, crevi, cretum, 3.*v.n.*, grow up, increase

Creusa, -ae, *f.*, Creusa, *the wife of the Trojan hero Aeneas*

crimen, -inis, *n.*, accusation, reproach

criticus, -a, -um, *adj.*, decisive, critical

cruciatus, -us, *m.*, torture, torment, punishment

crudelitas, -tatis, *f.*, cruelty

cruentus, -a, -um, *adj.*, bloody, blood-stained, bleeding

crux, crucis, *f.*, a cross; *especially,* the Cross of Christ

cubiculum, -i, *n.*, chamber

cubile, -is, *n.*, a bed, bedchamber; *in pl., Conf.* VIII, 12, 29, chambering

cultor, -oris, *m.*, worshiper

cultura, -ae, *f.*, cultivation, husbandry

cum, *conj.*; *temporal,* when, while, whenever; **cum tamen,** while nevertheless, while during this time; *causal,* because; *concessive,* although

cum, *prep. with abl.*, with

cumulate, *adv.*, copiously, abundantly

cunctabundus, -a, -um, *adj.*, delaying

cunctatio, -onis, *f.*, hesitation

cunctor, -ari, -atus sum, 1.*v.dep.*, delay, hesitate

cupa, -ae, *f.*, cask

cupiditas, -tatis, *f.*, desire, passionate longing, passion

cupido, -inis, *f.*, desire

cupio, -ere, -ivi (-ii), -itum, 3.*v.a.*, desire, long for, wish

cur, *interrog. adv.*, why? wherefore?

cura, -ae, *f.*, care, solicitude

curatio, -onis, *f.*, healing, cure

curiositas, -tatis, *f.*, curiosity

curo, 1.*v.a.*, care for, have concern for, watch over; heal, cure

curro, -ere, cucurri, cursum, 3.*v.n.*, run

cursus, -us, *m.*, course

custodio, -ire, -ivi (-ii), -itum, 4.*v.a.*, guard, protect

custos, -odis, *m.*, guardian, protector

Cyprianus, -i, *m.*, Cyprian, *bishop of Carthage, martyred 258 A.D.*

D

daemon, -onis, *m.*, demon

daemonium, -ii, *n.*, demon, devil

damnabilis, -e, *adj.*, worthy of condemnation, damnable, detestable

damno, 1.*v.a.*, condemn

David, *indecl.*, *m.*, David

de, *prep. with abl.*, from, down from, away from, out of; *in partitive sense*, from, of, out of; *of cause*, on account of, from; *fig.*, concerning, of, in regard to, as to

deambulo, 1.*v.n.*, take a walk

debeo, -ere, -ui, -itum, 2.*v.a.*, owe, be indebted to, ought, must; *p.p. as adj.*, **debitus, -a, -um,** due; *n. as subst.*, **debitum, -i,** a debt

debitor, -oris, *m.*, debtor

decem, *indecl. num.*, ten

decennium, -ii, *n.*, a period of ten years

decenter, *adv.*, decently, properly

deceptor, -oris, *m.*, deceiver

decerno, -ere, -crevi, -cretum, 3.*v.a.*, decide, resolve, resolve upon

decet, decere, decuit, 2.*v.impers.*, it is becoming, it is fitting

decido, -ere, -cidi, *no sup.*, 3.*v.n.*, fall

decimus, -a, -um, *adj.*, tenth

decipio, -ere, -cepi, -ceptum, 3.*v.a.*, deceive

declino, -are, -avi, -atum, 1.*v.n.*, decline, depart

decorus, -a, -um, *adj.*, beautiful

decrepitus, -a, -um, *adj.*, very old, decrepid

decumbo, -ere, -cubui, *no sup.*, 3.*v.n.*, fall ill

dedecet, -decere, -decuit, 2.*v.impers.*, it is unbecoming, it is unfitting

dedecus, -coris, *n.*, disgrace, shame, dishonor, infamy

dedignor, 1.*v.dep.*, disdain, scorn, refuse

dedoceo, -ere, -docui, -doctum, 2.*v.a.*, cause one to unlearn, unteach

deduco, -ere, -duxi, -ductum, 3.*v.a.*, lead down, bring down

defectus, -us, *m.*, defect, want, falling off, failing; *Conf.* IX, 11, 27, **defectus animae,** a swoon

defendo, -ere, -fendi, -fensum, 3.*v.a.*, defend

defensio, -onis, *f.*, defense

defero, -ferre, -tuli, -latum, *irr.v.a.*, render, defer, give

deficio, -ere, -feci, -fectum, 3.*v.n.*, fail, be wanting; *Conf.* V, 6, 10, be unable to answer; *Conf.* VI, 4, 6, *with* **ex nullo,** be wanting in nothing deflecto, -ere, -flexi, -flexum, 3.*v.a.*, turn, turn aside

deformis, -e, *adj.*, deformed; *n.pl. as subst.*, deformities

deformiter, *adv.*, shamefully, basely

defungor, -fungi, -functus sum, 3.*v.dep.*, die; *p.p. as adj.*, defunctus, -a, -um, dead

deiectio, -onis, *f.*, a casting down, dejection, degradation

deinde, *adv.*, then, thereupon, next

delectatio, -onis, *f.*, delight, that which causes delight, pleasure

delecto, 1.*v.a.*, please, delight

deleo, -ere, -levi, -letum, 2.*v.a.*, efface, destroy, blot out

deliciae, -arum, *f.pl.*, delight, pleasure

delictum, -i, *n.*, offense, sin, crime

deligo, -ere, -legi, -lectum, 3.*v.a.*, choose

deliramentum, -i, *n.*, nonsense, absurdity, trifle

deliro, 1.*v.n.*, dote, rave, rant

demens, -ntis, *adj.*, out of one's mind, insane, foolish

dementia, -ae, *f.*, madness, folly

demonstro, 1.*v.a.*, set forth, characterize

denique, *adv.*, finally, in short

dens, dentis, *m.*, tooth

densus, -a, -um, *adj.*, frequent

deploro, 1.*v.a.*, deplore, bemoan

depono, -ere, -posui, -positum, 3.*v.a.*, bury

deprecatio, -onis, *f.*, prayer, petition

deprecor, 1.*v.dep.*, entreat, beg of, beseech

deprehendo, -ere, -hendi, -hensum, 3.*v.a.*, catch, detect

depromo, -ere, -prompsi, -promptum, 3.*v.a.*, draw out

derideo, -ere, -risi, -risum, 2.*v.a.*, laugh to scorn, scoff at

descendo, -ere, -scendi, -scensum, 3.*v.n.*, come down, descend

desero, -ere, -serui, -sertum, 3.*v.a.*, desert, forsake, abandon

desertor, -oris, *m.*, one who abandons, deserter

desertus, -a, -um, *p.adj.*, deserted, abandoned, waste; *Conf.* II, 3, 5, uncultivated (*to keep the play on words in the Latin*); *n.pl. as subst.*, solitudes, wastes

desiderium, -ii, *n.*, longing, desire

desidero, 1.*v.a.*, long for, desire

desino, -ere, -sivi, -situm, 3.*v.a. and n.*, stop, cease, desist from

desperatio, -onis *f.*, despair

despero -are -avi -atum, 1.*v.n. and a.*, be without hope, despair, despair of

despicio, -ere, -spexi, -spectum, 3.*v.a.*, despise

destituo, -ere, -stitui, -stitutum, 3.*v.a.*, desert; *in pass.*, be deprived of

desum, -esse, -fui, -futurus, *irr.v.n.*, be absent, be wanting, be lacking, fail

desuper, *adv.*, from above

deterior, -ius, *comp. adj.*, worse

detestor, 1.*v.dep.*, detest, abominate, abhor

detraho, -ere, -traxi, -tractum, 3.*v.a.*, remove, take away; *fig.*, *Conf.* III, 11, 20, bring down, reduce

deus, -i, *m.*, a god, God; *voc.*, Deus meus, *used in Conf. in place of* mi Deus; Dominus Deus, the Lord God

devenio, -ire, -veni, -ventum, 4.*v.n.*, come to, arrive at

devito, 1.*v.a.*, avoid, shun

devolvo, -ere, -volvi, -volutum, 3.*v.a.*, roll down; *pass. with middle force*, roll on, pass on

dextera, -ae, (*sc.* manus), *f.*, right hand

diabolicus, -a, -um, *adj.*, diabolical

diabolus, -i, *m.*, devil, the Devil

dico, 1.*v.a.*, dedicate

dico, -ere, dixi, dictum, 3.*v.a.*, say, speak, tell, call

dictio, -onis, *f.*, style, diction, art of speaking; *Conf.* V, 13, 23, a trial theme

Dido, -onis, *f.*, Dido, *the traditional foundress of Carthage, enamored of Aeneas*

dies, -ei, *m. and f.*, day; de die in diem, from day to day, day by day

differo, -ferre, distuli, dilatum, *irr.v.a.*, put off, delay, postpone

difficilis, -e, *adj.*, difficult

difficultas, -tatis, *f.*, difficulty

diffido, -ere, -fisus sum, 3.*v.semidep.*, feel hopeless, despair

diffluo, -ere, -fluxi, -fluxum, 3.*v.n.*, flow away, waste away, be dissolved

diffugio, -ere, -fugi, *no sup.*, 3.*v.n.*, be dissipated, be dispersed

diffusus, -a, -um, *part. adj.*, diffused

digitus, -i, *m.*, finger

dignitas, -tatis, *f.*, dignity, honor; *of style*, majesty, stateliness

dignor, 1.*v.a.*, deign, be kind enough to

dignus, -a, -um, *adj.*, worthy

digredior, -gredi, -gressus sum, 3.*v.dep.*, go apart, go in different directions

dilanio, 1.*v.a.*, tear in pieces, tear asunder

dilectio, -onis, *f.*, love, pure affection

diligenter, *adv.*, diligently, assiduously, urgently

diligentia, -ae, *f.*, care, solicitude, attention

diligo, -ere, -lexi, -lectum, 3.*v.a.*, love, cherish; *Conf.* V, 13, 23, welcome

dimidius, -a, -um, *adj.*, half

dimitto, -ere, -misi, -missum, 3.*v.a.*, dismiss, send away; permit, suffer; pardon, forgive; give free course to; *with* habenas, give free rein

dirigo, -ere, -rexi, -rectum, 3.*v.a.*, direct; *Conf.* IX, 4, 7, make straight

dirimo, -ere, -emi, -emptum, 3.*v.a.*, divide, separate

dirrumpo, -ere, -rupi, -ruptum, 3.*v.a.*, break off, sever, tear away, separate

discedo, -ere, -cessi, -cessum, 3.*v.n.*, go away, depart

discerno, -ere, -crevi, -cretum, 3.*v.a.*, separate, distinguish, discern; cleave, dispel

discindo, -ere, -scidi, -scissum, 3.*v.a.*, tear asunder, divide

disciplina, -ae, *f.*, discipline, training, study, art

discipulus, -i, *m.*, pupil, student

disco, -ere, didici, *no sup.*, 3.*v.a.*, learn

discrimen, -inis, *n.*, danger, peril

discurro, -ere, -curri, -cursum,
3.*v.n.*, go in different directions
discutio, -ere, -cussi, -cussum,
3.*v.a.*, discuss, examine, scrutinize
diserte, *adv.*, eloquently
disertus, -a, -um, *part.adj.*, skilled in
speaking, eloquent; *Conf.* II, 3, 5,
cultivated
dispenso, 1.*v.a.*, dispense
dispersio, -onis, *f.*, dispersion; *Conf.*
II, 1, 1, moral disintegration
displiceo, -ere, -ui, -itum, 2.*v.n.*, dis-
please
dispono, -ere, -posui, -positum,
3.*v.a.*, arrange, determine
disputo, 1.*v.a. and n.*, discuss, dis-
pute, contend, discourse
dissensio, -onis, *f.*, disagreement,
dissent, difference of opinion
dissentio, -ire, -sensi, -sensum,
4.*v.n.*, differ, disagree
dissero, -ere, -serui, -sertum, 3.*v.a.*,
speak, argue, discourse
disserto, 1.*v.a.*, discuss, argue
dissimulo, 1.*v.a.*, dissemble, ignore
dissipo, 1.*v.a.*, disperse, dissipate
dissolute, *adv.*, dissolutely
dissolvo, -ere, -solvi, -solutum,
3.*v.a.*, untie, unravel; solve, answer
distabesco, -ere, -tabui, *no sup.*,
3.*v.n.*, melt away, sink
disto, 1.*v.n.*, differ
distortus, -a, -um, *part. adj.*, mis-
shapen, deformed
diu, *adv.*, long, for a long time
diuturnus, -a, -um, *adj.*, long
divinitas, -tatis, *f.*, Godhead
divinitus, *adv.*, from Heaven, by
Divine Command
divinus, -a, -um, *adj.*, divine; libri
divini, the Scriptures

divitiae, -arum, *f.*, riches
do, dare, dedi, datum, 1.*v.a.*, give,
offer, present, grant, permit; dare
manus, to yield, to surrender;
with vocem, utter
doceo, -ere, -ui, -tum, 2.*v.a.*, teach,
show, instruct
doctor, -oris, *m.*, teacher, doctor
doctrina, -ae, *f.*, teaching, instruction, knowledge; science, study,
art
doctus, -a, -um, *part.adj.*, learned,
well informed
documentum, -i, *n.*, proof
doleo, -ere, -ui, doliturus, 2.*v.n. and*
a., suffer, feel pain, pain, grieve
for, be sorry for
dolor, -oris, *m.*, suffering, sorrow,
grief, pain; dolor dentium, tooth-
ache
dolus, -i, *m.*, fraud, deceit
domesticus, -a, -um, *adj.*, of *or*
belonging to a house, domestic,
at home
domina, -ae, *f.*, mistress
dominicus, -a, -um, *adj.*, of *or* belonging to a master or mistress;
especially in Christian sense, of *or*
belonging to the Lord; dies
dominicus, the Lord's day, Sun-
day
dominus, -i, *m.*, lord, master, the
Lord
domitor, -oris, *m.*, tamer, van-
quisher
domus, -us, *f.*, house, home; family,
household; *loc.*, domi, at home
donec, *adv.*, until
dono, 1.*v.a.*, give, present; *of sin*,
forgive, remit
donum, -i, *n.*, gift

dormio, -ire, -ivi (-ii), -itum, 4.*v.n.*, sleep

dorsum, -i, *n.*, the back; *Conf.* VIII, 7, 16, a dorso meo, from behind my back

draco, -onis, *m.*, dragon

dubitatio, -onis, *f.*, doubt, uncertainty

dubito, 1.*v.n.* and *a.*, doubt, hesitate

duco, -ere, duxi, ductum, 3.*v.a.*,lead, attract, influence; *pass.*, *Conf.* VI, 3, 3, move

ductus, -us, *m.*, connection, direction, bent

dulce, *adv.*, sweetly, pleasantly, charmingly

dulcedo, -inis, *f.*, sweetness

dulcesco, -ere, 3.*v.n.*, become sweet

dulciloquus, -a, -um, *adj.*, sweetly speaking

dulcis, -e, *adj.*, sweet, pleasant

dulciter, *adv.*, agreeably, sweetly

dulcitudo, -inis, *f.*, sweetness

dum, *conj.*, while, until, as long as; provided that, if only; *in final sense*, in order that

dummodo, *conj.*, provided, provided only

dumtaxat, *adv.*, to this extent, only

duo, duae, duo, *num.adj.*, two

duodecim, *indecl.*, twelve

duodetricensimus, -a, -um, *adj.*, twenty-eighth

duplex, -icis, *adj.*, double, twofold

durus, -a, -um, *adj.*, hard

dux, ducis, *m.*, guide

E

ebrietas, -tatis, *f.*, drunkenness, inebriation

ebrius, -a, -um, *adj.*, drunk, intoxicated

ebullio, -ire, 4.*v.n.*, bubble up, boil up *or* over

ecce, *interj.*, behold!, lo!, see!

ecclesia, -ae, *f.*, a church, the Church

ecclesiasticus, -a, -um, *adj.*, of *or* belonging to the Church, ecclesiastical

eculeus, -i, *m.*, wooden rack *used as an instrument of torture*

edisco, -ere, -didici, *no sup.*, 3.*v.a.*, learn, learn thoroughly

edo, -ere, edidi, editum, 3.*v.a.*, put forth, utter, express; *of games*, give, put on

edomo, -are, -ui, -itum, 1.*v.a.*, break in

educo, 1.*v.a.*, rear, educate

effero, -ferre, extuli, elatum, *irr.v.a.*, carry out, carry to the grave

effervesco, -ere, -ferbui, *no sup.*, 3.*v.n.*, boil up *or* over, rage

effigies, -ei, *f.*, image, likeness

efflo, 1.*v.a.*, and *n.*, breathe out

effluo, -ere, -fluxi, *no sup.*, 3.*v.n.*, flow on, pass away, flow forth

effodio, -ere, -fodi, -fossum, 3.*v.a.*, dig up

effugio, -ere, -fugi, *no sup.*, 3.*v.n.* and *a.*, flee; flee from, avoid

effundo, -ere, -fudi, -fusum, 3.*v.a.*, pour out, pour forth

egens, -ntis, *part. adj.*, poor, needy

egeo, -ere, -egui, *no sup.*, 2.*v.n.*, be in want of, need

egestas, -tatis, *f.*, want, need, necessity

ego, mei, *pers. pron.*, I, myself

ei (*also* hei), *interj.*, an *exclamation*

of grief or fear, ah! alas!; *with* **mihi,**
ah me! woe is me!

eiulo, 1.*v.n.,* wail, lament

eiusmodi, *see* **modus**

electus, -a, -um, *part. adj.,* select,
choice; *m.pl. as subst.,* **electi,
-orum,** the chosen ones, the elect

elementum, -i, *n.,* element

elemosyna, -ae, *f.,* alms

eligo, -ere, -legi, -lectum, 3.*v.a.,*
choose, select

eliquo, 1.*v.a.,* distil, filter

eloquentia, -ae, *f.,* eloquence, oratory

eloquium, -ii, *n.,* manner of speech,
eloquence, declaration, pro-
nouncement; *pl.,* eloquent dis-
courses

eloquor, -loqui, -locutus sum, 3.*v.
dep.,* speak out, express

eluceo, -ere, -luxi, *no sup.,* 2.*v.n.,*
shine out; *fig.,* be apparent, be
manifest

emico, 1.*v.n.,* dart forth, leap forth

emigro, 1.*v.n.,* go out from, depart

emineo, -ere, -ui, *no sup.,* 2.*v.n.,*
stand out, be conspicuous, excel

emo, -ere, emi, emptum, 3.*v.a.,* buy,
purchase

emptor, -oris, *m.,* buyer, purchaser

enim, *conj., explaining a preceding
statement,* namely, for, in fact, indeed

enodate, *adv.,* clearly, plainly

enumero, 1.*v.a.,* number, enumerate

enuntio, 1.*v.a.,* disclose, announce,
express

enutrio, -ire, -ivi, -itum, 4.*v.a.,* rear,
bring up

eo, *adv.,* to that place, there; to that
point; on that account, for this

reason; **eo quod,** for the reason
that, because; *Conf.* II, 4, 9, **eo
. . . quo,** for this reason, that;
with comp., the more, *and correlatively with* **quo,** the more . . .
the more

eo, ire, ivi (ii), **itum,** *irr.v.n.,* go

episcopaliter, *adv.,* in the manner of
a bishop

episcopus, -i, *m.,* bishop

epistula, -ae, *f.,* letter, epistle

epulae, -arum, *f.pl.,* feast, feasting

equus, -i, *m.,* horse

eradico, 1.*v.a.,* uproot, root out

erga, *prep. with acc.,* towards

ergo, *adv.,* then, therefore, now (*il-
lative*)

eripio, -ere, -ripui, -reptum, 3.*v.a.,*
tear away, free, rescue

erro, 1.*v.n.,* wander, stray; *fig.* err,
be in error

error, -oris, *m.,* wandering; *fig.,* error, fault

erubesco, -ere, -rubui, *no sup.,*
3.*v.n. and a.,* blush with shame,
feel ashamed

erudio, -ire, -ivi (-ii), **-itum,** 4.*v.a.,*
instruct, educate

eruditus, -a, -um, *part. adj.,* learned,
erudite

eruo, -ere, -rui, -rutum, 3.*v.a.,* tear
away, rescue, deliver

eruptio, -onis, *f.,* a bursting forth

Esaias, -ae, *m.,* Isaias

esca, -ae, *f., frequently in pl.,* food,
victuals

esurio, -ire, *no perf.,* **-itum,** 4.*v.n.,* be
hungry

et, *conj.,* and, also; *frequently as
exact equivalent of* **etiam,** also,
even; **et . . . et,** both . . . and;

Conf. I, 15, 24, **sed et = sed etiam**

etiam, *conj.,* even now, still; and furthermore, even, also, likewise

etiamsi, *conj.,* even if, although

etsi, *conj.,* even if, although

Eva, -ae, *f.,* Eve

evado, -ere, -vasi, -vasum, 3.*v.n. and a.,* escape, avoid

evanesco, -ere, -nui, *no sup.,* 3.*v.n.,* vanish away

evangelicus, -a, -um, *adj.,* of or belonging to the Gospel

evangelium, -ii, *n.,* the Gospel

evectio, -onis, *f.,* a post-warrant

evenio, -ire, -veni, -ventum, 4.*v.n.,* happen

eversio, -onis, *f.,* overturning, (*wanton*) act of destruction, hazing, escapade

eversor, -oris, *m.,* overturner, wrecker

everto, -ere, -verti, -versum, 3.*v.a.,* overturn, overthrow, destroy

evigilo, 1.*v.n.,* wake, awake

evinco, -ere, -vici, -victum, 3.*v.a.,* prevail over, overcome

Evodius, -ii, *m.,* Evodius, *a fellow townsman and friend of St. Augustine, later bishop of Uzala in North Africa*

evolvo, -ere, -volvi, -volutum, 3.*v.a.,* unroll, *hence* read

ex (e), *prep. with abl.,* out of; *of place,* from, out of; *of source,* of, from; *of time,* from, since; ex quo (*sc.* tempore) since; *of cause,* from, on account of; *partitively,* out of, of; *Conf.* VI, 1, 1, with regard to; *ibid.,* **ex tanta parte,** in such a large degree; *Conf.* IX, 12, 32,

parva ex parte, in small measure; *Conf.* II, 3, 5, **ex fide,** in accordance with . . . ; *Conf.* III, 11, 19, **ex fide,** by virtue of . . . ; *Conf.* VI, 4, 6, **ex nullo,** in no respect: **ex invicem,** upon one another

exaestuo, 1.*v.n.,* be excited, be stirred

exagito, 1.*v.a.,* disquiet, excite, trouble

exardesco, -ere, -arsi, *no sup.,* 3.*v.n.,* blaze up; burn, be parched (*of thirst*); *fig.,* be inflamed, burn (*with desire*)

exaudio, -ire, -ivi (-ii), -itum, 4.*v.a.,* hear, hear favorably, listen to

excedo, -ere, -cessi, -cessum, 3.*v.n. and a..* withdraw, depart; go beyond, transgress; *Conf.* II, 3, 6, overtop, rise above

excellens, -ntis, *part. adj.,* lofty, excellent

excellenter, *adv.,* excellently, in a superior manner

excellentia, -ae, *f.,* superiority, excellence; preëminence, exalted station

excello, -ere, 3.*v.n.,* excel, surpass

excelsus, -a, -um, *part. adj.,* lofty, high

excessus, -us, *m.,* excess, aberration

excipio, -ere, -cepi, -ceptum, 3.*v.a.,* take up, receive, catch up, rescue

excito, 1.*v.a.,* arouse, excite, stimulate, animate, provoke

exclamo, 1.*v.n.,* shout out, cry out

excludo, -ere, -clusi, -clusum, 3.*v.a.,* shut out, exclude

excrucio, 1.*v.a.,* torture, torment

excubo, -are, -bui, -bitum, 1.*v.n.*, keep watch, stand guard

excuso, 1.*v.a.*, excuse

excutio, -ere, -cussi, -cussum, 3.*v.a.*, shake, shake down, shake off, tear away

exemplum, -i, *n.*, example

exeo, -ire, -ii (-ivi), -itum, *irr.v.n.*, go out, depart; come out, issue

exerceo, -ere, -cui, -citum, 2.*v.a.*, train, practice; *used of disease,* attack, rack

exercitatio, -onis, *f.*, practice

exercitatus, -a, -um, *part. adj.*, practiced, well-versed, trained

exhalo, 1.*v.a.*, breathe out, exhale

exhibeo, -ere, -hibui, -hibitum, 2.*v.a.*, show, manifest

exhorresco, -ere, -horrui, *no sup.*, 3.*v.a.*, shudder at, be horrified at

exhortatio, -onis, *f.*, exhortation

exigo, -ere, -egi, -actum, 3.*v.a.*, demand, exact

exiguus, -a, -um, *adj.*, small, slender, *n.sing. as subst.*, a little, a little bit

exilio, -ire, -ui (3rd *pers. sing. also* exilivit), *no sup.*, 4.*v.n.*, leap up, leap

eximo, -ere, -emi, -emptum, 3.*v.a.*, remove, deliver

existimo, 1.*v.a.*, think, judge

exitus, -us, *m.*, a going forth, departure; exit, way out; outcome, issue

exordium, -ii, *n.*, beginning

expavesco, -ere, -pavi, *no sup.*, 3.*v.n.*, be terrified

expecto, 1.*v.a.*, await, expect, look forward to

expedio, -ire, -ivi (-ii), -itum, 4.*v.a.*, explain, settle

experior, -iri, -pertus sum, 4.*v.dep.*, put to the test, experience, find

expers, -ertis, *adj.*, wanting in, without, having no knowledge of

expeto, -ere, -ivi (-ii), -itum, 3.*v.a.*, seek out; long for, desire, long

expleo, -ere, -plevi, -pletum, 2.*v.a.*, fulfill, complete, gratify

explico, 1.*v.a.*, explain, interpret, express

exploro, 1.*v.a.*, search out, examine; *p.p. as adj.*, confirmed, established, certain

expolitus, -a, -um, *part. adj.*, polished, elegant

expono, -ere, -posui, -positum, 3.*v.a.*, expound, explain

exquiro, -ere, -quisivi, -quisitum, 3.*v.a.*, search out, examine

exsecrabiliter, *adv.*, execrably

exsecrandus, -a, -um, *adj.*, abominable, detestable

exstinguo, -ere, -stinxi, stinctum, 3.*v.a.*, quench, destroy

extendo, -ere, -tendi, -tentum, 3.*v.a.*, extend, stretch out, stretch forth; *p.p. as adj.*, extentus, -a, -um, prolonged, intense

extinctio, -onis, *f.*, extinction, annihilation

exto, -are -titi, *no sup.*, 1.*v.n.*, stand out, be conspicuous; be

extollo, -ere, exsustuli, *no sup.*, 3.*v.a.*, praise, extol

extra, *prep. with acc.*, outside

extremus, -a, -um, *superl. adj.*, last; *n. sing. as adv.*, extremum, for the last time

exudo, 1.*v.n.*, sweat out

exulo, 1.*v.n.*, be an exile, live in exile

exultatio, -onis, *f.*, exultation

exulto, 1.*v.n.*, exult, rejoice exceedingly

exuo, -ere, -ui, -utum, 3.*v.a.*, draw away, put off; *pass. with middle sense,* free one's self from

F

fabella, -ae, *f.*, story; fabellae falsae, fables

fabrico, 1.*v.a.*, fashion, fabricate

fabula, -ae, *f.*, story, fable, fiction

fabulosus, -a, -um, *adj.*, fabulous

facies, -ei, *f.*, face, countenance

facile, *adv.*, easily

facilis, -e, *adj.*, easy

facinus, -oris, *n.*, deed, evil action, crime

facio,-ere, feci, factum, 3.*v.a. and n.*, make, do, create, cause to; *pass.*, **fio, fieri, factus sum,** be made, become, happen

factum, -i, *n.*, deed, act, exploit

facultas, -tatis, *f.*, power, skill

facundia, -ae, *f.*, eloquence

faeneus, -a, -um, *adj.*, of hay, of grass

fallacia, -ae, *f.*, deceit, deception

fallax, -acis, *adj.*, false, deceitful

fallo, fallere, fefelli, falsum, 3.*v.a.*, deceive

falsitas, -tatis, *f.*, falsity

falsus, -a, um, *part. adj.*, false, deceitful, pretended; *n. sing. as subst.*, **falsum,** -i, what is false, falsehood

fama, -ae, *f.*, fame, report

familiaris, -e, *adj.*, belonging to a household; intimate, friendly; *as subst.*, familiar acquaintance, friend; res **familiaris,** property, patrimony

familiaritas, -tatis, *f.*, intimacy, friendship

familiariter, *adv.*, familiarly, intimately

famis, -is, *f.*, hunger

famula, -ae, *f.*, servant, handmaid

famulor, 1.*v.dep.*, be a servant to, serve

fastidio, -ire, -ivi (-ii), -itum, 4.*v.n. and a.*, scorn, dislike, feel disgust at; *pres. part. as adj., Conf.* III, 2, 2, bored

fastidiosus, -a, -um, *adj.*, disdainful, that feels disgust for

fastidium, -ii, *n.*, scorn, disgust

fastus, -us, *m.*, pride, arrogance

fateor, -eri, fassus, 2.*v.dep.*, confess

fatuus, -i, *m.*, fool

Faustus, -i, *m.*, Faustus, *a famous Manichaean contemporary of St. Augustine*

faveo, -ere, favi, fautum, 2.*v.n.*, favor, be inclined to, be well disposed to

febris, -is, *f.*, fever

fecundus, -a, -um, *adj.*, fruitful

fel, fellis, *n.*, gall

felicitas, -tatis, *f.*, felicity, happiness

feliciter, *adv.*, happily

felix, -icis, *adj.*, happy, gracious

femina, -ae, *f.*, woman

femineus, -a, -um, *adj.*, of *or* belonging to a woman

fenestra, -ae, *f.*, window

fere, *adv.*, almost, nearly

feretrum, -i, *n.*, a bier

feriatus, -a, -um, *part. adj.*, unoccupied, at leisure, idle, disengaged, free

ferio, -ire, 4.*v.a.*, strike

ferme, *adv.*, almost, nearly

fero, ferre, tuli, latum, *irr.v.a.*, bear, carry, take up, endure; extol; *in pass.*, be carried along, go

ferrum, -i, *n.*, iron; an iron instrument; *hence Conf.* IX, 8, 18, **medicinale ferrum,** a surgeon's knife

ferula, -ae, *f.*, rod *or* ferule, *used in administering punishment*

ferveo, -ere, ferbui, *no sup.*, 2.*v.n.*, burn, glow; *pres. part. as adj.*, glowing, fervent

fervor, -oris, *m.*, heat

fessus, -a, -um, *adj.*, tired, weary

festinabundus, -a, -um, *adj.*, hastening, quick

festino, 1.*v.n.*, hasten

ficus, -i, *f.*, the fig tree

fidelis, -e, *adj.*, faithful, true, genuine, loyal, of *or* belonging to Faith; *as subst., m. or f.*, a faithful Christian, a faithful servant of God

fides, -ei, *f.*, faith, trust, fidelity; promise, pledge; *frequently in Christian sense*, Faith, the Christian religion

fiducia, -ae, *f.*, trust, reliance, confidence

fiducialiter, *adv.*, confidently

figmentum, -i, *n.*, fiction

figo, -ere, fixi, fixum, 3.*v.a.*, fix; *with* **genua,** kneel down

filia, -ae, *f.*, daughter

filius, -i, (-ii), *m.*, son

fingo, -ere, finxi, fictum, 3.*v.a.*, fashion, invent, frame; feign, pretend; *p.p. as adj.*, **fictus, -a, -um,** feigned

finio, -ire, -ivi, -itum, 4.*v.a.*, end, put an end to

finis, -is, *m.*, end; purpose, design

fio, *see* **facio**

firmitas, -tatis, *f.*, firmness, strength

firmo, 1.*v.a.*, secure, establish, strengthen

firmus, -a, -um, *adj.*, firm

flagello, 1.*v.a.*, scourge, chastise

flagellum, -i, *n.*, whip, scourge

flagitiosus, -a, -um, *adj.*, shameful

flagitium, -ii, *n.*, shame, infamy, vice

flagito, 1.*v.a.*, demand, ask ardently; *with* **ab, de,** of, from

flagrans, -ntis, *part. adj.*, eager, ardent

flagrantia, -ae, *f.*, ardor

flagro, 1.*v.n.*, burn, (*of an odor*) spread into the air; burn, be ardent, be filled with enthusiasm

flebilis, -e, *adj.*, tearful

fleo, -ere, flevi, fletum, 2.*v.n. and a.*, weep, mourn; bewail, lament

fletus, -us, *m.*, weeping

flo, 1.*v.n.*, blow, freshen

floreo, -ere, -ui, *no sup.*, 2.*v.n.*, bloom; *fig.*, flourish, prosper

flos, floris, *m.*, flower, bloom

fluctuatio, -onis, *f.*, wavering

fluctuo, 1.*v.n.*, waver, be in doubt

fluctus, -us, *m.*, wave

fluentum, -i, *n.*, stream

flumen, -inis, *n.*, river

fluxus, -us, *m.*, flux, stream; free flow, ardor (*of curiosity*)

foeditas, -tatis, *f.*, foulness, deformity, impurity

foedus, -a, -um, *adj.*, foul, base, vile

fomentum, -i, *n.*, balm, lenitive

fomes, -itis, *m.*, kindling wood, fuel; incentive

fons, fontis, *m.*, fountain, source

for, fari, fatus sum, 1.*v.dep.*, speak

foras, *adv.*, without, forth, out

forem, *see* sum

foris, *adv.*, without, outside; **foris a**
as prep., outside, outside of

forma, -ae, *f.*, form, appearance

formido, 1.*v.a.*, dread, fear

formo, 1.*v.a.*, form, fashion

fornicatio, -onis, *f.*, fornication

fornicor, 1.*v.dep.*, commit fornication

fortasse, *adv.*, perhaps, perchance

forte, *abl. of* fors, *used as adv.*, by
chance

fortis, -e, *adj.*, strong, brave, steadfast, redoubtable

fortiter, *adv.*, strongly, vigorously,
resolutely

forum, -i, *n.*, forum

fovea, -ae, *f.*, pit

fragilis, -e, *adj.*, unstable

frater, -tris, *m.*, brother; *in pl., often
in sense of* the Christian brethren

fraudulentus, -a, -um, *adj.*, deceitful, fraudulent

fremo, -ere, -ui, -itum, 3.*v.n.*,
shudder, shake

freno, 1.*v.a.*, curb, check

frequens, -ntis, *adj.*, frequent; *of a
person,* who is often at a place,
frequently present

frequenter, *adv.*, often

frequento, 1.*v.a.*, frequent, do *or*
make use of frequently, repeat;
with elemosynas, give . . . often

frigidus, -a, -um, *adj.*, cold

frons, -ntis, *f.*, expression of countenance, face

fructus, -us, *m.*, fruit

frumentum, -i, *n.*, grain, wheat

fruor, frui, fructus sum, 3.*v.dep.*,
enjoy

frustatim, *adv.*, piecemeal, in pieces

frux, frugis, *f.*, fruit

fuco, 1.*v.a.*, paint, dye; disguise

fugio, -ere, fugi, fugiturus, 3.*v.n.
and a.*, flee, escape; avoid, flee
from, shun

fugitivus, -i, *m.*, fugitive

fumus, -i, *m.*, smoke

fundo, -ere, fudi, fusum, 3.*v.a.*,
pour, pour out; *fig.*, pour forth

fundus, -i, *m.*, base, foundation,
depth

funus, -eris, *n.*, funeral; corpse;
death

fur, furis, *m.*, thief

furiosus, -a, -um, *adj.*, mad, raging,
furious

furor, -oris, *m.*, madness, fury

furor, -ari, -atus sum, 1.*v.dep.*, steal

furtim, *adv.*, furtively, secretly

furtum, -i, *n.*, theft

G

garrio, -ire, -ivi (-ii), -itum, 4.*v.a.*,
prate, babble

gaudeo, -ere, gavisus sum, 2.*v.semidep.*, rejoice, be delighted, be
glad; *pres. part. as adj., Conf.* III,
2, 2

gaudium, -ii, *n.*, joy

gehenna, -ae, *f.*, hell

gemitus, -us, *m.*, groan, groaning,
lamentation

gemo, -ere, -ui, -itum, 3.*v.n.*, sigh,
groan

gena, -ae, *f.*, cheek

gens, gentis, *f.*, race, nation; *in pl.,
Conf.* VIII, 7, 17, the world; *in pl.
also,* the Gentiles, the Pagans

genu, -us, *n.*, knee

genus, -eris, *n.*, race, kind

germanitus, *adv.*, faithfully, truly
germanus, -a, -um, *adj.*, true
gero, -ere, gessi, gestum, 3.*v.a.*,
carry in one's self, have; *of age*,
pass, be in; carry out, discharge;
in pass., be done, come to pass
Gervasius, -ii, *m.*, Gervasius, *a
martyr whose body was found by
St. Ambrose*
glacialis, -e, *adj.*, covered with ice, icy
gloria, -ae, *f.*, glory
glorior, 1.*v.dep.*, glory, pride one's
self in, boast
gnarus, -a, -um, *adj.*, knowing,
having knowledge of
gradatim, *adv.*, step by step, gradually
Graecus, -a, -um, *adj.*, of the Greeks,
Greek
grammatica, -ae, *f.*, grammar; grammatica graeca, Greek literature
grammaticus, -a, -um, *adj.*, of *or*
relating to grammar *or* to a
grammarian; grammaticus, -i, *m.*,
a teacher of grammar
grandis, -e, *adj.*, huge, great, grand
granditer, *adv.*, strongly
grandiusculus, -a, -um, *adj.*, pretty
well grown up, rather big
gratia, -ae, *f.*, favor, benefit, grace;
especially in pl., thanks; gratias
agere, to give thanks; *abl.*, gratia,
for the sake of, on account of
gratis, *ab. pl. of* gratia *as adv.*, for
nothing, gratis, without provoca-
tion
gratulatorie, *adv.*, in a congratulat-
ing manner
gratulor, 1.*v.dep.*, rejoice
gratus, -a, -um, *adj.*, pleasing,
pleasant

gravidus, -a, -um, *adj.*, full, heavy
gravis, -e, *adj.*, heavy, grievous;
grave, serious, venerable
graviter, *adv.*, heavily, violently,
seriously, deeply
gressus, -us, *m.*, step, stage, progress
grex, gregis, *m.*, flock, multitude,
congregation
gula, -ae, *f.*, the gullet, throat; *fig.*
gluttony
gurges, -itis, *m.*, abyss, whirlpool
gymnasium, -ii, *n.*, school

H

habena, -ae, *f.*, rein
habeo, -ere, -ui, -itum, 2.*v.a.*, have,
hold, possess, enjoy; account,
consider, judge
habito, 1.*v.n.*, dwell
habitus, -us, *m.*, dress
hac, *adv.*, here, on this side, on the
one hand; hac atque hac, hither
and thither, on this side and on
that
haereo, -ere, haesi, haesum, 2.*v.n.*,
cling, cleave
haeresis, -is, *f.*, heresy
haesitatio, -onis, *f.*, hesitation
haesito, 1.*v.a.*, stick fast; hesitate
harena, -ae, *f.*, sand; arena
haurio, -ire, hausi, haustum, 4.*v.a.*,
drink down, drain
hebetudo, -inis, *f.*, dulness, stupidity
herba, -ae, *f.*, herb
heremus, -i, *f.*, desert
hic, *adv.*, here
hic, haec, hoc, *dem. adj. and pron.*,
this (*of what is near in time, place,
or thought*), this one, he, she, it;
hoc est, that is, namely
Hierusalem, *indecl.*, *f.*, Jerusalem

hilaresco, -ere, 3.*v.n.*, enliven, divert, give pleasure to

hilaris, -e, *adj.*, cheerful, joyous

hinc, *adv.*, hence; from this, on this account

hodiernus, -a, -um, *adj.*, of this day; in hodiernum, to this day, to the present time

Homerus, -i, *m.*, Homer, *the greatest of Greek epic poets*

homo, -inis, *c.*, human being, man

honeste, *adv.*, honorably, uprightly, nobly

honesto, 1.*v.a.*, honor, adorn; *Conf.* IV, 8, 13, simul honestari, being respected in turn, receiving attention in turn

honestus, -a, -um, *adj.*, honorable, virtuous, becoming

honor, -oris, *m.*, honor, respect

honoro, 1.*v.a.*, honor

hora, -ae, *f.*, hour

horreo, -ere, -ui, *no sup.*, 2.*v.n.*, shudder, be filled with horror; *Conf.* IV, 7, 12, appear horrible, look hideous

horribilis, -e, *adj.*, horrible

horror, -oris, *m.*, fear, terror, awe

hortatorius, -a, -um, *adj.*, encouraging, cheering

Hortensius, -ii, *m.*, Hortensius, *the title of a dialogue of Cicero, of which only fragments are extant*

hortulus, -i, *m.*, a little garden

hortus, -i, *m.*, a garden

hospes, -itis, *m.*, host, owner

hospitium, -ii, *n.*, lodging

hostis, -is, *m.*, enemy

huc, *adv.*, hither, here; up to this time

huiusmodi, *see* modus

humanitas, -tatis, *f.*, humanity

humaniter, *adv.*, humanly, in a manner becoming humanity

humanus, -a, -um, *adj.*, of man, human; *n. pl. as subst.*, humana, -orum, human things, the lot of man

humilio, 1.*v.a.*, make low; *p.p. as adj.*, humiliatus, -a, -um, humbled

humilis, -e, *adj.*, low

humilitas, -tatis, *f.*, humility

hymnus, -i, *m.*, hymn

I

iaceo, -ere, -ui, -itum, 2.*v.n.*, lie, be situated

iacto, 1.*v.a.*, toss, cast, drive hither and thither; send forth, utter; vaunt, flaunt, boast of

iaculo, -are, -avi, -atum, 1.*v.a.*, hurl, cast

iam, *adv.*, now, already, presently; non iam, not indeed, no longer (*and similarly with other negatives*); iam vero, what is more, besides, moreover

ibi, *adv.*, there, then; in that matter

ibidem, *adv.*, at the same time

ictus, -us, *m.*, blow, stroke

idem, eadem, idem, *dem. pron. and adj.*, the same

ideo, *adv.*, for this reason, therefore

idoneus, -a, -um, *adj.*, suitable, fit, capable

Iesus, *gen. and voc.*, Iesu, *m.*, Jesus

igitur, *adv.*, therefore

ignarus, -a, -um, *adj.*, ignorant, not knowing

ignis, -is, *m.*, fire; *fig.*, fire of passion

ignominiosus, -a, -um, *adj.*, ignominious, shameful

ignorantia, -ae, *f.*, ignorance

ignoro, 1.*v.a.*, not know, be ignorant

ignotus, -a, -um, *adj.*, unacquainted with; *as a subst.*, *m.*, *Conf.* III, 3, 6, a newcomer, a freshman

illac, *adv.*, there, on that side, on the other hand

ille, illa, illud, *dem. adj. and pron.* (*referring to what is remote from speaker*), that; he, she, it; *of what follows*, this, these; ille aut ille, this or that

illic, *adv.*, there

illicitus, -a, -um, *adj.*, illicit, unlawful, forbidden

illuc, *adv.*, thither, to that place

imago, -inis, *f.*, image, representation

imber, -bris, *m.*, rain, tempest

imbuo, -ere, -ui, -utum, 3.*v.a.*, initiate, instruct, imbue

imitor, 1.*v.dep.*, imitate, mimic

immineo, *see* inmineo

immitto, -ere, -misi, -missum, 3.*v.a.*, set, sow

immo, *adv.*, nay, on the contrary; immo vero, nay rather, nay even

immolo, 1.*v.a.*, immolate, sacrifice

impedio, *see* inpedio

impendeo, -ere, 2.*v.n.*, impend, be close at hand, threaten, menace

impendo, -ere, -pendi, -pensum, 3.*v.a.*, expend, lay out for, spend, employ, devote

imperator, -oris, *m.*, emperor

imperito, 1.*v.a.*, command, rule

imperium, -ii, *n.*, power, command

impero, 1.*v.a.*, command, order

impetus, -us, *m.*, impetus, violence, force, violent current

impleo, -ere, -evi, -etum, 2.*v.a.*, fill; *fig.*, fulfill, carry out

imus, *superl. adj.*, *see* inferus

in, *prep. with acc.*, into, *with abl.* in. *With acc.*, into, towards, to, among, upon, against; *of purpose*, to, for, for the purpose of, unto; *Conf.* I, 11, 17, in remissionem peccatorum, unto the remission of sins; *Conf.* VIII, 12, 28, in finem, to the end, forever; *Conf.* VIII, 12, 30, in melius, for the better. *With the abl.*, in, within, among, on, at; *of time*, in, during; *of other relations*, in, in the case of, with reference to; *sometimes bordering on the instrumental*, by

inanis, -e, *adj.*, vain, empty; *n. sing. and pl. as subst.*, vanity, emptiness, vain things

inanitas, -tatis, *f.*, emptiness, inanity, vain thought

inauditus, -a, -um, *adj.*, strange, new

inbecillus, -a, -um, *adj.*, weak, tender, unstable, unresisting

incautus, -a, -um, *adj.*, unwary, rash

incendium, -ii, *n.*, burning

incertus, -a, -um, *adj.*, uncertain

incessus, -us, *m.*, entrance

incido, -ere, -cidi, *no sup.*, 3.*v.n.*, chance upon, happen; *with* in and *acc.*, fall in with, fall among, meet

incipio, -ere, -cepi, -ceptum, 3.*v.a.*, begin

inclino, 1.*v.a.*, incline, bend, bend down

incolumitas, -tatis, *f.*, safety, wellbeing

incommodum, -i, *n.*, disadvantage, inconvenience, detriment inconparabiliter, *adv.*, incomparably

inconprehensibilis, -e, *adj.*, incomprehensible

incorruptus, -a, -um, *adj.*, uncorrupted

incorruptibilis, -e, *adj.*, incorruptible

incredibilis, -e, *adj.*, incredible, unbelievable

increpo, -are, -ui, -itum, 1.*v.n.* and *a.*, utter rebuke, make reproach against, blame

incumbo, -ere, -cubui, -cubitum, 3.*v.n.*, lean upon

incuriosus, -a, -um, *adj.*, unconcerned, careless

incurro, -ere, -curri (-cucurri), -cursum, 3.*v.n.*, run upon; *with* in *and acc.*, fall in with, chance upon

incutio, -ere, -cussi, -cussum, 3.*v.a.*, strike into, inspire in

indago, 1.*v.a.*, search out, seek for, find out

inde, *adv.*, from there, thence, from this, from these; next, then

indico, 1.*v.a.*, point out, state, make known, announce

indigentia, -ae, *f.*, want, need

indigeo, -ere, -ui, *no sup.*, 2.*v.n.*, want, need, be in need of

indignatio, -onis, *f.*, indignation, anger

indignor, 1.*v.dep.*, be indignant, be angry

indignus, -a, -um, *adj.*, unworthy

indo, -ere, -didi, -ditum, 3.*v.a.*, give, assign a name to

indocilis, -e, *adj.*, indocile, unfit

indoctus, -a, -um, *adj.*, unlearned, ignorant

induo, -ere, -dui, -dutum, 3.*v.a.*, put on; *in pass. with middle sense*, clothe oneself

ineo, -ire, -ii (-ivi), -itum, *irr.v.n.*, begin; ab ineunte aetate, from early youth

infans, -antis, *c.*, infant

infantia, -ae, *f.*, infancy

infelicitas, -tatis, *f.*, misfortune, unhappiness

infelix, -icis, *adj.*, unhappy

inferus, -a, -um, *adj.*, low; *superl.*, infimus *and* imus, lowest, deepest, the depths of; *m. pl. as subst.*, the lower regions, Hell

infidus, -a, -um, *adj.*, unfaithful, untrue; false; *n. pl., as subst.* Conf. III, 3, 5, false things, *i.e.* infidelity (*in respect to beliefs and practices contrary to the Christian Religion*)

infirmitas, -tatis, *f.*, infirmity; *Conf.* VI, 3, 3, trouble, difficulty

infirmus, -a, -um, *adj.*, weak; *masc. sing. as subst., Conf.* VIII, 12, 30, one who is weak

inflammo, 1.*v.a.*, set on fire, inflame

inflatus, -a, -um, *part. adj.*, puffed up, proud

influo, -ere, -fluxi, -fluxum, 3.*v.n.*, flow in

infremo, -ere, -fremui, *no sup.*, 3.*v.n.*, groan

infundo, -ere, -fudi, -fusum, 3.*v.a.*, pour into, infuse

ingemesco, -ere, -gemui, *no sup.*, 3.*v.n.*, groan, sigh

ingemino, 1.*v.a.*, double, redouble

ingenium, -ii, *n.*, natural disposition, character, talent, mental power, genius

ingens, -ntis, *adj.*, huge, extraordinary, very great

ingero, -ere, -gessi, -gestum, 3.*v.a.*,
bring before; submit; urge upon,
press upon

ingravesco, -ere, 3.*v.n.*, become
more serious, increase, grow worse

ingredior, -gredi, -gressus sum,
3.*v.dep.*, enter, enter upon, go in

inhabito, 1.*v.a. and n.*, inhabit, dwell

inhianter, *adv.*, eagerly

inhio, 1.*v.n.*, gape for, pant for

inhonestus, -a, -um, *adj.*, shameful

inimica, -ae, *f.*, an enemy

inimice, *adv.*, inimically, in a hostile
manner

inimicitia, -ae, *f.*, enmity

inimicus, -i, *m.*, enemy

iniquitas, -tatis, *f.*, iniquity

initio, 1.*v.a.*, initiate into

iniuriosus, -a, -um, *adj.*, injurious,
wrongful

inlecebra, -ae, *f.*, allurement

inlecebrosus, -a, -um, *adj.*, enticing,
inviting

inlicitus, *adj.*, *see* illicitus

inludo, -ere, -lusi, -lusum, 3.*v.n.*,
make sport, amuse one's self with

inlumino, 1.*v.a.*, illuminate

inmanis, -e, *adj.*, vast, frightful,
horrible

inmineo, -ere, 2.*v.n.*, be close upon,
be imminent, be close at hand

inmoderate, *adv.*, immoderately,
without moderation

inmoror, 1.*v.dep.*, pause, linger, tarry

inmortalitas, -tatis, *f.*, immortality

inmundus, -a, -um, *adj.*, unclean,
impure

inmutabilis, -e, *adj.*, immutable, unchangeable

innecto, -ere, -nexui, -nexum, 3.*v.a.*,
tie, weave

innocens, -entis, *adj.*, innocent,
blameless

innocentia, -ae, *f.*, innocence

innotesco, -ere, -notui, *no sup.*,
3.*v.n.*, become known

innovo, 1.*v.a.*, renew

innumerabilis, -e, *adj.*, innumerable

inoboediens, -ntis, *part. adj.*, diso-
bedient

inolitus, -a, -um, *part. adj.*, ingrown

inopia, -ae, *f.*, want, need, indigence

inopinate, *adv.*, unexpectedly

inopinatus, -a, -um, *adj.*, not expected, unexpected

inops, -opis, *adj.*, needy, without
resources, poor; lacking, wanting in

inordinatus, -a, -um, *adj.*, inordinate

inpatiens, -ntis, *part. adj.*, impatient,
unwilling

inpedio, -ire, -ivi (-ii), -itum, 4.*v.a.*,
hinder, prevent, impede, stop

inpello, -ere, -puli, -pulsum, 3.*v.a.*,
drive, push

inpendeo, *see* impendeo

inpendo, *see* impendo

inperitia, -ae, *f.*, lack of knowledge,
ignorance

inperitus, -a, -um, *adj.*, ignorant,
untrained

inpertio, -ire, -ivi (-ii), -itum, 4.*v.a.*,
give, furnish

inpetro, 1.*v.a.*, ask, obtain

inpietas, -tatis, *f.*, impiety

inpingo, -ere, -pegi, -pactum, 3.*v.a.*,
push, thrust, drive

inplico, 1.*v.a.*, entangle, catch

inprobus, -a, -um, *adj.*, monstrous,
unbearable

inpudens, -entis, *adj.*, shameless

inpudenter, *adv.*, shamelessly, im-
pudently

inpudicitia, *f.*, impurity

inpune, *adv.*, with impunity

inquam, *v.def.*, say

inquietudo, -inis, *f.*, restlessness, feverishness, disquietude

inquietus, -a, -um, *adj.*, disturbing, distressing, restless

inquisitio, -onis, *f.*, investigation, inquiry

inquisitor, -oris, *m.*, inquirer, investigator

inrideo, -ere, -risi, -risum, 2.*v.a.*, ridicule, laugh at, mock, scoff at

inrisio, -onis, *f.*, derision

inrisor, -oris, *m.*, mocker

inrumpo, -ere, -rupi, -ruptum, 3.*v.n.*, break in, burst in

inruo, -ere, -rui, *no sup.*, 3.*v.n.*, rush into; enter

insania, -ae, *f.*, madness, insanity

insanio, -ire, -ivi *and* ii, -itum, 4.*v.n.*, rage, be beside one's self, be mad

insanus, -a, -um, *adj.*, unsound in mind, mad, insane, senseless

insatiabilis, -e, *adj.*, that cannot be satisfied, insatiable

inscribo, -ere, -scripsi, -scriptum, 3.*v.a.*, inscribe, entitle

insector, 1.*v.dep.*, attack, rail at, mock insolently

insero, -ere, -serui, -sertum, 3.*v.a.*, put in, introduce, insert

insidiae, -arum, *f. pl.*, deceit, fraud

insigne, -is, *n.*, mark, badge

insinuo, 1.*v.a.*, introduce, make known, inform; *Conf.* IX, 4, 12, *pass. with middle sense*, make its way into, force itself into

insipientia, -ae, *f.*, folly; *Conf.* I, 9, 14, harm

insolitus, -a, -um, *adj.*, unwonted, unusual, unheard of

inspiro, 1.*v.a.*, inspire, breathe in, infuse; *with dat.*, inspire into, breathe into, inspire in

instauro, 1.*v.a.*, restore, refresh

instituo, -ere, -ui, -utum, 3.*v.a.*, determine, decide, resolve; institute, establish, ordain

institutio, -onis, *f.*, arrangement, plan

insto, -are, -steti, -staturus, 1.*n. and a.*, press, press on, urge, insist, threaten; *impers.*, *Conf.* I, 14, 23, instabatur mihi, I was threatened

instruo, -ere, -struxi, -structum, 3.*v.a.*, instruct

insultatio, -onis, *f.*, insult, insolence

integre, *adv.*, wholly, entirely

integritas, -tatis, *f.*, integrity

intellectus, -us, *m.*, meaning, sense

intellego, -ere, -lexi, -lectum, 3.*v.a.*, know, perceive, understand

intemperans, -ntis, *adj.*, intemperate, unrestrained

intemperantia, -ae, *f.*, intemperance, unrestraint

intempestus, -a, -um, *adj.*, unseasonable; nocte intempestiva, at the dead of night

intendo, -ere, -tendi, -tentum, 3.*v.a.*, strain, extend, direct; *with* animum, apply one's mind, direct one's thoughts to

intente, *adv.*, attentively

intentio, -onis, *f.*, attention, intention

intentus, -a, -um, *part. adj.*, attentive, eager; intent

inter, *prep. with acc.*, between, among; *Conf.* VIII, 6, 15, in the midst of, during interblandiens, -ntis, *part. adj.*, giving a caress for, returning thanks for

intercido, -ere, -cidi, *no sup.*, 3.*v.n.*, fall down, collapse, perish

intercurro, -ere, -cucurri *and* -curri, -cursum, 3.*v.n.*, intervene

interdum, *adv.*, sometimes

interea, *adv.*, meantime, meanwhile; nevertheless

intericio, -ere, -ieci, -iectum, 3.*v.a.*, put between

interim, *adv.*, meanwhile, for a time

interior, -oris, *adj.*, interior, inner; *n. pl. as subst.*, depths; *Conf.* III, 5, 9, deeper *or* hidden meaning

intermissio, -onis, *f.*, respite, interruption

intermitto, -ere, -misi, -missum, 3.*v.a.*, interrupt

internus, -a, -um, *adj.*, internal

interpello, 1.*v.a.*, make intercession to

interpono, -ere, -posui, -positum, 3.*v.a.*, interpose

interpretatio, -onis, *f.*, interpretation, explanation

interpretor, 1.*v.dep.*, interpret, conclude

interrogo, 1.*v.a.*, ask, question, inquire of

intime, *adv.*, most deeply, from one's innermost being

intimus, -a, -um, *superl. adj.*, inmost, most secret; *n. pl. as subst.*, intima, -orum, the innermost parts

intra, *prep. with acc.*, within

intro, 1.*v.a. and n.*, go into, enter

introduco, -ere, -duxi, -ductum, 3.*v.a.*, introduce

introeo, -ire, -ivi (-ii), -itum, *irr.v.n.*, go into, enter

intueor, -eri, -tuitus sum, 2.*v.dep.*, look at, gaze at, look to, consider, give attention to

intus, *adv.*, within, inside

inusitatus, -a, -um, *adj.*, unusual, strange

invado, -ere, -vasi, -vasum, 3.*v.a.*, rush upon, rush in upon

invalesco, -ere, -valui, *no sup.*, 3.*v.n.*, become heavy, weigh down

invenio, -ire, -veni, -ventum 4.*v.a.*, find, discover

inventio, -onis, *f.*, finding, discovery

investigabilis, -e, *adj.*, not to be traced, unsearchable

investigo, 1.*v.a.*, investigate, search into

invicem, *adv.*, reciprocally, one another; **ex invicem**, upon one another

invideo, -ere, -vidi, -visum, 2.*v.n. and a.*, envy, be jealous of

invidia, -ae, *f.*, hatred, jealousy, ill-will

invisibilis, -e, *adj.*, invisible

invito, 1.*v.a.*, invite

invitus, -a, -um, *adj.*, unwilling, against one's will

invocatio, -onis, *f.*, invocation

invoco, 1.*v.a.*, invoke

involvo, -ere, -volvi, -volutum, 3.*v.a.*, roll about, entangle

iocum, -i, *n.*, joke, jest, pleasantry

ipse, ipsa, ipsum, *intens. pron.*, self, even; himself, herself, itself; *emphatic*, he, she; *sometimes with force of* hic, ille, is, *or* idem

ira, -ae, *f.*, anger

irascor, irasci, iratus sum, 3.*v.dep.*, be angry, be enraged

iratus, -a, -um, *part. adj.*, angry

irrideo, *see* **inrideo**

is, ea, id, *dem. pron. and adj.*, he, she, it, they; this, that, these, those

iste, ista, istud, *dem. pron. and adj.*, that; he, she, they, these, those; *in Conf. frequently used as equivalent of* **hic** *and* **is**

istuc, *adv.*, thither

ita, *adv.*, so, thus, in that way

Italia, -ae, *f.*, Italy

Italicus, -a, -um, *adj.*, of *or* belonging to Italy, Italian

itaque, *adv.*, and so, and thus; therefore

item, *adv.*, likewise, in like manner

iter, itineris, *n.*, journey

iterum, *adv.*, again, the second time

itidem, *adv.*, in like manner, likewise

iubeo, -ere, iussi, iussum, 2.*v.a.*, order, command, bid

iucunditas, -tatis, *f.*, pleasantness, pleasure

iucundo, 1.*v.a.*, give pleasure to; *pass. with middle sense*, enjoy one's self

iucundus, -a, -um, *adj.*, delightful, pleasing

iudicium, -ii, *n.*, judgment

iudico, 1.*v.a.*, judge

Iuno, -onis, *f.*, Juno, *queen of the gods, consort of Jupiter*

ius, iuris, *n.*, right, law

iuste, *adv.*, justly, rightly

Iustina, -ae, *f.*, Justina, *Roman empress, mother of Valentinian II, and defender of Arianism in the last quarter of the 4th Century A.D.*

iustitia, -ae, *f.*, justice

iustus, -a, -um, *adj.*, just

iuvenalis, -e, *adj.*, of *or* belonging to a youth, youthful

iuvenis, -is, *m.*, a youth, young man

iuventus, -tutis, *f.*, youth; young people, youth

iuxta, *adv.*, near, close by; *prep with acc.*, near, close to

L

labor, labi, lapsus sum, 3.*v.dep.*, slip, glide, fall

labor, -oris, *m.*, work, labor, toil, weariness

laboriosus, -a, -um, *adj.*, difficult, irksome

laboro, 1.*v.n.*, suffer, be afflicted with

labrum, -i, *n.*, lip

lac, lactis, *n.*, milk

lacrima, -ae, *f.*, tear

lacrimosus, -a, -um, *adj.*, tearful, piteous

laetitia, -ae, *f.*, joy, joyfulness, delight

laetor, 1.*v.dep.*, be glad, rejoice

laetus, -a, -um, *adj.*, joyful

laguncula, -ae, *f.*, bottle, flagon

languor, -oris, *m.*, languor, illness

lapso, 1.*v.n.*, slip, slide, stumble

laqueus, -i, *m.*, a snare

lassitudo, -inis, *f.*, weariness

lateo, -ere, -tui, *no sup.*, 2.*v.n. and a.*, be concealed, be hidden; be unknown to

latine, *adv.*, in Latin

Latinus, -a, -um, *adj.*, Latin; **litterae Latinae,** the Latin language, Latin

latus, -eris, *n.*, side

laudabilis, -e, *adj.*, praiseworthy

laudabiliter, *adv.*, praiseworthily, in a praiseworthy manner
laudo, 1.*v.a.*, praise
laus, laudis, *f.*, praise
lavacrum, -i, *n.*, bath (*of Baptism*), *Conf.* I, 11, 17
lavo, 1.*v.a. and n.*, wash
laxo, 1.*v.a.*, loosen, slacken, relax
lectio, -onis, *f.*, reading
lectus, -i, *m.*, bed
legitimus, -a, -um, *adj.*, lawful; *n. pl. as subst.*, legitima, -orum, precepts, commands
lego, -ere, legi, lectum, 3.*v.a.*, read
lenio, -ire, -ivi (-ii), -itum, 4.*v.a.*, soften, make smooth
leo, -onis, *m.*, lion
lepor (depos), -oris, *m.*, grace, charm
letalis, -e, *adj.*, deadly, mortal
lex, legis, *f.*, law; the Law
levo, 1.*v.a.*, raise
libenter, *adv.*, willingly, freely
liber, libri, *m.*, book
liber, -era, -erum, *adj.*, free
libere, *adv.*, freely, openly
liberalis, -e, *adj.*, liberal
liberi, -orum, *m. pl.*, children
libero, 1.*v.a.*, liberate, set free, deliver
libertas, -tatis, *f.*, liberty, freedom
libet, -ere, libuit, *or* libitum est, 2.*v.n.impers.*, it pleases, it is agreeable
libido, -inis, *f.*, passion, inordinate desire
licentia, -ae, *f.*, license, wantonness
licentiosus, -a, -um, *adj.*, unbridled, licentious
licet, -ere, licuit, licitum est, 2.*v.n. impers.*, it is allowed, it is permitted

ligneus, -a, -um, *adj.*, of wood, wooden
lignum, -i, *n.*, wood, tree
ligo, 1.*v.a.*, tie, bind
limen, -inis, *n.*, threshold, door, entrance
limes, -itis, *m.*, boundary, bound, limit
limosus, -a, -um, *adj.*, muddy, slimy
limus, -i, *m.*, slime, mire
lingua, -ae, *f.*, tongue, language
linguosus, -a, -um, *adj.*, wordy, tonguey
lis, litis, *f.*, contest, struggle
litigiosus, -a, -um, *adj.*, litigious; fora litigiosa, lawsuits in the forum
litigo, 1.*v.n.*, quarrel
littera, -ae, *f.*, letter of the alphabet; *pl.*, litterae, -arum, letters (*one's A B C's, Conf.* I, 8, 13), rudiments; a writing, writings; a letter, epistle; literature; *Conf.* I, 13, 20, litterae graecae, the Greek Language
litteratura, -ae, *f.*, literature
litteratus, -a, -um, *adj.*, learned
litus, -oris, *n.*, the seashore
locus, -i, *m.*, place, position; a place *or* passage in a book
locutio, -onis, *f.*, speaking, manner of expression, style
longe, *adv.*, far, far away, far off; *with comp.*, far, by far; a longe, from afar
longinquus, -a, -um, *adj.*, distant, remote, of long duration, long; de longinquo, from afar
longus, -a, -um, *adj.*, long; *with* fabula, tedious, endless
loquacitas, -tatis, *f.*, loquacity:

aniles loquacitates, old women's gossiping

loquax, -acis, *adj.,* loquacious, babbling, prating

loquor, loqui, locutus sum, 3.*v.dep.,* speak, utter, say

lora, -orum, *n. pl.,* reins

lubricus, -a, -um, *adj.,* slippery, perilous; *n. sing. as subst.,* **lubricum, -i,** a slippery place, slippery ground

lucens, -ntis, *part. adj.,* shining, bright

lucror, 1.*v.dep.,* gain

lucrum, -i, *n.,* gain, profit

luctamen, -inis, *n.,* struggle, combat

luctor, 1.*v.dep.,* strive, struggle

luctuosus, -a, -um, *adj.,* sorrowful, doleful; *n. pl. as subst.,* sorrowful things

luctus, -us, *m.,* mourning, grief

ludicer (and **ludicrus**), **-cra, -crum,** *adj.,* playful, sportive, absurd; *n. sing. as subst.,* **ludicrum, -i,** show, spectacle

ludificatio, -onis, *f.,* deception, disillusionment

ludo, -ere, lusi, lusum, 3.*v.n.,* play, play at

ludus, -i, *m.,* a game, sport; *pl.,* the public games, spectacles

lumen, -inis, *n.,* light

luminosus, -a, -um, *adj.,* luminous

luna, -ae, *f.,* the moon

lusorius, -a, -um, *adj.,* used for play, gaming

lutum, -i, *n.,* mire, filth

lux, lucis, *f.,* light, the light of day, life

M

macero, 1.*v.a.,* afflict, torment

machinamentum, -i, *n.,* invention, device

maculosus, -a, -um, *adj.,* defiled, polluted

Madaura, -ae, *f.,* or **Madauri, -orum,** *m.,* Madaura, a city in Numidia

maerens, -ntis, *part. adj.,* mournful, lamenting, sad

maeror, -oris, *m.,* grief, sorrow

maestitia, -ae, *f.,* grief, sorrow

maestitudo, -inis, *f.,* sorrow

maestus, -a, -um, *adj.,* sad, grief-stricken

magis, *comp. adv.,* more, rather

magister, -tri, *m.,* schoolmaster, teacher

magisterium, -ii, *n.,* teaching, office of teaching

magnus, -a, -um, *adj.,* great; *comp.,* maior; *Conf.* III, 3,6, maior, head, first in rank (*in a school*); *Conf.* I, 8, 13, maiores homines, one's elders, grown-ups; *also* maiores alone, *Conf.* IX, 8, 18; *superl.,* maximus

malivolus, -a, -um, *adj.,* malicious, malevolent

malo, malle, malui, *irr.v.,* prefer

malum, -i, *n.,* evil, misfortune

malus, -a, -um, *adj.,* bad, evil; *comp.,* peior; *superl.,* pessimus

mancipium, -i, *n.,* slave

mando, 1.*v.a.,* entrust, commit, enjoin

mane, *adv.,* in the morning

maneo, -ere, mansi, mansum, 2.*v.n.,* remain, stay, abide

Manichaeus, -i, *m.*, Manichaeus *or* Mani *the founder of Manichaeism*

Manichaeus, -a, -um, *adj.*, Manichaean; *m. sing. as subst.*, Manichaeus, -i, a Manichaean; *m. pl. as subst.*, Manichaei, -orum, the Manichaeans

manifesto, 1.*v.a.*, make manifest, reveal

manifestus, -a, -um, *adj.*, manifest, clear, evident

mano, 1.*v.n.*, flow, run

manus, -us, *f.*, hand

mare, -is, *n.*, the sea

marinus, -a, -um, *adj.*, of *or* relating to the sea

marito, 1.*v.a.*, impregnate

maritus, -i, *m.*, spouse, husband

martyr, -yris, *c.*, martyr

mater, -tris, *f.*, mother

maternus, -a, -um, *adj.*, of *or* relating to a mother, maternal

matrimonium, -ii, *n.*, marriage, matrimony

maxime, *superl. adv.*, especially

medicamentum, -i, *n.*, medicine, remedy

medicina, -ae, *f.*, medicine

medicinalis, -e, *adj.*, of *or* pertaining to medicine, medical

medicus, -i, *m.*, physician

Mediolanensis, -e, *adj.*, of *or* belonging to Milan; *m. pl.*, the Milanese

Mediolanium, -i, *n.*, Milan

meditor, 1.*v.dep.*, consider, meditate on

medulla, -ae, *f.*, *sing. and pl.*, marrow

melior, *comp. adj.*, see bonus

melius, *comp. adv.*, see bene

membrum, -i, *n.*, member, limb

memini, -isse, *def.v.a.*, remember, recall

memor, -oris, *adj.*, mindful

memoria, -ae, *f.*, memory; *Conf.* V, 8, 15, a shrine

memoro, 1.*v.a.*, mention

mendacium, -ii, *n.*, lie, falsehood, deception

mendax, -acis, *adj.*, lying, deceitful

mens, mentis, *f.*, mind, intellect

mensa, -ae, *f.*, table; mensa lusoria, gaming table

mentior, -iri, -itus sum, 4.*v.dep.*, lie

merces, -cedis, *f.*, money, allowance, fee, salary, recompense, reward

meribibula, -ae, *f.*, winebibbess

meritum, -i, *n.*, reward, merit

merso, 1.*v.a.*, immerse

merum, -i, *n.*, wine (*unmixed with water*)

-met, *an emphatic enclitic suffix added to personal pronouns*

meticulosus, -a, -um, *adj.*, terrifying, fear-inspiring

metuo, -ere, -ui, -utum, 3.*v.a. and n.*, fear, dread

metus, -us, *m.*, fear, dread

meus, -a, -um, *poss. adj. and pron.*, my, mine, my own; *m. sing. voc.*, mi (*also* meus; *see* deus)

militia, -ae, *f.*, military *or* civil service; career *or* profession; militia saecularis, the service of the world, worldly service

milito, 1.*v.n.*, serve (*of both military and civil service*)

minime, *superl. adv.*, see parum

ministerium, -ii, *n.*, office, ministration

ministro, 1.*v.a.*, minister, distribute

minor, *comp. adj.*, *see* **parvus**

minus, *comp. adv.*, less, not; *see* **parum**

mirabilis, -e, *adj.*, admirable, wonderful, marvelous, extraordinary, strange; *n. pl. as subst.*, wondrous works

miraculum, -i, *n.*, wonder, miracle

miror, 1.*v.dep.*, wonder at, admire, marvel

mirus, -a, -um, *adj.*, strange, wonderful

misceo, -ere, miscui, mixtum, 2.*v.a.*, mix, mingle, intermingle

miser, -era, -erum, *adj.*, unfortunate, wretched

miserabilis, -e, *adj.*, miserable, wretched

miserabiliter, *adv.*, miserably

miseratio, -onis, *f.*, pity, compassion, mercy

misere, *adv.*, miserably, wretchedly

misereor, -eri, misertus sum, 2.*v.dep.*, feel pity for, take pity on

miseria, -ae, *f.*, misery, affliction

misericordia, -ae, *f.*, mercy, pity

misericorditer, *adv.*, mercifully

misericors, -cordis, *adj.*, merciful

miseror, 1.*v.dep.*, pity, have compassion on

mitigo, 1.*v.a.*, mitigate, soften

mitis, -e, *adj.*, gentle, kind, mild

mitto, -ere, misi, missum, 3.*v.a.*, send; put forth

moderamen, -inis, *n.*, control, direction

moderate, *adv.*, moderately, simply

modeste, *adv.*, modestly

modicus, -a, -um, *adj.*, moderate, little; *n. as subst.*, a little, a small quantity

modo, *adv. of time*, but now, now, just now

modus, -i, *m.*, measure, mean, manner, way, fashion; *Conf.* III, 5, 9, simple style; eiusmodi, of this kind, of that kind; huiuscemodi *and* huiusmodi, of this kind, of such a kind, such

moenia, -ium, *n. pl.*, walls

moleste, *adv.*, with trouble *or* difficulty; moleste habeo, take it ill, be annoyed

molestia, -ae, *f.*, impatience

molestus, -a, -um, *adj.*, annoying, disagreeable, be opposed

mollitia, -ae, *f.*, weakness

momentum, -i, *n.*, moment

monachus, -i, *m.*, monk

monasterium, -ii, *n.*, monastery

moneo, -ere, -ui, -itum, 2.*v.a.*, advise, admonish, warn

monitus, -us, *m.*, warning, admonition

Monnica, -ae, *f.*, Monnica, *mother of St. Augustine*

mons, montis, *m.*, mountain

monumentum, -i, *n.*, monument

morbus, -i, *m.*, disease, malady

morigerus, -a, -um, *adj.*, obsequious, benevolent

morior, mori (moriri), mortuus sum (moriturus), 3.*v.dep.*, die

mors, mortis, *f.*, death

mortalis, -e, *adj.*, mortal

mortalitas, -tatis, *f.*, mortality

mortifico, 1.*v.a.*, mortify

mortuus, -a, -um, *adj.*, dead; *Conf.* V, 8, 14, deadly, death-bringing

mos, moris, *m.*, custom, usage; de more, according to custom

motus, -us, *m.*, motion, movement, action; emotion
moveo, -ere, movi, motum, 2.*v.a.*, move; affect, trouble
mox, *adv.*, soon; **mox ut,** as soon as
mulceo, -ere, mulsi, mulsum, 2.*v.a.*, charm, delight, allure
muliebris, -e, *adj.*, of *or* belonging to a woman
multipliciter, *adv.*, in manifold *or* various ways
multiplico, 1.*v.a.*, multiply, increase many times
multus, -a, -um, *adj.*, much, numerous, many; *n. pl. as subst.*, **multa, -orum,** many things; *comp.* **plus,** *superl.* **plurimus;** *comp.pl.*, **plures,** several; *n. acc. sing. as adv.* **multum,** much, very; *n. abl. sing. as adv.* **multo,** much, by much, far
mundatio, -onis, *f.*, cleansing
mundus, -i, *m.*, the world; **hic mundus,** this world (*as opposed to Heaven and eternity*)
municeps, -cipis, *m.*, a citizen (*of a municipium*)
municipium, -ii, *n.*, municipal town, municipality
munus, -eris, *n.*, gift; favor, grace
murmur, -uris, *n.*, murmur
murus, -i, *m.*, wall
muscipula, -ae, *f.*, *and* **muscipulum, -i,** *n.*, trap, pitfall
mussito, 1.*v.n. and a.*, speak in a low tone, murmur
mutatio, -onis, *f.*, change
muto, 1.*v.a.*, change
mutus, -a, -um, *adj.*, mute, dumb
mysterium, -ii, *n.*, mystery
mysticus, -a, -um, *adj.*, mystic

N

nam, *conj.*, for
namque, *conj.*, for (*more emphatic than* **nam**)
nanciscor, -i, nactus sum, 3.*v.dep.*, obtain
narratio, -onis, *f.*, narration, story
narro, 1.*v.a.*, tell, relate
nascor, nasci, natus sum, 3.*v.dep.*, be born
natura, -ae, *f.*, nature
naturalis, -e, *adj.*, natural
nauta, -ae, *m.*, sailor
navigatio, -onis, *f.*, voyage
navigo, 1.*v.n.*, sail, voyage
navis, -is, *f.*, boat, ship
ne, *neg. adv. and conj.*, not; that . . . not, in order that . . . not, lest
ne, *adv.*, not; **ne . . . quidem,** not even
-ne, *enclitic interrog. part.*, whether, (*in direct questions, usually omitted in English translation*)
Nebridius, -ii, *m.*, Nebridius, a fellow countryman and friend of Augustine
nebula, -ae, *f.*, cloud, mist
nec (neque), *conj.*, not, and not, also not, nor; **nec . . . nec,** neither . . . nor; *Conf.* II, 4, 9, **nec** (= **ne . . . quidem**), not even; *also, Conf.* IX, 8, 17
necdum, *adv.*, not yet
necessarius, -a, -um, *adj.*, necessary
necesse, *indecl. adj.*, necessary; **with est,** it must be, it is necessary
necessitas, -tatis, *f.*, necessity, compulsion, need, necessity
neco, 1.*v.a.*, kill
neglego, -ere, -lexi, -lectum, 3.*v.a.*, neglect, disregard

nego, 1.*v.a.*, say no, say . . . not, deny

negotiosus, -a, -um, *adj.*, busy, occupied with business

negotium, -ii, *n.* business, affair, task; *Conf.* II, 3, 5, concern, sacrifice

nemo, -inis, *c.*, no one, nobody

nempe, *adv.*, forsooth, to be sure

nemus, -oris, *n.*, a wood, grove

nepos, -otis, *c.*, grandchild

nequam, *adj., indecl. in positive*, vile, dissolute, worthless, wicked; *superl.*, **nequissimus, -a, -um**

nequaquam, *adv.*, by no means, in no wise

nescio, -ire, -ivi (-ii), *no sup.*, 4.*v.a.*, not know, be ignorant, be unacquainted with; **nescio quis,** — **cuius,** *etc.*, I know not who, some, some . . . or other; *Conf.* VIII, 6, 15, **nescio quando,** some time or other

nihil, *indecl.*, nothing; *as adv.*, not at all, by no means

nimie, *adv.*, very, exceedingly

nimirum, *adv.*, doubtlessly, certainly

nimis, *adv.*, too much, too, excessively, exceedingly

nisi, *conj.*, unless, if not, except; **nisi quia,** except because, unless that; **nisi cum,** unless when, except when

nocens, -ntis, *part. adj.*, guilty, wicked; *as m. subst.*, guilty person

nodus, -i, *m.*, knot

nolo, nolle, nolui, *irr.v.*, be unwilling, not wish

nomen, -inis, *n.*, name, appellation

nominatus, -a, -um, *part. adj.*, renowned, celebrated

non, *adv.*, no, not

nondum, *adv.*, not yet

nonne, *interrog. adv., expecting an affirmative answer*, (is) not? (does) not?

nonnullus, -a, -um, *adj.*, some, several

nonus, -a, -um, *adj.*, ninth

nosco, -ere, novi, notum, 3.*v.a.*, become acquainted with; learn; *in perfect tenses*, know; *with infin.*, know how

noster, -tra, -trum, *poss. adj. and pron.*, our, ours, of us

noto, 1.*v.a.*, censure

notus, -a, -um, *part. adj.*, known, well-known

novem, *indecl.*, nine

novitas, -tatis, *f.*, newness, novelty

novus, -a, -um, *adj.*, new, novel, strange

nox, noctis, *f.*, night

nubo, -ere, nupsi, nuptum, 3.*v.n.*, marry, (*used of the woman*)

nudo, 1.*v.a.*, uncover, disclose, reveal

nudus, -a, -um, *adj.*, bare

nugae, -arum, *f. pl.*, trifles, play

nugatorius, -a, -um, *adj.*, trifling, worthless; *n. pl. as subst.*, silly things, trifling things

nugor, 1.*v.dep.*, jest, trifle

nullus, -a, -um, *adj.*, no, none; *m. and f. as subst.*, no one, nobody

numero, 1.*v.a.*, number, enumerate

numerus, -i, *m.*, number; in pl., *Conf.* V, 7, 12, mathematics, astronomy

numquam, *adv.*, never, by no means, not at all

numquid, *interrog. particle used to*

introduce a question whether the answer expected be negative or affirmative

nunc, *adv.,* now

nuntio, 1.*v.a.,* announce

nusquam, *adv.,* nowhere

nutabilis, -e, *adj.,* unstable, fragile

nutrio, -ire, -ivi, -itum, 4.*v.a.,* nourish, sustain

nutritor, -oris, *m.,* one who rears, one who brings up; *Conf.* VIII, 6, 15, sub Ambrosio nutritore, under the fostering care of Ambrose

nutrix, -tricis, *f.,* nurse

nutus, -us, *m.,* nod; *of the eyes,* winking; *fig.,* command, will; ad nutum, at one's will *or* pleasure

nux, nucis, *f.,* nut

O

o, *interj.,* oh! O!

ob, *prep. with acc.,* because of, on account of

obfusco, 1.*v.a.,* obscure

obicio, -ere, -ieci, -iectum, 3.*v.a.,* propose, offer, put, charge against, cast up, throw in one's teeth; *p.p. n. pl. as subst.,* **obiecta, -orum,** charges, objections

oblatio, -onis, *f.,* offering, oblation

obliviscor, oblivisci, oblitus sum, 3.*v.dep.,* forget

obnubilo, 1.*v.a.,* overcloud, darken

oborior, -oriri, -ortus sum, 4.*v.dep.,* arise

obscure, *adv.,* obscurely

obsecro, 1.*v.a.,* beseech, implore; *often used practically as an interjection*

obsequium, -ii, *n.,* obedience, allegiance, service, attention

obsequor, -sequi, -secutus sum, 3.*v.dep.,* comply with, be indulgent; be obsequious, be obedient

obsum, -esse, -fui, *irr.v.n.,* harm, injure

obsurdesco, -ere, -surdui, *no sup.,* 3.*v.n.,* become deaf; be deaf, not give ear

obtempero, 1.*v.n.,* obey, submit to

obtero, -ere, -trivi, -tritum, 3.*v.a.,* trample, tread upon

obtineo, -ere, -tinui, -tentum, 2.*v.a.,* obtain, possess

obtundo, -ere, -tudi, -tusum, 3.*v.a.,* dull, weaken, make hoarse

obviam, *adv.,* in the way; *hence with verb of motion,* against, face to face; in obviam, *same meaning*

occido, -ere, -cidi, -cisum, 3.*v.a.,* kill

occulte, *adv.,* secretly, in secret

occultus, -a, -um, *adj.,* hidden; *n. pl. as subst.,* secrets; *Conf.* VIII, 11, 25, one's inmost being; in occulto, in secret

occupo, 1.*v.a.,* seize, occupy, engage

occurro, -ere, -curri, -cursum, 3.*v.n.,* meet; *of words (to the mind of the speaker),* occur, come into, present themselves; occur, happen

oculus, -i, *m.,* eye

odi, odisse, osurus, *v.def.a.,* hate, detest

odiosus, -a, -um, *adj.,* hateful, odious, tedious

odium, -ii, *n.,* rancor

odor, -oris, *m.,* odor

offendo, -ere, -fendi, -fensum, 3.*v.a.,* offend

offensio, -onis, *f.,* offense, that which gives offense; *Conf.* II, 2, 4, disgust, discontentment

offero, -ferre, obtuli, oblatum, *v.irr.
a.*, present, offer
officina, -ae, *f.*, workshop
officium, -ii, *n.*, courtesy, kindness,
duty, office
olens, -ntis, *part. adj.*, smelling,
fragrant
oleum, -i, *n.*, oil
olim, *adv.*, now for a long time, once
omnimodus, -a, -um, *adj.*, of every
kind, in every way
omnino, *adv.*, entirely, wholly, certainly, indeed
omnipotens, -entis, *adj.*, omnipotent
omnis, -e, *adj.*, all, every; *n. pl.*, all
things, everything
onero, 1.*v.a.*, weigh down, oppress
onerosus, -a, -um, *adj.*, burdensome
onus, oneris, *n.*, burden, load
onustus, -a, -um, *adj.*, loaded, laden
operor, 1.*v.dep.*, work, act
opes, -um, *f. pl.*, wealth, resources
opifex, -ficis, *m.*, artisan
opinor, 1.*v.dep.*, be of opinion,
believe, suppose
oportet, -ere, oportuit, 2.*v.impers.*,
it behooves, it is necessary
oportune, *adv.*, opportunely, season-
ably
oportunus, -a, -um, *adj.*, opportune,
suitable
opperior, -iri, -pertus sum, 4.*v.dep.*,
await
oppidum, -i, *n.*, town
oppono, -ere, -posui, -positum,
3.*v.a.*, place before
oppugno, 1.*v.a.*, attack, oppose,
combat
optimus, *superl. adj.*, *see* bonus
opto, 1.*v.a.*, wish, desire

opulentus, -a, -um, *adj.*, rich,
opulent
opus, *n. indecl.*, necessity, need; opus
est, it is necessary, there is need
opus, -eris, *n.*, work, toil, deed,
action
oraculum, -i, *n.*, oracle
oratio, -onis, *f.*, oration; prayer
oratoria, -ae, *f.*, the oratorical art,
oratory
orbis, -is, *m.*, circle; orbis terrae
and orbis terrarum, the world,
mankind
ordinator, -oris, *m.*, ordainer, one
who ordains, orderer
ordinatus, -a, -um, *part. adj.*,
orderly, regular
ordino, 1.*v.a.*, ordain; *Conf.* I, 6, 7,
foreordain
ordo, -inis, *m.*, order, arrangement,
course, cycle
Orestes, -ae, *and* -is, *m.*, Orestes,
*son of Agamemnon and Clytaem-
nestra, whose friendship with Pylades became proverbial*
orfanus, -i, *m.*, orphan
orientalis, -e, *adj.*, of *or* belonging to
the East; orientales partes, the
East, the Orient
originalis, -e, *adj.*, original
orior, oriri, ortus sum, 4.*v.dep.*,
arise, begin
oro, 1.*v.a.*, pray, entreat
os, oris, *n.*, mouth; countenance;
in pl., *Conf.* VI, 1, 1, lips
os, ossis, *n.*, bone
ostendo, -ere, ostendi, ostensum,
3.*v.a.*, show, indicate, reveal
Ostia, -orum, *n. pl.*, Ostia
otiose, *adv.*, idly, without effect, to
no purpose

otiosus, -a, -um, *adj.*, free, at leisure

otium, -ii, *n.*, leisure, ease, period of idleness; tranquillity, repose

P

pactum, -i, *n.*, agreement, compact; pactum et placitum, compact and agreement

paedagogus, -i, *m.*, pedagogue

paene, *adv.*, almost, nearly

paenitet, -ere, -uit, *no sup.*, 2.*v.a.im-pers.*, be sorry, repent, regret

pagina, -ae, *f.*, page

palaestra, -ae, *f.*, palaestric art

palam, *adv.*, openly, publicly

palatium, -ii, *n.*, palace, imperial court

palmes, -itis, *m.*, vine-sprout

panis, -is, *m.*, bread

par, paris, *adj.*, equal

paracletus, -i, *m.*, the Paraclete

paratus, -a, -um *adj.*, prepared, ready

parens, -entis, *c.*, parent, mother, father

pareo, -ere, parui, paritum, 2.*v.n.*, obey

parilis, -e, *adj.*, like, similar

pario, -ere, peperi, partum, 3.*v.a.*, bear, bring forth

pariter, *adv.*, equally, in like manner, alike, together with, at the same time

pars, partis, *f.*, part; *pl.*, a side (*in an argument, etc.*)

particula, -ae, *f.*, small part, particle

partior, -iri, partitus sum, 4.*v.dep.*, share

parturio, -ire, -ivi (-ii), *no sup.*, 4.*v.a.*, be in labor, be in travail, bring forth

parturitio, -onis, *f.*, parturition

parum, *adv.*, too little, not enough; *comp.*, minus, less, not; *superl.*, minime, very little, not at all

parvulus, -a, -um, *adj.*, small, young little; *as subst. m.*, parvulus, -i, child

parvus, -a, -um, *adj.*, small, young, little; *comp.*, minor, minus; minor (natu), younger; *superl.*, minimus

pasco, -ere, pavi, pastum, 3.*v.a.*, feed, satisfy; *as v.dep.*, pascor, pasci, pastus sum, feed on

passer, -eris, *m.*, sparrow

passim, *adv.*, in a disorderly fashion, promiscuously

pateo, -ere, -ui, *no sup*, 2.*v.n.*, be open, lie open, have space

pater, -tris, *m.*, father

paterne, *adv.*, paternally, like a father

paternus, -a, -um, *adj.*, of *or* relating to a father, paternal

patior, pati, passus sum, 3.*v.dep.*, suffer, bear, endure, experience

patria, -ae, *f.*, one's country, native land

Patricius, -ii, *m.*, Patricius, *father of St. Augustine*

patrius, -a, -um, *adj.*, paternal; *Conf.* IX, 13, 36, sepulchrum patrium, a tomb in her own country

patrona, ae, *f.*, protectress, patroness

paucus, -a, -um, *adj.*, *mostly pl.*, few

paulatim, *adv.*, little by little, gradually

paulisper, *adv.*, a little while

paulo, *adv.*, by a little, a little

paululum, -i, *n.*, a very little; post paululum, after a little while, shortly; *as adv.*, a little, for a little while

Paulus, -i, *m.*, Paul

pauper, -eris, *adj.*, poor; *m. pl. as subst.*, the poor

pausatio, -onis, *f.*, rest, period of rest

pax, pacis, *f.*, peace

peccator, -oris, *m.*, sinner

peccatum, -i, *n.*, sin

pecco, 1.*v.n.*, commit a fault, sin

pectus, -oris, *n.*, breast, heart

pecunia, -ae, *f.*, money

pello, -ere, pepuli, pulsum, 3.*v.a.*, drive out, expel

pendeo, -ere, pependi, *no sup.*, 2.*v.n.*, hang, hang down; *fig.*, *Conf.* IV, 4, 8, depend on; be in suspense, be hesitant

pendo, -ere, pependi, *no sup.*, 3.*v.n.*, hang; *fig. with* **ex,** depend on

penetro, 1.*v.a. and n.*, penetrate, pierce into, enter

penitus,*adv.*, entirely, wholly, deeply

penuria, -ae, *f.*, want, need, indigence

per, *prep. with acc.*, through, over, across; *of time*, through, during; *of agency, means, cause, and manner*, through, by means of, on account of

perago, -ere, -egi, -actum, 3.*v.a.*, complete, finish, end

percipio, -ere, -cepi, -ceptum, 3.*v.a.*, acquire, learn, receive

percutio, -ere, -cussi, -cussum, 3.*v.a.*, strike

perditio, -onis, *f.*, ruin, perdition

perditus, -a, -um, *part. adj.*, thoroughly corrupt, abandoned, profligate

perdo, -ere, -didi, -ditum, 3.*v.a.*, lose

perdomo, -are, -domui, -domitum, 1.*v.a.*, conquer, subdue completely

perduco, -ere, -duxi, -ductum, 3.*v.a.*, lead, bring to

peregre, *adv.*, in a foreign country, abroad

peregrinatio, -onis, *f.*, sojourn, stay; coming, journey, pilgrimage

peregrinor, 1.*v.dep.*, sojourn

peregrinus, -a, -um, *adj.*, foreign, strange

pereo, -ire, -ivi(-ii), -itum, *irr.v.n.*, perish, be lost

perexiguus, -a, -um, *adj.*, very little

perfectus, -a, -um, *part. adj.*, perfect

perficio, -ere, -feci, -fectum, 3.*v.a.*, perform, complete, accomplish

pergo, -ere, perrexi, perrectum, 3.*v.n.*, proceed, advance

periclitor, 1.*v.dep.*, be in danger, be in peril

periculosus, -a, -um, *adj.*, dangerous, perilous

periculum, -i, *n.*, danger, peril

peritus, -a, -um, *adj.*, experienced, expert, skilful at, well versed in; *as m. subst. with* iuris, one skilled *or* learned in the law

permaneo, -ere, -mansi, -mansum, 2.*v.n.*, remain, continue

permitto, -ere, -misi, -missum, 3.*v.a.*, permit

perniciosus, -a, -um, *adj.*, pernicious

perpetior, -peti, -pessus sum, 3.*v.a.*, endure, put up with

persequor, -sequi, -secutus sum, 3.*v.dep.*, persecute

persona, -ae, *f.*, person, character, personage; **ex persona,** under the name of

persuadeo, -ere, -suasi, -suasum,
2.*v.a.*, persuade, convince
pertendo, -ere, -tendi, -tentum,
3.*v.n.*, go on, proceed
perturbo, 1.*v.a.*, disturb, throw into
confusion, terrify
pervenio, -ire, -veni, -ventum, 4.*v.n.*,
come, arrive, reach, attain to
perventio, -onis, *f.*, arrival
perversitas, -tatis, *f.*, perversity
perverto, -ere, -verti, -versum,
3.*v.a.*, destroy, pervert, overturn
pes, pedis, *m.*, foot
pestifer, -fera, -ferum, *adj.*, deadly,
pernicious, mortal
pestilentia, -ae, *f.*, pestilence, unwholesomeness
petitio, -onis, *f.*, request, petition
peto, -ere, -ivi (-ii), -itum, 3.*v.a.*,
seek, ask
phantasma, -atis, *n.*, phantasm
philosophia, -ae, *f.*, philosophy
philosophus, -i, *m.*, philosopher
pie, *adv.*, piously
pietas, -tatis, *f.*, dutiful love, filial
piety, piety, devotion
piget, -ere, piguit, 2.*v.impers.a.*, it
troubles, it displeases
pila, -ae, *f.*, ball, game of ball
pilula, -ae, *f.*, little ball
pinna, -ae, *f.*, wing
pirus, -i, *f.*, pear tree
pius, -a, -um, *adj.*, pious
placeo, -ere, -ui, -itum, 2.*v.n.*,
please, delight; *impers.*, it pleases,
it is one's pleasure, it seems best;
pres. part. as adj., pleasing
placide, *adv.*, calmly, serenely
placitum, -i, *n.*, convention, agreement, principle
plaga, -ae, *f.*, blow, stroke

planctus, -us, *m.*, weeping, lamentation
plane, *adv.*, clearly; wholly, entirely
plango, -ere, planxi, planctum, 3.*v.a.*,
lament, bewail, weep for
plausus, -us, *m.*, applause
plebs, plebis, *f.*, the multitude;
especially in a Christian sense, the
Christian people, the faithful
people of God
plecto, -ere, 3.*v.a.*, punish
plenitudo, -inis, *f.*, fulness
plenus, -a, -um, *adj.*, full, full of
plerumque, *adv.*, generally, often
plerusque, -aque, -umque, *adj.*,
usually in pl., very many, many
ploratus, -us, *m.*, weeping
ploro, 1.*v.n. and a.*, lament, cry for
grief; weep over, grieve for
plus, pluris, *comp. adj.*, see multus
poculum, -i, *n.*, cup
poena, -ae, *f.*, penalty, punishment
poenalis, -e, *adj.*, penal, painful
poeta, -ae, *m.*, poet
poeticus, -a, -um, *adj.*, poetical
polliceor, -eri, -itus sum, 2.*v.dep.*,
promise
polus, -i, *m.*, the sky, the heavens
pomeridianus, -a, -um, *adj.*, in the
afternoon, afternoon
pomum, -i, *n.*, a fruit; *pl.*, fruit
pondus, -eris, *n.*, weight, burden;
authority, firmness
pono, -ere, posui, positum, 3.*v.a.*,
put, place, lay, lay down, bury;
set down, state
Ponticianus, -i, *m.*, Ponticianus, *an
acquaintance of Augustine*
popularis, -e, *adj.*, popular, to the
people

populus, -i, *m.*, the people; *especially in sense of* the Christian people

porcus, -i, *m.*, pig

porro, *adv.*, forward, further; again, moreover

portio, -onis, *f.*, portion, part

porto, 1.*v.a.*, carry

posco, -ere, poposci, *no sup.*, 3.*v.a.*, ask, request

possum, posse, potui, *irr.v.n.*, can, be able, have power

post, *adv.*, after, afterwards; *as prep. with acc.*, after

postea, *adv.*, afterwards

posteaquam, *conj.*, after that

postmodum, *adv.*, after, afterwards

potens, -entis, *adj.*, powerful, mighty; having power, able

potestas, -tatis, *f.*, power; *in pl.*, *Conf.* VI, 3, 3, high authorities, high personages; **in potestate**, under one's power, at one's disposal

potius, *adv.*, *only in comp. and superl.*, rather, more; *superl.*, potissimum, chiefly, above all

poto, 1.*v.a. and n.*, drink

prae, *prep. with abl.*, before, in front of; on account of, because of; more than

praebeo, -ere, -ui, -itum, 2.*v.a.*, offer, furnish, give

praecaveo, -ere, -cavi, -cautum, 2.*v.a.*, guard against beforehand, prevent

praecedo, -ere, -cessi, -cessum, 3.*v.n.*, go before, precede

praeceps, -cipitis, *adj.*, headlong, with headlong speed

praeceptum, -i, *n.*, command, precept, commandment

praecido, -ere, -cidi, -cisum, 3.*v a.*, cut off, cut away

praecipio, -ere, -cepi, -ceptum, 3.*v.a.*, admonish, teach

praecipitium, -i, *n.*, precipice

praeclare, *adv.*, excellently; in a high position *or* capacity

praecordia, -orum, *n. pl.*, the breast, heart

praeda, -ae, *f.*, prey

praedestino, 1.*v.a.*, predestine, ordain beforehand

praedicator, -oris, *m.*, preacher

praedico, 1.*v.a.*, predict, foretell; say, proclaim, glorify, preach; praise, commend

praedico, -ere, -dixi, -dictum, 3.*v.a.*, announce before, predict

praeditus, -a, -um, *adj.*, endowed, furnished

praedium, -ii, *n.*, estate

praefectus, -i, *m.*, prefect

praegrandis, -e, *adj.*, very great, mighty

praeloquor, -loqui, -locutus sum, 3.*v.dep.*, speak beforehand

praemium, -ii, *n.*, reward

praenuntiator, -oris, *m.*, one who announces beforehand, a foreteller

praeparo, 1.*v.a.*, make ready, provide, prepare

praepono, -ere, -posui, -positum, 3.*v.a.*, place before, prefer; place over; *p.p. as subst.*, *m.*, praepositus, -i, a superior, one placed over others

praesens, *part. adj.*, present; *n. pl. as subst.*, present things, transitory things

praesentia, -ae, *f.*, presence

praesertim, *adv.*, especially

praesto, -are, -stiti, -stitum, 1.*v.a.*, ~~give, furnish~~

praestruo, -ere, -struxi, -structum, 3.*v.a.*, construct before, prepare before

praesumo, -ere, -sumpsi, -sumptum, 3.*v.a.*, presume, suppose; take for granted, feel confident

praeter, *prep. with acc.*, beyond, except, apart from, outside of

praetereo, -ire, -ii (-ivi), -itum, *irr.v.a. and n.*, pass over, omit; *of time*, pass, go by; *p.p. as adj.*, praeteritus, -a, -um, gone by, past; *n. pl. as subst.*, praeterita, -orum, the past

praetermissio, -onis, *f.*, intermission

praetermitto, -ere, -misi, -missum, 3.*v.a.*, omit, pass over, neglect

praeterquam, *adv.*, beyond, besides, except

praevaleo, -ere, -valui, *no sup.*, 2.*v.n.*, prevail

praevenio, -ire, -veni, -ventum, 4.*v.a.*, surpass, excel

pravus, -a, -um, *adj.*, crooked; evil

preces, -um, *f.pl.*, *see* prex

premo, -ere, pressi, pressum, 3.*v.a.*, press upon, press down, repress, close

prenso, 1.*v.a.*, seize

pressus, -us, *m.*, pressing, pressure

pretiosus, -a, -um, *adj.*, precious

pretium, -ii, *n.*, price; *Conf.* IX, 12, 32, redemption

prex, precis, *f.*, *usually*, *pl.*, prayer, petition

primo, *see* prior

primor, -oris, *adj.*, foremost part,

tip; *Conf.* IX, 8, 18, **primoribus labris**, with the tips of the lips

primum, *see* prior

primus, *see* prior

prior, -oris, *adj.*, former, earlier, first; *n.*, prius, *as adv.*, before, sooner, earlier, first; *superl.*, primus, first, foremost; **primae** (*sc.* partes), the first part, chief role; *n. sing. as adv.*, primum, first, in the first place; *abl. sing. as adv.*, primo, first, at first

pristinus, -a, -um, *adj.*, former, previous; *n. pl. as subst.*, one's old way of life

prius, *see* prior

priusquam, *conj.*, before

privo, 1.*v.a.*, deprive of

pro, *prep. with abl.*, before, in front of, in behalf of, for; instead of, in return for; on account of, for the sake of; in comparison with, in proportion to; **pro invicem,** for each other

probabilis, -e, *adj.*, probable

probo, 1.*v.a.*, prove, approve

procedo, -ere, -cessi, -cessum 3.*v.n.*, proceed, appear

procella, -ae, *f.*, storm

procellosus, -a, -um, *adj.*, stormy

procuratio, -onis, *f.*, obtainment, procuration

procuro, 1.*v.a. and n.*, take care for, attend to

produco, -ere, -duxi, -ductum, 3.*v.a.*, prolong

profero, -ferre, -tuli, -latum, *irr.v.a.*, propose, present, bring forth

professio, -onis, *f.*, profession, calling; *Conf.* VIII, 6, 14, teaching, expounding proficio, -ere, -feci, -fectum, 3.*v.n.*, make progress, advance

proficiscor, -ficisci, profectus sum, 3.*v.dep.*, set out

profluo, -ere, -fluxi, -fluxum, 3.*v.n.*, flow, flow forth

profundum, -i, *n.*, depth, abyss, the deep

profundus, -a, -um, *adj.*, deep, profound

prohibitio, -onis, *f.*, prohibition

proicio, -ere, -ieci, -iectum, 3.*v.a.*, throw forth, cast, cast down, throw before, cast to

proloquor, -loqui, -locutus sum, 3.*v.dep.*, speak out, speak out of

promissio, -onis, *f.*, a promise

promitto, -ere, -misi, -missum, 3.*v.a.*, promise

promo, -ere, prompsi, promptum, 3.*v.a.*, bring forth, produce; utter, express

propalo, 1.*v.a.*, bring to light

prope, *adv.*, near; nearly, almost; *comp.*, propius

propero, 1.*v.n.*, hasten

propheta, -ae, *m.*, prophet

propinquo, 1.*v.n.*, draw near

propior, -ius, *comp. adj.*, nearer; *superl.*, proximus, very near, nearest; *Conf.* VIII, 11, 25, de proximo, very near

propono, -ere, -posui, -positum, 3.*v.a.*, propose, put before

propositum, -i, *n.*, intention, resolution

proprius, -a, -um, *adj.*, one's own, peculiar to a person

propter, *prep. with acc.*, on account of; propter quod, *conj.*, for the reason that, because

propterea, *adv.*, on that account, therefore

prorsus, *adv.*, entirely, absolutely

prorumpo, -ere, -rupi, -ruptum, 3.*v.n.*, rush forth, burst forth

prospecto, 1.*v.a.*, look forth upon, view

prosterno, -ere, -stravi, -stratum, 3.*v.a.*, cast down; *pass. with middle sense*, prostrate one's self

Protasius, -ii, *m.*, Protasius, *a martyr whose body was found by St. Ambrose*

protectio, -onis, *f.*, protection

protego, -ere, -texi, -tectum, 3.*v.a.*, protect

proterve, *adv.*, wantonly, insolently

proturbo, 1.*v.a.*, disturb, attack, outrage

provenio, -ire, -veni, -ventum, 4.*v.n.*, come forth, turn out, happen

providentia, -ae, *f.*, providence; *Conf.* VIII, 12, 29, provision

provideo, -ere, -vidi, -visum, 2.*v.a.*, provide, arrange

provisio, -onis, *f.*, store, provision, repository

provoco, 1.*v.a.*, provoke, excite

proximus, *see* propior

prudenter, *adv.*, prudently, wisely

prudentia, -ae, *f.*, prudence

prurio, -ire, 4.*def.v.n.*, itch

pruritus, -us, *m.*, itching, itch

psalmus, -i, *m.*, psalm

psalterium, -ii, *n.*, the Psalter

pubertas, -tatis, *f.*, puberty

publicus, -a, -um, *adj.*, public

pudet, pudere, puduit, puditum, 2.*v.a.*, *impers.* it causes shame, one is ashamed; one disdains

pudor, -oris, *m.*, shame

puella, -ae, f., girl

puer, -eri, m., boy, child

puerilis, -e, adj., boyish, youthful, childish

pueritia, -ae, f., boyhood

puerulus, -i, m., little boy, child

pulcher, -chra, -chrum, adj., beautiful, noble; n. as subst., pulchrum, -i, beauty

pulchritudo, -inis, f., beauty

pulso, 1.v.a., beat, knock at

punctum, -i, n., point, moment (of time)

punio, -ire, -ivi (-ii), -itum, 4.v.a., punish

purgo, 1.v.a., purge, cleanse, purify; p.p. as adj., purgatus, -a, -um, purified, pure

puto, 1.v.a., think, consider, suppose; occasionally used parenthetically

putredo, -inis, f., putridity, rottenness

Pylades, -ae, and -is, m., Pylades, friend of Orestes

Q

qua, adv., which way, in what manner, how, where

quadrigae, -arum, f. pl., chariot, car

quadrupes, -pedis, c., quadruped

quaero, -ere, quaesivi, quaesitum, 3.v.a., ask, seek

quaeso, -ere, quaesivi, no sup., with acc. or absol., beg, entreat

quaestio, -onis, f., question, problem, inquiry

quaestiuncula, -ae, f., petty question

quaestus, -us, m., emolument, income

qualis, -e, pron. and adj.; interrog., of what sort?, what kind of?; rel., as, such; talis . . . qualis, such . . . as

quam, adv.; interrog., how?, how much?; rel., as much as, than; with superl., as possible; correlatively with tam, as, as much . . . so much

quamdiu, interrog. adv., how long?

quamquam, conj., although, and yet

quamvis, adv. and conj., however, however much, although

quando, adv. and conj.; temporal, when; causal, Conf. IV, 4, 8, because, since

quandoquidem, conj., because, since, when

quanto, see quantus

quantuluscumque, -acumque, -umcumque, adj., however small, how little soever

quantum, see quantus

quantus, -a, -um, interrog. and rel. adj., how much, how great, what a; as great as; correlative with tantus, as; n. acc. sing. as adv., quantum, how much, how greatly, so far as, as; abl. as adv., quanto, by how much, how much, by as much as, the more (see tantus); in quantum, in so far as

quare, interrog. adv., wherefore?, on which account?, why?

quasi, adv., as if, just as, as it were

quatenus, adv., how far, up to what point

quattuor, indecl., four

-que, enclitic conj., and

quemadmodum, interrog. and rel. adv., in what manner?, how?; just as, as querella, -ae, *f.*, complaint

questus, -us, *m.*, complaint, lament

qui, quae, quod, *rel. pron.*, who, which, that, what

qui, quae, quod, *interrog. adj.*, what?, what sort of?

quia, *conj.*, because, that

quicumque, quae-, quod-, *indef. rel. pron. and adj.*, whoever, whatever, whichever

quidam, quae-, quid- (quod-), *indef. pron. and adj.*, a certain person *or* thing; a certain, a kind of; *often to be translated*, so to speak, as it were

quidem, *adv.*, truly, indeed, at least, surely

quies, -etis, *f.*, rest, repose

quiesco, -ere, quievi, quietum, 3.*v.n.*, rest, be silent

quiete, *adv.*, quietly, peacefully

quietus, -a, -um, *adj.*, quiet, peaceful

quilibet, quae-, quod- (quid-), *indef. pron.*, any you will, any one; *as interrog.*, whoever, whatever

quindecim, *indecl.*, fifteen

quinquagesimus, -a, -um, *adj.*, fiftieth

quinque, *indecl.*, five

quippe, *adv.*, in fact, truly; *ironically*, forsooth

quis, quid, *interrog. pron.*, who?, what?, which?; *also as interrog. adj.*, what?, which?; quid, why?; ut quid, why?; quid est quod, why is it that?

quis (qui), qua (quae), quid (quod), *indef. pron. and adj.*, any one, anything, any

quisnam, quae-, quid-, *interrog. pron. and adj.*, who?, which?, what indeed?

quisquam, quae-, quid- (quic-), *indef. pron.*, any, anyone, anything

quisque, quae-, quid- (quod-), *indef. pron. and adj.*, each one, everyone, each, every

quisquis, quaequae, quicquid (quidquid), *indef. rel. pron. and indef. adj.*, whoever, whatever, some

quo, *interrog. and rel. adv.*, whither, to what place, in what place; to what end; *with comp.*, by what, the more; wherefore, on which account

quo, *conj.*, to the end that, in order that, that the (more); because, that

quod, *conj.*, because, since, that, as to the fact that

quominus, *conj.*, by which the less, in order that not, from

quomodo, *adv.*, in what way, how

quondam, *adv.*, once, one time

quoniam, *conj.*, since, inasmuch as

quoque, *conj.*, also, too

quot, *indecl. adj.*, how many, as many as, as

quotquot, *indecl. num.*, however many, as many as

quousque, *adv.*, until which time, till when

R

rabies, -ei, *f.*, madness, fury

rapio, -ere, rapui, raptum, 3.*v.a.*, snatch, carry off, sweep away, seize, storm

rarus, -a, -um, *adj.*, rare

ratio, -onis, *f.*, reckoning, computation, explanation; method, manner, way; cause, reason

reatus, -us, *m.,* guilt

recedo, -ere, -cessi, -cessum, *3.v.n.,* depart from, go away from, leave, retire

recens, -ntis, *adj.,* recent, fresh

recessus, -us, *m.,* remoteness, secrecy

recipio, -ere, -cepi, -ceptum, *3.v.a.,* receive, take

recito, *1.v.a.,* recite, read out, declaim

recogitatio, -onis, *f.,* recollection, survey

recolo, -ere, -colui, -cultum, *3.v.a.,* recall, remember, survey

recondo, -ere, recondidi *(and* **recondi), -ditum,** *3.v.a.,* conceal, hide

recordatio, -onis, *f.,* recollection

recordor, *1.v.dep.,* recall, recall to mind

recreo, *1.v.a.,* restore, revive, recover, refresh

recte, *adv.,* rightly

rector, -oris, *m.,* ruler, master, moderator

rectus, -a, -um, *adj.,* right, true

recupero, *1.v.a.,* recover

recuso, *1.v.a.,* refuse

recutio, -ere, -cussi, -cussum, *3.v.a.,* drive back, repel

redamo, -are, *1.v.n.,* love in return

redarguo, -ere, -gui, -gutum, *3.v.a.,* blame for, charge with

reddo, -ere, -didi, -ditum, *3.v.a.,* give back, return, repay, render

redemptor, -oris, *m.,* redeemer

redeo, -ire, -ivi (-ii), -itum, *irr.v.n.,* go back, return

reditus, -us, *m.,* return

redoleo, -ere, -ui, *no sup.,* *2.v.a.,* be redolent of

reduco, -ere, -duxi, -ductum, *3.v.a.,* bring back, recall

refello, -ere, refelli, *no sup.,* *3.v.a.,* refute, confute, disprove

refero, -ferre, -tuli, -latum, *irr.v.a.,* carry back, refer, put, apply, employ

reficio, -ere, -feci, -fectum, *3.v.a.,* recreate, restore, refresh

reformido, *1.v.a.,* fear, dread

reformo, *1.v.a.,* reform

refrango, *(and* **refringo), -ere, -fregi, -fractum,** *3.v.a.,* break, destroy; check, weaken, abate

refugio, -ere, -fugi, -fugitum, *3.v.n. and a.,* flee; avoid, shun, draw back from

refugium, -ii, *n.,* refuge

refundo, -ere, -fudi, -fusum, *3.v.a.,* pour out, pour into, refund, pay back

regenero, *1.v.a.,* regenerate

regimen, -minis, *n.,* discipline

regius, -a, -um, *adj.,* of *or* belonging to an emperor or empress, imperial

regnum, -i, *n.,* kingdom

regula, -ae, *f.,* rule

reicio, -ere, -ieci, -iectum, *3.v.a.,* reject

relabor, -labi, lapsus sum, *3.v.dep.,* slip back

relaxo, *1.v.a.,* loosen

religio, -onis, *f.,* religion

religiosus, -a, -um, *adj.,* religious, holy

relinquo, -ere, -liqui, -lictum, *3.v.a.,* leave, abandon

reliquiarium, -ii, *n.,* remnant, heritage

remaneo, -ere, -mansi, -mansum, 2.*v.n.,* remain

remeo, *no sup.,* 1.*v.n.,* go back, return

remissio, -onis, *f.,* remission

remitto, -ere, -misi, -missum, 3.*v.a.,* remit

remote, *adv.,* afar off, at a distance

removeo, -ere, -movi, -motum, 2.*v.a.,* remove; *p.p. as adj.,* **remotus, -a, -um,** removed, afar off, not connected with

renascor, -nasci, -natus sum, 3.*v.dep.,* be born again

renitor, -niti, 3.*v.dep.,* oppose, resist

renuntio, 1.*v.n.,* report, announce

reparo, 1.*v.a.,* renew, restore, repair

repello, -ere, repuli, -pulsum, 3.*v.a.,* spurn, reject

repente, *adv.,* suddenly, unexpectedly

repentinus, -a, -um, *adj.,* sudden, unexpected

reperio, -ire, -peri, -pertum, 4.*v.a.,* find out, discover

repeto, -ere, -ivi (-ii), -itum, 3.*v.a.,* attack again, repeat

repletus, -a, -um, *part. adj.,* filled, full

reprehendo, -ere, -hendi, -hensum, 3.*v.a.,* reprove, find fault, criticize

reprehensio, -onis, *f.,* reprehension, condemnation

reprimo, -ere, -pressi, -pressum, 3.*v.a.,* check, repress

requies, -etis, *f.,* rest, repose

requiesco, -ere, -quievi, -quietum, 3.*v.n.,* rest, repose

requiro, -ere, -quisivi, -quisitum, 3.*v.a.,* seek, seek for, desire, call on

res, rei, *f.,* thing, matter, affair, fact, circumstance, undertaking; *pl.,* nature, circumstances, property; **re vera,** indeed, in truth, truly

resarcio, -ire, -sarsi, -sartum, 4.*v.a.,* repair, restore; fill again

resisto, -ere, -stiti, *no sup.,* 3.*v.n.,* resist, oppose

resolutio, -onis, *f.,* dissolution

resolvo, -ere, -solvi, -solutum, 3.*v.a.,* deliver, resolve

resorbeo, -ere, 2.*v.a.,* suppress, repress

respicio, -ere, -spexi, -spectum, 3.*v.a. and n.,* look back at, look behind, observe, reflect upon

respiro, 1.*v.a. and n.,* take breath, breathe in

respondeo, -ere, -spondi, -sponsum, 2.*v.a.,* reply, answer, respond

responsum, -i, *n.,* reply, response

restituo, -ere, -stitui, -stitutum, 3.*v.a.,* restore

resto, -are, -stiti, *no sup.,* 1.*v.n.,* be left, remain

restringo, -ere, -strinxi, -strictum, 3.*v.a.,* confine, restrict, restrain

resuscito, 1.*v.a.,* raise up again

retardo, 1.*v.a.,* delay, detain

retineo, -ere, -tinui, -tentum, 2.*v.a.,* keep, preserve, retain, hold fast, hold back

retorqueo, -ere, -torsi, -tortum, 2.*v.a.,* turn *or* cast back

retribuo, -ere, -ui, -utum, 3.*v.a.,* requite, give one back his due

retro, *adv.,* back, backwards

reus, -i, *m.,* defendant; one who is

liable, one who is in danger (*because of wrongdoing*)

revalesco, -ere, -valui, *no sup.,* 3.*v.n.,* grow strong again, regain strength

revelo, 1.*v.a.,* reveal

reverbero, 1.*v.a.,* check

reverto, -ere, -verti, -versum, *and* **revertor, -verti, -versus sum,** 3.*v.n.,* come back, return

revivesco, -ere, revixi, *no sup.,* 3.*v.n.,* be restored to life

revoco, 1.*v.a.,* recall

revolo, 1.*v.n.,* fly back

rex, regis, *m.,* king; *Conf.* IX, 7, 15, emperor

rhetor, -oris, *m.,* rhetor, teacher of rhetoric

rhetorica, -ae, (*sc.* **ars**), *f.,* rhetoric

rhetoricus, -a, -um, *adj.,* of *or* belonging to rhetoric, rhetorical

rideo, -ere, risi, risum, 2.*v.a. and n.,* laugh, laugh at

rigo, 1.*v.a.,* moisten, wet

rimor, 1.*v.dep.,* search into, penetrate into

rixa, -ae, *f.,* quarrel, struggle

robuste, *adv.,* strongly, firmly

rodo, -ere, rosi, rosum, 3.*v.a.,* eat away, gnaw, consume

rogo, 1.*v.a.,* ask, inquire of; beseech, pray

Roma, -ae, *f.,* Rome

rudis, -e, *adj.,* inexperienced

rumino, 1.*v.a.,* ruminate, feed upon

rumpo, -ere, rupi, ruptum, 3.*v.a. and n.,* break, break asunder, burst

ruo, -ere, rui, rutum, 3.*v.n.,* rush blindly, fall down, fall to ruin

rursum, *adv.,* again, anew

rursus, *adv.,* again, anew

rus, ruris, *n.,* the country, country estate

S

sacerdos, -otis, *m.,* priest

sacramentum, -i, *n.,* sacrament, rite, mystery

sacrificium, -ii, *n.,* sacrifice

sacrifico, 1.*v.a. and n.,* offer sacrifice, sacrifice; *impers., Conf.* I, 17, 27

sacrilegus, -a, -um, *adj.,* sacrilegious

saecularis, -e, *adj.,* secular, worldly

saeculum, -i, *n.,* age, generation; the world, *especially in the phrase* **hoc saeculum,** this world, *as opposed to Heaven and Eternity;* **in saeculum,** forever

saepe, *adv.,* often

saevio, -ire, -ivi (-ii), -itum, 4.*v.n.,* be furious, rage, be violently angry

saevus, -a, -um, *adj.,* cruel, harsh, savage

sagax, -acis, *adj.,* sagacious, shrewd

sagina, -ae, *f.,* surfeit, superfluity

sal, salis, *m.,* salt

salio, -ire, salui, saltum, 4.*v.n.,* spring up, leap

saltem, *adv.,* at least, at all events; **nec saltem,** not even

saluber, -bris, -bre, *adj.,* healthful, salutary

salubriter, *adv.,* wholesomely, healthily, in a salutary manner

salus, -utis, *f.,* safety, health, salvation

salutaris, -e, *adj.,* salutary

salutifer, -fera, -ferum, *adj.,* salutary

salvator, -oris, *m.,* saviour; *especially,* Our Saviour, *Jesus Christ*

salvus, -a, -um, *adv.,* well, sound

sancte, *adv.*, holily

sanctus, -a, -um, *adj.*, sacred, holy; *m. pl. as subst.*, sancti, -orum, saints

sane, *adv.*, clearly, certainly

sanguis, -inis, *m.*, blood

sanitas, -tatis, *f.*, health, soundness of mind, sanity

sano, 1.*v.a.*, heal

sanus, -a, -um, *adj.*, sound, healthy, wholesome; *with* ab, free from, unaffected by

sapidus, -a, -um, *adj.*, savory

sapiens, -entis, *adj.*, wise

sapientia, -ae, *f.*, wisdom

sapio, -ere, -ii, *no sup.*, 3.*v.a.*, taste of, savor of; hold, harbor

sapor, -oris, *m.*, taste

sarcina, -ae, *f.*, burden, load

sartago, -inis, *f.*, frying-pan, kettle

satago, -ere, -egi, -actum, 3.*v.n.*, be anxious, be solicitous

satio, 1.*v.a.*, satisfy, satiate, fill

satis, *adv.*, enough, sufficiently, quite

saucio, 1.*v.a.*, wound

scaevus, -a, -um, *adj.*, unfortunate, perverse

scalpo, -ere, scalpsi, scalptum, 3.*v.a.*, scratch; *fig.*, tickle

scatebra, -ae, *f.*, a bubbling up

scenicus, -a, -um, *adj.*, belonging to the stage, scenic, represented on the stage

sceptrum, -i, *n.*, sceptre, dominion, authority

schola, -ae, *f.*, school; in scholam dare, to put to school

scholasticus, -i, *m.*, student

scientia, -ae, *f.*, knowledge

scintillo, -are, -avi, *no sup.*, 1.*v.n.*, sparkle, gleam, flash

scio, scire, scivi, scitum, 4.*v.a.*, know, know how

sciscitor, 1.*v.dep.*, ask, inquire into

scribo, -ere, scripsi, scriptum, 3.*v.a.*, write; scriptum est (*referring to Scripture*), it is written

scriptito, 1.*v.a.*, copy often

scriptum, -i, *n.*, a writing; scripta vetera, the books of Scripture, the Old Testament

scriptura, -ae, *f.*, a writing; *especially, sing. and pl.*, the Scripture, the Scriptures

scrutator, -oris, *m.*, investigator, examiner

secedo, -ere, -cessi, -cessum, 3.*v.n.*, go apart, withdraw

secludo, -ere, -clusi, -clusum, 3.*v.a.*, shut off, keep away

secreto, *adv.*, secretly, in private

secretum, -i, *n.*, secret, mystery

secretus, -a, -um, *adj.*, remote, concealed, hidden, secret, mysterious, deep

secta, -ae, *f.*, a school *or* sect of philosophy; a religious sect

sector, 1.*v.dep.*, strive after, pursue eagerly

secundum, *prep. with acc.*, according to

securitas, -tatis, *f.*, security, freedom from care

securus, -a, -um, *adj.*, free from care, untroubled, secure

sed, *conj.*, but, yet; sed et, but also (=sed etiam); sed tamen, but nevertheless, but yet

sedatus, -a, -um, *part. adj.*, moderate, restrained

sedecim, *indect.*, sixteen

sedeo, -ere, sedi, sessum, 2.*v.n.*, sit

sedes, -is, *f.*, abode, home

sedo, 1.*v.a.*, check, keep down

seduco, -ere, -duxi, -ductum, 3.*v.a.*, seduce, corrupt

seductio, -onis, *f.*, seduction

seductorius, -a, -um, *adj.*, seductive, attractive

sedulo, *adv.*, busily, zealously

segnis, -e, *adj.*, slow, slothful, laggard

semen, -inis, *n.*, seed

semisaucius, -a, -um, *adj.*, half-wounded

semper, *adv.*, always, forever

sempiternus, -a, -um, *adj.*, eternal, everlasting

Seneca, -ae, *m.*, Seneca, *great Latin philosopher and poet, c.* 4 *B.C.*—65 *A.D.*

senecta, -ae, *f.*, old age

sensibilis, -e, *adj.*, sensible, perceptible, *n. pl. as subst.*, sensible things

sensim, *adv.*, gradually, little by little

sensus, -us, *m.*, feeling, perception, thought, sense, consciousness, inclination, desire

sententia, -ae, *f.*, thought, sentiment; *Conf.* I, 8, 13, phrase, sentence; *Conf.* VIII, 12, 28, in hac sententia, in this tenor

sentio, -ire, sensi, sensum, 4.*v.a.*, perceive, feel, see, learn, understand, think; *absol.*, *Conf.* I, 20, 31, experience sensation, have consciousness; *p.p. in n. pl. as*

subst., sensa, -orum, thoughts, ideas, feelings

seorsum, *adv.*, apart, separately

separo, 1.*v.a.*, sever, separate

sepono, -ere, -posui, -positum, 3.*v.a.*, put aside

septem, *indecl.*, seven

sepulchrum, -i, *n.*, grave, sepulchre

sequor, sequi, secutus sum, 3.*v.dep.*, follow, pursue

serenitas, -tatis, *f.*, clearness, serenity

serenus, -a, -um, *adj.*, tranquil, serene

sermo, -onis, *m.*, speech, conversation, discourse; word; sermon

sermocinor, 1.*v.dep.*, converse, discuss, discourse

serpens, -ntis, *c.*, serpent

servio, -ire, -ivi (-ii), -itum, 4.*v.n.*, serve, obey, be a slave; *Conf.* VI, 3, 3, with infirmitatibus, give assistance in difficulties

servitus, -tutis, *f.*, slavery

servo, 1.*v.a.*, keep, preserve

servus, -i, *m.*, servant

severitas, -tatis, *f.*, severity, sternness, strictness

severus, -a, -um, *adj.*, stern, severe, harsh

sextus, -a, -um, *adj.*, sixth

si, *conj.*, if; whether, to try whether

sic, *adv.*, so, thus, in this way

siccitas, -tatis, *f.*, dryness

sicco, 1.*v.a.*, make dry, dry up

siccus, -a, -um, *adj.*, dry, tearless

sicut, *or* sicuti, *adv.*, as, just as, as if

sidus, -eris, *n.*, star

significo, 1.*v.a.*, signify, indicate

signo, 1.*v.a.*, mark, seal, sign

signum,- i, *n.*, sign, symbol, mark

silentium, -ii, n., silence
sileo, -ere, -ui, no sup., 2.v.a. and n., not speak of, keep silent about; keep silent
silvesco, -ere, 3.v.n., grow rankly, run to a wild growth in
similis, -e, adj., like, similar
simul, adv., at the same time, at once, together
sine, prep. with abl., without
singuli, -ae, -a, distr. adj., separate, single, individual
sino, -ere, sivi, situm, 3.v.a., allow, suffer, permit
sinus, -us, m., bosom
sitis, -is, f., thirst
sive, conj., or; correlatively, sive . . . sive, either . . . or
sobrius, -a, -um, adj., sober, virtuous
societas, -tatis, f., society, fellowship, association; Conf. IV, 4, 7, with studiorum, community of interests
socio, 1.v.a., unite, associate
socius, -ii, m., fellow, companion, comrade, associate; sharer
sol, solis, m., the sun
solacium, -ii, n., solace, comfort
solamen, -inis, n., solace, consolation
soleo, -ere, solitus sum, 2.semidep., be wont, be accustomed
solidus, -a, -um, adj., solid, substantial, strong
solitudo, -inis, f., solitude
solitus, -a, -um, adj., ordinary, customary; n. sing. as subst., the customary, what is usual; n. pl. as subst., one's accustomed life or tasks

sollicitudo, -inis, f., care, solicitude, anxiety
solum, adv., alone, only; non solum . . . verum etiam, not only . . . but also
solum, -i, n., soil, ground
solus, -a, -um, adj., alone, only, sole
solutus, -a, -um, part. adj., unbound, free; with verba, free from the fetters of meter, hence, prose; weakened, tired
solvo, -ere, solvi, solutum, 3.v.a., free, sever; make payment for; break down, destroy; solve
somnium, -ii, n. dream
sonitus, -us, m., sound
sono, -are, sonui, sonitum, 1.v.n. and a., sound, give forth a sound; sound, utter
sonus, -i, m., sound
sopor, -oris, m., deep sleep
sorbeo, -ere, sorbui, no sup., 2.v.a., suck in, sip
sordeo, -ere, sordui, no sup., 2.v.n., be despised
sordes, -ium, f. pl., filth, defilement, baseness, sordidness
sordido, 1.v.a., defile, pollute
sordidus, -a, -um, adj., filthy, vile
sors, sortis, f., lot, fortune, destiny
spargo, -ere, sparsi, sparsum, 3.v.a., sprinkle, distribute
spatior, 1.v.dep., walk, walk up and down
species, -ei, f., beauty
spectaculum, -i, n., show, spectacle, sight; spectacle (in the theater or circus)
spectator, -oris, m., spectator
specto, 1.v.a., look at, look on at, see, behold

sperno, -ere, sprevi, spretum, 3.v.a.,
spurn, despise

spero, 1.v.n. and a., hope, hope for;
with in and abl. (also with in and
acc.), hope in

spes, spei, f., hope

spiritalis, -e, adj., spiritual

spiritaliter, adv., spiritually, in a
spiritual sense

spiritus, -us, m., breath; Conf. I,
13, 20, wind; a (bad) spirit;
especially, with or without sanctus,
the Holy Spirit, the Holy Ghost

spiro, 1.v.n., breathe

splendidus, -a, -um, adj., shining,
radiant, resplendent

sponsa, -ae, f., betrothed woman,
fiancee

stabilis, -e, adj., stable, unchanging

statim, adv., at once, immediately

statuo, -ere, statui, statutum, 3.v.a.,
determine, resolve

statura, -ae, f., stature

sterilis, -e, adj., sterile

sterno, -ere, stravi, stratum, 3.v.a.,
cast down, prostrate

stimulus, -i, m., spur, goad

sto, -are, steti, statum, 1.v.n., stand

stoliditas, -tatis, f., stolidity, dulness

stomachus, -i, m., stomach

strenue, adv., actively, zealously

strepitus, -us, m., noise, tumult;
bustle; Conf. III, 6, 10, rattle

stridor, -oris, m., clanking

studeo, -ere, -ui, no sup., 2.v.n.,
be eager, be diligent, apply one's
self, study, be a student

studiose, adv., studiously, zealously

studium, -ii, n., zeal, effort; pursuit,
study, interest

stultus, -a, -um, adj., foolish, stupid

stupefactus, -a, -um, part. adj.,
astounded, astonished

stupeo, -ere, -ui, no sup., 2.v.n. and
a., be astonished, be amazed;
wonder at, be amazed at

suadeo, -ere, suasi, suasum, 2.v.a.,
advise, recommend

suave, adv., sweetly, pleasantly

suaveolentia, -ae, f., sweet odor,
fragrance

suaviloquentia, -ae, f., sweetness of
speech

suavis, -e, adj., sweet

suavitas, -tatis, f., sweetness, pleasantness, charm

sub, prep. with acc. and abl., under,
beneath

subditus, -a, -um, part. adj., subject

subdoceo, -ere, -docui, -doctum,
2.v.a. and n., to teach as an assistant, to act as an assistant teacher

subeo, -ire, -ii, -itum, irr.v.a., go
under, take upon one's self

subigo, -ere, -egi, -actum, 3.v.a.,
subdue, subject

subito, adv., suddenly, unexpectedly

sublimitas, -tatis, f., elevation,
honor

submitto, -ere, -misi, -missum,
3.v.a., lower, let down

submurmuro, 1.v.n., murmur softly

subrepo,-ere, -repsi, -reptum, 3.v.n.,
steal upon, grow upon unawares

substantia, -ae, f., substance

substerno, -ere, -stravi, -stratum,
3.v.a., strew or spread beneath

substomachor, 1.v.dep., be somewhat
angry or vexed

subsum, -esse, -fui, irr.v.n., be at
hand, exist

subtilis -e adj., subtle

subtiliter *adv.*, accurately
subtraho, -ere, -traxi, -tractum, 3.*v.a.*, withdraw, draw away
subvenio, -ire, -veni, -ventum, 4.*v.n.*, help, succor
succedo, -ere, -cessi, -cessum, 3.*v.n.*, follow, succeed, take the place of
successus, -us, *m.*, an advancing, advance, progression
succutio, -ere, -cussi, -cussum, 3.*v.a.*, strike softly, pluck softly at
sudarium, -ii, *n.*, handkerchief
sudor, -oris, *m.*, sweat, perspiration
sufficio, -ere, -feci, -fectum, 3.*v.n.*, be enough, be sufficient, meet the demands of
suggero, -ere, -gessi, -gestum, 3.*v.a.*, suggest; *Conf.* VIII, 12, 28, *in pass. with middle sense*, suggest itself
sugo, -ere, suxi, suctum, 3.*v.a.*, suck
sui, *reflex. pron., 3rd pers.*, of himself, herself, itself, themselves
sum, esse, fui, futurus, *irr.v.n.*, be; forem, *etc., equivalent to* essem; *future part. as adj.*, futurus, -a, -um, future, coming
summe, *adv.*, in the highest degree, most eminently
summus, *see* superus
sumptuose, *adv.*, sumptuously
sumptus, -us, *m.*, cost, expense; expenses, funds
super, *prep. with acc. and abl.*, over, above, upon, on, more than, concerning
superbe, *adv.*, proudly, with pride, presumptuously
superbia, -ae, *f.*, pride
superbus, -a, -um, *adj.*, proud

supererogo, 1.*v.a.*, pay more than one's due
superexalto, 1.*v.n.*, be exalted above
superfluo, -ere, -fluxi, *no sup.*, 3.*v.n.*, overflow
supernus, -a, -um, *adj.*, supernal, celestial
supero, 1.*v.a.*, overcome, defeat
superstitio, -onis, *f.*, superstition
superstitiosus, -a, -um, *adj.*, superstitious
superus, -a, -um, *adj.*, above, high; *comp.*, superior, -oris; *superl.*, supremus, last, extreme, *and* summus, highest, supreme, greatest
supervenio, -ire, -veni, -ventum, 4.*v.n.*, chance in upon, come upon unexpectedly
suppeto, -ere, -ivi (-ii), -itum, 3.*v.n.*, be present, be in store, suffice
supplex, -plicis, *adj.*, humble, pious
supplicium, -ii, *n.*, punishment, torture
supplico, 1.*v.a.*, supplicate, entreat suppliantly
supra, *adv., of time*, before, farther back; *prep. with acc.*, above, upon
surgo, -ere, surrexi, surrectum, 3.*v.n.*, rise, rise up
suscipio, -ere, -cepi, -ceptum, 3.*v.a.*, take up, raise up, receive
suspendium, -ii, *n.*, suspense
suspendo, -ere, -pendi, -pensum, 3.*v.a.*, support, hold in suspense; *in pass. with middle sense*, be in suspense, hang upon; *p.p. as adj.*, suspensus, -a, -um, in suspense, intent

suspiro, 1.*v.n.*, sigh for, sigh after; breathe out

sustentaculum, -i, *n.*, nourishment

suus, -a, -um, *poss. pron.*, his, her, its, their; his own, her own, *etc.*

syllaba, -ae, *f.*, syllable

Symmachus, -i, *m.*, Symmachus

T

tabesco, -ere, tabui, *no sup.*, 3.*v.n.*, waste away

taceo, -ere, -ui, -itum, 2.*v.n. and a.*, be silent; keep silent about, pass over in silence

tacite, *adv.*, silently, in silence

taediosus, -a, -um, *adj.*, disgusting, loathsome

taedium, -ii, *n.*, weariness, impatience, loathing

talis, -e, *pron. adj.*, such, of such a kind

tam, *adv.*, so, so much, so very; **tam . . . quam,** so much . . . as

tamdiu, *adv.*, *correlatively with* **donec,** *etc.*, so long

tamen, *adv.*, yet, still, nevertheless, however

tametsi, *conj.*, even if, although

tamquam, *adv.*, as if, as it were, as, like, just as

tandem, *adv.*, at length, at last, finally

tango, -ere, tetigi, tactum, 3.*v.a.*, touch

tanquam, *see* **tamquam**

tantillus, -a, -um, *adj.*, so little, so small

tantum, *see* **tantus**

tantummodo, *adv.*, only

tantus, -a, -um, *adj.*, so great, so much; as great, as much; *n.acc. sing. as adv.*, **tantum,** only, merely; *abl.*, **tanto,** *with comp.*, by so much, the more; *correlatively with* **quanto,** the more . . . the more; **in tantum,** to such a degree; **non tantum . . . verum etiam,** not only . . . but also

tardo, 1.*v.a., and n.* delay

tardus, -a, -um, *adj.*, tardy, late

tegimentum, -i, *n.*, covering, cover

tego, -ere, texi, tectum, 3.*v.a.*, cover

temere, *adv.*, rashly

temperantia, -ae, *f.*, modesty

temporalis, -e, *adj.*, temporal

temptatio, -onis, *f.*, suffering, trial; temptation

tempto, 1.*v.a.*, attempt, try

tempus, -oris, *n.*, time, point of time; period; the (proper) time, occasion

temtamentum, -i, *n.*, temptation

temulentus, -a, -um, *adj.*, drunken

tenebrae, -arum, *f.pl.*, darkness

teneo, -ere, tenui, tentum, 2.*v.a.*, have, hold, keep; *with* **memoria** (*also without* **memoria**), remember, recall

tener, -era, -erum, *adj.*, tender

tento, *see* **tempto**

tenuis, -e, *adj.*, small, slight; of narrow *or* small means

tenus, *prep. with abl.*, up to, as far

tepide, *adv.*, without warmth, feebly

termino, 1.*v.a.*, end, finish

terra, -ae, *f.*, land, earth, ground, dust, clay; *pl.*, **terrae,** the world

terrenus, -a, -um *adj.*, of *or* belonging to earth, earthly; *n. pl. as subst.*, earthly things

terror, -oris, *m.*, fear, terror; *in pl.*,

Conf. I, 14, 23, threatening expressions

tertius, -a, -um, *adj.,* third

testatus, -a, -um, *part. adj.,* attested, manifest

testimonium, -ii, *n.,* testimony, proof

testor, 1.*v.dep.,* bear witness

Teucri, -orum, *m. pl.,* the Trojans

texo, -ere, texui, textum, 3.*v.a.,* weave; *fig.,* construct, compose

Thagastensis, -e, *adj.,* of *or* belonging to Thagaste, *a city in Numidia*

theatricus, -a, -um, *adj.,* of *or* belonging to the theater, theatrical

thesaurus, -i, *m.,* treasure, treasury

Tiberinus, -a, -um, *adj.,* of *or* belonging to the Tiber; **Ostia Tiberina,** Ostia at the mouth of the Tiber

timeo, -ere, -ui, *no sup.,* 2.*v.a. and n.,* fear, dread; be afraid

timor, -oris, *m.,* fear

tolerantia, -ae, *f.,* patience

tollo, -ere, sustuli, sublatum, 3.*v.a.,* take up, take; lift up, extol

tormentum, -i, *n.,* an instrument of torture; torture, punishment

torqueo, -ere, torsi, tortum, 2.*v.a.,* torture, torment

tortuosus, -a, -um, *adj.,* crooked; *n. pl. as subst., Conf.* IX, 4, 7, tortuous ways

torus, -i, *m.,* marriage bed

tot, *indecl. num.,* so many

totus, -a, -um, *adj.,* the whole, all, entire

tracto, 1.*v.a.,* treat, discuss, explain

traditio, -onis, *f.,* tradition

trado, -ere, -didi, -ditum, 3.*v.a.,* deliver over, give; hand down, relate

tragicus, -a, -um, *adj.,* of *or* belonging to tragedy, tragic, terrible; *n. pl. as subst.,* tragic things

traho, -ere, traxi, tractum, 3.*v.a.,* draw, trail, attract

tranquillus, -a, -um, *adj.,* tranquil, at peace, calm

transeo, -ire, -ii (-ivi), -itum, *irr.v.a. and n.,* cross, cross over, pass, pass over to; *of time,* pass

transfero, -ferre, -tuli, -latum, *irr.v.a.,* transfer, remove

transfluo, -ere, -fluxi, *no sup.,* 3.*v.n.,* flow out

transgredior, -gredi, -gressus sum, 3.*v.dep.a.,* pass over

transgressor, -oris, *m.,* a transgressor; *Conf.* I, 17, 27, *with adjectival force,* transgressing

transigo, -ere, -egi, -actum, 3.*v.a.,* complete, finish, perform; *p.p. as adj.,* **transactus, -a, -um,** completed, past

transilio, -ire, -ui, (-ii), *no sup.,* 4.*v.n.,* leap over, hasten over

transitorius, -a, -um, *adj.,* transitory

transmarinus, -a, -um, *adj.,* beyond the sea, across the sea

transverbero, 1.*v.a.,* pierce, transfix

trepidatio, -onis, *f.,* anxiety, fear

trepido, 1.*v.n. and a.,* be agitated, be excited; fear

tres, tria, *num. adj.,* three

Treveri, -orum, *m.,* the town of the Treveri, *the modern* Treves

tribuo, -ere, tribui, tributum, 3.*v.a.,* bestow, give

tricenarius, -a, -um, *adj.,* of *or* con-

taining thirty; *with* **aetas,** one's
thirtieth year
~~tricesimus, -a, -um,~~ *adj.,* thirtieth
tristis, -e, *adj.,* sad
tristitia, -ae, *f.,* sorrow
triumpho, 1.*v.n. and a.,* triumph,
triumph over
Troia, -ae, *f.,* Troy, *an ancient city
in Asia Minor made famous in
literature through the epic poems
of Homer and Vergil*
tu, tui, *pers. pron.,* thou, you
Tullianus, -a, -um, *adj.,* Tullian, *i.e.,*
Ciceronian (*Cicero belonged to the
gens Tullia*)
tum, *adv.,* then
tumeo, -ere, 2.*v.n.,* be puffed up,
swell
tumor, -oris, *m.,* puffed up pride
tumultuor, 1.*v.dep.,* make a great
noise *or* stir
tumultus, -us, *m.,* disturbance,
tumult
tunc, *adv.,* then, at that time; *often
used practically as an adj.*
turba, -ae, *f.,* turmoil, confusion;
throng
turbidus, -a, -um, *adj.,* deeply excited, in mental anguish
turbo, 1.*v.a.,* disturb, confuse, trouble; *p.p. as adj.,* **turbatus, -a, -um,**
disturbed, perturbed
turbulentus, -a, -um, *adj.,* bois-
terous, turbulent, violent, fearful
turgidus, -a, -um, *adj.,* swollen,
inflated; **turgidus spiritus,** the
spirit of pride
turpis, -e, *adj.,* foul, shameful, base,
low
turpitudo, -inis, *f.,* shame, shameful-
ness, turpitude

turris, -is, *f.,* tower
tutela, -ae, *f.,* protection, guardian-
ship
tutus, -a, -um, *adj.,* safe, secure
tuus, -a, -um, *poss. pron.,* thy, your;
thine, yours
tyfus, -i, *m.,* pride

U

uber, -eris, *n.,* breast
uber, -eris, *adj.,* fertile, fruitful,
abundant
uberius, *comp. adv.,* more abundantly
ubertim, *adv.,* copiously
ubi, *interrog. and rel. adv.,* where;
wherewith, by which; when, as
soon as
ubicumque, *adv.,* anywhere
ubique, *adv.,* everywhere
ubiubi, *adv.,* wheresoever
ulcerosus, -a, -um, *adj.,* ulcerous,
full of ulcers
ullus, -a, -um, *pron. adj.,* any, anyone
ultimus, -a, -um, *superl. adj.,* last
ultio, -onis, *f.,* revenge
ultra, *adv.,* further, farther; *prep.
with acc.,* beyond, more than
umbra, -ae, *f.,* shadow, darkness;
ghost, shade
umbrosus, -a, -um, *adj.,* shady;
Conf. II, 1, 1, dark, shunning the
light of day
umerus, -i, *m.,* the shoulder
unanimis, -e, *adj.,* of one mind, of
one manner
unde, *interrog. and rel. adv.,* whence,
from what source; whence, from
which, from whom; from what
reason, why

undetricesimus, -a, -um, *adj.*, twenty-ninth

undevicensimus *and* undevicesimus, -a, -um, *adj.*, nineteenth

undique, *adv.*, from all sides; on all sides, everywhere

unguentum, -i, *n.*, ointment

ungula, -ae, *f.*, iron claw (*used as an instrument of torture*)

unicus, -a, -um, *adj.*, only

unigenitus, -a, -um, *adj.*, only-begotten

unitas, -tatis, *f.*, unity

universitas, -tatis, *f.*, universe, world

universus, -a, -um, *adj.*, altogether, whole, entire

unquam, *adv.*, ever; **nec unquam**, and never

unus, -a, -um, *num. adj.*, one

unusquisque, unaquaeque, unumquodque (*and* -quidque), *indef. pron.*, each one, each and every one, each

urbanitas, -tatis, *f.*, urbanity, fine manners

urbs, urbis, *f.*, city

urgeo, -ere, ursi, *no sup.*, 2.*v.a.*, press hard, drive on, urge on, force

usitatus, -a, -um, *part. adj.*, customary, usual, ordinary

uspiam, *adv.*, anywhere

usque, *adv.*, even to, up to, all the way; **usque ad**, up to; *Conf.* IX, 6, 14, to the point of; *Conf* I., 9, 14, **usque ab**, . . . even by . . .

usquequaque, *adv.*, wholly, entirely

usquequo, *interrog. adv.*, how long

usura, -ae, *f.*, usury, interest

usus, -us, *m.*, use, pursuit

ut (uti), *adv. and conj.; as adv.*, as, just as; *introducing a question,* how; *expressing time*, when, as soon as; *as conj. with subj. of purpose,* in order that, that, to; *of result*, so that, that; *of concession*, although

uterque, utraque, utrumque, *pron. adj.*, each (*of two*), both

uterus, -i, *m.*, the womb

utilis, -e, *adj.*, useful, profitable

utilitas, -tatis, *f.*, use, advantage, usefulness, utility

utiliter, *adv.*, usefully, profitably

utique, *adv.*, indeed, in fact, certainly

utor, uti, usus sum, 3.*v.dep.*, use, employ, make use of, enjoy, have

ut quid, (*used as an equivalent of* quid *or* cur), why, for what reason

utrum, *conj.*, whether; **utrum . . . an,** whether . . . or

utrumnam, *conj.*, whether

uxor, -oris, *f.*, wife

V

vaco, 1.*v.n.*, be idle, be free from, be at leisure

vado, -ere, 3.*v.n.*, go, depart

vae, *interj. expressing pain, sorrow, or anger,* alas! woe!; *absol. or with dat.*

vagabundus, -a, -um, *adj.*, wandering

vagus, -a, -um, *adj.*, wandering, restless

valde, *adv.*, very, very much, exceedingly

Valentinianus, -i, *m.*, Valentinian II, *Roman emperor of the West,* 375–392 *A.D.*

valeo, -ere, -ui, -iturus, 2.*v.n.*, be strong, be well; avail, prevail; *often with infin., like* possum, be

able, can; *pres. part. as adj.*,
valens, -ntis, able, strong, capable
of
valetudo, -inis, *f.*, health, state of
health
valide, *adv.*, strongly
vanitas, -tatis, *f.*, emptiness, vanity
vanito, 1.*v.n.*, be vain; *used only in
pres. part. pl. as subst.*, *Conf.* VIII,
11, 26, vanitates vanitantium,
vanity of vanities (*lit.*, vain
things)
vanus, -a, -um, *adj.*, vain, empty; *n.
pl. as subst.*, vain things, vanities
vapulo, 1.*v.n.*, be whipped, be
beaten
varius, -a, -um, *adj.*, various,
diverse, different, changing
vasculum, -i, *n.*, vessel
-ve, *enclitic*, or, or perhaps
vehemens, -ntis, *adj.*, strong, stern,
resolute
vehementer, *adv.*, severely, violently, vehemently, exceedingly
vel, *conj.*, or (*not exclusive*); vel . . .
vel, either . . . or; neque . . .
vel, neither . . . nor; even, indeed, surely
velamentum, -i, *n.*, covering, veil
vellico, 1.*v.a.*, pluck at
velo, 1.*v.a.*, envelop, veil
velum, -i, *n.*, sail, covering, curtain
velut, *adv.*, as, even as, just as, as it
were
venditor, -oris, *m.*, seller, vender
vendo, -ere, -didi, -ditum, 3.*v.a.*, sell
venio, -ire, -veni, ventum, 4.*v.n.*,
come; *Conf.* II, 8, 16, mihi venit
in mentem, came into my mind
ventosus, -a, -um, *adj.*, empty, vain,
vainglorious

ventus, -i, *m.*, wind; vento facto,
when a (favorable) wind had
arisen
vepres, -is, *m.*, thornbush, briar
verber, -eris, *n.*, *usually in pl.*, whip,
scourge
verbum, -i, *n.*, word, expression,
saying
vere, *adv.*, truly, really
verecundia, -ae, *f.*, modesty, bash-
fulness, timidity
Verecundus, -i, *m.*, Verecundus,
*an old teacher of grammar and
friend of Augustine who owned a
country estate at Cassiciacum near
Milan*
Vergilius, -ii, *m.*, Vergil, *the great
Roman poet, author of the Aeneid*
veridicus, -a, -um, *adj.*, veracious,
true
veritas, -tatis, *f.*, truth
vero, *adv.*, in truth, really; but, but
in fact
verso, 1.*v.a.*, turn hither and thither,
twist
versus, -us, *m.*, verse
versutus, -a, -um, *adj.*, subtle,
deceitful
verto, -ere, verti, versum, 3.*v.a. and
n.*, turn
verum, *adv.*, but, but in truth, still,
yet; verum tamen, notwith-
standing, nevertheless; non solum
. . . verum etiam, not only . . .
but also
verus, -a, -um, *adj.*, true, genuine,
real; *n. sing. as subst.*, verum, -i,
what is true, the truth
vesania, -ae, *f.*, madness, frenzy
vespere, *abl. of* vesper *as adv.*, in the
evening

vester, -tra, -trum, *poss. adj. and pron.,* your, yours

vestigium, -ii, *n.* trace, track; *Conf.* I, 20, 31, impression, copy, image

vestio, -ire, -ivi (-ii), -itum, 4.*v.a.,* cover, clothe, adorn; *Conf.* I, 17, 27, become, fit

vestis, -is, *f.,* garment

veto, -are, vetui, vetitum, 1.*v.a.,* prevent, forbid

vetus, -eris, *adj.,* old, ancient

vetustas, -atis, *f.,* age, decay, *Conf.* I, 4, 4, in vetustatem perducens, leading into decay = making weak, humiliating

vexo, 1.*v.a.,* trouble, torment

via, -ae, *f.,* way, road; *fig., Conf.* I, 9, 14, ways (*of knowledge*); way, manner

viator, -oris, *m.,* traveller

vicinia, -ae, *f.,* vicinity

vicinus, -a, -um, *adj.,* near, neighboring; *fig., Conf.* III, 11, 20, specious

vicissim, *adv.,* in turn

victima, -ae, *f.,* victim

victoria, -ae, *f.,* victory

victoriosus, -a, -um, *adj.,* victorious

victrix, -icis, *f.,* victress; *as adj.,* victorious

videlicet, *adv.,* evidently, of course, namely

video, -ere, vidi, visum, 2.*v.a., see,* behold; *pass.,* seem, appear, seem best

vidua, -ae, *f.,* widow

vigeo, -ere, 2.*v.n.,* thrive, flourish, be strong

vigilans, -ntis, *part. adj.,* watchful, vigilant

vigilia, -ae, *f.,* watch

vigilo, 1.*v.n.,* awake, wake, be awake; watch

vilesco, -ere, vilui, *no sup.,* 3.*v.n.,* become worthless, fade away

vilis, -e, *adj.,* vile, of no account, base

villa, -ae, *f.,* villa, country house

vincio, -ire, vinxi, vinctum, 4.*v.a.,* bind

vinco, -ere, vici, victum, 3.*v.a.,* conquer, vanquish, defeat

vinculum, -i, *n.,* bond, fetter

vindemialia, -ium, *n. pl.,* the Vintage Festival

vindico, 1.*v.a.,* claim; *with* **de,** take vengeance on; *impers. with* **in** *and acc., Conf.* I, 9, 15, punishment was exacted of

vinea, -ae, *f.,* vineyard

vinulentia, -ae, *f.,* fondness for wine, winebibbing

vinum, -i, *n.,* wine

violenter, *adv.,* violently, by force

violentus, -a, -um, *adj.,* violent, impetuous, strong; *with* **consuetudo,** all-powerful

vir, viri, *m.,* man, husband

virga, -ae, *f.,* rod

virginitas, -tatis, *f.,* virginity

virgo, -inis, *f.,* virgin, maiden

virilis, -e, *adj.,* of *or* belonging to a man

virtus, -utis, *f.,* virtue, power

vis, vis, *f.,* strength, force, violence, influence

viscera, -um, *n.pl.,* viscera, vitals

viscum, -i, *n.,* bird-lime

visio, -onis, *f.,* a vision

visum, -i, *n.,* a vision

vita, -ae, *f.,* life, existence

vitalis, -e, *adj.,* of *or* relating to life, vital

vitaliter, *adv.*, vitally; after a living manner

vitiosus, -a, -um, *adj.*, corrupt, wicked

vitium, -ii, *n.*, vice

vituperatio, -onis, *f.*, blame, censure, vituperation

vitupero, 1.*v.a.*, blame, censure

vivifico, 1.*v.a.*, quicken, make alive

vivo, -ere, vixi, victum, 3.*v.n.*, live

vix, *adv.*, hardly, scarcely

vocatio, -onis, *f.*, a calling

voco, 1.*v.a.*, call, name

volatile, -is, *n.*, a flying thing, bird

volo, velle, volui, *no sup.*, *irr.v.a.*, wish, will, desire, mean

volubilis, -e, *adj.*, mutable, changeable

volumen, -inis, *n.*, roll, book

voluntarius, -a, -um, *adj.*, voluntary; *n. pl.*, *as subst.* free offerings

voluntas, -tatis, *f.*, will, wish, desire

voluptas, -tatis, *f.*, pleasure, delight, enjoyment

voluto, 1.*v.a.*, roll, turn, tumble about

volvo, -ere, volvi, volutum, 3.*v.a.*, roll, set in motion; throw headlong; *pass. with middle sense*, roll, revolve

vorago, -inis, *f.*, abyss, whirlpool

votum, -i, *n.*, vow, prayer; wish, desire

vox, vocis, *f.*, voice, cry, sound; word

vulnero, 1.*v.a.*, wound

vulnus, -eris, *n.*, wound

vultus, -us, *m.*, expression, countenance

Z

zelo, 1.*v.a. and n.*, be jealous, love with a jealous love

Tomb of St. Augustine in S. Pietro in Ciel d'Oro, Pavia.
Fourteenth century.

INDEX

INDEX

Ablative, use of in place relations without prepositions, 34; of duration of time, 34–35; special features in use of ablative absolute, 35

Abstracts, use of in Late Latin, 21–22, 25

Academics, *see* New Academy

Accusative, extension in use of with verbs, 31

Adeodatus, 7, 117, 170, 174; part of in *De Magistro*, 175

Adjectives, substantival use of, 25; use of positive of for superlative, 27

Adverbs, summary of use of, 27–29; adjectival, 27; of time, 27; of place, 27–28; of interrogation, 28; of negation, 28–29

Agentes in Rebus, 157

Alliteration, 17

Alypius, 8, 151, 154, 170, 171

Ambrose, St., influence of on A., 6; 20; 65; 67; 136; opponent of Symmachus, 140; historical significance of, 141; manifold duties of as bishop, 148; silent reading by, 148; introduction of antiphonal singing by, 176; struggle of with Empress Justina, 176; and hymnography, 177; hymn of, *Deus Creator Omnium* quoted by A., 189

Ambrosian Basilica, 176

Anadiplosis, 17

Anthony of Egypt, St., 7; 8; life of, 155; 167

Antimetathesis, 17

Antonomasia, 18

Aquilius Severus, 13

Arians, heresy of, 176

Aristotle, comparison of A. with, 10, 11; views of on the drama, 101

Assessores, 154

Asyndeton, 18

Athanasius, St., 8, 155

Augustine, St., outline of life of, 3–8; place of in world of thought, 9–12; style of, 14–17; familiarity of with the Scriptures, 52; problem of the conversion of, 53–55; criticism of rhetorical studies by, 74, 82–83, 87, 103, 116, 173; knowledge of Greek of, 85; school days of at Madaura, 95; reflections of on boyhood theft, 98–99; arrival of in Carthage, 100 ff.; views of on the drama, 101; head of class in school, 103; influence of the *Hortensius* on, 105; early distaste of for the style of the Scriptures, 108; a Manichaean disciple, 109 ff.; return of to Thagaste, 111; a Manichaean "Hearer," 115; professor of rhetoric at Carthage, 116; suffering of on death of friend, 121 ff.; life of at Carthage, 125; association of with Faustus, 131; journey of to Rome, 133 ff.; called to Milan as professor of rhetoric, 141; influence of St. Ambrose on, 142 ff.; resumption of Catechumenate by, 144; resignation of professorship by, 169–170; inability of to understand *Isaias*, 173; discourse of with St. Monnica at Ostia, 182–183

Carthage: Site of Punic harbors and early city, from Bursa hill. At back: Bou-Kornëin mt. (Punic Baal site) and modern Tunis.